Essays on Gogol

ESSAYS ON

GOGOL

Logos and the Russian Word

Edited by Susanne Fusso and Priscilla Meyer

Northwestern University Press / Evanston, Illinois

Northwestern University Press
Evanston, Illinois 60208-4210

A portion of Frederick T. Griffiths's and Stanley J. Rabinowitz's "The Death of Gogolian Polyphony: Selected Comments on *Selected Passages from Correspondence with Friends*" appeared in slightly different form in their *Novel Epics: Gogol, Dostoevsky, and National Narrative*, published by Northwestern University Press, 1990. Copyright © 1990 by Northwestern University Press. Alexander Zholkovsky's "Rereading Gogol's Miswritten Book: Notes on *Selected Passages from Correspondence with Friends*" appears in his *Text Counter Text*, published 1994, and appears here by permission of Stanford University Press. Copyright © 1994 by the Board of Trustees of the Leland Stanford Junior University.

First paperback printing, 1994

Printed in the United States of America

ISBN 0-8101-1009-1 cloth
ISBN 0-8101-1191-8 paper

Library of Congress Cataloging-in-Publication Data

Essays on Gogol : logos and the Russian word / edited by Susanne Fusso and Priscilla Meyer.
p. cm.—(Studies in Russian literature and theory)
"Papers presented at the Logos of Gogol : Poetics, Aesthetics, Metaphysics, a conference . . . at Wesleyan University on 9–10 April 1988"—P. vii.
Includes bibliographical references and index.
ISBN 0-8101-1009-1 (alk. paper). — ISBN 0-8101-1191-8 (pbk.: alk. paper)
1. Gogol', Nikolaĭ Vasil'evich, 1809–1852—Criticism and Interpretation—Congresses. I. Fusso, Susanne. II. Meyer, Priscilla. III. Gogol', Nikolaĭ Vasil'evich, 1809–1852. IV. Series
PG3335.Z8E84 1992
891.78'309—dc20 91-38937
CIP

The paper used in this publication meets the minimum requirements of the American National Standard for Information Sciences—Permanence of Paper for Printed Library Materials, ANSI Z39.48-1984.

Gogol's Selfless Logo: G

Contents

Acknowledgments

THIS VOLUME collects the papers presented at "The Logos of Gogol: Poetics, Aesthetics, Metaphysics," a conference we organized that took place at Wesleyan University on 9–10 April 1988. A great many people contributed to that splendid event whom it is our pleasure to thank. Funding was provided by Colin Campbell from his Presidential Discretionary Fund, by the Soros Foundation–Soviet Union, and by gifts from Mrs. Joseph Mahoney and Mrs. Charles Stanwood. The head chefs at the conference banquet were Sergei Bunaev, Dean of Humanities at the Pedagogical Institute of Irkutsk, and Yuz Aleshkovsky of Middletown; music was provided by Bejun Mehta and Elizabeth Sawyer; Mary Lou Nelles gave administrative assistance. We are grateful to the respondents, Professors Victor Erlich, Donald Fanger, Robert Jackson, and Duffield White, for their participation in the conference. Professor Gavriel Shapiro kindly lent his expertise on some questions of translation, and Joan Jurale of Wesleyan's Olin Library was, as always, extremely helpful. Other essential aid was generously proffered by Anya Reeve, Howard Stern, and William Trousdale. Susan Harris, Ruth Melville, and Lee Prater Yost of Northwestern University Press provided valuable assistance in the preparation of the collection for publication. We thank Oxford University Press for permission to reprint the illustration on p. 116 from H. Steinhaus, *Mathematical Snapshots* (New York: Oxford University Press, 1969), p. 103.

A NOTE ON TRANSLITERATION AND BIBLIOGRAPHY

This book uses the transliteration system employed by the *Slavic Review*, except in the case of the familiar forms of Gogol, Dostoevsky,

Tolstoy, Herzen, and Meyerhold when they appear in the body of the text.

All references to Gogol's Russian texts are drawn from the Academy of Sciences *Polnoe sobranie sochinenii,* 14 volumes (Moscow and Leningrad, 1937–52); references in the text indicate volume number in Roman numerals, page number in Arabic.

For English translations of Gogol's works, we refer the reader to *The Complete Tales of Nikolai Gogol,* in 2 volumes, edited by Leonard J. Kent (Chicago: University of Chicago Press, 1985), which contains the tales from *Evenings on a Farm Near Dikanka, Mirgorod,* and the Petersburg stories; for his essays see *Nikolai Gogol: Hanz Kuechelgarten, Leaving the Theater and Other Works,* edited by Ron Meyer (Ann Arbor, Mich.: Ardis, 1990), and *Arabesques,* translated by Alexander Tulloch (Ann Arbor, Mich.: Ardis, 1982); for the plays see *The Theater of Nikolai Gogol,* translated by Milton Ehre and Fruma Gottschalk (Chicago: University of Chicago Press, 1980). The best translation of *Dead Souls,* by Bernard Guilbert Guerney, will soon become available again from Northwestern University Press.

A Key to Titles of Gogol's Works Mentioned in the Articles

Hans Kuechelgarten (1829)	Gants Kiuchel'garten
Evenings on a Farm near Dikanka	*Vechera na khutore bliz Dikan'ki*
Part 1 (1831)	
The Fair at Sorochintsy	Sorochinskaia iarmarka
St. John's Eve	Vecher nakanune Ivana Kupala
A May Night, or the Drowned Maiden	Maiskaia noch', ili utoplennitsa
The Lost letter	Propavshaia gramota
Part 2 (1832)	
Christmas Eve	Noch' pered Rozhdestvom
A Terrible Vengeance	Strashnaia mest'
Ivan Fedorovich Shponka and His Aunt	Ivan Fedorovich Shpon'ka i ego tetushka
A Bewitched Place	Zakoldovannoe mesto
Mirgorod (1835)	*Mirgorod*
Part 1	
Old-World Landowners	Starosvetskie pomeshchiki
Taras Bulba	Taras Bul'ba

English	Russian
	Part 2
Vii	Vii
The Tale of How Ivan Ivanovich Quarreled with Ivan Nikiforovich	Povest' o tom, kak possorilsia Ivan Ivanovich s Ivanom Nikiforovichem
	STORIES
Nevsky Prospect (1835)	Nevskii Prospekt
The Portrait (1835; 1842)	Portret
The Diary of a Madman (1835)	Zapiski sumasshedshego
The Nose (1836)	Nos
The Coach (1836)	Koliaska
The Overcoat (1842)	Shinel'
Rome (1842)	Rim
PLAYS AND	*RELATED PIECES*
The Inspector General (1836)	*Revizor*
Marriage (1842)	*Zhenit'ba*
Leaving the Theater after the Performance of a New Comedy (1842)	Teatral'nyi raz''ezd posle predstavleniia novoi komedii
The Denouement of *The Inspector General* (1846)	Razviazka *Revizora*
ARTICLES FROM	*"ARABESQUES" (1835)*
Sculpture, Painting and Music	Skul'ptura, zhivopis' i muzyka
On the Middle Ages	O srednikh vekakh
On the Teaching of World History	O prepodavanii vseobshchei istorii
A Glance at the Composition of Little Russia	Vzgliad na sostavlenie Malorossii
A Few Words about Pushkin	Neskol'ko slov o Pushkine
On Present-Day Architecture	Ob arkhitekture nyneshnego vremeni
Al-Mamun	Al-Mamun
Life	Zhizn'
Schlözer, Müller, and Herder	Schletser, Miller i Gerder
The Songs of the Ukraine	O Malorossiiskikh pesniakh

Thoughts on Geography	Mysli o geografii
The Last Day of Pompeii	Poslednii den' Pompei
On the Movements of Peoples at the End of the Fifth Century	O dvizhenii narodov v kontse V veka

ESSAYS

Woman (1830)	Zhenshchina
Boris Godunov ([1831]/1890)	*Boris Godunov*

NOVELS

The Hetman (one chapter) (1831)	*Get'man*
Dead Souls (1842)	*Mertvye dushi*
Selected Passages from Correspondence with Friends	*Vybrannye mesta iz perepiski s druz'iami*

A Key to Titles of Gogol's Works

Susanne Fusso and Priscilla Meyer

Introduction

1. THE FACE OF RECENT GOGOL SCHOLARSHIP

IN HIS valuable 1974 essay on the history of Gogol criticism, Robert A. Maguire described a situation that has since changed in at least two respects. First, Maguire noted that "the distinguishing mark of criticism in this century . . . has been specialization as against generalization, the diorama as against the panorama."[1] Since the mid 1970s a number of important surveys have appeared that attempt to view Gogol's works as a whole and to define the general laws of his artistic universe (Karlinsky; Mann, *Poetika*; Peace). Donald Fanger's *Creation of Nikolai Gogol,* in particular, brilliantly summarizes the critical work that preceded it and presents a well-defined reading of Gogol's life and art that subsequent scholars have found it necessary either to build on or to react against. One aspect of the reaction may be a turn back toward the specialization that Maguire viewed as the hallmark of the twentieth century, a return to detailed concentration on individual works rather than global surveys of the entire oeuvre (see, e.g., Mann, *V poiskakh*; Rancour-Lafferiere, *Overcoat*; Smirnova; Woodward, *Dead Souls*).

Even more significant is the change that has taken place in the years since Maguire was able to make the following statement: "Generally speaking, [Soviet] critics since [the publication of the Academy of Sciences edition of Gogol's works, 1937–52] have trodden the well-worn paths of socialist realism."[2] Fortunately, it is no longer true that the Western critic turns to Soviet Gogol scholarship only for the wealth of its resources in literary history and textual criticism while maintaining a healthy skepticism toward its ideological and theoretical underpinnings. Now, thanks to the work of the Tartu structuralists and semioticians, the ongoing rediscovery of the Bakhtin legacy, and the highly original studies by Iurii Mann and Sergei Bocharov, Western scholars are finding inspiration in Soviet theory above all.[3]

Soviet stereotypes about Western scholarship (at least in print) may be more difficult to dismantle. An extremely interesting review of Western Gogol scholarship begins by lamenting that "few Western Gogol scholars exceed the limits of the circle formed by the names Merezhkovskii, Rozanov, Belyi, the early Eikhenbaum, Gippius, and, finally, Nabokov."[4] (One might counter that this is not such a bad circle to be trapped in.) Western Gogol scholars are predictably scolded for "primitive Freudianism" and "repetition of the old precepts of Formalism."[5] Still, the very fact that a detailed forty-three-page discussion of Western critical works has appeared in a Soviet publication is a sign of change. A change in the attitudes of the Soviet literary-critical establishment can also be observed in the planning of a new *Complete Works* of Gogol at the Gorkii Institute of World Literature in Moscow. The editor in chief, Iurii Mann, and the assistant editor, Sergei Bocharov, have stated the principle that the commentary, which is to constitute about forty percent of the text of the edition, must take into account Western scholarship on Gogol. In connection with work on the edition, they plan to publish a series, *Gogolevskii sbornik: Materialy i issledovaniia,* to include Russian translations of works by Western scholars.

In the past ten years both Soviet and American scholars, as well as the émigrés who form an important link between the Russian and American traditions, have been continuing, expanding, and modifying the major approaches to Gogol that have long dominated the field.[6] New life has been injected into one of the oldest approaches, literary history, by Mann, who leaves no document unexamined, no memoir unread, in his endeavor to illuminate the genesis, evolution, and reception of *Dead Souls* (see his *V poiskakh*). Gogol's biography and his possible sources continue to attract scholarly attention (Kjetsaa; Shapiro; Shustov; Zolotusskii), and the venerable genre of "Gogol and ______" is still alive. We have not only the traditional comparisons with Pushkin, Dickens, Walter Scott, Belyi, Bulgakov, and Nabokov but also comparisons with St. Paul, Thomas Pynchon, and Malcolm Lowry (see, respectively, Makogonenko; Cox, "Writer as Comic"; Urnov; Altshuller; Keys; Papernyi; Chebotareva; Chudakova; Milne; Bowie; Keil; Weisenburger; Hadfield).

The tracing of folkloric motifs in Gogol's works has long been a favorite pursuit of scholars, and it continues to provide material for new interpretations and insights (Ivanov; Oinas; Shapiro, "Transformation"; Voropaev). The "deep" unconscious structures revealed in

Gogol's affinities with folk Ur-texts have attracted the attention of modern psychoanalytic critics, who have greatly surpassed their forebear I. D. Ermakov in sophistication and depth (Cox, "Geographic Tensions"; Rancour-Laferriere). Simon Karlinsky's psychosexual approach to the interpretation of Gogol's texts, an approach pioneered by Hugh McLean in the late 1950s, has proved both controversial and thought-provoking.

The consideration of the ethical and spiritual dimension of Gogol's works is emerging from its decades-long eclipse in both the Soviet Union and the West. Now, however, the accent is on sensitive and attentive readings of Gogolian texts rather than on abstract philosophical speculation (Bocharov, "Zagadka"; Deutsch; Gregg; Krivonos; Nosov; Sobel; Weiskopf). Scholars interested in this dimension are concerned to deny the notion of a drastic difference between the early, "secular" Gogol and the religious fanatic of the last years (see the essay by Priscilla Meyer in the present volume). In seeking to restore the unity of Gogol's career they pay close and respectful attention to his nonfictional works. While doing so, they fulfill one of the tasks called for by Maguire: "[Gogol's] non-fictional writings are largely unexplored. . . . their deeper connections with the fictions have not been really probed—connections that depend not so much on paraphrasable common ideas, but, say, on structure and imagery."[7] The essays by Susanne Fusso, Frederick Griffiths and Stanley Rabinowitz, Mikhail Weiskopf, and Alexander Zholkovsky in the present collection are explorations of this "largely unexplored" realm of Gogol's oeuvre. Another forgotten realm reclaimed by critics of this stamp, particularly Bocharov, is the legacy of Russian religious thought and non-Marxist philosophy of the years 1890–1930 (see Bocharov's essay in this collection).

The Formalists and their associates and heirs have by no means disappeared from the scene: *Russkaia literatura* recently published an excerpt from an unpublished paper by V. Ia. Propp that uses Gogol as the springboard for a theory of comedy; L. I. Eremina has produced a study of Gogol's language that is clearly (and admittedly) indebted to the work of V. V. Vinogradov; and M. N. Virolainen has achieved brilliant results from a painstakingly detailed analysis of the language and style of "Old-World Landowners."[8] Western structuralism has paid relatively little attention to Gogol (see Bernheimer; Pomorska), but beginning in 1968 with his highly influential essay on artistic space in Gogol, Iurii Lotman has laid the foundation for a truly rewarding structuralist approach. Central to Lotman's investigations is the idea that "there is a logic in the development of artistic ideas, and a new thought, as a rule, is the transformation of a certain original invariant."[9] Although Mann has his differences with Lotman, his analyses (particularly in *Poetika Gogolia*) rely on the same search for the invariants of Gogol's poetic world, a search that has allowed him to map that world with unparalleled thoroughness.[10]

The "sociological approach" to Gogol has as a rule been a euphemism for the Marxist approach. William Mills Todd III has decisively broken that rule with his own subtle brand of sociological criticism, which reads *Dead Souls* in the context of the ideologies and institutions of early nineteenth-century Russia. In his review of the work, Fanger summarizes its theoretical interest in terms that may also remind one of Lotman's readings of the "text" of Russian culture (especially in "O Khlestakove"):

> On Todd's showing, the designations of "container" (Russian gentry culture of the early nineteenth century with its French ideals) and "contained" (the significant fictions of the period) turn out to be interchangeable. So, to the extent that both the culture and its novels may be regarded as texts, this whole book could be characterized as a model exercise in the exploration of intertextuality, shedding new and revealing light on the several "discourses" involved, and on their interpenetration.[11]

A different kind of intertextuality—literary parody—concerns Efraim Sicher in his playful and amusing Bakhtinian reading of "The Nose."

Critics of postmodern and deconstructionist orientation have so far had almost nothing to say about Gogol, although the fragmentation and rhetorical deviousness of his texts would seem to be ideally suited to their mode of inquiry.[12] Finally, a productive feminist approach to Gogol has yet to be fully elaborated (but see Heldt), perhaps because his vision of Woman is apparently so simplistic and repugnant.

The Soviet tendency toward positivistic accumulation of historical data can at times reach absurd extremes, as in a study that seeks to illuminate Gogol's life and work by a detailed description of the "material culture" of Nezhin, down to the shape of the cornices on its buildings, but at its best it offers exhilarating revelations, as in Zolotusskii's analysis of the journalistic sources of "The Diary of a Madman."[13] The same can be said for the Western tendency to impose preconceived theory upon texts: in the case of James Woodward, the investigator's symbolic constructs at times engulf and ultimately efface the object of investigation. On the other hand, Karlinsky's provocative biographical speculations, whatever their intrinsic value, lead him to always solid, often revelatory readings of the

Gogolian text. What is clear is that the very best studies build compelling theories on the foundation of close reading and careful attention to the social and historical background.

2. THE LOGOS OF GOGOL

> A lot of nonsense does go on in the world . . . but nonetheless, when you think about it, there is something in all this.
> —"The Nose"

Scholars have taken both points of view—yes, Gogol's work is a lot of nonsense! some insist, while others have looked for what there might be in all this. The strange difficulties presented by Gogol's texts call into question the very nature of interpretation: have we just not discovered the right set of concerns, or is the attempt to do so totally inappropriate to the work? Both assumptions are represented in the present volume. The pro-nonsense party proposes several ways to interpret Gogol's troublesome text *Selected Passages from Correspondence with Friends,* while others believe that profound meaning may be uncovered in Gogol's texts if their language, imagery, and motif systems can be related to his philosophy, in which aesthetic and religious thought are continuous. The critical tradition established by Belinskii regards Gogol's later work as the product of a great writer whose religious fanaticism had turned him into a misguided would-be prophet; this interpretation was challenged by Konstantin Mochul'skii in 1934 in *Gogol's Spiritual Path (Dukhovnyi put' Gogolia).* Showing Gogol's religiosity to be the single most important aspect of his creative personality, Mochul'skii responds sympathetically to the crisis that led him to write *Selected Passages.* Certainly Gogol's view of the relationship among the writer, human existence, and God is central to any reading of his work. Gogol's logos is the focal subject of inquiry here.

Logos has had a variety of meanings. In the tradition of Plato and Aristotle, the concept is associated with the division between a higher reality and the material world, a topos of Romantic thought present in Gogol's earliest writing. In Christian thought, in the New Testament, logos is the message of eternal life and truth, the Word of God, of which Christ is the personification. Christ at once reveals the existence of the Father and is himself the truth of the Father.

It is clear from Gogol's voluminous correspondence that he expected his works to affect his Russian audience as the Revelation affected Christianity; Gogol saw his works, fictional or otherwise, as the manifestation of divine truth. Short of incarnation, how might the artist represent the unrepresentable? As John Kopper puts it in his essay, "Gogol's texts ask these questions, but more important, they *are* these questions." In this he comes close to Saul Morson's view of Gogol's texts as being about the hermeneutic process but rewarding it with their radical uninterpretability.

The conference "The Logos of Gogol" set out to identify systems of thought that define Gogol's sense of his literary mission and to formulate approaches to Gogol's work capable of accommodating new readings. One set of articles investigates Plato, the German Romantic philosophers, Russian cultural myth, and the aesthetics of English landscape designers, showing their specific contributions to individual works by Gogol. The essays are mutually illuminating, sharing points of contact in their discussion of Gogol's work as a deliberation on and reflection of the relationship between ideal beauty and its distorted reflection in the everyday and explicating Gogol's relationship to Platonic and Neoplatonic thought. The group of essays is unusual in taking seriously the degree to which Gogol consciously incorporated the important philosophical texts of his time into his apparently folksy or absurd fiction. The essays suggest that Gogol's texts are the very thing they are about—*Arabesques* is a "picturesque" garden, the mute scene in *The Inspector General* is itself an apocalypse, the *Dikanka* tales represent the limits of the knowable, *Dead Souls* is a duplication of Russia's boundlessness.

Mikhail Weiskopf finds precise correspondence between Plato's images and Gogol's: the famous cave metaphor from Plato's *Republic* underlies "The Tale of How Ivan Ivanovich Quarreled with Ivan Nikiforovich"; "the chariot of the soul" of the *Phaedrus* becomes the troika in *Dead Souls.* Weiskopf distinguishes the utopian Plato of the *Republic* from the Romantic Plato of the *Timaeus* and *Phaedrus.* The examination of the intricate resonance between the *Phaedrus* and Gogol's "Woman" is all the more convincing in that it is supported by the Stoics' understanding of logos, which differentiates between the idea that remains a thought and the idea once it is expressed in words. In "Woman" the infinite idea of woman (Sophia) becomes man when embodied in an artistic work. Gogol's mission was to embody the Idea in art so that there would arise in the reader the "infinite disembodied idea of the artist," as he says in "Woman." Gogol's conclusion to *Dead Souls*, then, is his solution to the problem of the nature of Russia: "The Russian idea is itself infinity, undefinedness, that is, the Romantic idea as such," Weiskopf writes.

Platonic ideas reached Gogol directly as well as through the German Romantics, and Weiskopf is careful to identify these different routes. John Kopper recasts the division between the real and the ideal in terms of Kant's phenomenal and noumenal, showing the special nature of the *Dikanka* tales to lie in their conflation of these categories. The problem of interpretation of the later tales, Kopper suggests, comes from the absence of the second term of the opposition: the phenomenal is visible but the noumenal absent: after all, the "thing-in-itself" is unrepresentable.

But it can be hinted at, and several of the essays suggest how to interpret systems within Gogol's texts as pointing to the divine or the sublime. Katherine Lahti recasts the conventional opposition animate/inanimate as the contrast between natural and man-made, emphasizing the made-ness of the multiplicity of things in Gogol's texts and its relationship to the word that represents it, itself a "thing" that subverts the categorization. The "pithily spoken Russian word" of the peasant in *Dead Souls* has the status of peasant songs and of a crow's flight—while they appear to have earthly agents, all come from a higher source, like Gogol's *poema* itself.

The same ambiguity between man-made and natural underlies Susanne Fusso's analysis of the English garden. Capability Brown's highly organized landscaping reflects an idea of beauty that is sterile because it is so purely man-made; the sublime inspires terror because it implies a monumental unknowable force outside man. Uvedale Price's theory of the picturesque prescribes both control and lack of control of nature's forces, allowing nature to express itself independently of the gardener. Fusso relates these ideas both to *Arabesques* as a collection (a picturesque garden) and to Pliushkin's garden in *Dead Souls*.

The opposition between the earthly and the divine also motivates Gogol's scenes of petrification. Iurii Mann shows that the moments in which characters become frozen with terror or amazement are representations of "man's conflict with a supernatural force." Uniting all the characters in prolonged silence, these scenes take place at the boundary between life and death, between an earthly and a higher power. Mann finds the mute scene of *The Inspector General* to contain the essence of Gogol's poetics, a realization of the transition from the temporal to the eternal, from chaos to unity.

Mann's technique of identifying constants in Gogol's work is employed in Priscilla Meyer's identification of the Russian concept of the False Pretender in many of Gogol's works, from the Ukrainian "May Night" through *The Inspector General* to "The Overcoat." The approach assumes Gogol to be no less seriously devoted to revealing divine will in his early texts than he was in *Selected Passages*, where he felt reduced to direct statement by the incomprehension of his audience. The result is a rereading of Akakii Akakievich's role in "The Overcoat."

Criticism has continually wrestled with the problem of Gogolian nonsense, whether that refers to the absurd surrealism of the tales or to the incomprehensibility of his more publicistic work, and the definition of the genre of the latter is itself problematic. Gary Saul Morson's essay contends that Gogol's "nonsense" is devised precisely to reject systematization. Showing how Gogol establishes categories only to deny their validity, Morson goes against the current of "semiotic totalitarianism" that would establish a system of meaning for all of culture and proposes instead the accumulation of detail for each text, each life, as a method of interpretation, a method he calls "prosaics." He reads *Dead Souls* as a hermeneutic parable whose hero is the process of explanation itself, and "The Nose" as designed to resist any interpretation whatsoever.

Two other theoretical essays also examine Gogol's "nonsense": both take as their text the *Selected Passages.* Alexander Zholkovsky proposes using Susan Sontag's idea of "camp" to analyze Gogol's collection, which he calls a miswritten book, a failed piece of journalism that should best be read as a form of popular fiction; Stanley Rabinowitz and Frederick Griffiths, using Bakhtin's concept of polyphony, accuse Gogol of resorting to the monologic discourse of Bakhtin's "totalitarian epic" as a means of justifying himself as a writer and spiritual teacher while blaming his audience for his failure. Rabinowitz and Griffiths and Zholkovsky agree with Gogol's idea, voiced in a letter to Zhukovskii, that he has become one of his own characters; in *Selected Passages*, he is seen as suffering the delusions of grandeur of Poprishchin. Cathy Popkin also identifies Gogol with his characters, as endless word gluttons filling the page and derailing the argument with digressions that frustrate the reader in the manner of Jean Paul.

The critical essays dwell on the nonsensicality of Gogol's work, while the close readings examine the relationship of Gogol's religious philosophy to his literary creation. The portrait of the artist that emerges is of a much more conscious thinker than scholars, dazzled by Gogol's nonsense, have typically taken him to be. In touching up Gogol's rather unflattering portrait, the present collection may uncover hitherto hidden features of the author's thought and suggest rewarding new lines of investigation.

WORKS CITED IN INTRODUCTION

Altshuller, Mark. "The Walter Scott Motifs in Nikolay Gogol's Story *The Lost Letter.*" *Oxford Slavonic Papers*, n.s., 22 (1989): 81–88.

Bernheimer, Charles C. "Cloaking the Self: The Literary Space of Gogol's 'Overcoat.' " *PMLA* 90 (1975): 53–61.

Bibikhin, B. B., R. A. Gal'tseva, and I. B. Rodnianskaia. "Literaturnaia mysl' zapada pered 'zagadkoi Gogolia.' " In *Gogol': Istoriia i sovremennost' (k 175-letiiu so dnia rozhdeniia)*, edited by V. V. Kozhinov et al., pp. 390–433. Moscow, 1985. (Reprinted from *Voprosy literatury*, 1984, no. 3: 126–61.)

Bocharov, S. G. "O stile Gogolia." In *Teoriia literaturnykh stilei: Tipologiia stilevogo razvitiia novogo vremeni: Klassicheskii stil'*, edited by N. K. Gei et al., pp. 409–45. Moscow, 1976.

———. "Perekhod ot Gogolia k Dostoevskomu." In his *O khudozhestvennykh mirakh*, pp. 161–209. Moscow, 1985.

———. "Zagadka 'Nosa' i taina litsa." In his *O khudozhestvennykh mirakh*, pp. 124–60. Moscow, 1985. (Reprinted in *Gogol': Istoriia i sovremennost'* [*k 175-letiiu so dnia rozhdeniia*], edited by V. V. Kozhinov et al., pp. 180–212. Moscow, 1985.)

Bowie, Robert. "Nabokov's Influence on Gogol." *Journal of Modern Literature* 13 (1986): 251–66.

Chebotareva, V. A. "O gogolevskikh traditsiiakh v proze M. Bulgakova." *Russkaia literatura*, 1984, no. 1: 166–76.

Chudakova, M. O. "Gogol' i Bulgakov." In *Gogol': Istoriia i sovremennost' (k 175-letiiu so dnia rozhdeniia)*, edited by V. V. Kozhinov et al., pp. 360–88. Moscow, 1985.

Cox, Gary. "Geographic, Sociological, and Sexual Tensions in Gogol's Dikan'ka Stories." *Slavic and East European Journal* 24 (1980): 219–32.

———. "The Writer as a Stand-up Comic: A Note on Gogol and Dickens." *Ulbandus Review*, no. 2 (1979): 45–61.

Debeaux, Anne. "Les âmes mortes ou le roman inachevé." *Europe* 648 (1983): 170–76.

Deutsch, Judith. "The Zaporožian Cossacks of Nikolay Gogol': An Approach to God and Man." *Russian Literature* 22 (1987): 359–77.

Eremina, L. I. *O iazyke khudozhestvennoi prozy N. V. Gogolia*. Moscow, 1987.

Fanger, Donald. *The Creation of Nikolai Gogol*. Cambridge, Mass.: Harvard University Press, 1979.

———. Review of William Mills Todd's *Fiction and Society in the Age of Pushkin*. *Slavic and East European Journal* 31 (1987): 106–8.

Frantz, Philip E. *Gogol: A Bibliography*. Ann Arbor, Mich.: Ardis, 1989.

Gippius, V. V. *Gogol*. Edited and translated by Robert A. Maguire. Ann Arbor, Mich.: Ardis, 1981.

Gogol, Nikolai. *Dead Souls*. Edited by George Gibian. New York: Norton, 1985.

Gogol': Istoriia i sovremennost' (k 175-letiiu so dnia rozhdeniia). Edited by V. V. Kozhinov et al. Moscow, 1985.

Gregg, Richard. "The Curse of Sameness and the Gogolian Esthetic: 'The Tale of the Two Ivans' as Parable." *Slavic and East European Journal* 31 (1987): 1–9.

Gutsche, George, and Gavriel Shapiro, eds. *The Gogol Bulletin*. 1985–.

Hadfield, Duncan. "*Under the Volcano* and Gogol's 'Diary of a Madman.' " *Malcolm Lowry Review* 16 (1985): 78–83.

Heldt, Barbara. "*Dead Souls*: Without Naming Names." In *Nikolay Gogol: Text and Context*, edited by Jane Grayson and Faith Wigzell, pp. 83–91. New York: St. Martin's Press, 1989.

Ivanov, V. V. "Kategoriia 'vidimogo' i 'nevidimogo' v tekste: Eshche raz o vostochnoslavianskikh fol'klornykh paralleliakh k gogolevskomu 'Viiu.' " In *Structure of Texts and Semiotics of Culture*, edited by Jan van der Eng and Mojmir Grygar, pp. 151–76. The Hague: Mouton, 1973.

———. "Ob odnoi paralleli k gogolevskomu 'Viiu.' " *Uchenye zapiski Tartuskogo gosudarstvennogo universiteta*, issue 284, *Trudy po znakovym sistemam*, no. 5 (1971): 133–42.

Karlinsky, Simon. *The Sexual Labyrinth of Nikolai Gogol*. Cambridge, Mass.: Harvard University Press, 1976.

Keil, Rolf-Dietrich. "Gogol' und Paulus." *Die Welt der Slaven* 31 (1986): 86–99.

Keys, Roger. "The Unwelcome Tradition: Bely, Gogol and Metafictional Narration." In *Nikolay Gogol: Text and Context*, edited by Jane Grayson and Faith Wigzell, pp. 92–108. New York: St. Martin's Press, 1989.

Kjetsaa, Geir [Khetso]. "Gogol' kak uchitel' zhizni: Novye materialy." *Scando-Slavica* 34 (1988): 55–67.

Krivonos, V. Sh. "Pritcha o Kife Mokievich i ee rol' v 'Mertvykh dushakh.' " *Izvestiia Akademii nauk SSSR, Seriia literatury i iazyka* 44 (1985): 48–56.

Lahusen, Thomas. "De la tautologie (II): Gogol' ou l'attrait du vide (Essai d'analyse discursive)." *Russian Literature* 26 (1989): 267–96.

Lotman, Iu. M. "O Khlestakove." *Uchenye zapiski Tartuskogo gosudarstvennogo universiteta*, issue 361, *Trudy po russkoi i slavianskoi filologii*, no. 26, *Literaturovedenie* (1977): 19–53. (Translated as "Concerning Khlestakov," in *The Semiotics of Russian Cultural History*, edited by Alexander D. Nakhimovsky and

Alice Stone Nakhimovsky. Ithaca, N.Y.: Cornell University Press, 1985.)

———. "Povest' o Kapitane Kopeikine (rekonstruktsiia zamysla i ideino-kompozitsionnaia funktsiia)." *Uchenye zapiski Tartuskogo gosudarstvennogo universiteta,* issue 467, *Semiotika teksta: Trudy po znakovym sistemam,* no. 11 (1979): 39–42.

———. "Problema khudozhestvennogo prostranstva v proze Gogolia." *Uchenye zapiski Tartuskogo gosudarstvennogo universiteta,* issue 209, *Trudy po russkoi i slavianskoi filologii,* no. 9, *Literaturovedenie* (1968): 5–50. (Partial translation in Nikolai Gogol, *Dead Souls,* edited by George Gibian, pp. 577–83. New York: Norton, 1985).

Maguire, Robert A. "Gogol's 'Confession' as a Fictional Structure." *Ulbandus Review* no. 2 (1982): 175–90.

———. "The Legacy of Criticism." In his *Gogol from the Twentieth Century: Eleven Essays,* pp. 3–54. Princeton, N.J.: Princeton University Press, 1974.

Makogonenko, G. P. *Gogol' i Pushkin.* Leningrad, 1985.

Mann, Iu. V. *Poetika Gogolia.* Moscow, 1978.

———. *V poiskakh zhivoi dushi: "Mertvye dushi": Pisatel'-kritika—chitatel'.* Moscow, 1984.

McLean, Hugh. "Gogol's Retreat from Love: Towards an Interpretation of *Mirgorod.*" In *American Contributions to the Fourth International Congress of Slavists,* pp. 225-45. The Hague: Mouton, 1958.

Meyer, Priscilla, and Stephen Rudy, eds. *Dostoevsky and Gogol: Texts and Criticism.* Ann Arbor, Mich.: Ardis, 1979.

Milne, Lesley. "Gogol and Mikhail Bulgakov." In *Nikolay Gogol: Text and Context,* edited by Jane Grayson and Faith Wigzell, pp. 109–26. New York: St. Martin's Press, 1989.

Mochul'skii, Konstantin. *Dukhovnyi put' Gogolia.* Paris: YMCA Press, 1934.

Nabokov, Vladimir. *Nikolai Gogol.* New York: New Directions, 1944.

———. "Nikolai Gogol'." Translated by E. Golyshev. *Novyi mir,* 1987, no. 4: 173–227.

Nosov, V. D. *"Kliuch" k Gogoliu.* London: Overseas Publications Interchange, 1985.

Oinas, Felix J. "The Transformation of Folklore into Literature." In *American Contributions to the Eighth International Congress of Slavists, Zagreb and Ljubljana, September 3–9, 1978.* Vol. 2, *Literature,* pp. 587–603. Edited by Victor Terras. Columbus, Ohio: Slavica, 1978.

Papernyi, V. M. "Andrei Belyi i Gogol': Stat'ia pervaia." *Uchenye zapiski Tartuskogo Gosudarstvennogo Universiteta*, issue 604, *Edinstvo i izmenchivost' istoriko-literaturnogo protsessa. Trudy po russkoi i slavianskoi filologii* (1982): 112–26.

Peace, Richard. *The Enigma of Gogol: An Examination of the Writings of N. V. Gogol and Their Place in the Russian Literary Tradition.* Cambridge: Cambridge University Press, 1981.

Pliashko, L. A. *Gorod, pisatel', vremia: Nezhinskii period zhizni N. V. Gogolia.* Kiev, 1985.

Pomorska, Krystyna. "On the Problem of Parallelism in Gogol's Prose: 'A Tale of the Two Ivans.' " In *The Structural Analysis of Narrative Texts: Conference Papers,* edited by Andrej Kodjak et al., pp. 31–43. Columbus, Ohio: Slavica, 1980.

Propp, V. Ia. "Priroda komicheskogo u Gogolia (Publikatsiia V. I. Ereminoi)." *Russkaia literatura,* 1988, no. 1: 27–43.

Rancour-Laferriere, Daniel. "The Identity of Gogol's *Vij.*" *Harvard Ukrainian Studies* 2 (1978): 211–34.

———. *Out from under Gogol's "Overcoat": A Psychoanalytic Study.* Ann Arbor, Mich.: Ardis, 1982.

———. "Špon'ka's Dream Interpreted." *Slavic and East European Journal* 33 (1989): 358–72.

Shapiro, Gavriel. "Nikolai Gogol and the Baroque Heritage." *Slavic Review* 45 (1986): 95–104.

———. "A Note on Gogol's *Kniga vsyakoy vsyachiny* and the Comments on It." *Slavonic and East European Review* 65 (1987): 238–40.

———. "The Role of Facetiae in Gogol's Early Works." *Transactions/Zapiski of the Association of Russian-American Scholars in the USA,* no. 17 (1984): 69–74.

———. "The Transformation of the Lost Pipe Motif: Nikolai Gogol's 'Taras Bulba' and Leo Tolstoy's 'The Wood-Felling.' " *Die Welt der Slaven* 31 (1986): 174–82.

Shukman, Ann. "Gogol's *The Nose* or the Devil in the Works." In *Nikolay Gogol: Text and Context,* edited by Jane Grayson and Faith Wigzell, pp. 64–82. New York: St. Martin's Press, 1989.

Shustov, A. N. "Smert' Gogolia—obshchestvennaia utrata (poet N. A. Arbuzov o N. V. Gogole)." *Russian Literature* 28 (1990): 235–44.

Sicher, Efraim. "Dialogization and Laughter in the Dark, or How Gogol's Nose Was Made: Parody and Literary Evolution in Bachtin's Theory of the Novel." *Russian Literature* 28 (1990): 211–34.

Smirnova, E. A. *Poema Gogolia "Mertvye dushi."* Leningrad, 1987.

Sobel, Ruth. *Gogol's Forgotten Book: "Selected Passages" and Its Con-*

temporary Readers. Washington, D.C.: University Press of America, 1981.

Soviet Literature, 1984, no. 4. (Issue devoted to Gogol.)

Todd, William Mills III. *Fiction and Society in the Age of Pushkin: Ideology, Institutions, and Narrative.* Cambridge, Mass.: Harvard University Press, 1986.

Trahan, Elizabeth, ed. *Gogol's "Overcoat": An Anthology of Critical Essays.* Ann Arbor, Mich.: Ardis, 1982.

Transactions/Zapiski of the Association of Russian-American Scholars in the USA, no. 17 (1984). (Issue devoted to Gogol.)

Urnov, D. M. "Gogol' i Dikkens." *Izvestiia Akademii nauk SSSR, Seriia literatury i iazyka* 44 (1985): 38–47.

Vinogradov, V. V. *Gogol and the Natural School.* Translated by Debra K. Erickson and Ray Parrott. Ann Arbor, Mich.: Ardis, 1987.

Virolainen, M. N. "Mir i stil' ('Starosvetskie pomeshchiki' Gogolia)." *Voprosy literatury,* 1979, no. 4: 125–41.

Voropaev, V. A. " 'Mertvye dushi' i traditsii narodnoi kul'tury (N. V. Gogol' i I. M. Snegirev)." *Russkaia literatura,* 1981, no. 2: 92–107.

———. "Zametki o fol'klornom istochnike gogolevskoi 'Povesti o kapitane Kopeikine.' " *Filologicheskie nauki,* 1982, no. 6: 35–41.

Weisenburger, Steven. "The Origin of Pynchon's Tchitcherine." *Pynchon Notes* 8 (1982): 39–42.

Weiskopf, Mikhail [Vaiskopf]. " 'Nos' v Kazanskom sobore: O genezise religioznoi temy u Gogolia." *Wiener Slawistischer Almanach* 19 (1987): 25–46.

Woodward, James B. *Gogol's Dead Souls.* Princeton, N.J.: Princeton University Press, 1978.

———. *The Symbolic Art of Gogol: Essays on His Short Fiction.* Columbus, Ohio: Slavica, 1981.

Yelistratova, Anna. *Nikolai Gogol and the West European Novel.* Translated by Christopher English. Moscow, 1984.

Zolotusskii, Igor'. *Gogol'.* 2nd ed. Moscow, 1984.

———. *Trepet serdtsa: Izbrannye raboty.* Moscow, 1986.

Andrei Bitov

Being Buried Alive; or, Gogol in 1973

(From the cycle *Memoirs of Great Writers*)

VII

IT WAS THE 31st of December; the train was to arrive at 11:20; forty minutes to make it to the holiday table.

An hour before arrival the intercom came on. Shulzhenko sang, then someone else. Then one number came after another with no announcements in between, and all you could do was guess or not guess what they were going to sing or play. The next number was a reading. In the voice of a "people's artist" who had substituted extortion of responses for any sort of artistry, employing the mannerisms of Grandpa Shchukar,* winking and leaving time for audience reactions, the reader began to read a "classic." You knew right away that it was a classic from the way the artist stressed precisely the unimportant words: for instance, nouns were more important for him than verbs; he kept emphasizing the wrong words, but with the kind of confidence that only great fame, great name power, could give those superfluous words. But I just couldn't guess what that great name was, and this somewhat wounded my professional pride. I was thoroughly annoyed that I couldn't guess the text right away, but only through the prompting of the proper nouns, like "Kiev," "Khoma."† Even a mental exclamation directed at the performer—"I never knew how unrecognizable you could make a text!"—failed to mitigate this irritation of my vanity. I turned away and stopped listening. There was nothing in the nighttime window—the reflection showed the same train car, the same me. As always, the sixth and last hour of the trip was particularly tedious. People were getting tired as we approached the station. They got their things together too soon, put their coats on too soon, crowded into the aisle too soon. . . .

*A folksy character in a novel by Mikhail Sholokhov.
†Khoma Brut is the hero of Gogol's "Vii," which is set in and around Kiev.

"And suddenly it became quiet in the church; one could hear wolves howling in the distance, and soon heavy footsteps resounded through the church. With a sidelong glance, he saw . . . " It's strange after all, I thought, a train on New Year's Eve, Vii. . . . Distilled weirdness.

The train started to rock and jump on the switches more violently, choosing its own personal branch, its own private dead end in the delta of the railway. And the reader continued, liquidating the horror with his cheery voice, emphasizing the inexhaustible folk imagination, its life-affirming force. . . . How did he manage it?—this really was a kind of artistry. At any rate, he was worthy of his title, he corresponded to it.

"With horror Khoma noticed that his face was made of iron,"* the reader joyfully exclaimed, and then there was a click on the loudspeaker and, seeming so natural this time, a railroad voice announced:

"The train is arriving at hero-city Leningrad."

The platform. A little flowerbed-grave at the end of the track. Eleven-twenty-five on the station clock. A monument with an outflung arm: "There he is!"

And his face was made of iron.

EXTERNAL INSPECTION OF A BOOK

Gogol in the edition of A. F. Marks, vol. 4—"Two scenes excluded from the first edition because they slowed down the action of the play." The scene with Rastakovskii.† Interested, I look to see whether Rastakovskii has remained anywhere in the canonical text. I leaf through, I don't find him, I get bored, I slam the book shut. What's this?

"Bound at the 'Niva' Bindery," I read at the bottom of the cover. Yes, it's neatly bound. They used to bind things neatly *then*. It's nice to hold in your hand. Greenish blue calico, the gold hasn't all worn off yet. The colophon is a convolvulus flower, like a question. There's no price on the back. But—what's this?

I closed Gogol, but here's Gogol again. Under that flower is printed, "Drawing approved by the Government." That is, this very flower has been approved. It's small comfort that *then* the govern-

*Khoma is destroyed by a glance from the gnome Vii, a stout creature covered with black earth, with eyelids that hang down to the ground and a face made of iron.

†In his 1842 *Collected Works*, Gogol included two scenes that had been omitted from the first edition of *The Inspector General*. Rastakovskii is a character who appears in one of the scenes.

ment had pretty good taste; after all, the colophon is rather pretty. "Approved by the Government." We are compatriots.

THE LITTLE CASE IN THE LITTLE BOX

It has always seemed to me, I have always flattered myself, that I have an easy time finding any passage I need in a book. Even a book I read long ago, in an unfamiliar edition. One-two-three, I open it, I take a look, here it is. The only thing that's hard is not to notice this wonderful ability in yourself.

There are authors whose waters close up immediately behind the reader's stern; an impression remains, even a shock, but it is almost as immediately impossible to differentiate as the closed book itself. Dostoevsky for one. While I read, I forget the words in which it was written. But even in Dostoevsky I can immediately find the passage I need. The problem is just to remember which passage I want to find. For instance, a duel. Where does he have a duel? Not there, not there, and not there. It must be *The Possessed.* Where in *The Possessed?* Not here and not here.

It would seem as if we remember all the details in Gogol. Since childhood each image has been distinct, outlined. But with him I can never find it, can never open the volume at the place I need.

Once I had the idea of using the description of Chichikov's traveling case as an epigraph. What could be more distinct than that object! There it stands on my table, like the work of a pop artist. The epigraph will be like that too, like a decal! Joyfully I rushed to that distinct place in *Dead Souls* where the case stood. It wasn't there. There was only the word *case,* with either a hint that it was a remarkable case, or a promise that it would be mentioned again. Renouncing with difficulty the place where it had always stood for me (the place where Chichikov installs himself in the hotel room), I set off for the next place where it might be—but it wasn't there either. This disheartened and wounded me; reluctantly I proposed a third place and was almost pleased when it failed to show up there as well. I began to turn pages far and wide, getting carried away against my will and rereading individual chapters—the case was nowhere to be found! But I remembered it as if I had seen it! I spent a whole day in this bitterness, not even getting down to work. Toward evening I had already begun to stumble across only the passages I had reread, and the place where the case *had* to be—I already knew almost by heart. But the case wasn't there, as if it had been swallowed up by the earth . . . or rather by the page, between the lines. I had already begun to think about this unusual artistic phenomenon, a sort of almost holographic effect (a technological anticipation!) by which Gogol, without expending any energy, has forced us to *see* in a literal, physical way. The occasion for rereading *Dead Souls* from such an unaccustomed angle, in such a nonsequential way—for that occasion alone one could give thanks to chance and not feel put out. And the day is over. . . . Almost pleased, I put the book aside, daydreaming about the power of an artistic image. Drifting toward sleep, I leafed through the book like a deck of cards, as if running a fingernail along piano keys. . . . What's this? Really? It can't be! The living Gogol grinned from the page, and what did I see there! I could hear him giggling, his long nose buried in his shoulder. . . .

Korobochka!* The case was located in "Korobochka"! I wonder why I wasn't drawn to reread just that "Korobochka" chapter, why I thought the case just couldn't be in it? All I know is that it was the only chapter I didn't reread on that "utterly wasted" day.

But that's not enough—I did say that I heard laughter in my room. For what did I see when I finally found the ill-starred piece of luggage?

" 'She's worn me out, the damned old hag!' he said, resting a bit and unlocking his case. The author is sure that there are readers so curious that they would even like to know the plan and internal arrangement of the case. Well, why not satisfy them? Here it is, that internal arrangement. . . . "

Gogol giggled.

P.S. Just now as I was writing all this, I decided to also check the phrase that I heard in the train car and remembered very distinctly, about the "iron face." And what do you know? The business with the case was almost repeated, with the difference that "Vii" is a little shorter. I found that phrase at the very top of the next-to-last page, after having refused to engage in superficial searches and rereading it straight through from the beginning. Well, I don't regret it.

It's very hard to find anything in Gogol, right up to meaning; Gogol somehow shrinks from your touch, wriggles away. He hides, and when you finally find him it won't be right, it won't be him: it isn't that you have found him, but that he thrust himself out where you didn't expect him, where there was no place for your ideas of him, where he wasn't yesterday. That Gogol is no longer where you remember him; *this* one is not where you expect him. The order in which Nozdrev and Sobakevich appear is not obvious, and where

*Korobochka, the name of one of the characters in *Dead Souls*, is also a Russian word meaning "little box." Thus the heading to this section means both "The Little Case in the 'Korobochka' Chapter" and "The Little Case in the Little Box."

Pliushkin is—you'll just never find out. And no matter how many pages you leaf through, no matter how you try to learn *about* Gogol, there will remain in your room only the trace of a laugh, the shadow of a nose, and the smell of a bit of unholy power.

REMISSION OF SINS

So then, being buried alive is a condition for the immortality of the corpse.

However, the desire to see something satanic, infernal, even the unholy power in the audacity of Gogol's art is the desire to flatter oneself. We are not like him, not to that extent, on the other hand we aren't devils; we are people, with our weaknesses, peccadilloes, the inconclusiveness of our efforts and deeds, but—people. It is as though, according to our pathetic bookkeeping and limited range, to make up for our dimness, our laziness, our weakness, our belonging to the human race, we are guaranteed forgiveness, remission of sins; weakness is our earthly investment in the heavenly cooperative. But a person who does not forgive himself for his sufferings, who does not replace conscience with suffering, who does not console himself with suffering, who has not expiated anything with that suffering because he has seen clearly that these things, suffering and conscience, are separate—suffering is life, and conscience is God, and there is no way to fix things up, and conscience cannot be bought off by suffering—to us such a person is in the grip of arrogance and the devil. Gogol's suffering seems somehow quite just to us because he is not a person.

Rozanov has a "fallen leaf" about the fact that he, Rozanov, can imagine anything you like about Gogol—this, and this, and this (he enumerates what seem to be highly virtuous, rare, heroic things)—but he can't bring himself to imagine "Gogol crossing himself."*

But here are Gogol's final lines:

"Have mercy on me a sinner, forgive me, Lord! Bind Satan again with the mysterious force of the invincible cross!

"How can I act in order to consciously, gratefully, and eternally remember in my heart the lesson I have received?"

How can I act. . . .

This is more than crossing oneself.

Translated by Susanne Fusso

**Fallen Leaves* is a collection by the critic and philosopher V. V. Rozanov (1856–1919).

Sergei Bocharov

Around "The Nose"

> Skryeshi ikh v taine litsa Tvoego ot
> miatezha chelovecheska. —Ps. 30:21
>
> In the covert of thy presence [*litso*, "face"]
> thou hidest them from the plots of men.
> —Ps. 31:20

THESE REMARKS are a continuation of my attempt to connect the famous enigma of "The Nose" with Gogol's philosophy of humanity, an attempt begun in my article "Zagadka 'Nosa' i taina litsa" ("The Enigma of 'The Nose' and the Mystery of the Face").[1] That article had two initial premises. The first was that careful attention must be paid to the very character of the story's strange subject, the very choice of such an absurd and ridiculous subject, the nose itself with its specific physical and physiological character, which for some reason so intrigued Gogol that he continually touched upon it in artistic texts, letters, and album notes. In these persistent jokes on the theme of the nose there is some point we have not yet deciphered, and it seems possible to speak of a special complex of the nose in Gogol. Of course this complex and this point are present in the story "The Nose."

But—and here lies the second premise of that earlier article—in Gogol this theme of the nose has a significance that transcends the object itself. To understand this strange story there are two equally important requirements: to deal with the "nose" not merely as a comical object but as a highly expressive and in its way weighty object for Gogol; and also not to get stuck on it, that is, not to find oneself in the position of the characters in the story, who are hopelessly bewildered by this object and this word: "He started to rub his eyes and grope: a nose, a nose indeed!" (III:50). In the literature on Gogol there is an authoritative work that, one might say, gets stuck on "the nose" in just this way: the well-known study by V. V. Vinogradov.[2] To explain the story Vinogradov introduces an encyclopedic volume of material on the motif of the nose in language and in the literature of Gogol's era. His study of the story consists entirely of this "nosological" commentary; the plot is deduced from linguistic puns connected with "the nose." In Vinogradov's work there is much useful material and many lively observations, but faced with the enigma of "The Nose" it is just as powerless as the characters in the story are when faced with the events that happen in it. Like the police officer in the story who adduces his nearsightedness as justification for not immediately recognizing the departing gentleman as Major Kovalev's nose, Vinogradov's meticulous analysis is a nearsighted one, since it looks no further than "its nose" and does not depart from the sphere of the story's apparent action.

Yes, one must pay literary-critical attention to the nose in Gogol, but at the same time one must go beyond the nose and see where it leads us in the world of Gogol's images. It leads us, as we may discover with surprise, to the mysteries of Gogol's anthropology. And above all it naturally leads us to the problem of the image of the human face in Gogol. The best introduction to this theme of *the face* in Gogol is a quotation from Innokentii Annenskii's article on "The Portrait":

> Gogol wrote two stories: one he devoted to the *nose*, the other to the *eyes*. . . . If we place these two emblems—of *corporeality* and of *spirituality*—side by side and imagine the figure of Major Kovalev, who for unknown reasons bought himself a medal, and the shade of Chartkov, who dies in insane delirium, then we feel if only for a moment all the impossibility, all the absurdity of a being who combines in himself nose and eyes, body and soul. . . . But indeed it may be that a sort of higher *humor of creation*, no longer accessible to us, is manifested here, and that the enigma of man, tormenting for us, is solved as simply as possible in the sphere of the higher categories of existence.[3]

The critic-poet's meditation is remarkable for the sensitivity with which it corresponds to the *picture of humanity* that saturates all of Gogol's work in a sort of fragmented and dissolved form. The expression "kartina cheloveka" ("picture of humanity")—the title of an anthropological work by A. Galich, which appeared precisely when Gogol's "Nose" was being written (1834)—seems felicitous as a definition of that artistic conception of man as a physical-spiritual being, a conception that seems to be scattered about the world of Gogol as the red jacket is scattered in pieces about the fairground in "The Fair at Sorochintsy"[4]—scattered in innumerable features and details which do not submit to rational transcription, but in each and every one of which, in the words of Andrei Belyi, "the dog is buried" ("the point lies").[5] It is a purely artistic picture of humanity, which in the late Gogol was only partly transformed into a more rational anthropology, psychology, and morality.

Annenskii comments on this Gogolian artistic anthropology, and his commentary is itself almost an artistic one. What does Annenskii do? From two so different stories he take two emblems of the face of man—the fantastically isolated nose and eyes—and as if by force combines them into a single *image of the face.* But this image of the face contains discord and the grotesque: after all, it has been put together from the disconnected material of two different works, and these parts, which had fallen away and are now pulled together, preserve their separateness even while forming part of a single image, part of the face. Annenskii attempts to synthesize a face out of Gogol's material, but in this synthesis there is no Grace-ful unity, for "sintez vsegda blagodaten" ("synthesis is always full of Grace," from unpublished notes on Gogol by V. N. Toporov). This discord in the human being may be understood in connection with various philosophical traditions—either according to Christian anthropology, as a sinful corruption of God's image in man (according to the Christian conception, God's image unites soul and body in man by Grace); or according to the idea that Annenskii suggests, the classical idea of a higher "humor of creation." Both philosophies are apparently relevant to Gogol's anthropology, but the idea of God's image has primary significance. Gogol wrote of "chelovek, kak predstavitel' obraza Bozhiia" ("man as the representative of God's image," VIII:240), and we cannot read his picture of humanity without correlating it with the Christian conception of the image bestowed on each person, which a person may either cultivate into the godlike or damage and distort.

The human face as represented by Gogol is a major topic for reflection, and it is strange that there are (almost) no studies on it, and that those who write about Gogol have not paid sufficient attention to it. Meanwhile the attention paid to the human face by the author himself is unusual in a number of respects. Above all, in Gogol there are many faces, descriptions of faces, and actions that physically touch the human face. This is a sort of center of attraction in his world, a center of high tension. No one has yet done a detailed inventory and analysis of the various cases, which seem to constitute a definite typology in Gogol. Therefore, we must base ourselves on a few selected examples that reveal a certain tendency.

This tendency can be seen, first of all, in an exceptional attention precisely to the external physical human face, to the very flesh of the face, to its bodily makeup and bodily perceptibility. Next, the portrait of the face is never neutral in Gogol. It is as far as possible from being a simple dispassionate description; it is displaced and deformed by the author's gaze. The direction of the displacement is expressed and generalized by the author himself in the epigraph to *The Inspector General:* "Na zerkalo necha peniat', koli rozha kriva" ("Don't blame the mirror if your own mug is crooked"). In "The Denouement of the *Inspector General,*" in explaining this epigraph, Gogol made it clear that it applies in general to any and all faces in contemporary human society. To the offended Semen Semenych's question, "Is my mug really crooked?" Fedor Fedorych answers, "But, my friend, Semen Semenych, again you're asking a strange question. After all you're like the rest of us sinners, you're no beauty. One can't come right out and say that your face is a model of perfection. No matter how you look at it, it's sort of lopsided, and whatever's lopsided is also crooked [*chto koso, to uzh i krivo*]" (IV:125). Evidently, Semen Semenych has an ordinary, everyday face, well, maybe a little lopsided, but Gogol's mirror shows him this external lopsidedness, multiplied by internal lopsidedness, as an insultingly crooked mug. This insult to the human face has a serious and even lofty basis in late Gogol. In general a certain evolution may be observed in the character of Gogol's depiction of the face, which has three stages.

The first stage is exemplified by *Evenings on a Farm near Dikanka.* Here people deal unceremoniously with each other's faces, and an entire collection of coarse synonyms is used to designate the face—*morda, rozha, kharia, rylo, obrazina, lichina* (slang words meaning "mug," "snout"). At times almost no distinction is made among people, beasts, and demons. But all these abundant external desecrations of the face do not cause internal damage to the human personality, which has not yet become a particular problem. The most vivid of these insults to humans are caused by the power of darkness, as is the case with Grandfather in "A Bewitched Place," when his "mug" is "glued up" and spat on, splattered with garbage and festooned with watermelon rinds. Reading *Don Quixote,* Thomas Mann was shocked by the story of the cottage cheese that Sancho accidentally left in his master's helmet. At the most pathetic moment the whey begins to trickle down the face of the Knight of the Mournful Countenance, who delivers a speech on the occasion, thinking that his brain has melted. Mann is amazed by "Cervantes's intemperate cruelty," the way his "inventiveness runs riot in ridiculous and humiliating pitfalls, into which the high-minded hero then tumbles and most comically disgraces himself."[6] Gogol's Grandfather, splashed with garbage and festooned with rinds, is in a similar situation, but this does not mean such a severe ordeal for his dignity because Grandfather is not Don Quixote, and the whole incident is explained as a prank by the power of darkness: "Again Satan will spit in your eyes" (I:315).

Nevertheless, there are occasions in *Dikanka* as well when one senses keenly that the human face is being touched in an unseemly, impossible fashion, as in the case of the bodies piled up in Solokha's sacks: "The poor clerk did not even dare to express his pain through coughing and wheezing when a heavy peasant sat almost on his head and placed his boots, covered with frost, on either side of his temples" (I:219). Of course this is only an external operation, and again the Devil's tricks are behind it. But it is a sort of trying-out of the piquant possibilities in such treatment of the human face. In general one may say of *Dikanka* that although this humiliation of the face is still of a comparatively innocent character, the very operation and, so to speak, method and technique of this humiliation, leveling, and mixing of the human face with the most external, alien, and dirty things have already been richly elaborated.

In the second and principal period of Gogol's work, a process takes place that has been discovered and described by Iurii V. Mann: the Devil as an active subject and cause of fantastic action disappears from Gogol's world, but that world becomes fantastic from within, strange in a Gogolian manner. "The fantastic has receded into everyday life, things, people's behavior and their way of thinking and talking. . . . The fantastic has receded into style."[7] One may continue this statement: it has receded and taken root in the faces of Gogol's people and in the style of their depiction. There is no Devil who jests with the human face, but the fantastic nature of the most inventive *unmotivated* deformations of the human face (like the disappearance of the nose from Kovalev's face) becomes all the deeper and more destructive of the human image. These deformations are diverse and constitute yet another typology in Gogol.

One may recall Dostoevsky's remark that the Devil is fighting with God and the battleground is men's hearts. Gogol also saw his human being at the center of a battle between powerful spiritual forces. But Gogol's human being is corporeal, more external than Dostoevsky's, and the battleground is also brought out to the exterior—to the human face. We may say of Gogol, paraphrasing Dostoevsky: the battleground is men's *faces*.

There is a discussion of virtue in the *Protagoras* in which Plato speaks of two different types of relationship between parts and the whole, and he introduces as an example the difference between the parts of a lump of gold and the parts of the face. If the various virtues ("wisdom, temperance, courage, justice, and holiness," 349b) may be regarded as "parts" (manifestations) of virtue as such, it is "not like the parts of a lump of gold all homogeneous with each other and with the whole of which they are parts, but like the parts of a face, resembling neither the whole nor each other and each having a separate function" (349c).[8] Thus, as the model of the noblest type of unity of parts with the whole Plato chooses none other than the *face*, with its precious qualitative variety of the parts and their harmonized unity.

This Platonic face may be taken as the philosophical background against which one may analyze Gogolian deformations. Gogol has an entire spectrum of violations of the classical type: There is the frankly anti-Platonic case—a face completely without parts or features, bare, somehow unarticulated (in folk demonology such is the face of the Devil, the face of a demon, bare and empty, "smooth as an egg"):[9] "And if you stand before me, I see only that you have a face, but I notice neither nose nor beard, nothing" (III:66) (spoken by the above-mentioned policeman in "The Nose," also referring to his nearsightedness). Or the case in which, even if the features of the face are in place and described in detail, the equilibrium among them is destroyed, as in the famous "kuvshinnoe rylo" ("jug's snout"), where "vsia seredina litsa . . . poshla v nos" ("the entire middle part of the face ran mostly to nose," VI:143), and in a whole collection of Gogolian faces recalling "badly baked bread" (VI:229). (Indeed if we consider Gogol's own commentary in "The Denouement of the *Inspector General*," it becomes clear that under Gogol's gaze the most seemingly ordinary faces undergo such a dislocation. All faces have an inevitable "lopsidedness": "Whatever's lopsided is also crooked" [IV:125]—such is the direction in which the dislocation moves.) The very outline of the face is deformed and moreover is described in a very detailed, careful, and meticulous way, as in the following experimental portrait, in the fragment "Fonar' umiral" ("The Lamp Was Dying Down"):

> A face in which one could not discern a single angle, but which all the same was not marked by light, rounded outlines. The forehead did not fall straight down to the nose, but was completely sloping, like an ice-covered hill for sledding. The nose was its continuation—large and blunt. There were lips, only the upper lip stuck out further. There was no chin at all. From the nose a diagonal line ran right to the neck. It was a triangle whose apex was located at the nose: such faces express stupidity more than anything else. (III:331)

Finally, the most extreme case: the absence of the face from the place where it should be, a hole instead of a face, as in the famous description of Petrovich's snuffbox, "with the portrait of some general, but it is impossible to say which general, because the place where the face had been was poked through by someone's finger and then pasted over with a small rectangular scrap of paper" (III:150). This description is deeply terrifying, terrifying in the very depths of its comedy, because such a refined invention is not just an attack by someone's finger on the sacredness of the human face (even if only a portrait), but an artistic attack on it by the writer.

What, in fact, is the source of these deformations? Gogol's characters love to talk about bad mirrors, in which "your mug comes out looking lopsided" (V:15). Here Podkolesin is speaking, but the narrator, too, speaks of typical mirrors that reflect "a kind of flat cake instead of a face" (VI:62). In the final analysis the author says to his characters plainly: Don't blame the mirror, this is what your inner face is like. The deformation of the face appears as an unmotivated, fundamental attribute of the Gogolian world which arises both from the objective state of that world and the Gogolian person and from the author's subjective view of them. Both the view and the world, in their unique interconnection, are the source of this unusual and challenging depiction of humanity.

Thus, insulting the human face—whether by deed, word, or, most profoundly, depiction—forms one of the striking and inexplicable oddities of Gogol's world. In early works it is motivated by the action of a fantastic negative force, "the Devil"; later it appears as an unmotivated general property of the depicted world. Finally, in late Gogol this way of treating the face acquires a new function. In the hands of the writer-preacher it becomes a conscious method of educating a humanity that has stagnated. Late Gogol begins, on the part of the author, lyrically to address and present to his characters and then to modern humanity in general this image of the face as evidence. Through the same means of insulting the face, seemingly borrowed from his own world of images, he seeks now to heal and save humanity; the evil of the human face's desecration must now directly serve goodness and salvation. Instead of filthy inn and tavern mirrors that distort the images of his characters, now he places directly before them the pure mirror of his own art, and it, alas, reflects the same crooked mug. It is as if Gogol borrows the language of his characters when in *Selected Passages from Correspondence with Friends* he advises the "Russian landowner," "Do not beat your serf. It's no great art to bash him in the mug. . . . But know how to really get his goat with a word," and shows how to do it: "Akh ty, nevymytoe rylo!" ("Oh, you unwashed snout!" VIII:323–24). The indignant Belinskii quite justly recalled Gogol's characters as the source of this way of expressing oneself and of educating humanity: "From what Nozdrev or Sobakevich did you overhear this."[10] Finally, in an entirely lyric manner Gogol presents humanity with salvation in the form of a *slap in the face* (*opleukha*): "Oh, how we sometimes require a public slap in the face, given in view of all!" (VIII:348). S. T. Aksakov told Gogol about M. P. Pogodin's reaction: "Jesus Christ teaches us that if someone smites us on the cheek we should meekly turn to him the other also; but where does he teach us to give slaps in the face?" (XIII:234). "I would like to know how you would contrive to answer him," Aksakov added.[11]

Indeed, it would not be easy to answer. Pogodin's contrast of Gogol's slap in the face with the gospel turning of the cheek was a sensitive objection, because, intentionally or not, the gospel cheek served as a model for Gogol's slap, but a somehow inverted one. Gogol, for whom, as we have seen, the human face was an attractive—perhaps even morbidly attractive—center of artistic attention, must have experienced with heightened intensity this commandment and the role accorded in it to the face, the unbearable corporeal concreteness that was necessary here in order to convey the scope of the spiritual feat, of this "vysshee liubomudrie" ("higher philosophy"), as John Chrysostom called it.[12] This is not the only instance in the Gospel of the motif of the humiliation of the face. Christ himself endures it in reality, when people slap his cheek and spit in his face.

I venture to note here, realizing that the comparison is perhaps inappropriate, that precisely these motifs and these actions are rather frequently employed in the world of Gogol's characters. Indeed the writer himself experiences such urges in relation to the faces of his countrymen, especially in the first months after his departure from Russia in 1836. See his letters to Pogodin: "But in Russia there is such a large collection of disgusting mugs that it became unbearable for me to look at them. Even now I feel like spitting when I remember them" (XI:60); "people born to be slapped in the face" (XI:77). He hopes that Zhukovskii will avoid meeting "those physiognomies that one just has to spit on" (XI:76). These direct and live reactions are still far from the future slap in *Selected Passages*, although they are on the road to it. The "slap" in *Selected Passages* is already an entire idea that relates strangely to the gospel cheek. In fact, when he calls for *putting forward* (*vystavit'*) one's face for a public slap (VI:241), Gogol expects of contemporary humanity precisely the spiritual feat of offering one's cheek. Nevertheless, Pogodin's retort to Gogol hit the nail on the head, because the gospel commandment does not give one the right to subject the face of one's neighbor, *another's* face, to such an ordeal. One must note that the very stylistic incompatibility of the word *lanita* ("cheek," Old Church Slavic) and the word *opleukha* ("slap in the face," colloquial) constitutes a venomous retort and is close to the essence of the matter. Gogol accepted the objection; with regard to the catastrophe of *Selected Passages* he turned the themes of Khlestakovism, the mirror, and the slap against himself: "I said this somewhere in a letter, although I did not even know then that I myself would receive this public slap in the face. My book is precisely a slap in my face" (XIII:302). It turned out that he offered his cheek to his own slap, becoming like his character, the soldier's wife in *The Inspector General*, who gave herself a beating.

Of course, these observations do not constitute a complete outline of the theme of the face in Gogol, but we have discerned a clear-cut tendency, a pointedly dominant feature. What role then, does the face, displayed in this manner, play in Gogol's entire picture of humanity? As is appropriate for the face, it plays a capital and central role—that is why this distorted image is filled with such high intensity. Do we not, in fact, sense in all these examples, in a kind of inside out, inverted way, the quite special, unique value of this location where all these scandalous things happen in Gogol, do we not sense it as the locus of human dignity? Gogol writes about the defamed sacredness of "zvan'ie i mesto" ("calling and place," VIII:291), but the central defamed sacredness in his world is the face.

Gogol's picture of humanity is full of physical detail; human flesh, its elements and members, and the methods of depicting this flesh carry disproportionate significance in that picture. But it is important that all of a person's flesh leads to the face; the coordination and correlating of any part of the body with the head and face, which lead the body, are always of great importance. For example, the "fist the size of a civil servant's head" which the robber puts "right up against the mouth" of Akakii Akakievich (III:161) produces a rather complicated effect: it is the double effect of correlating both sizes and qualities—the physical weapon of force and robbery with the "fragile weapon of the civil servant's intellect."[13] Thus this fist not only is placed up against the civil servant's face but is in a sense flouting this puny face itself. It is as if the physical member recalls the face, even though it is removed from it in the hierarchy of the body's composition, and through these bodily mediators it refers covertly to the face. This "fist the size of a civil servant's head" is the sort of quantum of Gogol's picture of the world by means of which a significance emerges that is almost inaccessible to rational interpretation, but which in fact communicates quite a bit of information. Our understanding of Gogol depends on our ability to "read" such quanta.

If in one direction all a person's flesh leads to the face, in the opposite direction the flesh is mixed up, as if by contiguity, with the world of things. Here is another Gogolian quantum, this time an erotic one. The suitors in *Marriage,* spying through a crack at the betrothed's toilette: "Nothing is visible, gentlemen. And you can't make out what that white thing is, a woman or a pillow" (V:30). Human corporeality, torn away from the *image* as humanity's inner form and task, thereby torn away from the *face* as the focus, center, and "representative" of the image in humanity—this corporeality, disintegrating into parts and members, losing form, seems to be striving in the opposite direction from the face, toward confusion and identification with inanimate materiality.

The face itself may also be torn away from the image. P. A. Florenskii offered in his works an analysis of the face (*litso*) that has lost contact with the visage (*lik*). Not without reason does he mention Gogol in this connection:

> Suddenly the face of our interlocutor, which had led into the depths of the personality, is covered with an ontological film and, as if torn away from its own essence, appears to us as an external thing. The gaze, which had penetrated into the infinity of the gaze meeting it, suddenly comes up against the moist convexity of the eyeball and skims blindly over the skin, inspecting the pores of the face. Then does not the personality, integral and united in its fullness, seem to us like a poorly tied bundle of separate signs? During such blackouts [*zatmenie*], one's own name, while preserving its linguistic substance, receives a different internal fulcrum, and having lost its ownership, becomes a common noun.[14]

As an example Florenskii mentions the masks of Gogol's characters, "whose names inevitably turn into common nouns and consequently display not so much the persons named as the thought devices of the namer, so that through his devices only he himself is displayed."

In Florenskii's analysis of the face, as well as in his distinctions among the visage (*lik*), the face (*litso*), and the mask (*lichina*) in his "Ikonostas" ("The Iconostasis"), we may in fact seek a philosophical commentary on Gogol's deformations. The face as "an external thing"—is this not the semantic background without which the enigma of "The Nose" cannot be deciphered? Does not the perplexing universal blackout in the story refer us to that "blackout" (*zatmenie*) described by Florenskii? Florenskii has what one might call a special philosophical sensitivity to the face as the central "locus" of that struggle between spiritual power and inert matter which for him pervades the life not only of humanity but of the cosmos. And he was able to describe this struggle as a dramatic action taking place on the material space of the human face, conveying at the same time the physical concreteness of this action. This is easy to perceive in the fragment cited above (think only of that gaze coming up against the moist convex surface of the eyeball), or in the following description: "Everything in the face that is not the face itself is pushed aside by the pulsing stream that bursts through the thick crust [*kora*] of materiality by means of the energy of the image of God."[15] Let us recall how frequently this same "crust" appears in Gogol's meditations on humanity and in his artistic descriptions: "We must constantly be afraid lest the crust that envelops us become stronger and finally become so thick that [living forces and impressions] truly cannot break through it" (XI:196). Florenskii studied the phenomenon of the breaking away of the human being's membrane from its nucleus, the "outer" person from the "inner" person, a phenomenon that Gogol was the first Russian writer and thinker to discover and depict. "The phenomenon of personality breaks away from its essential nucleus, exfoliates, and becomes a shell."[16]

This takes us back to the enigma of "The Nose." In my earlier article, "The Enigma of 'The Nose,'" I assumed that this enigma could be deciphered only with the help of the face, that is, by broadening our view from the part to the whole, and putting in place of the nose as an imaginary object and an imaginary theme the face as a real object and the most real theme in Gogol's art. The bifurcation of the nose in the story, by virtue of its utter absurdity, refers us to the face, for it is the essence of the face to combine this ambiguity, of which "the nose" is of course completely devoid. It is the face that harbors the possibility of that bifurcation and splitting analyzed by Florenskii. Meanwhile, in the plot of the story this possibility is absurdly realized by the nose, although it is not the nose's calling. " 'Face' is a hierarchical word";[17] and in this strange story the entire hierarchy of meanings of the word *face* is attributed to the nose—from object to subject, from something purely physical (in the extreme case, a blind material thing)[18] to a sovereign personality, and a socially prominent one to boot.

"Every kingdom divided against itself is brought to desolation" (Matt. 12:25)—it would seem that this universal truth is relevant even to "The Nose." Again we turn to the articles on Gogol by Innokentii Annenskii, who presented a picture of how the kingdom of the human image was divided against itself in Gogol's works. Annenskii speaks of the two people merged by life within each person: "One—tangible . . . the other—enigmatic, secret—the crepuscular, indivisible, incommunicable essence of each of us. But this second person is precisely that which gives us life and without which the whole world would sometimes truly seem like a mere jest of the Devil." And so of these two people, Gogol tore the first, the tangible one, away from the second, the crepuscular one, leaving the latter in shadow; he developed "typical corporeality," so that "the first, tangible one *would now answer for both.*"[19]

Again the critic-poet's penetration gives us a more reliable key than many scholarly studies. Let us employ Annenskii's image and say that in this story the nose answers for the face and for those two, "merged by life," who in the human image are after all united and merged most closely and above all in the face. In Gogol's story the nose answers for the entire human face, which contains both "the nose" and "the soul." But from this proceeds—as the insane consequence—the bifurcation of the nose and thus the impossible action of the story.

This obvious absurdity bears witness to something; it bears witness to somc kind of mistake, some kind of "blackout" that has given rise to this imaginary event. By the same token it bears witness to a certain truth that lies beyond the boundaries of this imaginary world. It bears witness to that Gogolian logic according to which "mistakes themselves already give us an idea how to avoid them, the characterless gives us an idea of the characteristic, petty and banal things call forth bold and unusual things in opposition, descending into the depths gives an idea of ascending upward and vice versa" (VIII:72).

Thus the hypertrophy of the nose "gives an idea" of the face and, further, of that internal contradiction in the human image which is the face, directed not only to the external world (and the emblem of this thrusting outward is the nose) but also inside and into the depths of the face, into its internal plane, in the direction, so to speak, of an inverse hypertrophy of the nose. If one may present the fantastic of "The Nose" as the result of an extremely one-sided understanding of humanity as completely external, turned outward, if the "blackout" that gives rise to the impossible plot is this total externalization of the internal, then according to the same logic described so expressively by Gogol himself,[20] must not such a story "call forth in opposition" a certain idea of another plane of human existence and another polarity of the human essence?

A remarkable document by a reader of Gogol's era has been preserved, but it has passed completely unnoticed in the literature on Gogol. This document, the response of A. M. Bukharev (Archimandrite Feodor), Gogol's interlocutor at the end of the 1840s, attests to the fact that Gogol's "joke," as Pushkin called it when he published it in *Sovremennik* (The Contemporary), truly does give one an idea of this other plane of human existence, strangely turning our gaze "with the pupils directed into the soul":

> Even your story "The Nose" reminded me that sometimes, having forgotten what my life is and what I should do in life, I sometimes bustle about, make a fuss, bother other people, and then it turns out that I am seeking nothing other than my own nose, and when I finally feel that it is back in its place, I calm down, as if I had found some great treasure. . . . This joke of yours is really hilarious! For example, we undertake to reform others, we try this or that key, and the key is perhaps closer to us than our own nose, in the true disclosure, already accomplished for us, of the mystery of our own ego. This thought seems to come to me of its own accord as I read your "Nose."[21]

These last words are particularly remarkable. So simply, "of its own accord," comes this profound idea, which interpretations of Gogol have not yet reached after a century and a half. And the very process of deepening the idea and the impression is so simply, one might say ingenuously, described: the hilarious joke depicts for us the empty and external activity that fills our lives, and turns us from such activity to that which is "closer to us than our own nose," to "*edinomu na potrebu*" ("the only thing we need"). This transition from a ludicrous event to the inner task of humanity and "the mystery of our own ego" takes place so naturally, and in this ingenuously penetrating retelling the absurd, puzzling story suddenly takes on the simple features of something like a gospel parable!

If we now turn to the text of "The Nose," we find a key passage that points the way to deepening our own perception. It is the objection of the "desperate Major" to the analogy offered by the clerk in the newspaper office ("Last week we had just such a case," i.e., a runaway black poodle turned out to be a runaway treasurer): "Now really, I am not placing an advertisement about a poodle, but about my own nose: that means *almost the same as about my own self* [*o samom sebe*]" (III:61, emphasis added).

In order to appreciate the significance of this passage, we must study the role of this existential formulation in the language of Gogol—writer and journalist, "artist-thinker" and "thinker-artist" (as Apollon Grigor'ev distinguished the two aspects of Gogol in his article on *Selected Passages*).[22] An example: In "Vii" the hero Khoma Brut has a conversation with the father of the dead maiden. After telling of his orphanhood (he never knew his father or mother), he offers a definitive characterization of himself: "And I don't have the right kind of voice, and *I myself am the Devil knows what* [*sam ia—chort znaet chto*]" (II:197, emphasis added). This is an important admission when it comes to explaining what happens to him: in "Vii," for the first time in Gogol (simultaneously with the first Petersburg stories) there appears a protagonist who must solve an inner problem; he has been chosen for an ordeal by the mysterious powers of life, and he is presented with a demand on his personality.[23] The outcome of the ordeal depends on what this "I myself" in Khoma Brut turns out to be. Thus in making such an admission about himself, he is speaking of the inner deficiency that will determine his fate.

Another example, from *Selected Passages:* Gogol says of the haughty, arrogant person that "he will run away from himself [*ot samogo sebia*] straight into the Devil's hands" (VIII:298). Sin tears a person away from himself, and in place of the whole person it creates, as it were, two figures. Gogol imagines this so vividly—in the form of spatial separation and loss of contact, the distancing or "running away" of the outer person from the inner one. It is as though within himself the person scatters in all directions, away from "his own self." Such a scene is sketched in the early article "*Boris Godunov*: A Narrative Poem by Pushkin": "People who seem to have forever run away from their own world of the soul, a world hidden within themselves and incomprehensible to them" (VIII:149). The action of "The Nose" is the realization of this scene.

Kovalev's retort to the newspaper clerk marks out a reverse path: at the critical moment the "runaway" person seems to guess what he has "run away" from. "About my own nose: that means almost the same as about my own self." The remarkable word here is "almost": it measures the amplitude of Gogol's picture of humanity at its extreme points—from the nose to the inner existential center. It is like a rickety, unreliable little bridge from the outer person to the inner one. By means of this indeterminate word they are simultaneously distinguished and linked, but linked somehow vaguely and obscurely, so that they are "almost" equated and again mixed together. The entire outline of Gogol's anthropology is encompassed by this speech of Kovalev's.

Thus, "I myself" ("sam ia"), "about my own self" ("o samom sebe"): this Gogolian existential formulation has yet to be studied thoroughly. It plays a highly significant role, especially in *Selected Passages* and the texts associated with it. Even in "Vii" and "The Nose" we have seen that it creates a moment of intensity in the text. It removes us from the empirical person, presented through an abundance of bodily details (not devoid of psychological details as well, but they too are on the same plane as the body; one might call them "body-psychological"). It removes us from this external picture of man, so highly developed in Gogol's works, to a certain secret nucleus that transcends and lies beyond the boundaries of that picture but always remains perceptible. Outside this nucleus, without feeling it or taking it into account, Gogol's picture of humanity cannot exist either. Even Major Kovalev dimly perceives in himself this independent individual core. In Gogol's hero it does not have a means of expression or disclosure, but it does have an inalienable existence. Thus in *Dead Souls* it is "only the inanimate body" of the deceased public prosecutor that first gives an idea of his soul: "It was only then that they realized with sympathy that the deceased did indeed have a soul, although because of his modesty he never gave evidence of it" (VI:210). Gogol did not know how to depict the "inner world," even when he wished to do so in his attempts at lyricism. "I saw him with the eyes of my soul," he writes of his dying friend in the fragment "Nochi na ville" ("Nights at a Villa," III:324). This is a rare attempt, exceptional for Gogol the artist, at direct lyrical expression, an attempt to speak directly of that secret world—"the soul"—and to show and depict it directly. But it is a symbolic rather than a psychological depiction, making use of a bodily image—those symbolic "eyes of the soul," thanks to which the soul becomes a "face" and one may look and see out of the soul directly, bypassing external membranes.

In the psychological conception of late Gogol, in *Selected Passages* and "The Denouement of the *Inspector General*," the existential formulation "my own self" serves to separate the layers of the human image, to exfoliate the inauthentic from the authentic. At the same time, the formulation itself undergoes and reflects the same sort of exfoliation. In a tautological and antinomian fashion it may be applied not only to what is authentic in man (this is more common in Gogol) but also to the inauthentic. The person "himself" is affirmed as a place in which one must collect oneself ("to collect all of oneself in oneself [*vsiu sebia v sebe*] and hold onto oneself," VIII:341) and in which one may even erect a monument (in "Zaveshchanie" ["Testament"] the author forbids the erection of an external monument to himself after his death and instead asks the reader to erect a monument "within himself" ["v samom sebe," VIII:219]).[24] But it also may be overcome, must be overcome. This is the subject of advice given by Gogol on educating humanity—"popreknut' ego im zhe samim" ("to reproach him by his own self," VIII:351). And in the aesthetic program of late Gogol, the viewer must turn his laughter at the characters "na samogo sebia, protivu sobstvennogo litsa" ("onto his own self, against his own persona"), for a Russian has "otvaga otorvat'sia ot samogo sebia i ne poshchadit' dazhe samogo sebia" ("the courage to tear himself away from his own self and not to spare even his own self," IV:136).

Behind Gogol's existential formulation and this internally contradictory use and fulfillment of it stood the tradition of the ascetic literature of the church fathers. Gogol was quite familiar with this literature, in which the formulation was elaborated in just such an antinomian fashion. "That which is most dear to us in a person, that which makes him 'himself,' is indefinable, because in its nature there is nothing that could be related strictly to the personality, which is always unique, incomparable, and 'matchless,' " writes Vladimir Losskii, interpreting the patristic conception of image and likeness. At the same time Losskii distinguishes this higher conception of the personality from the lower conception of individuality and of the special idea of *samost'* ("the self," Gk. *autotēs*) that has developed in fallen humanity. In the ascetic literature of the Eastern church this idea of "the self" designates the condition characteristic of historical humanity, which confuses personality with individuality ("and the term 'egoism' does not convey the true meaning of this term").[25] Twentieth-century Russian philosophy has subjected this idea of "the self" to new analysis, and the stimulus for such an analysis was Russian literature, especially Dostoevsky, but also Gogol to a lesser degree.

Finally, in evaluating Gogol's formulation from a philosophical perspective, one must mention Carl Jung's doctrine of "true selfhood." Jung distinguishes between two spiritual instantiations: the "mask" (the "persona"), "that which a person, in essence, *is not, but for which* he is taken by himself and other people";[26] and "the self" (*das Selbst*), the deep "ego" (and even "superego"). This distinction is without doubt closely related to the internal conflict in the human image that was so strangely and uniquely expressed in Gogol's "The Nose," as well as to the formulation "about my own self" in that work. It is not by chance that S. Averintsev, in setting forth Jung's conception of human spiritual life "as an inner drama with a multitude of characters," recalls (along with Western European writers of the twentieth century) Gogol and Dostoevsky.[27]

Jung's "self," however, as a kind of authentic instantiation, does not contain in itself that self-contradictory, antinomian character that Russian philosophy of our century observes in the analogous phenomenon and idea. In a recent study of Dostoevsky's *Besy* (*The Possessed*) that analyzes the conflict between face and mask in the central character, Lena Szilard demonstrates that in approaching such phenomena, "religious philosophy and modern analytic psychology" meet and mark themselves off from one another, both in terminology and in substance (she compares the positions of S. Bulgakov and Jung). In the Russian philosophical tradition, in which Gogol is included as an essential but as yet unappreciated link, the principle that he conveyed by the formulation "one's own self," a person "himself," is evaluated in a dual manner. On the one hand, it is affirmed as the principle of authenticity in a person, an inner fulcrum that certifies the reality of the personality; and at the same time it is to be overcome, as a dangerous principle of proud self-affirmation, self-identity, self-sufficiency and enclosure in oneself, which cuts a person off from other people and from the world.

For Dostoevsky, says Bakhtin, "a person never coincides with himself . . . , the true life of the personality is accomplished seemingly at the point of that noncoincidence of a person with himself."[28] This is incontrovertibly true; however, it did not keep Dostoevsky from directly inheriting Gogol's formulation. It appears in his most crucial ideological statements, such as the Pushkin speech: "Truth is not outside you, but within you [*v tebe samom*]; find yourself in yourself [*sebia v sebe*], subordinate yourself to yourself, master yourself."[29] We cannot yet adequately distinguish and appreciate in the language of Dostoevsky, the religious moralist, the legacy of Gogol, the journalist and moralist—his vocabulary, his intonation (independent of Dostoevsky's direct evaluations of *Selected Passages*). Wherever a didactic position arises in Dostoevsky, Gogol's imagery is revived, for example in Makar Ivanovich Dolgorukii's discussion of a person without "blagoobrazie" ("a noble appearance"): "Sometimes he would throw himself all about, and would stop noticing his own self [*samogo sebia*]."[30] Is this not, in its artistic provenience and even in the language of characterization, the same Gogolian person who has torn himself away from "his own self" ("samogo sebia")?

Gogol's existential formulation suggests yet another philosophical parallel. We do not know whether Gogol knew the works of his countryman Grigorii Skovoroda. His name does not appear in Gogol's works, but Gogol could have read him and probably knew about him by tradition and from Ukrainian researchers with whom he was acquainted, as well as from their publications in journals.[31] Independently of whether Skovoroda had any influence on Gogol, however, striking similarities can be detected not only between Skovoroda's search for the true and "precise" ("tochnyi") person and the moral thought of late Gogol, which as Iurii Loshchits has noted, "sometimes almost 'quotes' Skovoroda."[32] There are also broader similarities, not local but general, similarities not of individual motifs and verbal formulations but of systems of imagery—similarities, one might say, in the two writers' *picture of humanity*. For Skovoroda was also a thinker-artist, and he created his own picture of humanity; his philosophy was an anthropology, and his philosophical conception was the image of humanity that he created and that pervaded all his works.

The existential formulation of "one's own self" as the authentic person constitutes the center of Skovoroda's "wisdom-loving":

> And not to understand one's own self [*sebe samago*], word for word, is the same thing as to lose one's self. If there is a treasure buried in your house and you do not know about it, word for word, it is as though it did not exist. Thus to come to know one's self, and to seek out one's self, and to find a person—all mean the same thing.[33]

Combining Greek and biblical mythology in his world, Skovoroda builds a central opposition, two embodiments of two approaches to life that are expressed in terms of the direction of a person's gaze: either Narcissus, the person who has wisely fallen in love "with himself [*v samago sebe*] and his own center," or Michal, who "scattered her glances about the streets through the window of her father's house" ("The World is Michal's Street," pp. 27–29). These two orientations—the centripetal and the centrifugal, the latter expressed through the gesture of looking outward and all around (and also into a mirror, which amounts to the same thing), the complete turning of a person's face outward, the movement of running away from "one's own self"—these two orientations constitute the coordinates of Gogol's image of man. (They are revealed in different ways in the tragic "Vii" and the absurdly comic "Nose.")

The "interiority of Skovoroda's thought," as it is defined by the early twentieth-century religious philosopher V. F. Ern, the author of a book on Skovoroda, is as it were the inverse function of a minutely detailed corporeal image of humanity.[34] Paradoxically, the main arguments for the inner, invisible, and uniquely "precise" person are provided by the bodily members of the empirical person, which are enumerated and considered as everything that the person "himself" *is not.* In the dialogue "Narcissus" one interlocutor frightens the other by doubting his corporeal existence. To the question, "Do we really not have a head and nostrils?" he answers, "A head and nostrils? Know that we lack the entire person." And later: "You will say that I have neither ears nor eyes." "Yes, I already said long ago that you do not exist at all." The imaginary fragmented existence of man as a being consisting of separate members is systematically contrasted with the postulate that there is a whole person, the whole person, who may only be sought beyond this reality of bodily members. The passage from Skovoroda quoted above compares the loss of one's self to a treasure hidden in one's house; his corporeal metaphor for this loss is the following:

> And if you wish to know, then know that the way we see people is as if someone were to show you a single human foot or heel, having covered the head and the rest of the body. . . . Can one come to know *a person* by his heel alone? And just as you see nothing of your own eye but its extremities, thus have you never seen your ear, nor your tongue, nor your arms nor your legs, nor your other parts, your entire body, except for its extremities, called the heel, tail, or shadow. . . . Thus can you say that you have come to know yourself? You have lost yourself. You have neither ears, nor nostrils, nor eyes, nor all of you, except your shadow alone. (Pp. 32–33)

How can one not recall "The Nose" when reading this! It is not just this hypertrophy of the heel as a substitute for the whole person, presaging the hypertrophy of the nose. It is not just the connection formed by all this coarse bodily imagery, which can apparently be explained by both authors' connection with a common cultural origin—Ukrainian folk culture, the Ukrainian puppet theater, "a grotesque conception of the body."[35] The point is also the similarity in the way this imagery is used, its poetic and philosophical function in the two anthropologies—Skovoroda's and Gogol's. Skovoroda also has something like his own negative anthropology: corporeal images bear negative witness to the existence of other persons. "But since we see on all people without exception the external members, which also attest to their core . . . ," (p. 49). The "interiority of thought" has as its point of departure the entire external picture, "bolvaneiushchiia vneshnosti" ("material externalities," p. 51), the body of man, his "corporeal idol [*bolvan*]." Skovoroda has a beautiful fragment about this "idol," which is perhaps the best known of his texts, thanks to Leskov, who used it as the epigraph to his story "Zaiachii remiz" ("The Rabbit Warren"). The "corporeal idol" is placed at the center of the world (the center of Skovoroda's world) surrounded by "a wreath of a hundred mirrors," and within them he is "master of a hundred views," of copies and doubles, but even their single original, himself, is only a shadow—"telesnyi nash bolvan i sam est' tol'ko ten' istinnago *cheloveka*" ("our corporeal idol is himself only a shadow of the true *person*," p. 194). One recalls the mirror reflections of "corporeal idols," Gogol's characters, and the true mirror that the writer places before them. This is not an echo of individual motifs, but a deeper and more general echo of essence—an echo of anthropologies, of pictures of humanity, of their contours and their structures as a whole. But the direct and indeed almost quoted echoes are also telling. Skovoroda: "An essence that lives without a center is like a boat without a harbor" (p. 187). Gogol: "And external life in itself is the opposite of inner life; when under the influence of passions a person is drawn without a struggle by the streams of life, when he has no center within himself on which he might rest in order to overcome the very sufferings and sorrows of life" (XII:196).

In his book Ern draws a straight line from Skovoroda to Dostoevsky, not mentioning Gogol at all:

> In his anthropology Skovoroda distinctly separates empirical man from man as he can be comprehended by the intellect, and sees in the study and mastery of the latter the highest and main goal of his philosophy. What do the works of Dostoevsky engrave with lofty spiritual beauty, if not the blinding radiance of this intellectually comprehensible [*umopostigaemyi*] man in the tragic darkness of sinful, criminal life? What if not this does his fiery anthropologism elevate to a world-historical height?[36]

This comparison could be reinforced by the remarkable fact that "the man in man" (*chelovek v cheloveke*)—the basic idea of Dostoevsky's poetic philosophy—already appears in Skovoroda, who wrote that the human heart "is the most precise man in man [*v chelóveke chelovek*], and all the rest is peripheral." Along this path from one "man in man" to the other, however, was Gogol, and his absence from the outline, with which Ern's book concludes, of the connections between Skovoroda's thought and the further movement of Russian thought, creates a lacuna. If one compares it with Skovoroda, Gogol's picture of humanity is connected more concretely and intimately, more corporeally, one may say, than Dostoevsky's "fiery anthropologism." Most important, on the path from Skovoroda's "man in man" to Dostoevsky's "man in man," Gogol's picture of humanity was the most important event.

To provide the grounds for this thesis would be to open a new and larger topic. Within the framework of the present remarks and in concluding them, one may just say in summary that in a profound fashion, the way for Dostoevsky's poetic anthropology was paved by that *bifurcation* of the human image that Gogol produced. The significance of this painful operation in the history of Russian literature has not been sufficiently appreciated, as in general the anthropological aspect of Gogol's work has been little noticed and virtually unexamined (the omission of Gogol from Ern's sketch is no accident).

What sort of anthropology could there be in such a warped image? This general impression gave birth, especially in early twentieth-century criticism, to the opposition of Dostoevsky's vivid anthropologism to Gogol's peculiar artistic "inhumanity." "In one there are faces without souls, in the other—the faces of souls," wrote

Viacheslav Ivanov in formulating their "polar opposition."[37] One may, after all, read this as the dialectical formulation not just of their opposition but of a contradictory line of succession in the history of our literature. Strictly speaking, it is the formulation of Gogol's division of the image "which calls forth in opposition" (as if realizing the logic of Gogol's negative anthropology) Dostoevsky's artistic answer. For Gogol's division and dismantling of the image posed a question and called for an answer. "Faces without souls"—yes, at its extreme this is "The Nose." But let us recall how this story was read by A. M. Bukharev—as a story addressed to the inner person and speaking to a person's inner task. "No esli vneshnii nash chelovek i tleet, to vnutrennii so dnia na den' obnovliaetsia" ("Though our outer nature [*chelovek*, "person"] is wasting away, our inner nature is being renewed every day," 2 Cor. 4:16). Let us grasp these holy words: for Gogol's division of the image follows this spiritual model. It is a sharp division; in producing it Gogol unfolded the outer man in detail, while in Annenskii's words he left the inner man in shadow and secrecy. But he discovered thereby—thanks to the division—that person grasped by the intellect, the man in man, who for Gogol remained in the dark and silent depths. Those depths had to be illuminated by self-consciousness and the word, to acquire a "face" ("the faces of souls," in Ivanov's words; recall how Gogol tried to depict the face of the soul symbolically in the lyric fragment "Nights at a Villa").

Thus for Dostoevsky's "fiery anthropologism" Gogol's terrible dismemberment within the image was a prerequisite and even precondition of no small importance. It seems that in a strange way Gogol's negative anthropology signified at the same time an extreme exteriorization and simplification of the image of humanity (against the background of Pushkin's integral, spiritual-corporeal, complex-simple person) and a new and mysterious complication and deepening of it. In Gogol, man, so material and primitive, became mysterious and problematic in a way that he had never been in our literature before.

Translated by Susanne Fusso

John Kopper

The "Thing-in-Itself" in Gogol's Aesthetics: A Reading of the *Dikanka* Stories

> No matter what anyone did, her legs would go their own way, and something forced her to dance.
>
> They may sow it properly, but there's no saying what it is that comes up: not a melon—not a pumpkin—not a cucumber, the devil only knows what to make of it.
>
> —*Dikanka*

THE SENTENCES concluding the two volumes of Gogol's *Evenings on a Farm near Dikanka*, used as an epigraph to this essay, mark the emergence of a unique voice in world literature. The wild register of its obsessions is unmistakable. Legs dancing by themselves, communicating their motion to other legs at the bidding of an unseen choreographer, foreshadow the many places in Gogol's later works where his characters are infected and possessed by a contagious automatism. The melons and pumpkins of the second passage are not so much an example of but a metaphor for another characteristically Gogolian device, the sudden deflection of narrative, where a change in either plot or authorial tone erupts into the story without preparation and diverts the tale into new channels. If the marionette-like legs of volume 1 exemplify the inhuman in Gogol, the enchanted vegetable patch of volume 2 is a very emblem of Gogol's writing, where the expectations planted in the reader's head may be precipitiously and violently subverted by the story.

The conclusions of the two story sets of 1831 and 1832 are a reminder that many of the stylistic and thematic issues Gogol addresses in later works receive preliminary attention in *Dikanka.* While Nabokov eccentrically dismissed *Dikanka* as "the juvenilia of the false humorist," a work in which Gogol "was skirting a very dreadful precipice," most students of Gogol have tended to look upon the two volumes of pseudo-Ukraininan tales as an anticipatory step toward the major pieces of the years 1836–42.[1] The common thread seen in the stories has differed with the age and the critic: Vissarion Belinskii used *Dikanka*'s reliance on village *realia* and dialectal color to annex it ex post facto to the "Natural School," and twentieth-century readers like Vasilii Gippius and Iurii Mann have seen in *Dikanka* the origin of certain character types and Gogol's initial exploration of the fantastic, respectively. The unnerving flavor of the passages certainly gives a foretaste of Gogol's characteristic mixture of realism and magic. But it offers more. Behind the nonsense of these lines are concealed a metaphysic and an aesthetic peculiar to Gogol and highly unusual in their nineteenth-century context. It is difficult to make hasty generalizations about the construct of mind in a century that began with Austen mocking the faculty of intuition and Zhukovskii exalting it, and closed with Zola and Tolstoy betraying a skittish horror of the power of sexual drives even as an Artsybashev promoted their balanced expression. But uniting virtually all nineteenth-century European writing is a conviction that the human mind is a prodigiously capable instrument, however fettered by external constraints and buffeted by internal impulses. It is this tradition that Gogol transgresses in *Dikanka* in order to produce an aesthetic of inscrutability.

The involuntary multiplication of an action and the sudden redirection of plot are symptomatic of a new approach to both experience and the art that imagines it. They represent Gogol's fictional articulation of a long-standing problem in Western thought, the relationship between sensible and supersensible experience, things "seen" and "unseen." In the philosophical discourse of Gogol's time the first term of these pairs was known as the "phenomenon" and the second as the "noumenon," a Platonic opposition resurrected by Kant and used in Germany as a dividing line in determining philosophical allegiances for two generations after him. Although originally used by Kant as criteria of epistemology, "phenomenon" and "noumenon" acquired value in aesthetic debate of the late eighteenth and early nineteenth centuries as a result of Kant's *Critique of Judgment* (1790). Indeed, a characteristic feature of European aesthetics as it responded to Kant was its unfading attention to these categories. During the fifty years preceding Gogol's writerly debut, and for the first time since the Middle Ages, the ability of art to render supersensible experience legibly—or at the very least to refer to that experience even as it remained beyond mimetic transcription—became a central subject of discussion in European letters. It would persist as a topic of polemical reflection throughout the first three quarters of the nineteenth century, from the English Romantic poets' exaltation of the creative power of "imagination" to the pitiless reformulation of the limits of reason carried out by Russia's most profound students of Romantic philosophy, Dostoevsky and Tolstoy. The duel between the evidence of the senses and the evidence of the spirit in *The Brothers Karamazov,* and the representations of death in Tolstoy's two major novels and in a host of his short stories, all reflect late-century, Russian investigations of the phenomenal/noumenal polarity.

Although a detailed description of the usage of these terms in nineteenth-century philosophy would be out of place here, certain features of the opposition require refinement if one is to understand Gogol's peculiar achievement.[2] Kant was led to reintroduce to philosophy the terminological antithesis of phenomenon and noumenon when arguing against the power of reason to constructively resolve metaphysical—or supersensible—problems. In part a desire to "quarrel in print" with Plato led Kant to use these words and no other. They gave him an opportunity to refute the doctrine of ideal forms presented in the *Phaedo* and the *Theaetetus.* If for Plato the intelligible was only what could be thought (a "noumenon"), Kant ascribed intelligibility only to what was made manifest to the senses (a "phenomenon"). His first *Critique, A Critique of Pure Reason,* explored our means of knowing nature and therefore dealt exclusively with phenomena. Kant described the noumenon as a limiting concept (*Grenzbegriff*) beyond which reason could not stray.

> Whatever lies beyond the sphere of phenomena is (to us) empty; that is, we have an understanding which *problematically* extends beyond that sphere, but no intuition, nay not even the conception of a possible intuition, by which, outside the field of sensibility, objects could be given to us, and our understanding could extend beyond that sensibility in its assertatory use. The concept of a noumenon is therefore merely *limitative.*[3]

Kant sometimes used "noumenal" to refer to concepts like "God" and "freedom," which are not subject to the constitutive categories that the mind imposes upon sense experience. But in its other meaning for Kant, the noumenon is the dimension of an object of experience that exceeds its appearance. The noumenon is the limit to phenomenal experience, and since Kant did not believe in an intuition of objects that transcended sensible cognition, it is completely inaccessible to the mind.

> The concept of a noumenon is not therefore the concept of an object, but only a problem, inseparable from the limitation of our sensibility,

> whether there may not be objects independent of its intuition. This is a question that can only be answered in an uncertain way, by saying that as sensuous intuition does not embrace all things without exception, there remains a place for other objects, that cannot therefore be absolutely denied, but cannot be asserted either as objects of our understanding, because there is no definite concept for them.[4]

This noumenon Kant also referred to as the *Ding-an-sich*, or "thing-in-itself": "We cannot possibly know [the existence of the thing that appears] by the senses as it is in itself. . . . By sensuous perception appearances only, and not things themselves, are given to the understanding for reflection."[5] Kant was careful to describe the noumenon as a contentless boundary term, a concept that limits the object but is not itself an object.

Consternation over an apparent self-contradiction in the concept of noumenon—that something unknowable could be known, if only to the extent of knowing that it *is* unknowable—immediately led a generation of philosophers to revision.[6] Two major strategies emerged for banishing the uncomfortable term. One could promote a more powerful reason than Kant accepted and thereby encompass all reality within the one purview of an omnipotent rational function, or one could create an alternate form of cognition like "supersensible intuition." Thus one could either deny, like Hegel, that there was a limit to reason ("the real is rational"), or propose with Schelling that reason could be circumvented. Hegel's position remained of marginal interest in Russian literature before the time of Chernyshevskii, although the nascent intelligentsia of the 1830s, including Belinskii, Bakunin, and Herzen, briefly found the idea intriguing.[7] Schelling on the other hand had an immediate and prodigious influence on Russian letters. Arguing from a neo-Platonic position, Schelling describes the manifest world of finite things as the shadow of an ideal essence, which in turn reflects what he terms the Absolute. The Absolute is infinite and unified, displaying indifferentiation (*Indifferenz*).[8] Schelling denies that intelligence is limited by anything not itself: the Absolute can be known through intuition, of which art is the privileged vehicle. Art intuits the unitary infinite in the plural finite, discovering the universal through the particular: "Representation of the absolute with absolute indifference of the universal and the particular *in the particular* is art."[9] (This agrees with Kant's assertion that art is a phenomenally grounded statement about a noumenal world.) Since the Fall—a lapse from the Absolute—man is deprived of direct access to *Indifferenz*, but a symbolic order like art, acting upon his reason, can mediate the distance. This last claim derives from Herder, who saw language as the vehicle of a "foreign awareness."[10]

For Kant, presumably, any realm of experience that *can* be reached, by whatever means, is by definition part of phenomenal experience.

> Understanding and reason may be applied to phenomena, but it is very questionable whether they can be applied at all to an object which is not a phenomenon, but a noumenon. . . .
>
> When *we* . . . say that the senses represent objects to us as they *appear*, and the understanding as they *are*, the latter is not to be taken in a transcendental, but in a purely empirical meaning, namely, as to how they, as objects of experience, must be represented, according to the regular connection of phenomena, and not according to what they may be, as objects of the pure understanding, apart from their relation to possible experience, and therefore to our senses. This will always remain unknown to us.[11]

Kant and Schelling differ only in their belief in intuition. Schelling sustains Kant's idea that there are various kinds of experience but gives the name of "intuition" to the faculty that understands what "pure reason" cannot. He continues the Kantian tradition of a noumenon, subject not to a primary mode of understanding (Kant's *Verstand* and *Vernunft*) but to a privileged adjunct faculty, which for Schelling includes art. For this reason, the "noumenon" remains in Schelling, but the "thing-in-itself" disappears. He rejects the idea of an unknowable reality and retains some notion of the "thing-in-itself" only to deny that it is problematic. This line of thought embodies the essence of what can be distinguished as a "Romantic" aesthetic.

The most obvious philosophical forebear of the *Dikanka* stories is Schelling. In the *Dikanka* stories the noumenal world is so close to phenomenal experience that no special cognitive power like intuition is needed to make it accessible. The stories persistently conflate sensual and transsensual reality. They thereby disarm the potential of "the otherwordly" itself to become a subject of investigation. Witches live on the edge of the village and play cards in "The Lost Letter"; devils appear as gypsies in "The Fair at Sorochinsty" and as the rowdy strangers in town in "St. John's Eve." In "Christmas Eve" Vakula the blacksmith abuses the devil and threatens him with a beating. But Gogol does not limit himself to the more patent models of noumenality represented by the spirit world. He submits to similar demystification the imperial throne, often treated in Russian literature before Tolstoy as a noumenal realm (in Pushkin's *The Captain's Daughter*, for example, where Grinev cannot "see" Catherine the Great when he is before her). In "The Lost Letter" we hear about the throne (Empress Catherine eats dumplings) and in "Christmas Eve" we see it. The "domesticated spirits" of the *Dikanka* stories have been noted often enough.[12]

Because of the magic element in *Dikanka*, Gogol scholars have frequently stressed his filiation with Tieck, Arnim, Brentano, and other masters of the German *Kunstmärchen*. But while the suspense of the *Kunstmärchen* usually rides on the postponed and spectacular discovery that a past action was indeed supernatural, *Dikanka* takes the supernatural perfectly for granted. Moreover, its persistent conversion of noumenal reality into appearance rarely entails the loss of semantic differentiation between the two, as often takes place in the fairy tale. Fairy tales with magic elements normally assume the pervasiveness of magic.[13] The *Dikanka* stories, by contrast, carefully delimit the spheres of natural and supernatural behavior and use their intersection to generate plot. Apparent or real supernatural acts propel most of the stories. "The Fair at Sorochintsy" makes the devil's red jacket a talisman to be traced from beginning to end. Almost every section of "A Terrible Vengeance" follows a new interference of the sorcerer in quotidien reality. Both "Christmas Eve" and "St. John's Eve" are driven by a series of pacts and promises made with supernatural forces: gold in exchange for a murdered child, a trip to Petersburg in exchange for a vow not to make the sign of the cross. And a number of the stories climax with a moment of transport between the noumenal and phenomenal worlds. In "A May Night" Levko awakens from his encounter with the drowned maiden to find he still has the letters she gave him, and in "A Bewitched Place" the grandfather moves unscathed into and out of the noumenal realm.[14] The "bewitched place" of this last tale is an appropriate emblem for the reality construct used in most of the stories. *Dikanka* is a magic reading space where one finds the conventions of the fairy tale and an inchoate realist narrative tradition intertwined. For the reader the peculiar flavor of the stories lies in the *Dikanka* characters' failure to disengage the noumenal from their historically grounded experience in the Ukrainian countryside, a territory with perfectly unmagical historical and geographical coordinates.

If there is an analogy for the reality construct of Gogol's *Dikanka* stories, it would not be found in the fairy tale, where a distinctly independent realm of natural law does not exist; or in the *Kunstmärchen*, which demands a reader's passage from incredulity to belief; or, for that matter, in the gothic romance, which reverses the conventions of the *Kunstmärchen* in its progress from credulity to skepticism and explanation. Because *Dikanka* rarely problematizes and never compromises belief in the noumenal, it survives as a deliberately conceived vestige of a historical period that accepted the supernatural as natural, an era that distinguished sensible and supersensible but was not confounded by their interpenetration. In Schiller's terms, the *Dikanka* stories present a studiously "sentimental" image of the supernatural. (It would seem that the classical world, particularly ancient Greece, is an important intertext for Gogol, who uses "the Ukraine" in *Dikanka* to represent an order of belief that writers of his age typically associated with Homeric antiquity.)

The imagery of the stories supports the central theme of the *Dikanka* universe: the interaction of separate worlds. Nature and the human appear as obverses of one another: "Her hair curled and fell over her shoulders like a pale gray mist; a faint flush colored her lips like the scarcely perceptible crimson glimmer of dawn glowing through the white transparent sky of morning" (I:258/150).[15] In "May Night" heaven and earth touch: "The moon looks out from the center of the sky; the immense dome of heaven stretches further, more inconceivably immense than ever; it glows and breathes; the earth is all bathed in a silvery light" (I:159/55). In "A Terrible Vengeance" what lies beyond the horizon is suddenly made visible: "In all directions even the ends of the earth had become visible. Far off was the dark blue of the Odessa lagoon and beyond that lapped the waters of the Black Sea" (I:275/167).

Gogol's style also reflects his effort to bring the noumenal to light. Perhaps the strongest "noumenal" experience of the act of reading is recognizing a guiding hand in storytelling. In general, by foregrounding the relation of text production and reception, the *Dikanka* stories disclose the noumenal dimension of reading. The text ceases to be the world and becomes contingent upon discourse about authorship, text production, and transmission. Holding to ample precedents in the tradition of the seventeenth and eighteenth centuries, Gogol thematizes—especially in "St. John's Eve"—the moments of textual circulation: telling, writing, misquoting, publishing, reading and failing to read, losing the text, and so forth. This metatextual dimension in Gogol's work may be tame and inherited, but it is eminently appropriate to the overarching enterprise of the *Dikanka* stories—to bring "heaven" down to "earth." As a mode of storytelling in which the tale and the manner of narration mutually sustain each other, the *Dikanka* stories most resemble latter-day renditions of myth like Ovid's *Metamorphoses* and Joyce's *Finnegans Wake.* In all three cases a universe deriving from myth (where noumenon and phenomenon are one, argued Schlegel, and the infinite and finite blend together, according to Schelling) is debased by the voices of narration, which alter the reception of myth without challenging the mythical content. The noumenological experience in *Dikanka* is made human but not discarded.[16]

For the most part, the *Dikanka* stories are an exposition, with some modification, of the "Romantic" perspective—not strictly identifiable with any German philosopher after Kant, but most nearly based on Schelling's thought. Because *Dikanka* is largely about the domestication of the noumenal, it reproduces the Romantic enterprise. And like much Romantic art, it thematizes the aesthetic experience itself. In Gogol's art, Schelling's views become not simply an aesthetic philosophy but a program for creation. The majority of the *Dikanka* stories go beyond merely corroborating the theory and realize the Romantic aesthetic. The plots *do* what artistic appreciation uses intuition to accomplish, and dissolve the noumenal and phenomenal in a universal vision. Furthermore, in a litotes that confirms Schelling's conviction about the capabilities of intelligence, the *Dikanka* stories in the main deny that intelligence needs even to reach anything not itself. They simplify Schelling's theory by suggesting that no special cognitive power is needed to make the noumenal part of sense experience. Is there anyone who *can't* see a devil in the *Dikanka* villages?

• • •

At the beginning of his career, then, Gogol would appear to use the opposition of phenomenon and noumenon consistently. There are elements in the *Dikanka* stories, however, that suggest that the relation between phenomenon and noumenon is more vexed. In "The Bewitched Place" the grandfather cannot return in this world to the exact spot he occupied in another, and the riches he acquires "there" become swill "here."[17] The casual ease with which disguises are assumed and discarded—a mark of the unveiling of the noumenal—is replaced in "A Terrible Vengeance" by the rupture of a presupposed unity—body and soul. Within Katerina a noumenal realm is opened that is accessible to Danilo but remains closed to Katerina herself. Supersensible experience unfolds from *within* the subject as a fractious and resistant subconscious.

The stories betray other traces of an unusual aesthetic. They don't appear so much to be out of control—a quality sometimes attributed to the Gogolian text—as under the sway of a diseased mentality, inclined to indulge in trivial and repetitive discourse that forces the narrative to swell and bulge. In most cases in the *Dikanka* stories the reader can quickly identify the origin of these divagations as "Dikankan." The obsession with food, for example (which is carried *into* the noumenal realm in one story—see "St. John's Eve," I:138/34), is shared alike by the town's narrators and protagonists. But two other textual tendencies appear to be the unique product of an abnormal narrative mentality: "multiplication" and plot redirection, the features of *Dikanka* with which this essay opened. We will take up these two features in turn.

In "Ivan Fedorovich Shponka and His Aunt" Ivan Shponka's wives multiply in his dreams. The devil as pig multiplies in "The Fair at Sorochintsy," and the dancers in "St. John's Eve"—there are a lot of dancers in *Dikanka*—multiply everywhere. In the mid and late 1830s Gogol will use to great advantage the reduplication of terms: the presence of a second Ivan Ivanovich in "The Story of How Ivan Ivanovich Quarreled with Ivan Nikiforovich" ("not *the* Ivan Ivanovich but the other one, who squinted," II:265/410), the nose, the overcoat, and in "The Diary of a Madman" both the king of Spain and Spain itself. Gogolian multiplications are underdetermined, and their effect consistently unsettling. An example is the dance at Sorochintsy. In this passage, the peculiar declension from animacy and individuation to indifferentiation and death is motivated by the rule of duplication, according to which "more means same."

> Several couples surrounded the happy pair and formed an impenetrable dancing wall around them.
>
> A strange feeling, hard to put into words, would have overcome anyone watching how everything was transformed, like it or not, into a scene of unity and harmony, at one stroke of the bow of the fiddler, who had long twisted mustaches and wore a homespun jacket. Men whose sullen faces seemed to have known no gleam of a smile for years were tapping with their feet and wriggling their shoulders; everything was heaving, everything was dancing. But an even stranger and more disturbing feeling would have been stirred in the heart at the sight of old women, whose ancient faces breathed the indifference of the tomb, shoving their way between the young, laughing, living human beings. Caring for nothing, indifferent, long removed from the joy of childhood, driven by drink alone, which like the puppeteer with his lifeless automaton, made them do things that seem human; yet they slowly wagged their drunken heads, dancing after the rejoicing crowd, not casting one glance at the young couple. (I:135–36/32)

The passage begins with a spreading epidemic of liveliness, but its animation is undermined by the neuter pronoun: not "everyone was transformed, everyone was heaving, everyone was dancing," but "everything was transformed, everything was heaving, everything was dancing." Behavior is automatic, gesture not human but human-like, and the action is authored by "drink." The phrase "like it or not"—normally a cliché—acquires on rereading a sinister nuance, and the passage ends with deprivation (the morpheme "without" [*bez*] occurs four times), the nonliving ("lifeless automaton"), drunkenness, and the grave.

Such multiplications of action frequently precede instances of a second peculiarity of Gogol's style, the redirection of plot. In comparison to its treatment in Gogol's later works, plot redirection has received little attention in *Dikanka* criticism, and for good reason.[18] The reader is sometimes briefly kept in ignorance of the course of events by characters' disguises, but the stories in general keep the reader ahead of the characters' discoveries. The epistemological premise of most of the stories is classic comedy: an omniscient perspective on present action, coupled with ignorance of the future, induces the active reader to create possible plot combinations in anticipation of their realization or denial. "A Terrible Vengeance," however, runs against this convention. The story is characterized by major gaps (the circumstances leading to the sorcerer's imprisonment are given in half a sentence) and a narrative so rudimentary ("a sequence of disturbances created by the sorcerer") that the forward-thinking reader is left the vague assignment of guessing where the plot will end. Moreover, the conclusion produces a complete surprise. The interference of the sorcerer is swept up into a historical context that could never be deduced from plot information, and the thematized "terrible vengeance" turns out to be exacted by one ancestor of the sorcerer, Ivan, upon another, Petro, neither of whom was hitherto identified. Very few unclear textual places are "recuperated" by this ending.[19] The conclusion of "A Terrible Vengeance" is morally divorced from the story of Katerina and Danilo. Furthermore, the sorcerer himself is a victim, for the terrible vengeance is a punishment meted out *even* upon the sorcerer. "A Terrible Vengeance" is often dismissed by critics as one of the more derivative and—because it is absolutely humorless—least Gogolian of the *Dikanka* stories.[20] But its relatively primitive plot structure (Gogol would never return to the complexity of "Christmas Eve" or "A May Night"), together with the outrageous ending, presage the developing concerns of the mature writer.

The multiplications of objects in stories like "The Fair at Sorochintsy" and the redirection of plot in "A Terrible Vengeance" point to an interesting convergence between Gogol and Kant, the father of the phenomenon-noumenon controversy. Both textual effects lead to a radical severance of phenomenon and noumenon, with the result that the stories appear to "fall out" of a Romantic aesthetic. In "A Terrible Vengeance" resort to a noumenal world at the end accounts for but does not justify the particular suffering of Katerina and Danilo. This would seem to be a moral question, but it is an epistemological one as well. In the other *Dikanka* stories—most notably "St. John's Eve" and "Christmas Eve"—those punished are the transgressors. In the gothic tradition from which "A Terrible Vengeance" sometimes borrows, the punished are often innocent. Horace Walpole's *The Castle of Otranto* (1765), Charles Brockden Brown's *Wieland* (1798), and Heinrich von Kleist's "The Beggarwoman of Locarno" (1811) exemplify this axiology of the gothic. But in violation of the standard gothic schema, the accounts of Danilo and Katerina on the one hand and Petro and Ivan on the other are independent. Even the sorcerer, the mediator between the two narratives, is unwitting in his role. The force of "A Terrible Vengeance" lies precisely in there being *no* communication between a defined noumenal sphere—in this case the atemporal transcendence of divine justice—and the phenomenal. The fissure between the two is complete. Explanation does not lead to understanding; "seeing" is not "realizing." What brings terror to "A Terrible Vengeance" is the imposition of a noumenal order that cannot be grasped by the understanding. This order resembles Kant's "thing-in-itself," which is apprehended as a logical category but cannot be understood because it is without content. "A Terrible Vengeance" restores the "thing-in-itself" through denying noumenal experience the virtue of comprehensibility.[21]

Gogol's "return to Kant" in the plot redirections of "A Terrible Vengeance" represents an important moment in his career. In subsequent works he will increasingly pursue the ambiguities of Kantian epistemology: that there is a limit to understanding, but no content to what one cannot understand. With the exception of "Taras Bulba," all the stories in *Mirgorod* expansively develop Gogol's interest in solving the riddle of the "thing-in-itself." "Old-World Landowners" and "The Two Ivans" are appropriate brackets to the collection. Both take surprise turns at the end, suggesting a mysterious presence in the story. In "Old-World Landowners" the shift is now accompanied by narratorial reflection:

> Good old people! But my account of them is approaching a very melancholy incident which transformed forever the life of that peaceful nook. This incident is the more impressive because it arose from such an insignificant cause. But such is the strange order of things; trifling causes have always given rise to great events, and on the other hand great undertakings frequently end in insignificant results. Some military leader rallies all the forces of his state, carries on a war for several

> years, his generals cover themselves with glory; and in the end it all results in gaining a bit of land in which there is not room to plant a potato; while sometimes two sausage makers of two towns quarrel over some nonsense, and in the end the towns are drawn into the quarrel, then villages, then the whole kingdom. (II:27–28/219)

Here Gogol refers to a causal force that operates outside our knowledge. Events are determinate, not random, but the laws governing them cannot be discovered. The ruling principle is simply "the strange order of things." This impersonal motivation results in the disjuncture of normal cause-and-effect relationships: at the origin of the trivial is the grand event, and vice versa. After Pulkheriia Ivanovna's death, the narrator adheres to his own theory about events by introducing a hopelessly inapt anecdote, beginning with the question "What grief does not time bear away?" (II:33/224). While the subject of this nested narrative recovers after a year from his loss in love, the figure likened to him is Afanasii Ivanovich, who continues to lament the death of his wife after five years. In this way the narrator trivializes the grief of Afanasii Ivanovich with the confusing introduction of material, alien and unmotivated, from another plane. "Old-World Landowners" proposes that awareness of the inexplicability of events does not mitigate their effect. "The Two Ivans" confounds understanding in a similar way, proceeding swiftly from the madcap comedy of frivolous lawsuits to a forlornly pessimistic epilogue, which presages the world of grim self-deceived litigants in Charles Dickens's *Bleak House*. The world of farce in "The Two Ivans" lies beneath "a tearful sky without one gleam of light" (II:276/420). In both instances the stories pose the same question: does passion or habit govern behavior? But they then render the question extraneous. Passion implies an internal motivation and habit a lack of motivation, but "Old-World Landowners" and "The Two Ivans" suggest that motivation is external and unknowable.

"Vii" codifies Gogol's position in programmatic fashion.[22] Khoma Brut, tellingly called "the Philosopher," confronts two exclusive orders of magic, the divine and the diabolic. When the divine unmasks the diabolic, the diabolic cannot see the human subject. Revelation, or insight into the noumenal, removes the subject from any imprisoning, objectifying gaze. As soon as Khoma Brut recites his prayers, for example, the dead girl is revealed as a decaying corpse, but at that moment the girl cannot see him. At the climax of the story, however, Vii is hustled in and the tale ends with the institution for the first time of reciprocal sight, which causes the Philosopher's death. Having dealt almost exclusively hitherto with the masks and disguises of the "noumenological plot," the Philosopher comes face-to-face with the "thing-in-itself," and Gogol's message is clear. The "thing-in-itself" cannot be known.[23]

We can leave "Vii" here with its concluding metaphysical paralysis and turn to the aesthetic relation with Kant that Gogol establishes through use of multiplication. I noted above that Schelling claims art to mediate between the finite and the infinite. Kant's debt to empiricism makes him shy of totalizing concepts, but he also assigns art a mediating role and argues that art joins the subjects of his first two critiques, nature and morality. As a form of judgment, aesthetic taste bridges the spheres of determinism (man in nature) and freedom (moral man): "Between the realm of the natural concept, as the sensible, and the realm of the concept of freedom, as the supersensible, there is a great gulf fixed, so that it is not possible to pass from the former to the latter (by means of the theoretical employment of reason)." But between them lies judgment, "the faculty of thinking the particular as contained under the universal," which "even if it has no field of objects appropriate to it as its realm . . . with its concept of a *finality* of nature, provides us with the mediating concept between concepts of nature and the concept of freedom."[24] This idea was immensely influential. Schelling claims after Kant that intelligence, through art, perceives itself as the union of freedom and necessity: "The basic character of the work of art is that of an *unconscious infinity* (synthesis of nature and freedom)."[25] Friedrich Schiller, the most faithful acolyte of Kantian aesthetics, retains Kant's bridge and places the "play drive" (*Spieltrieb*) between the natural and moral spheres.[26] At the same time he argues that beauty, the quality art possesses, allows man to remain an individual in a community: "The dynamic State can merely make society possible, by letting one nature be curbed by another; the ethical State can merely make it (morally) necessary, by subjecting the individual will to the general; the aesthetic State alone can make it real, because it consummates the will of the whole through the nature of the individual."[27] Thus art in Schiller's terms produces an interesting achronological marriage of Kant's and Schelling's ideas. Art suspends without resolution the conflicts both of the individual with the crowd, and of freedom and necessity. The examples of multiplication in Gogol suggest that the first terms in these paired opposites drop out. When the impulse to dance spreads at Sorochintsy, the individual disappears and with him a capacity for choice. Multiplication means the instantaneous loss of individuation—what is replicated exactly is no longer individual.

This theme blossoms in the Petersburg stories. "Nevsky Prospect," "The Nose," and "The Overcoat" involve searches, in and through crowds, for self-completion, but in all three stories crowds are the locus of spiritual defeat. In "Nevsky Prospect": "The extraordinary brightness and variety of the scene completely staggered [Piskarev]; it seemed to him as though some demon had crumbled the whole world into bits and mixed all these bits indiscriminately together" (III:23–24/433). In "The Nose" and "The Overcoat" the protagonists are literally looking for missing parts of themselves. But multiplication weakens the position of the individual. As sightings of the nose multiply, so does the crowd. In "The Overcoat" a wall covered with overcoats signals Akakii Akakievich's impending failure with the crowd partying upstairs.

The Petersburg tales represent the apotheosis of Gogol's philosophy. (1) In all three of the stories mentioned, Gogol opposes extending reason's jurisdiction or allowing the mind knowledge of anything different from itself, thereby in one stroke rejecting Hegel and Schelling. "Nevsky Prospect" follows a traditional Romantic plot of disabusal and shows that things fail to conform with one's external idea of them. But such a world of false correspondences, created by an epistemology that *believes* in correspondences, is foreign to "The Nose" and "The Overcoat," in which the self sees only itself and is concerned only with self-alienation. (2) A noumenal realm exists, to which ontological and moral questions may be referred but not answered (why do noses disappear?). This sphere of invisible motivation is the "thing-in-itself." (3) Gogol dismantles Kant's bridge of art by questioning whether there is a realm of freedom to which art could lead. By denying the accessibility of the object, Gogol implies that his characters can have no moral experience of freedom and his readers no aesthetic experience of the same. The *Indifferenz* of unity in Gogol is the indifference of the crowd.

To understand the epistemological assumptions of Gogol's *Dikanka* fictions—which ultimately pass into patterns of reading—it was useful to look at the role of the "thing-in-itself" in German philosophy, and to distinguish it carefully from the commoner uses of "noumenon" (as Schopenhauer, among others, failed to do). Departing from Hegel and Schelling, Gogol's fictions imply a belief in the "thing-in-itself" and a corresponding skepticism about the faculties, reason and intuition respectively, that led Hegel and Schelling to abandon it. In his progress beyond Schelling and his disengagement from the metaphysical conventions that sustained a number of his contemporaries in the 1830s—Boratynskii, Lermontov, and Tiutchev—Gogol approached a pure Kantianism. Increasingly in his fiction there intrudes "another side"—not heavenly, not higher, not more real—to which the reader is forbidden passage. Most of Gogol's work after *Dikanka* ceases to maintain an equipoise between two worlds. His fictions "limp" because one world is barred from the reader.

In historical terms Gogol's work is a rereading—or one might say misreading—of Romanticism, as represented by Schelling. By the time Gogol began to publish, German philosophy was sweeping the Russian intelligentsia, and essays in his *Arabesques* like "On the Teaching of World History," "On Present-Day Architecture," and "A Few Words about Pushkin" show the kind of popular simplifications that German philosophy underwent in its reception by an educated but philosophically unrefined culture. Karamzin's fatuous noncomprehension of Kant in 1789 bespeaks a mentality that completely misunderstood the project of philosophy.

The grand design of German philosophy in the fifty years from Kant's first *Critique* to the death of Hegel (1781–1830) had little to do with Russian life in Gogol's time. The achievement of German philosophy was to reunite metaphysics with the epistemological questions being raised by science, and to provide a model for the reconciliation of conflict. These two issues—the nature of phenomenal reality and the discovery of ways of controlling disorder through various strategies (the dialectic, special faculties of mind like intuition, cultural artifacts like art or religion, etc.)—reflect the two chief post-Renaissance activities of philosophy in a contemporary guise: the confrontation with an increasingly secular culture and the effort to order the inherently *dis*orderly social system of bourgeois power.[28]

As *Arabesques* shows, Gogol did not absorb anything particularly coherent from German philosophy, and his own art, especially some of the stories published in this same collection, seems unrelated to the theories he was so excited about propagating.[29] And yet his art goes to the heart of epistemology and raises explicitly the question of controlling chaos. How do we deal with what we don't know? When diversity conjures up visions of the uncontrolled proliferation of noses or the mindless stamp of drunken dancers, how dare we believe in order? Gogol's texts ask these questions, but more important, they *are* these questions. The generic instability of virtually any Gogolian text, from *Dikanka* to *Selected Passages from Correspondence with Friends*, its threatening disunity, and its continuing problematic status as a knowable phenomenon in literary history suggest that Gogol's art may not be the dumb rendering of experience that

German philosophy would have all art be, but an alert comment on certain current discourses in European culture and an original contribution to their exposition.

The oppositions that Russian literature most readily inherited from Germany were ethnicity/universality, civilization/nature, rational/nonrational, objective/subjective, and phenomenal/noumenal. As early as *Dikanka*, however, the Gogolian text begins to orbit about a question raised by the "thing-in-itself," how one represents the unrepresentable.[30] This focus leads Gogol increasingly to replace the German polarities with new, half-empty terms: empirical experience/X, morality/X, order/X. The result is a confusion of authority, authorship, and motivation. As Mann writes of "The Nose," "There is no direct accuser. There is no persecutor. But the persecution itself remains."[31]

No one has ever successfully answered the question "Whence the phenomenon of Gogol?" N. L. Stepanov asserts that the Gogolian grotesque owes nothing to the Romantic "double world" (*dvoemirie*) but is a "means of estranging, a comic hyperbole that unmasks the banality and inhumanity of ambient reality."[32] But this statement fails to explain the absence of the grotesque in the equally civic-minded Turgenev or Tolstoy. Throughout *Masterstvo Gogolia* Andrei Belyi sees Gogol's fiction as a projection of his own conflicted sense of self. This is assuredly true. But a more specific answer to the question "Whence Gogol?" may involve the oral nature of his universe. Most critics have recognized the privilege granted orality by Gogol. Belyi argues that sound precedes image or form (*obraz*) in the early Gogol.[33] The *Dikanka* tales are the oral performances of marginally literate people, and the essays of *Arabesques*, apparently their diametric opposite, are Gogol's most oral work of all—a pastiche in lecture form of Hamann, Herder, and Schelling. Gogol's resurrection of the "thing-in-itself" is an appropriate gesture for an artist inhabiting an oral medium, for it raises questions both about control ("How did pickles and caviar get here?"—to quote the most famous eruption of nonsense into a Gogolian plot, Anna Andreevna's exclamation in *The Inspector General*) and about the reality construct as altered by oral performance: "Now that something is said, can it be taken back, does it fit the occasion, can it be identified?" That is, questions of control and epistemology *are* the central questions of Gogol's orally based universe, and they happen to coincide with the project of German philosophy in Gogol's era. If Gogol successfully based his art on the notion of the "unrevised universe" and the lack of systematization inherent in oral literature, then the tragedy of his career in the 1840s lay in his failure to find an essence to the "thing-in-itself" (such as religion, nationalism, prophecy), long after his best work had established that it had no knowable content.

• • •

Not a philosopher by training or by bent, Gogol did not appropriate fiction, as an impatient traveler would an available carriage, to provide the serviceable frame for a grand philosophical undertaking. Yet his idiosyncratic approach to the nature of supersensible experience is to some degree the "cause" behind certain effects in his writing. And if his attitude toward the epistemologically opaque has left an imprint in his work, that same stamp can be felt in some of the important structures invented by Gogol criticism. Gogol's conception of the "thing-in-itself" reopens many questions posed by scholars of his work, three of which I would like briefly to address here: the idea of the "two Gogols," the periodization of his work, and "the Gogolian influence."

1. By the early twentieth century the language of German philosophy had come to underlie the question of the "two Gogols," now one of the critical commonplaces in Gogol scholarship. Robert Maguire recalls Belinskii's impassioned distinction between Gogol the artist of genius and Gogol the muddled thinker, and Andrei Belyi cites the important transit of later scholars from the topos of the divided artist to the theme of Gogol's divided worlds: "By locating the split of styles in a split of the soul, researchers underline the bivalence of all images in Gogol."[34] It is only with Soviet criticism, however, that the question of the "two Gogols" became an issue of a double world, the site of a Romantic metaphysic and the force determining a range of stylistic decisions. I. F. Volkov writes:

> The search for another world, distinct from that which really exists, provided Romantic art with grounds for using "universal" artistic forms, especially the fantastic, which was borrowed from the oral creations of the people, popular beliefs, and religious ideas. . . . The search for another world essentially meant a search for the sort of circumstances which would correspond to the Romantic character, as opposed to those circumstances alien to it which comprised the practical conditions of his life. In this lies the chief significance of the so-called double world in the figural structure of Romantic works of art.[35]

In the tradition of Meyer Abrams's differentiation between the natural and supernatural, Stepanov refers to the "two-planed aspect" ("dvuplannost") of Romantic literature and cites M. Gorlin's distinction between "everyday experience" ("byt") and a "magic world."[36] At the same time, narratological analyses of Gogol have led to an extended literature on his use of plot redirection. Belyi refers to the "split in the plot [*razdvoi siuzheta*] which is not carried through to the end," and Mikhail Khrapchenko remarks that "the principle of an unexpected shift in the narrative from one thematic and compositional plane to another is exploited by the writer" in a number of tales.[37] Iurii Mann alone, however, has successfully joined together these two aspects of doubling, the biplanar world and the biplanar plot. In his theory the Romantic tension between natural and supernatural now no longer stands apart from the devices of narrative but exerts a gravitational effect upon them. He sees the fantastic of Gogol's work of the early 1830s passing over into everyday description—not as an intrusion upon the reality construct but as a compositional principle.[38] The fantastic lingers on in the disruption of the subject in first-person narration (e.g., in "The Diary of a Madman"), in alogical trains of thought, and, in the sphere of the represented ("plan izobrazhaemogo"), in the involuntary movements of characters.

Mann's argument generally supports the conclusions of this essay. But his entry to the Gogolian supernatural by way of the fantastic unavoidably stretches the definition of the fantastic to include *any* violation of the conventional reality constructs and compositional commonplaces dictated by a later realist norm. The very features that Mann notes above show Gogol reacting *against* the inherited German fantastic and English gothic in order to produce unmotivated narrative disorder. Writing elsewhere Mann notes, "In *Dikanka* the demonological judgment echoes from within a world struggling toward sovereignty, and we are simply deprived of the firm vantage of a higher consciousness from which one could critically interpret and master that judgment." Though just, this statement leads its author to a timid conclusion: "The Romantic world excludes any possibility whatever of interpretations from the position of positivism or pragmatism."[39] This is simply to say that empiricism cannot answer all questions, but Kant always knew this, and Herder, Hamann, and Friedrich Schlegel had made it a premise of the Romantic rebellion. Not only reason but intuition and moral awareness fail in Gogol's universe.

2. As a second consequence of this study of Gogol's "thing-in-itself" one might review the traditional periodizations of his stories. Belyi charts Gogol's course from hyperbole to satire, and from representation of the devil to characterization of the bureaucracy: "The unclean becomes the circle of officialdom."[40] Mann remarks three

way stations in Gogol's use of Romantic devices: *Dikanka,* with its popular fantastic and folkloristic motifs; "Taras Bulba," an epic romanticism of heroic pathos and tragedy; and the Petersburg stories, where the romanticism of contrast and a satirical grotesque is finally infused with realist elements.[41] These periodizations account for many features of Gogol's style but impose an overly easy dialectic inevitability on Gogol's literary evolution. This essay has shown the presence in Gogol's writing of a compositional stance, dictated by a metaphysical position, that is already evident in the *Dikanka* stories and proves largely *resistant* to adaptation or exclusion in later works. As landmarks in Gogol's literary career "Vii" and "A Terrible Vengeance" play as critical a role as "The Two Ivans" and "Ivan Shponka." Our reading of *Dikanka* as a whole, with its astonishingly variegated repertoire of devices and tonalities, shows that it encompasses two persistent and typically Gogolian features: the swift decay in the manifest world of traces of the recognizably and characteristically human, and the apparently arbitrary, unpatterned dance of narratorial positions. They are—what Kant would never have allowed—the representation of the unrepresentable, an "outward and visible sign" not of the merely noumenal but of a noumenon that is turned away from the mind's gaze, Kant's "thing-in-itself." Because the defining quality of the "thing-in-itself" is its ability to elude grasp by the constitutive categories of human thought, Gogol inevitably conceives it as nonhuman. What passes for the inhuman and the inhumane in his work is more generally a reflex of the nonhumanity of supersensible experience. We "read" the invisible track of the "thing-in-itself" in the frequent collapse of authorship: actions without human motivation (e.g., the legs at Sorochintsy), and plot without consistent direction (e.g., the unconvincing revelations at the end of "A Terrible Vengeance," the melancholy turn of events in "Old-World Landowners").

3. An artistic undertaking as striking as Gogol's has had many imitators, and his influence is notable enough to have spawned the most popular folk genealogy of Russian letters, the distinction between a "Pushkin line" and a "Gogol line." Interest in the play between rational and irrational orders of experience is not by itself a defining feature of Gogol's literary legacy. It preoccupied "Pushkinians" like Tolstoy and Blok as much as it did Dostoevsky and Belyi. Any attempt to base Gogol's distinctiveness solely on his humor also runs into immediate difficulties. If one were to identify the microscopic depiction of slovenliness as a hallmark of Gogol's comic effect, then Pushkin's own "Count Nulin" would be Gogolian (whereas the converse is true). And an inclination to peremptory shifts in narrative

register—at least if it is taken by itself—virtually unites Pushkin and Gogol. What differentiates the two authors is the origin of these shifts. Pushkin's most signal display of plot redirection, *Eugene Onegin,* reflects the Sternean voice of the Enlightenment, a playful, lucid narrator willing to manipulate in full view the strings of his talent. Gogol's use of plot redirection, on the contrary, is as symptomatic a response to the Romantic revolution as Pushkin's is to a strongly eighteenth-century attitude toward the rational exercise of mind. The authority governing plot redirection in Gogol is usually invisible because it is designed to function beyond understanding. To some extent the mystery that we attach to Gogol's stories betrays our critical anxiety that all dark places in a text be illuminated. We continually try to resolve textual mysteries that function in Gogol's works by virtue of being unresolvable, and tend to accept as Gogol's unpredictability what is better understood as a motivated textual incomprehensibility.[42]

Later writers in the Gogolian line would use seemingly "unauthored" shifts in narrative register to very different effect. Dostoevsky—to take Bakhtin's insight—builds the grounds for an irreducible pluralism of voices (in the Christianity of Bakhtin, this is possible), and Belyi provides a sequential and dramatic "before and after" to the hero's *Bildung:* the chaos of the opening of *Kotik Letaev* is positioned against the theme of Kotik's emergent authorship, while the instability of both tone and point of view at the beginning of *Petersburg* disappears at the novel's end in the wise embrace of History. These authors use Gogol's device, but the results are antithetical to his: Dostoevsky creates a noumenal religious sphere where humanity and individuality find full legitimation, and Belyi, Hegel-like, triumphantly abolishes the noumenon and places all irrationalities within anthroposophy's absorptive jurisdiction over the real and knowable.

Belyi's use of a theory of reference to engender narrative is a reminder that Gogol's inspection of the "thing-in-itself" entails not only a semantic stance but a progression, and therefore constitutes a story. Iurii Lotman's typology of narrative is relevant to Gogol here. Lotman bases his typology on relationships between language and the object of representation, and at the same time uses his theory to account for the Romantic/realist opposition. This opposition is particularly dear to students of Russian literature, thanks to Chizhevskii's grandly schematic theory of the bipolar oscillation of literary periods and to Roman Jakobson's almost Manichaean distinction between the way of metonymy (realism) and the way of metaphor (Romanticism, symbolism). Lotman's gloss on this debate helps provide an alternate way of understanding Gogol's problematic status in literary histories. Discussing literature as an act of representation (the "secondary modeling system"), Lotman proposes that the recoding work of the text can be established through either of two semantic relationships.[43] One is external, the other internal. In the first, which Lotman aligns with realism, literature attempts a correspondence between objects and their representation, the sequence of representations in turn producing narrative. Lotman relates the second semantic process to the aesthetic of Romanticism, with its emphasis on the expressive rather than mimetic powers of the artist. Here literature builds up the object through an accretion of mental acts that do not undergo a step-by-step "check" against the evidence of sensory data.[44] If the *differens* behind Lotman's distinction is reference to a construct of world supposedly exterior to the subject, then Gogol's work is "realist," even to the inclusion of its devils, who as we saw are translated in *Dikanka* and *Mirgorod* from the noumenal to the phenomenal. But in Gogol the textual universe itself appears the product of a mental process, and hence is "Romantic." Yet this process fails in turn to be truly "Romantic" because its workings cannot be matched with a single and recognizable center of consciousness. Gogol uses the first semantic coding process of Lotman to objectify, among other things, a mental process that is unknowable. This is not a "realist" tendency at all.

With such a typology of narrative in hand, we can better explain Gogol's place outside the borders of a conventionally defined realism or Romanticism. The air there is rarefied but Gogol is not alone. His companion writers come from both the nineteenth and twentieth centuries. In Nabokov, there is a clear sense that behind the text lies an inverted world in which all the chaotic details of the work's semantic system *might* make sense.[45] Flaubert's prose, like Gogol's, often makes it difficult to answer the question "Who is telling the story?" The seemingly stable text of "Taras Bulba" presents an acute example of this problem, which recurs in masterpieces of Flaubertian ambiguity like *Salammbô* and *The Temptation of St. Anthony*. But the truer kin to the Gogolian narrative semantic are German—Kafka and Kleist. Like Gogol, both undo the received wisdom that the negation of the Enlightenment and rational idealism necessarily entails a romanticism. Gogol shares Kleist's deep skepticism about the powers of understanding (Kleist's reading of the *Critique of Pure Reason* in 1801 would lead him to consider suicide). Like Kleist, Gogol inverts both the Enlightenment *and* Romanticism. Nor does he find chaos a ripe term for domestication, as Tiutchev does. Disorder can invade at any time, not only the reality construct of fiction, but the writing itself: "There's no saying what it is that comes up" (I:316/206). Kafka on the other hand follows Gogol's realization that the very assumption of an unknowable sphere of experience puts in question the origin of power.[46]

Thus German aesthetics itself provides the means for going beyond the paired opposite phenomenon/noumenon, a polarity which is useful for inserting Gogol (correctly) into the Romantic movement, but which by itself is inadequate to distinguish Gogol from his contemporaries. The concept of the "thing-in-itself" is a critical hinge of his work. Moreover, his invocation of the "thing-in-itself" forestalls our facile critical equation of phenomenon/noumenon with real/ideal. Gogol never confused the "thing-in-itself" with the ideal. His effort in the late 1840s to unite his writer's mission to the institutions of church and state, a project that entailed conflating the noumenal with the ideal, sacrificed the "thing-in-itself" and silenced an unusual voice.[47]

• • •

In characterizing the aesthetic of *Dikanka* I have tried to emphasize its complexity. Even in the romanticism that lies at the core of the stories Gogol follows no single genre. The gothic, the fairy tale, and the fantastic contribute elements to a whole which is none of these. Besides these magic-based forms the stories contain yet another system, a realism founded on painstaking description. What lends some unity to this heavy aggregate of seemingly incompatible genres is the shared naïveté that both narrator and reader are expected to assume. The product of a post-Rousseau age that esteems the simplicity of popular culture, *Dikanka* transports to the Ukraine the sentimentalized view of antiquity created by artists like Winckelmann, Schiller, and Hölderlin in Germany and Gnedich, Zhukovskii, and Merzliakov in Russia.

But *Dikanka* also departs from the literary codes of turn-of-the-century Europe. It overturns the important premise of Romanticism that supersensible experience is somehow, some time, within reach. And it refurbishes the very concept of an unknowable dimension of experience which the nineteenth century would elsewhere sacrifice. In certain ways the *Dikanka* tales are already a final step for Gogol. In them he masters a Romantic aesthetic and grasps a radical means of rewriting it. The pastoral of a sentimentalized Ukrainian landscape, with its easy absorption of good and bad spirits, is disrupted by the periodic lightning of an invisible and unknowable presence. Gogol's readers have long sensed the clash between this presence and the quotidien experience of the characters, and a disharmony between this same presence and their comfortable, genre-founded expectations about the stories. The presence readers note is the shimmer of the "thing-in-itself." Gogol's return to Kant through the "thing-in-itself" sets his work outside the mainstream of most nineteenth-century literature and causes its strange, "grotesque" disequilibrium. With the production of a textual universe whose contours baffle character and reader, he embarks on an itinerary sufficiently sui generis as to defy exact comparison with contemporaries or schools. In *Dikanka* Gogol is already "Gogolian," the writer who delights and chills.

Priscilla Meyer

False Pretenders and the Spiritual City: "A May Night" and "The Overcoat"

"ALLOW HIM at least a drop of intelligence," says the actor Shchepkin apropos the author of the play in "The Denouement of *The Inspector General*" (IV:128). From Gogol's contemporaries to current critics, there has been a tendency unique in the reception of great works to patronize the author, to regard him as hopelessly out of touch with his own intentions. This reading is, of course, just what caused Gogol to write "The Denouement" and later the infamous *Selected Passages from Correspondence with Friends* in the first place. Yet if we follow the lead of Konstantin Mochul'skii and take Gogol at his word, he is completely, almost predictably, consistent.[1]

Letter 27 of *Selected Passages* is addressed "To One Occupying an Important Position" (VIII: 349). Around the same time, Gogol also wrote an article, "On Classes in the State" ("O sosloviiakh v gosudarstve"), with similar content. In these two pieces Gogol sets out his understanding of what an ideal ruler should be. In "On Classes" he writes: "A monarch is a personage [lit., "face"] who should live a different life from the ordinary worm. He should renounce his own self and his property like a monk; his sole good should be his blessing—the happiness of every last person in the kingdom; his person should be none other than holy" (VIII:490–91). In the letter from *Selected Passages* Gogol says that it is easy to fulfill the duties of a government official if one is a Christian and brings Christian wisdom into everything. Every official post must be occupied "in the name of God." Then one may simply act "as one's own head commands, [because] Christian humility will prevent self-willed blindness [*samoosleplenie*] (VIII:350). Note that the face, the head, and blindness are here linked specifically to a Christian vision, a point related to Sergei Bocharov's discussion of the role of the face in "The Nose" as emblematic of personal integrity.[2]

In the letter Gogol lists the negative tendencies a truly Christian governor will avoid: "You will no longer be moved by vanity, you will not be motivated by rank or rewards, you will stop thinking completely about showing off in front of Europe and making yourself into a historical personage" (VIII:349). Rather, the Christian ruler is a father to his subordinates, who will therefore love him. He will transmit that love to his superiors, and so on up the hierarchy, "so that [that love] will reach its rightful source, and the tsar who is beloved by all will transmit it triumphally before everyone to God Himself" (VIII:366).

These are the principles, couched in the same terms and conveyed by the same images, on which Gogol based his stories, from the Ukrainian supernatural folk tales to the Petersburg works. Iurii Mann has opened new avenues of inquiry by showing that there is a constant set of images associated with the supernatural throughout Gogol's work.[3] To this set may be added the concept of the False Pretender (*samozvanchestvo*). It is interesting that in the transposition from the Ukrainian to the Petersburg setting, *samozvanchestvo*, unlike the features discussed by Mann, continues to be clearly associated with the supernatural, however mundane the context, as a comparison of "A May Night" and "The Overcoat" reveals.

The structure and imagery of "A May Night" become more comprehensible when analyzed in terms of *samozvanchestvo*. Boris Uspenskii has described the phenomenon as follows.[4]

The title of tsar is distinct from all other titles, as it is created by God, not by man. The tsar is likened to Christ, whose name means "the anointed one," and is himself anointed. The parallelism is reflected in the paired expression heavenly tsar/earthly tsar.

Pretenders arose in Russia only after the role of tsar was sacralized. Because pretenders attempt to take that title which can only be bestowed by God, they are viewed as agents of the devil, themselves anointed by his demons. They are false gods, false idols. The real Tsar is an image of God, a living icon. False pretenders often base their claims on bodily signs, such as a birthmark in the shape of a cross, and the falsity of such claims is seen to be that their basis is in outward appearance rather than inner nature.

This idea is the source of the practice of the mummers (*riazhenye*) at Yuletide and Shrovetide. They would dress up as tsar and in other masks and go around the villages singing. Masqueraders would often wear the clothes of the opposite sex.

The "game of tsar," in which the tsar would force another man to dress up as tsar, to play the role of pretender, is known to have been played by Ivan the Terrible and Peter the Great. Both actual and play pretenders were sometimes unmasked and killed; otherwise they were punished by having their right hands cut off. Uspenskii suggests that in the "game of tsar," the tsar sheds his external signs in order to emphasize his own authenticity, his internal right to the throne. The popular view of Peter the Great as an Antichrist arose from the idea that he was masquerading in German dress. German or Polish dress was often used on icons to depict devils.

Pretenders arise particularly when the succession is broken. Uspenskii connects Pugachev's appearance at the time of Catherine's reign to the fact that, as a German, she was popularly considered to have no legitimate right to the throne.

This material, together with some pagan folklore, explains many of the details and structures of "A May Night, or the Drowned Maiden." Note, by the way, that two of the tales from the *Dikanka* collections are "St. John's Eve" and "Christmas Eve," times specifically related to Christian mummery rituals, and a third, "A May Night," is set at the time of pagan fertility rites in which the earth is supposed to join in marriage with the sky. Young men and women exchange wreaths and throw them into the water to divine the future of their union—whether it will endure, and whether it will produce children.[5]

"A May Night" is divided into six parts. The supernatural parts of the story are confined to parts 1, 5, and 6, in which the love story of Levko and Ganna is told. In keeping with Iurii Lotman's analysis, the magical (*volshebnyi*) world is associated with astral and natural phenomena and is clearly differentiated from the everyday (*bytovoi*) world.[6] In part 1, when Levko courts Ganna, "the evening . . . embraced the blue sky" (I:153). "The pond . . . held . . . the distant, dark sky in its cold embrace." The earth and the sky are joined, in keeping with the pagan belief. Ganna exclaims to Levko that the stars are God's angels looking out their heavenly windows at earth. "Not a single oak in our village reaches the sky. But they say . . . that somewhere there is . . . a tree whose top rustles in the sky itself and God goes down to earth on it at night before the holy day" (I:156). This idea is present in several mythologies. Viacheslav Ivanov mentions the tenth-century Old Icelandic poem, the *Völuspą* (Sybil's prophecy) and shamanistic beliefs as well as Ukrainian sources.[7]

Ganna's eyes are like stars, she wears a coral necklace, and Levko calls her "my little fish" (I:154). Ganna is thereby identified with the drowned maiden, who offers Levko corals and is herself a kind of "little fish": she lives in the pond but complains that her stepmother has made it impossible for her to "swim like a fish." Instead she "sinks to the bottom like a stone." In pagan lore sinking is a bad omen—if the wreath thrown into the water during the May night rites sinks, it signifies death and childlessness.

Part 1, then, establishes the pagan natural purity of the lovers Levko and Ganna, who are united in part 6 by the supernatural agency of the drowned maiden. The maiden appears in Levko's dream in part 5, where she sets him the task of identifying her stepmother, the witch in disguise, from among the maidens dancing by the pond. The dancing of circle dances is traditionally considered a way to ward off witches.[8] Levko succeeds in unmasking the witch, although she is disguised—she wears the same garments as the other girls. The witch shares an attribute of the false pretender: her hand has been cut off by her stepdaughter. Levko's triumph over the evil stepmother mirrors on the supernatural plane the realist plot of his vanquishing his father to win Ganna. The drowned maiden rewards Levko for unmasking the witch by giving him a note that aids him in unmasking his father. The note (and the written word is Gogol's means of communicating God's word) is the one link (besides the natural setting) between the supernatural sphere and the realistic plane of village life. Levko swears to Ganna that he will never tell anyone but her about the drowned maiden; their pure, supernaturally assisted love story is separated from earthly contact. Its magical context is deliberately pagan, folkloric, pre-Christian.

Parts 2, 3, and 4 of "A May Night" treat the realistic plane of events of that night in the village. The focus of these is Levko's father, the "mayor," literally, the "head." Part 2 is entitled "The Head," and the mayor is referred to throughout by this ambiguous title. Like the "nose" of Gogol's later story, the head designates both the part and the whole. Unlike "nose" (*nos*) the feminine signifier (*golova*) is somewhat at odds with its masculine signified. Furthermore, the word links the individual mortal occupying the rank of "head" to the God-given rank of "head" of the village, just as a head is at once a physical object and a divinely created locus of thought.

These contradictions are underscored at the first introduction of the "head." The drunken muzhik, Kalenik, who is dancing the gopak like a "wild boar," approaches the mayor's house: "I won't look at any old head . . . a head, a head. I'm my own head. May God kill me! God kill me, I'm my own head" (I:160). Kalenik, echoing the "head's" lasciviousness, tries to kiss the girls; the girls direct him to the house of the mayor as a joke, because the mayor too keeps trying to kiss the girls. Kalenik is associated with the diabolic by his dancing the gopak and by mention of the wild boar, and later is dressed in the diabolical black sheepskin.[9] In his drunken babble, he recognizes that his claim "to be his own head" is a challenge to God, witness the repeated phrase, "May God kill me!" In his assumption of God's role he reveals the mayor's function, but the key feature of rank is inverted: Kalenik (like Akakii Akakievich) is at the foot of the village social ladder, while the mayor is at its head. In this way Kalenik implicates the entire population as potential usurpers.

While Kalenik is unwittingly making his way to the mayor's house, the narrator describes the mayor (and note the description's resemblance to that of Petrovich in "The Overcoat"): "That head is an important personage in the village." But he abuses his power: "The peasant stands with his cap in his hand . . . while the head puts his grubby fingers in his birchbark snuffbox. The head is gloomy, stern-looking and doesn't like to talk a lot." He also preys on the female villagers: "The head is one-eyed, but nonetheless his one evil eye is a scoundrel and can spot a pretty villager from a long way off" (I:160–61). A widower, he lives with an alleged sister-in-law who is rumored not to be related to him.

Levko overhears his father trying to seduce Ganna and gathers the young men of the village to help him "bedevil . . . the head" ("pobesit' . . . golovu") (I:163). The God-fearing old women of the town cross themselves as the young men dress up, smear their faces, and go to the mayor's, where Levko sings a mocking song under his father's window.[10] They throw a brick in the window and shove the sister-in-law into Levko's black sheepskin coat so that she is mistaken for one of the masqueraders (the female in male garb of mummery rituals).

The mayor summons his police to hunt down the "devil in the black sheepskin" as an example to others: "Let them find out what power means! Who ordains the mayor [lit., "places the head," "ot kogo golova postavlen"] if not the tsar?" (I:171).

The divine origin of the "head's" power is precisely what the band of young men challenges, with Levko as the "pretender"; Levko is finally unmasked by his father, who grabs him by the collar, calls him a son of a dog and "devil's spawn" ("besovskoe rozhdenie") (I:177), and threatens to beat him. On the symbolic level, the son pretends to the heavenly aspect of his father's throne by preventing his seduction of Ganna, while the note that Levko hands his father from the drowned maiden indicts the mayor's abuse of his earthly office. In this way the corruption of office is associated with desecration of the transcendent powers through Ganna and the drowned maiden. The drowned maiden's note is supposedly from the "commissar," who scolds the mayor for being a corrupt fool and demands he mend his ways. The father who unmasks his son is in turn unmasked by the next higher authority, just as in the denouement of

The Inspector General. There Khlestakov is a parody of a false pretender. The mayor and his officials unmask Khlestakov; but at the denouement they themselves are about to be unmasked by the true inspector, the duality of whose earthly and divine nature is hinted at by the final mute scene. One understands, then, why Gogol wanted the mute scene to last for a full three minutes: so that the entire audience experience the terror of the Judgment Day.[11]

In "A May Night" the dual nature of the inspector is made more explicit. Levko and the reader know that this "commissar" is of supernatural origin. But Levko conceals the otherwordly origin of the note. He tells his father that the commissar gave it to him personally and plans to dine with the mayor. The "head" is not terrified of the "commissar's" advent as the mayor is in the mute scene; he reacts the way the mayor does to Khlestakov, using the commissar's visit as a pretext to vaunt his pride and fleece the villagers. In short, the mayor commits all the sins listed by Gogol in his letter, including "self-blindness" (*samoosleplenie*): the mayor repeatedly pretends to be deaf when he doesn't like what he hears. He does exactly that when, reading the note, he gets to the place where the commissar calls him a fool.

The top of the governmental hierarchy is, of course, God. And the note comes not from any commissar but from the spirit of the drowned maiden. The note helps effect the divine union of Levko and Ganna; it forces the father to relent—"The priest will marry you tomorrow" (I:179). It also bridges the gap between pagan water spirits and the Christian God who is the basis of state authority. The merging of the pre-Christian and the Christian worlds is effected in the final paragraph of "A May Night"; Levko gazes at the sleeping Ganna and makes the sign of the cross over her. Their supernaturally effected union, unconsummated within the story, exemplifies the kind of love that Gogol says should be the source of the tsar's love for God in *Selected Passages*: "Complete love must not belong to anyone on earth" (VIII:366).

This reading of "A May Night" as a tale about *samozvanchestvo* provides a useful model for the Petersburg stories.

The description of the "head" closely resembles that of Petrovich in "The Overcoat." Dmitrii Chizhevskii long ago found Petrovich to resemble the devil: he emerges from clouds of smoke, he has a hornlike toenail, his snuffbox general has no face.[12] Now we can augment this rather general concept of "devil" with details that relate Petrovich's diabolism specifically to *samozvanchestvo.*

There is a German motif in "A May Night" and "The Overcoat." Both the mayor's and Petrovich's houses are filled with steam or smoke when first described. When Kalenik enters the mayor's house, the mayor is sitting with a visiting wine distiller who has filled the room with clouds of smoke from his pipe. The distiller tells the mayor that the "damned Germans" have started distilling not with wood, like honest Christians, "but with some devilish steam" (I:165). When Akakii enters Petrovich's home, Petrovich's wife has filled the place with smoke from the kitchen. Petrovich calls his wife a German when arguing with her, while she calls him "a one-eyed devil," just as the mayor's sister-in-law calls the mayor. Petrovich also likes to malign the Germans—he says they invented the sock to get more money; in the Petersburg tale the accusation is mundane, economic. In the Ukrainian setting the German invention is a betrayal of Christianity and is directly associated, not with everyday smoke from the kitchen, but with the steam that rises, presumably, from hell.

The mayor's great pride in life is that he was once selected as a guide to Tsaritsa Catherine, a story he is known to recount repeatedly. The German motif in "The Overcoat" and the emphasis on the mayor's foolish pride in having been singled out by the German tsaritsa in "A May Night" together underscore the Russian image of the Germans as Antichrists and implicate the mayor and Petrovich as false pretenders. In "The Overcoat" the idea is reinforced by references to Peter the Great: clerks ritually repeat the joke about the tail being chopped off the horse of Falconet's monument, an icon of Tsar Peter erected by Tsaritsa Catherine. Petrovich used to be the peasant Grigorii (the same name as the false pretender Grishka Otrep'ev) and started calling himself Petrovich (son of Peter) when he was freed. The Important Personage's sins are also associated with Germans—his "ladyfriend for pleasant relations" is named Karolina Ivanovna.

Petrovich forces Akakii to buy the coat, and the coat draws Akakii into the world of the clerks. That this is a corruption is clear from Akakii's reaction to the erotic engraving he sees on the way to the party and to the motion-filled lady he starts to chase on his way home. As on Nevsky Prospect, woman breathes potential deception; in the German Romantic tradition, beauty may lead to the sublime, but it may also be the devil's bait that results in madness and death.

In "The Overcoat" Gogol inverts many of the systems of "A May Night," a method that he appears to have systematically applied in transforming his Ukrainian works into his Petersburg tales.[13]

The divine love that frames the unmasking of the false pretender–mayor in "A May Night" is travestied in Akakii's love for the overcoat, his "(female) life companion," the "radiant guest" that enlivens his life. The elevated supernatural world that is the province of

Levko's love story is also parodied in "The Overcoat," in which there appear to be all sorts of mundane ghosts running around in the afterlife, blinding three policemen with one sneeze, and stealing coats.

Akakii, like Levko, has his coat torn from his back, establishing a parallel between them. But the parallel is suggested in order to be reversed: Levko's father unmasks him as the "devil in the black sheepskin," the claimant to the throne, so to speak, but we recognize Levko's claim as legitimate because he is protected by higher, beneficent powers. Akakii's higher powers (his superiors in government service) not only fail to protect him but rake him over the coals. When the thieves take the coat off Akakii, they reveal that his claim to be a government servant was illegitimate: while he is not corrupt, neither does he serve in God's name—his zeal is directed to the letters alone. Like Chichikov and Petrushka, who will read anything at all indiscriminately, Akakii will copy anything but has no language of his own. After death he becomes bold but not transfigured: he seeks only revenge.[14]

The clerk party is the reverse of Levko's merriment with his band of friends. The clerks dress Akakii up and glorify his coat, elevating his trappings. But Levko's disguise is assumed in the name of justice, and his mummers' festivities are paralleled by the maidens' dancing in his dream. Levko puts on the black sheepskin coat; the disguised witch looks somehow blacker than the other maidens. The two disguises are implicitly compared: the mayor mistakes his sister-in-law for a witch because the "mummers" have dressed her in the black sheepskin, which the mayor pulls off of her. The dubious status of the mayor's "sister-in-law" suggests impure love. Levko preserves his pure love for Ganna from the mayor's impure advances by using the disguise of the black sheepskin that, like the note, links the earthly to the supernatural realms of the story.

Akakii's overcoat functions in the same manner. First it is stolen by thieves (as Levko's is removed by his father), and then it is stolen by a ghost from the earthly world (as the mayor is robbed of his authority by the drowned maiden). But the point is inverted: Levko's love for Ganna is divine; Akakii's for his overcoat is blasphemous, a travesty of man's immortal spirit.

"A May Night" begins and ends on the divine plane; "The Overcoat" is equally symmetrical. Akakii is introduced in the first segment as a newborn entering earthly life and is last seen after departing this life in the final section. Just as Gogol establishes a parallel between Levko and Akakii to show them to be opposites, he draws a parallel between their superiors: Akakii unmasks his tyrant, the Important Personage, in the same way that Levko unmasks his father, the mayor, who is also called an "important personage." The false claimants to high rank get their comeuppance with the aid of supernatural powers: both are unmasked by figments—the nonexistent commissar reveals the "head's" corrupt use of office; Akakii's ghost terrifies the unfeeling Important Personage. But the first is unrepentant, while the second "reforms."

The Important Personage, like the mayor, commits all the sins of pride Gogol enumerates in his letter to another such important personage cited above. The pattern of double exposure, then, is common to "The Overcoat" as well as to *The Inspector General* and "A May Night": first Levko appears to his father to be a false pretender to his father's throne, and then the father himself is shown to be a false pretender to the position of governor by a still higher authority, pointing ultimately to the highest authority of all. Akakii is revealed by the thieves to be a false pretender to the lowest ranks of clerkdom, having gained entrance to the party by virtue of his mask, his coat, but Akakii then unmasks his superior.

Both the mayor and the Petersburg authorities order their constables to catch the culprit "dead or alive," emphasizing the inappropriateness of ghost behavior at least as much as of Russian officialdom. A policeman seizes a ghost that is pulling the coat off a musician "who used to tootle the flute"—a remnant of the mummers' music. But the policeman stops to take snuff from his birchbark snuffbox and loses his hold on the ghost. In "A May Night" the mayor's abuse of his power was illustrated by his way of taking some of the muzhik's snuff from his birchbark snuffbox. The belief that one's spirit leaves the body during a sneeze, as well as the idea of the nose, eyes, and ears as entry passages to the soul, discussed by Bocharov, causes the snuff-taking motif in Gogol's work to be consistently associated with diabolical temptation. It is precisely at the tenuous intersection of the earthly and the spirit worlds that snuff appears in "The Overcoat." Interestingly, snuff emphasizes the tenuousness of the policeman's secular authority on the supernatural plane in "The Overcoat," whereas in "A May Night" snuff affirms the "head's" earthly power; this is the reverse of the tendency noted by Mann for the diabolical of the Ukrainian stories to become invisible in the mundane setting of the Petersburg tales.

"The Overcoat" selects the most humble character in the official hierarchy to play the role of false pretender: although Akakii has no pretensions, he nonetheless should serve God. As Gogol suggests, he was doomed from the start when, instead of choosing the name of one of the saints from the church calendar, his mother chose the dynastic route and named him for his father. Levko can't read but knows the legends. Akakii can barely read, barely speak, and values only the outward trappings of the letters he copies at home—the rank of the addressees. He does not even have the Russian peasant's talent for the "pithily spoken Russian word" that Gogol praises in *Dead Souls*. Language, the living word, spoken and written, is the means of redemption throughout Gogol's work, and Akakii has none. There is no hope for the salvation of his soul any more than of the mayor's: on his deathbed, Akakii "foulmouths" (Gogol's portmanteau word with the overtone of "blasphemes": *skvernokhul'nichal*), shocking his landlady by the conjunction of his foul words with the term "His Excellency." Akakii speaks for the first and last time in order to accuse the government hierarchy.

"A May Night" ends with the mayor's double, the drunken Kalenik, stumblingly searching for his home; "The Overcoat" ends with the mustachioed ghost, Akakii' s "double," threatening a policeman. The anticlimax shows the open-ended potential ascent heavenward or descent to the bottom among the mustachioed thugs of the pseudospirit world.

The parallel endings of "A May Night" and *The Inspector General* suggest that Gogol did not simply make up an arbitrary justification for his play after the fact, but that he was honestly attempting to tell the audience how they were misreading it. "The Denouement of *The Inspector General*" is itself based on the model of *samozvanchestvo*. Shchepkin's fellow actors want to crown him with a wreath. Presenting it to him, they insist *five times* that he put it "on his head," but he consistently refuses: "To put on a wreath among comrades equal to oneself—gentlemen, to do that one would have to have far too much self-assurance." The actors reply that none of them would be insulted by this because he has not thought only of himself, has constantly tried not only to play his role as well as possible but also to help others improve their roles, has never refused advice to anyone, and has loved the business of art more than any one of them has. Shchepkin's refusal suggests that he would be a false pretender were he to wear a wreath on his head; he knows he is not the tsar. He is instead the embodiment of Gogol's ideal governor, who has only played the theatrical role of the false pretender–mayor. He has played it so superbly because he understands through his art the author's idea of the "spiritual city." The actor says himself that "our spiritual city is worthy of the same thought that a benevolent sovereign gives to his kingdom" (IV:132). Gogol embodies in Shchepkin an ideal government inspector who plays his role as a benevolent father to his fellow actors. Gogol's portrait of the actor is an icon of an ideal, just as the tsar is God's earthly representative.

The model of the false pretender can be applied to "The Diary of a Madman." The main concern of the governor, "papa," is whether or not he will get the ribbon, the physical trappings of high office, as Madgie emphasizes in her assessment of the ribbon as salty and lacking in aroma. The governor is no better than Poprishchin, who assumes the role of the king of Spain precisely when the succession is in question. In "The Nose" Major Kovalev's nose "masquerades" as a person of higher rank, as shown by the buttons on his uniform, but is unmasked by the policeman; the nose's escapades in turn unmask Kovalev's pretensions ("and where—in church!").

The mummers' carnival inversion of top and bottom confirms the phallic associations of the nose that critics have discussed in psychological terms. As Uspenskii points out, mummers traditionally wore shaggy masks with male members substituted for noses. The sexual aspect can thus be integrated into the spiritual dimension of Gogol's work. The religious implications of mummery link the sexual material to significantly more of the tale's features than does a merely sexual-psychological approach. Kovalev is a mock tsar, a false pretender to the rank of major, not even a true "major," and in any case, one that was made in the Caucasus. His impotence extends from the ladies all the way to his spiritual aspect. Akakii's hemorrhoidal complexion is related to the same system of top/bottom inversion, and his spiritual emptiness, as represented by his substituting a coat for a beloved, is associated with his lustful impulses (the lascivious engraving, the woman all of whose parts were in extraordinary motion).[15]

"The Overcoat" begins with the tale of "a certain police inspector" whose "holy name was being pronounced decidedly in vain" (III:141). It ends with the partial reform of the Important Personage on the one hand, and with the intimidation of the policeman first by an adult suckling pig and then by the mustachioed ghost on the other. In between, we ascend the governmental hierarchy: first the commissioner recommended by Akakii's landlady as a churchgoing man turns out to be accusing instead of sympathetic (not following Gogol's advice "To One Occupying an Important Position"), then the inspector is impugned as a potential usurper of Akakii's coat, and finally the Important Personage proves to be devoted solely to his own glorification. The work of *Dead Souls* and *The Inspector General* is combined in "The Overcoat."

From the bottom to the top of the hierarchy, Gogol's government officials fail to perform their godly mission; they wear the trappings of God's servants but are representatives of the Antichrist. This is how Gogol represents the supernatural terror of the Ukrainian tales in everyday Petersburg. As Gogol has his character Shchepkin say, "It is the inspector who awaits us at the door to the grave that is terrifying. . . . Before this inspector nothing will be hidden because he is sent by higher command and will appear when it will be impossible to take even a single step backward. Suddenly there will open before you, within you, such horror that your hair will stand on end from terror" (IV:131).

Iurii Mann

Gogol's Poetics of Petrification

GOGOL'S SYMBOLIC system of petrification and loss of speech, which may appear to be a limited aspect of his art, in fact leads us to the fundamental characteristics of his poetics. In a certain sense this symbolic system is analogous to that "sculptural myth" investigated by Roman Jakobson. Jakobson demonstrated that the functioning of this myth determines to a significant degree the peculiar stamp of Pushkin's poetic personality.[1] We can hardly be mistaken if we assume an analogous dependence for Gogol as well. Even on the external level Gogol's works are marked in this regard—literally dozens of formulas of muteness (or petrification) fill his works: "Horror fettered everyone in the hut"; the mayor "was transfixed with astonishment"; "everyone stood rooted to the ground," and so on. And in *The Inspector General* the factor of petrification even determines the style and texture of an entire fragment—the so-called mute scene.

The symbolism of immobilization may play one of two roles in a work—either as the animation of a dead person or as the immobilization of a living one. Both forms are encountered in Pushkin. In Gogol only one appears: the immobilization of the living. Gogol has no "statues" that come to life, a plot device that is the basis of three "sculptural myths" of Pushkin (in *The Stone Guest, The Bronze Horseman*, and *The Golden Cockerel*).[2] On the other hand, Pushkin's plea, "let not the poet's soul of passion / grow cold, and hard, and stiff as stock, / and finally *be turned to rock* / amid the deadening joys of fashion" (emphasis added), finds both analogy and development in Gogol.[3] The Gogolian process is not multidirectional as in Pushkin but unidirectional: from living to dead, from mobile to immobile.

If we speak specifically of the formula of petrification, that is, of the compact verbal construction with which Gogol usually expresses this process, then we must define another distinguishing feature as well. The formula of petrification is always unexpected and sudden; it is inserted into the text without preparation, often with the help of the adverb *suddenly* (*vdrug*). In this sense it is close to Pushkin's "sculptural myth," but with a necessary adjustment: whereas in Pushkin it is the character's meeting with the statue (with the Bronze Horseman or the Stone Guest) that is "unexpected," in Gogol it is the transformation of the character himself into a statue.

When we address the question of the cause, or more precisely the original stimulus, for the above-mentioned transformation, we again discover a recurring feature. Let us take the earliest sketch for the formula of muteness, in the story "Bisavriuk, or St. John's Eve" (the periodical version): when the people saw the broken pieces of pottery in Petro's sacks, "they all stood for a long time with their mouths open and their eyes bulging like crows, not daring to move even a whisker, such terror did this amazing event inspire in them" (I:364). Petrification is linked with some very powerful experience or shock. But there is more: the shock is attended by bewilderment and loss of orientation, which in turn are engendered by some sort of incomprehensible factors, an interruption in the ordinary and natural course of life. The people in "St. John's Eve" become paralyzed because gold coins have turned into broken pieces of pottery and the cause of the metamorphosis is supernatural. It is exactly the same with Kovalev in "The Nose": "Suddenly he stood as if rooted to the spot by the door of a certain house" (III:54), because his own nose has appeared in human form and in the uniform of a state councillor. That is, in Gogol's words, an "inexplicable phenomenon" ("iavlenie neiz"iasnimoe") had taken place, both for Kovalev and for any other ordinary consciousness. It is significant, moreover, that several cases of petrification in Gogol are directly provoked by a character's encounter with a supernatural person or with people who have fallen under supernatural influence. Thus Danilo in "A Terrible Vengeance," upon seeing the sorcerer's meeting with Katerina, felt that "his limbs became fettered; he tried to talk, but his lips moved without a sound" (I:258). Chartkov also freezes at the sight of the usurer-devil coming out of the picture frame in "The Portrait."

Such is the usual motivation of Gogol's formulas of petrification. There are very few exceptions, and if we look closely we find that many such exceptions, either indirectly or in a veiled fashion, originate from the same source, so to speak. In *Dead Souls,* part 2, Chichikov and his traveling companions, instead of arriving at Koshkarev's house, end up at Petukh's: "Chichikov was transfixed"; Selifan and Petrushka also "opened their mouths and opened their eyes wide" (VII:49). It would seem to be an ordinary traveling mix-up. Why then the formula of petrification? As I have already had occasion to point out, in Gogol's works cases of traveling confusions and mix-ups, a person's going astray in an unfamiliar or even a familiar locality, are causally connected with the intrigues of the devil.[4] "Vish', kak rastianul, vrazhii syn, satana, dorogu!" ("Just look how he's stretched out the road, the evil one, the Satan!" I:166), complains the drunken Kalenik in "A May Night" when he cannot find his way home. All of this sheds light on the consternation of Chichikov and his companions when they lose their way, although of course the direct participation of the "evil one" in the plot of *Dead Souls* is not intended.

Alongside the phenomena described above, which we may term lower forms of petrification, Gogol's works present examples of other, higher forms. Their peculiar property is their motivation, which preserves the tinge of the supernatural but receives a different, higher expression. Such is the action of feminine beauty. Here, by the way, is a parallel between Pushkin's poem "Beauty" (1832) and Gogol's story "Rome" (1842). In Pushkin: "meeting her, you are embarrassed, you will suddenly stop involuntarily . . . ," and so on. In Gogol: "And having met her [Annunziata] they stop as though rooted to the spot: the foppish nobleman with the flower in his hat, uttering an involuntary exclamation; and the Englishman in the green mackintosh . . . and the artist with the Vandyke beard" (III:218). In Pushkin, the person who meets the beauty lives an intense life; not for a minute does a profound inner working cease in him. The Gogolian character falls out of, is temporarily removed from, the course of time.

An analogous state overcomes Chartkov in front of the masterpiece of painting exhibited in the Academy of Arts, and also "a certain young man" in "The Overcoat," when he hears Akakii Akakievich's words "leave me alone, why do you insult me" (III:143). In all three cases the action is again illuminated by the participation of a higher force, which places its stamp on feminine beauty and art and Christian compassion alike. But this is a good and divine force; therefore we call such formulas of petrification higher ones.

Both lower and higher forms, however, have roughly the same manner of exposition, the same style, one may even say the same technique. A person receives a blow from outside. He freezes, "as if stunned by a thunderclap" ("Ivan Fedorovich Shponka," I:306), is transfixed (*stolbeneet,* a particularly frequent verb in Gogol), remains "as if rooted to the spot" (*kak vkopannyi,* Taras Bulba, Kovalev, Vakula, etc.). He seems to be pierced by an arrow or struck by lightning (the young man in "The Overcoat": "he stopped as if pierced," III:144). He is deprived of speech; he freezes in the most unexpected pose with an interrupted word or movement—"with mouth agape," "with fingers stretched wide," and so on (the gossip in "The Fair at Sorochintsy"). The words *strakh* (terror), *strannyi* (strange), and *porazhennyi* (struck) are ambiguously connected in Gogol. The poetics of petrification is the language of terror and horror, or at least of extreme affect.

Gogol's formula of petrification always strives toward an extreme—not only an emotional extreme but also a temporal and spatial one. Here is an example from *Dead Souls*. Chichikov informs Manilov that he intends to acquire dead peasants: "Manilov immediately dropped his chibouk on the floor and, having opened his mouth, remained with his mouth agape for several minutes. The two friends . . . remained motionless, fixing their eyes on one another like those portraits that used to be hung opposite each other on either side of a mirror in the old days" (VI:34). The length of the petrification draws attention to itself: "for several minutes" the characters remain in a completely motionless pose! The power of petrification over both participants in the action is also characteristic. Manilov has reason to experience shock: no one has ever approached him with such a strange proposal. But why does Chichikov freeze "for several minutes"? Has Manilov's reaction struck him? Or has he frozen "for company," as if a sort of virus of petrification has infected him too? Such scenes in Gogol do not lend themselves to simple psychological decoding according to formally understood rules of verisimilitude.

Here is yet another example of the formula of petrification, introduced at the height of a quarrel between two friends ("The Tale of How Ivan Ivanovich Quarreled with Ivan Nikiforovich"):

> The entire group presented a forceful picture: Ivan Nikiforovich, standing in the middle of the room in his complete beauty without any adornment. The peasant woman, with mouth agape and expressing on her face the most senseless expression, full of terror! Ivan Ivanovich with hand upraised, as Roman tribunes are depicted! This was an extraordinary moment! A magnificent spectacle! And meanwhile there was only one spectator: it was a boy in an immense frock coat, who was standing there rather calmly and picking his nose. (II:238)

One is struck by the clearly sculptural nature of the scene, reinforced by a direct reference to classical models, which lends the entire depiction a mixed Roman-Mirgorodian coloration. Also characteristic is the fact that the scene is introduced at a certain critical moment, when the quarrel has reached its apogee, a moment that cannot have failed to strike both the participants in the quarrel and its involuntary female witness. Finally, there is the characteristic tendency to broaden the action to an extreme, while the very exception (the boy picking his nose) proves the rule: the difference between those who are petrified and those who maintain freedom of movement is like the difference between adults and a child who does not yet understand the significance of what has taken place.

The sources of the Gogolian formula of petrification are very diverse: there is the classical mythological plastic art of numbness and of "mute sorrow" (in the tragedies of Aeschylus); the poetics of Romanticism, especially German Romanticism (one may observe analogous phenomena in Hoffmann and Tieck); and the pictorial language of the Ukrainian tales of V. T. Narezhnyi. In this spectrum of traditions and sources, Pushkin's "sculptural myth" also had an influence on Gogol, either directly or indirectly. It is significant that in his characterizations of Pushkin's poetry the author of *The Inspector General* invariably highlighted such qualities as sculpturality and plasticity. And in the article "V chem zhe nakonets sushchestvo russkoi poezii . . . " ("What Finally Is the Essence of Russian Poetry . . . ") Gogol interpreted the scene of the lyric subject's appearance "before the ancient statues with lyres and compasses in their hands" in Pushkin's poem "At the beginning of life I remember school" as an expression of an exceptional poetic breadth, an ability "to respond to everything" ("na vsë otklikat'sia," VIII:384).

Breadth defines the category of sculpturality in Pushkin, filled with various colors and diversely directed tendencies. But Gogol takes from Pushkin's many-colored palette a single color—that which expresses man's conflict with a superpersonal force—and he intensifies this color over and over again.

We may now turn to the "mute scene" in *The Inspector General.*[5] Gogol ascribed extraordinary significance to it and considered its failure on stage almost as the failure of the entire performance. This scene embodied so much for the author of *The Inspector General!* So much was connected with it, and so much thinking had gone into it! What is more, we may regard this scene as one of the nodes in which the artistic philosophy of Gogol's oeuvre as a whole is concentrated. Such an approach is chronologically justified as well: although the first bare sketching of the scene is contained in the 1835–36 text (the first draft version of *The Inspector General*), Gogol continued to comment on it and give explanations of it right up to and including the works of the mid 1840s: "The Denouement of *The Inspector General*" and "Preduvedomleniia dlia tekh, kotorye pozhelali by sygrat' kak sleduet 'Revizora' " ("Cautionary Remarks for Those Who Would Like to Perform *The Inspector General* Correctly"). In the strictly textual sense, the mute scene is only a single extensive stage direction; but in the perspective of Gogol's entire oeuvre one is justified in approaching it in its extratextual aspect as well, that is, by bringing in his later commentaries and interpretations.

Let us speak first, however, of the meanings that may be elicited from the text itself. These meanings are entirely in accord with what we already know about the formula of petrification. Here too the genesis of the mute scene is equivalent to a sudden blow from outside, coming from one side or, more precisely, from above ("The uttered words strike like a thunderclap," IV:95). Here too petrification is tantamount to paralysis, with the preservation of queer and utterly uncomfortable poses, with speech either falling mute or seeming to be broken off in the middle of a word (Dobchinskii and Bobchinskii freeze "with mouths agape and staring at each other with bulging eyes," IV:95). Here too petrification strives to expand as far as possible in time, encompassing "a minute and a half" (or even "two to three minutes," according to the "Otryvok iz pis'ma . . . " ["Fragment from a Letter . . . "], IV:103), which is almost unthinkable for a mute mise-en-scène. Finally, here too the mute scene is universal in its action: it strikes both the main and the secondary characters, as well as those who are not mentioned in the list of dramatis personae. There are and can be no exceptions.

The higher meaning of the mute scene, however, is also conditioned by the fact that beyond the textual meanings it contains other, implied meanings.

The occasion for the mute scene is the introduction of specific people and levels of authority. There is the "gendarme," who appears with strict orders; there is the Petersburg "civil servant"; finally, there are the "signed orders" ("imennoe rasporiazhenie"), that is, the will of the tsar, which authorize the bearer to take certain measures as yet undefined. In the texts accompanying *The Inspector General* it is also definitely declared *who* is to punish the mayor and company: "Everyone finally turned pale and was shaken when finally faced by that terrible law which closes the play and which looks equally upon the powerful and the powerless" ("Leaving the Theater after the Performance of a New Comedy," draft version, V:387). "Them bosses were pretty bold, but they all turned pale when the tsar's execution came!" ("Nebos', prytkie byli voevody, a vse pobledneli kogda prishla tsarskaia rasprava!" "Leaving the Theater," final text, V:146). In short, it is government action and Russian law. But looking back to the final scene of his comedy, Gogol prophesied, "Our actions will be inspected not by a senator but by him who cannot be bribed by anything and who has a completely different view of everything" (letter of 6 Dec. 1849 to A. O. Smirnova, XIV:154). The concept of an earthly power, albeit a high one, has given way to a superhuman, heavenly power.

To continue: On the one hand, we seem to have the conclusion only of a defined scenic action limited in time (one day in all!) of those events connected with the expectation, reception, and send-off of the (false) inspector general, and also with the sensation of the misfortune that has befallen all the townspeople. The error is a major one, each person experiences agonizing moments, but their lives do not after all end here. But on the other hand . . . "It seemed to me that the final scene represents the final scene of life, when conscience will force us to suddenly look ourselves straight in the eye and take fright at our very selves" (second version of the ending of "The Denouement of *The Inspector General*," IV:133).

All his life, especially in his last years, Gogol thought about the concluding moment, the fatal boundary of individual existence. "The constant thought of death educates the soul in an amazing manner, gives one strength for life and for spiritual feats in life" (letter to his mother of 25 Jan. 1847 [N.S.], XIII:194). And this spiritual element, which Gogol called *pamiat' smertnaia* (mortal memory), enters into the mute scene's quality of moral warning. But by this very fact the system of temporal coordinates is made more complex: the finale as the last scene of the act is present tense; as "the last scene of life," it is the future, perhaps even the distant future.

We are dealing with the conclusion of a certain life event (or even life-fate) of specific persons, the characters in the play. But precisely because the horizon of the play includes the whole town, and for Gogol the town has a self-propelling function, the significance of the finale is also broadened, to the extent of including the "last scene of life" of all humanity.

In petrification Gogol sees an attribute not only of a single person or group of persons but of human corporations, societies, and even of human history. "Then it seemed as if history had frozen and turned into geography: a monotonous life, moving in its parts and motionless as a whole, could be considered a geographical property of the country" ("A Glance at the Composition of Little Russia," VIII:41). A geographical map is the mute scene of history from which life has been castrated, leaving only an empty shell, turning the dynamic into the static. Here is another unexpected example—foreign mountains where "a knight of inhuman height" ("bogatyr' s nechelovech'im rostom") dwells:

> Their aspect is also marvelous: did not the fervent sea run out of its wide shores during a storm, throwing its shapeless waves up in a whirlwind, and did they not *become petrified* [*okamenev*] and remain motionless in the air? Did not heavy storm clouds break away from the sky and pile themselves up on the earth? ("A Terrible Vengeance," I:271–72, emphasis added)

The outline of mountains and ridges is equated with frozen waves or clouds, a mute scene of the sea or sky. Identical processes develop along three parallel lines in the physical, moral, and historical worlds, leading to a single finale—the mute scene.

The mute scene symbolizes retribution for crimes or misdemeanors, a sort of moral-juridical realization of the proverb "vsem sestram po ser'gam" ("each sister gets a pair of earrings," roughly, "everyone will get his"). The moral effect of restored justice must be rooted in the proportionality of transgression and punishment. But as we already know, one of Gogol's fictional spectators of the mute scene speaks not of punishment but of "execution" ("rasprava"). In another passage the question of why *The Inspector General* does not produce a cheering impression is specifically posed:

> The very appearance of the gendarme, who, like a sort of executioner, appears at the door, this petrification, induced in everyone by his words announcing the arrival of the real inspector general, who will exterminate them all, wipe them off the face of the earth, finally destroy them—all this is inexplicably terrifying! I confess to you in faith, *à la lettre,* not one tragedy has ever evoked in me such a sad, oppressive, cheerless feeling. (IV:127–28)

"Exterminate," "wipe off the face of the earth," "finally destroy" . . . none of these words leaves any room for discrimination or mercy.

Gogol's imagination was always captured by scenes of natural cataclysms that destroy cities and countries. In this regard the mute scene is related to such characteristic Gogolian images as earthquake and volcanic eruption. There is a parallel between his early article "The Last Day of Pompeii" and the finale of *The Inspector General*: in essence, the first draft of the mute scene was given precisely in this article; its main principle—the combination of universal immobility and petrification with endless diversity and individualization of poses—was grasped. "This entire group, which has stopped at the moment of shock and which expresses a thousand different feelings" (VIII:110). (Cf. Gogol's words about the mute scene: "These poses must not encounter each other and must be diverse and different" ["Cautionary Remarks," IV:119].) Something else is also anticipated in this article about Briullov: the independence of the effect of petrification from the degree and nature of the character's guilt, from its presence or absence. It is true that in *The Inspector General* the moral basis for the "retribution" is not entirely eliminated, for in the group of petrified people there are no people "in white raiment," in the words of Revelation—no righteous ones. But in the treatment of the Briullov painting the question of guilt and retribution is shunted aside: "Nam zhalka nasha milaia chuvstvennost', nam zhalka prekrasnaia zemlia nasha" ("We feel sorry for our dear sensuality, we feel sorry for our beautiful earth," VIII:112); the artist "has presented man in as beautiful a form as possible; his woman breathes everything that is best in the world. . . . And this beauty, this crown of creation, ideal of the earth, must perish in the general destruction together with a despised creature who is not worthy even to crawl at her feet" (VIII:112).

It is interesting that the motif of earthquake is also present in *The Inspector General,* in Khlestakov's drunken speech: "I pass through the department—it's simply an earthquake" (IV:50). Jakobson wrote apropos of Maiakovskii that the same image may be given first in ironic form and then in pathetic form or vice versa. "This is not an outrage upon yesterday's faith, it is two aspects of a single symbolism—the tragic and the comic, as in the medieval theater."[6] The comic image of earthquake in Khlestakov's speech corresponds to the noncomic (or, more precisely, to the not entirely comic, breaking with the comic) image of catastrophe in the finale of *The Inspector General,* and outside the bounds of the play to the earthquake in the article "The Last Day of Pompeii," in the finale of "A Terrible Vengeance," and finally in the article "Predmety dlia liricheskogo poeta v nyneshnee vremia" ("Subjects for the Lyric Poet of Today," in the analysis of Iazykov's poem "Zemletriasen'e" ["Earthquake"]). In turn, the noncomic images tend to be of two varieties: one with a moral element (the finale of *The Inspector General,* "A Terrible Vengeance," the treatment of Iazykov's poem), the other without, or at least with an inactive one (the treatment of Briullov's painting). But in all cases there is preserved a certain autonomy of retribution from any element of guilt, an autonomy connected to the universal breadth of the catastrophe. In "A Terrible Vengeance": "Poshlo triasenie po vsei zemle. I mnogo pooprokidyvalos' vezde khat. I mnogo zadavilo narodu" ("There was a shock over all the earth. And everywhere many huts were overturned. And many people were crushed," I:278). In the article on Iazykov: "v etu tiazheluiu godinu vsemirnogo zemletriasen'ia" ("in that difficult year of universal earthquake," VIII:278). Even in Khlestakov's speech: "vse drozhit, triasetsia kak list (*Gorodnichii i prochie triasutsia ot strakha*)" ("everything trembles and quakes like a leaf [*The Mayor and the others quake from fear*]," IV:50; emphasis added).

In addition, the mute scene of *The Inspector General* is connected with such favorite Gogolian images as the orchestra and the chorus, a certain everyday theatrical or religious action. These images are also presented sometimes comically or ironically, sometimes completely seriously. Examples of the former are the scenes of collective snoring in "Taras Bulba" ("Everything that was lying in various . . . corners began to snore and sing," II:286) and, even more, the dog orchestra in the Korobochka chapter of *Dead Souls* ("The dogs began to bark in all possible voices," VI:44). Examples of a different semantic and emotional coloration, entirely serious and pathetic, include the theatrical spectacle, which unites in itself both actors and spectators, for all those gathered may "vdrug potriastis' odnim potriasen'em, zarydat' odnimi slezami i zasmeiat'sia odnim vseobshchim smekhom" ("suddenly be shaken with a single shock, begin to sob the same tears, and begin to laugh with a single universal laughter," in "O teatre, ob odnostoronnem vzgliade na teatr i voobshche ob odnostoronnosti" ["On the Theater, on a One-Sided View of the Theater, and on One-Sidedness in General"], VIII:268). To the same group of images belongs collective prayer (one of its first depictions in the novel *The Hetman* is, by the way, close to the mute scene: "It was like the painting of a great artist, all full of movement, life, and action and at the same time motionless," III:278). Particularly important is the collective observance of the liturgical rite (*deistvo*)* as the embodiment of "order and harmony" ("Razmyshleniia o bozhestvennoi liturgii" ["Meditations on the Divine Liturgy"]).

The examination of the mute scene from the perspective of images of the chorus and of theatrical and religious rite illuminates anew antithetical facets of the scene. On the one hand, it emerges as if under the sign of a harsh and thoroughgoing negativity. After all, it is the reaction of people who are bad, vulgar, or at any rate burdened with human vices and weaknesses, to all that has happened. On the other hand, that reaction contains precisely the property that Gogol always considered to be valuable and even indispensable for true history, namely, collectivity, universality, concertedness. The mute scene is a sort of negative sign of a positive essence, an indication of its absence, or, to put it differently, of its presence in a special, extremely travestied, and strange form. In the article on Briullov's

*In the seventeenth century *deistvo* was the term for a dramatic spectacle; earlier it meant a religious rite that had a theatrical character.—TRANS.

painting Gogol wrote, "Its thought belongs completely to the taste of our age, which in general, as if sensing its terrible fragmentation, strives to unite all phenomena into general groups and chooses powerful crises that are felt by the whole mass" (VIII:109). In the mute scene of *The Inspector General,* it is precisely through a state of crisis that the general fragmentation is overcome and the lost unity restored.

The concept of crisis unites the mute scene with yet another Gogolian category, conveyed by the verb *porazhat'* (to strike)—"the uttered words strike . . . everyone." The ambiguity of the category lies in the potential of a multitude of sources for the action: one may be struck by thunder, earthquake, lightning (all these are present in Gogol), but also by the wrath of God. One may also be struck by the troika, for its origin is otherworldly ("the spectator, struck by a divine miracle, has stopped: is it not lightning cast down from the sky?" VI:247). One may also be struck by lofty art and the beauty of woman: "Not in vain has it been determined that all are alike struck by beauty" ("Zhenshchina v svete" ["Woman in Society"], VIII:226). Andrei Siniavskii has noted that ideas of the unearthly nature of beauty are not enough for Gogol (cf. Zhukovskii: "Prekrasnoe zdes' ne doma" ["The beautiful is not at home here"]); at certain moments beauty descends to earth, overtaking the spectator. I would add that through the effect of "being struck" the connection between mortals and the superpersonal principle is realized—in its good action (according to Gogol, beauty is called upon to ennoble, although it may also destroy) or in its punishing function, in its completely serious or in its travestied form.

When applied to the mute scene, the verb *to strike* is polyvalent in a different sense as well, for it assumes both the condition of the characters and the supposed effect on the spectators. "The unusual strikes everyone, but only when it arrests attention boldly, sharply, and all at once" ("On Present-Day Architecture," VIII:66). Gogol's efforts as a commentator and director were aimed at making the mute scene, in response to these demands, unite the two parts of the world that are divided by the footlights.

From all that has been said, the apocalyptic coloration of the mute scene is evident. This casts a significant light on many facets of the scene, beginning with the catastrophic nature of the moment (the very image of elemental disaster and of earthquake is, of course, apocalyptic; "and the same hour was there a great earthquake," Rev. 11:13) and ending with the universality of the action and the punishment. "Through the offense of one many be dead" (Rom. 5:15). "By the offense of one, judgment came upon all men to condemnation"

(Rom. 5:18). The unity of human history and the collective nature of responsibility outweigh the empirical concept of unequal personal guilt. The alternation of temporal levels is also important here: like the Apocalypse, which combines the present, past, and future in the single moment of St. John the Divine's vision, the mute scene unites the present tense of the plot finale with the future tense of fate, both individual and collective.

In this sense as well, the mute scene is the quintessence of Gogol's poetics, which strives to realize the transition from the temporal to the eternal, from the individual to the universally human, from the travestied and caricatured to the catastrophic, and finally, from fragmentation and chaos to unity and harmony. One may speak of the transcendental nature of Gogol's poetics, for the necessity of transition lies at its basis, although it is very difficult both for readers to comprehend and for scholars and theater directors to interpret. Here also the mute scene serves as a model example.

In 1851 S. P. Shevyrev attested that "the mute scene . . . which we only read . . . is never performed . . . on stage, perhaps because it is difficult or even impossible to perform it."[7] Practically the entire theatrical history of the comedy confirms this conclusion: the mute scene has been compressed, speeded up, shortened in length, and sometimes even simply ignored. Apparently this can be explained not only by the fact that, as V. I. Nemirovich-Danchenko believed, it is almost impossible theatrically and emotionally to sustain the required several minutes of the mute scene but also, and most important, by the very nature of the scene.

The plastic depiction of petrification requires a contrast between material and form. Sculpture, for instance, as Jakobson reminds us, does not favor the reproduction of inanimate objects because by virtue of the lifelessness of its material and (in distinction to painting) the three-dimensionality of its form, it entirely merges with these objects and supplants them. "Only the opposition between the lifeless, motionless mass out of which the statue is modeled, and the mobile, animate being which the statue represents, creates a sufficient distance between the subject and its representation."[8] This is what makes the sculptural depiction of humans and animals successful.

There would seem to be no problem with the mute scene. The characters are not "mobile," still less are they "animate," but they are represented by living actors; in short, the necessary contrast is present, although in a different form. In reality, however, the case is somewhat different. After all, we perfectly realize the feigned character of the actors' lifelessness and deduce from it the illusory nature of the petrification of the characters themselves. The contrast is smoothed over to the detriment of graphic and emotional force. In this regard one may appreciate the boldness and innovation of Meyerhold's treatment of the mute scene in his 1926 production.

As we know, Vsevolod Meyerhold replaced the actors in the finale with dolls—a device that for its boldness and simplicity Andrei Belyi compared to the stroke "of the double Cretan ax that chops off heads," for here "the archaic, coarse grotesque is more subtle than subtle." "Zhivoiu kartinoiu dat' potriasen'ia nel'zia: tol'ko mertvoi; dlia etogo molniei nado ubit' ispolnitelei, ne ubivaemykh zhalkim zhandarmom" ("To convey shock through a tableau vivant is impossible: only a tableau mort will do; for this one must use lightning to kill the performers, who aren't killed by the pitiful gendarme").[9] Elsewhere, by the way, Belyi speaks of the heightened apocalyptic coloration toward which Gogol strove in the finale: "Vsë povyshaet konets 'Revizora' do groma 'apokalipticheskoi truby.' Etogo i khotel Gogol' " ("Everything raises the end of *The Inspector General* to the thunder of the 'apocalyptic trumpet.' This is what Gogol wanted").[10]

Let us add that in Meyerhold's treatment the significance of the concept "to strike" was also restored—I have in mind the striking of the spectators. Here is how the effect is described by Erast Garin, who played the role of Khlestakov:

> [At first] the audience broke out in applause; after all the actors were doing a great job of standing there. . . . Gradually the applause died out, a pause ensued, then absolute silence. The spectators peered at the actors, someone moved from the audience toward the stage. . . . Someone on tiptoe, quietly, as if through crossfire, ran toward the orchestra. And suddenly a whole row of spectators, rising in agitation, went up to the stage.[11]

Meyerhold presented a literal transformation of the animate into the inanimate, giving substance to Gogol's metaphor. But at the same time he gave it a character of complete determinacy and finality. Did the author of *The Inspector General* desire such finality?

One is struck by the fact that Gogol always compared the mute scene not with a sculptural group but with a tableau vivant—probably not only with the aim of instructive clarity for the actor-performers. In the tableau vivant life has been stopped, but at the same time we recognize in the frozen figures and faces the features of people who are familiar and not at all alien to us. The popularity of tableaux vivants in the Russian cultural practice of Gogol's time enriched them with an intimate significance, a "domestic semantics," for in the frozen figures it was important for the observer to discover not only a character but also his close acquaintance or even a relative. The mute scene is of course not a tableau vivant, but the comparison with the latter subtly conveys the combination of sharp determinacy with inexhaustibility and ineffability that is peculiar to Gogol's poetics. Shevyrev was probably right: the mute scene will always be more complete in reading than in performance, for it is a sign of the untranslatability (incomplete translatability) of the Gogolian text into another graphic or conceptual set. At the same time, it is a sign of the indecipherability of Gogol's art, which we can only comprehend as a kind of eternal problem, never entirely solved.

Translated by Susanne Fusso

Duffield White

Khlestakov as Representative of Petersburg in *The Inspector General*

"What are you laughing at? You're laughing at yourselves!"

HOW DO WE "laugh at ourselves" when we experience Gogol's *Inspector General?* In the commentary on the play that he wrote soon after its first performance in 1836, "Leaving the Theater after the Performance of a New Comedy," Gogol suggested that comedy should create such an all-inclusive collective sense of life on stage that the audience will feel included, implicated in what it laughs at: "Comedy should cohere spontaneously, in all its mass, into one great, inclusive knot. The plot should embrace all the characters, not one or two—and touch upon the things that stir all of them, to whatever degree" (V:142).[1] Gogol noted that he had not found this ideal model of comedy embodied in any recent works of Russian or European drama, but that the classical model of Aristophanes' comedies had been an inspiration to him (V:143/181). In 1925 Viacheslav Ivanov wrote an article that follows this lead and compares *The Inspector General* to the Old Comedy of Aristophanes:

> Its similarity to the Old Comedy of the fifth century . . . is that its action is not limited to a circle of personal relationships, but, rather, presents these relationships as components of a collective life and embraces a whole social microcosm, self-contained and self-sufficient, which stands symbolically for any social confederation, and of course reflects, as in a mirror, just that social confederation to whose entertainment and edification the comic action is directed. (As the epigraph to *The Inspector General* has it: "There's no use grumbling at the mirror if your own mug is crooked.")[2]

While Ivanov's article powerfully asserts the spirit of Aristophanic comedy as an abstract ideal, Iurii Mann's *Komediia Gogolia "Revizor"* (Gogol's Comedy "The Inspector General") makes the convincing case that this ideal model is in fact embodied in Gogol's play. Mann shows how Aristophanes' model of comedy is consistent with Gogol's idealist philosophical thoughts about the role of the artist in cultural history. He suggests that when Gogol commented on the contemporary significance of Briullov's painting "The Last Day of Pompeii," he may have been identifying for himself both the nature of the cultural crisis that it was his role as artist to resolve in his art and the outline of a method for achieving this resolution: "The basic idea [of Briullov's "The Last Day of Pompeii"] is in keeping with the taste of our age, which generally, as if aware of its terrible fragmentation, strives to gather all phenomena together into general groups and selects powerful crises which are felt by the whole mass of society."[3] According to Mann, Gogol conceived of fragmentation or alienation as the condition of modern Russian history, which he, as an artist, was obliged to transform into an ideal experience of collective unity. This condition was expressed by Gogol in a number of striking images, such as, "It's as if an enormous carriage has arrived at an inn, and each passenger, who has spent the whole long journey closed up in himself, enters into the common room only because there's nowhere else to go" (Mann, p. 12). Mann notes that Gogol might have chosen to represent the alienation and fragmentation of contemporary society directly by choosing a form of artistic expression that was also fragmented, but instead, "the more heavily burdened he became with his vision of the fragmentation of life, the more he spoke of the need for a broad synthesis in art" (p. 13).

Gogol's first move in this direction was to conceive of Russian society in the synthesizing, collective image of a *sbornyi gorod* (composite town). In contrast to the settings of earlier satires on provincial town officials by Russian playwrights, this "composite town" of *The Inspector General* is based upon "a striving to embrace *maximally* all aspects of the life of society and of government" (Mann, p. 19). It includes, in a pyramidal structure, virtually all of Russia's social estates: the peasants like Khlestakov's servant, Osip, and the mayor's servant, Mishka, poor townspeople like the widow the mayor has just beaten, the merchants from whom the mayor extorts bribes, landowners like Bobchinskii and Dobchinskii, middle-ranking provincial bureaucrats (who may also be landowners) like the mayor, the superintendent of schools, the director of charitable institutions, the postmaster, and finally, lower-ranking provincial functionaries like the district doctor and the police. Not only are the social estates of Russian society represented here, but also, contrary to the norms of satiric comedies that preceded it, *The Inspector General* makes no effort to present its town as "an isolated island of sin and corruption" in an otherwise virtuous society (p. 23).

The only social estates excluded from the play's cast of characters are the clergy (which, according to Mann, were generally not represented in Russian theater at the time) and the military. The exclusion of the military makes sense, according to Mann, insofar as the military chain of command was separate from the civilian bureaucracy, and Gogol was interested in representing the political system that extended throughout the civilian bureaucracy, from the heights of Petersburg ministries (with their inspector generals) to the lowest ranks of the mayor's police (p. 21).

Having imagined the whole of Russian society in terms of a cast of characters that constituted a "composite town," Gogol still had to imagine an event, a plot, that would create a sense of unity amid the fragmentation and alienation that pervade this town. Mann treats the idea for a plot that Gogol took from Pushkin (traveling landowner is mistaken for a government inspector) not primarily as a literary device (such mistaken identity plots were conventional in low comic vaudevilles of the period) but rather as the real "situation" in which "the wholeness of society would expose rather than hide the 'terrible fragmentation' that existed in the life of society" (p. 31). The real "situation of the inspector general" (in which government inspectors from Petersburg routinely inspected provincial towns) provided Gogol with a real, prosaic, unmelodramatic incident that would have the effect of the extraordinary, melodramatic event of the eruption of Vesuvius in Briullov's painting "The Last Day of Pompeii." Like the bolt of lightning that illuminates the characters in Briullov's painting, the inspector general's visit to Gogol's composite town would "lock together the collective group of people even as they were experiencing the increasingly terrible fragmentation of their social life" (p. 32).

Mann quotes at length from Gogol's "Leaving the Theater after the Performance of a New Comedy" to prove that when Gogol substituted the plot inherent in "the situation of the government inspector" for the conventional love plot of comedy, he was engaged in an artistic revolution, not just against the mediocre norms of comedy in Russian theater, but against the conventions of the "best writers of comedy" such as Molière. Even in "the best writers of comedy," according to Gogol, the love plot reduced the focus of comedy to personal relations between individuals rather than to "general" collective relationships that embrace all the characters and mirror the collective relationships within society and within the audience that watches the play (Mann, p. 44).

Mann proposes implicitly that audiences should recognize their own inclusion in "the great inclusive knot" of *The Inspector General.*

They should recognize that they share with the characters on stage a collective condition of social fragmentation; they should empathize with the terror of exposure and the delusionary hysteria that the characters experience in the "situation of the inspector general"; they should recognize that they are "laughing at themselves" when the town is collectively exposed in its reading of Khlestakov's letter at the end of act 5; and finally, along with the characters on stage, in the final scene of the play they should become "dumbstruck" both by a sense of collective guilt for human history and by a realization that the collective fate of humanity is now in God's hands.

Mann's study is persuasive in suggesting that *The Inspector General* be read as "collective" comedy and in abstractly defining the plot of the play as the movement of a fragmented, alienated Russian collective toward a unified religious condition of apocalyptic awareness. However, there are a number of other ways one can define the collective experience the play creates. The following analysis will look at how *The Inspector General* creates a comic, collective sense of Russian culture by "drawing together into a single knot" Russia's confused, muddled sense of the role of Petersburg in Russian history and culture.

Rather than conceptualizing the cultural crisis addressed by the play as the "fragmentation" of individuals in society, this analysis will define the crisis as a groping away from old, uncertain values associated with provincial life toward new, uncertain values associated with the modern world of Petersburg. It will emphasize the extent to which, through the character of Khlestakov, the play represents the contemporary social reality of Petersburg as one side of the divided Russian collective.

The cast of characters representing this collective is divided between, on the one hand, Khlestakov, Osip, and (at the very end of the play) the offstage appearance of the real inspector general, all of whom have just arrived from Petersburg, and, on the other hand, the inhabitants of the mayor's town (all of whom have apparently never been to Petersburg).

The setting of the play is one place, the mayor's town, but through monologues, stage directions, and letters it opens out to reveal the space outside the town, which stretches all the way to Petersburg: in the mayor's announcement at the beginning of act 1 that a government inspector is on his way to the town from Petersburg; in Osip's monologue about Petersburg at the beginning of act 2; in Khlestakov's monologue about Petersburg in act 3; in Khlestakov's and Osip's exit out of town at the end of act 4; in Khlestakov's intercepted letter in act 5, transmitting his ironic sense of the town to his writer friend in Petersburg; and finally, in the announcement at the end of the play that "a government inspector has arrived from Petersburg by imperial decree and demands that you present yourself to him at once."

The simplest way to define the plot of the play is as the confused conflict between the mayor's town and Khlestakov, who is mistaken for the inspector general from Petersburg, but who has in fact been living in Petersburg and whose Petersburg experience filters into the play in Osip's opening monologue in act 2 and in Khlestakov's own drunken monologue in act 3.

Interpretations of Khlestakov's interaction with the town vary widely but usually center on the plot device of mistaken identity. Critics have noted that although mistaken identity plots were conventional in low comic genres of Gogol's time, Khlestakov's is an unusual case of mistaken identity. Conventionally, mistaken identity is attributable to clever deception by the character in Khlestakov's position in the plot or simply to circumstances more suggestive than the ones that make Bobchinskii and Dobchinskii conclude that Khlestakov is the inspector general (he is an official from Petersburg and he has a thoughtful expression, so he must be the inspector general).

According to V. V. Gippius, the lack of intentional deception on Khlestakov's part has the effect of depersonalizing, and thereby making typically social, the dramatic conflict between him and the mayor's town: "If he were a deliberate cheat, as is Pustolobov in Kvitka's play *A Victor from the Capital* . . . then the point of the exposé would be blunted. Instead of confusion arising from society itself and being therefore *typical*, there would be just an artificial muddle created by the malevolence of a particular individual."[4] This model views Khlestakov as a blank screen onto which the town projects its notions of the power and authority of Petersburg. It is valid up to a point: the mayor and the other townspeople do consistently project their own versions of the inspector general onto Khlestakov, and they might continue to do so regardless of who he "really" is.

However, the character and actions of the "real" Khlestakov are also significant in a number of ways: first, insofar as he has been in Petersburg and his experience of that place filters into the play through his and Osip's monologues, he introduces a sense of the *actual* Petersburg that counters the townspeople's projected images; second, he and Osip are the only characters in the play who belong to both worlds—Petersburg and the provinces—and move freely back and forth between the two (thereby qualifying for the role of heroes, according to Claude Lévi-Strauss's and Iurii Lotman's definition of heroes as characters who cross the boundaries between the defining binary oppositions that structure a culture); and third, as a character who is grotesquely reduced psychologically (stupid, frivolous, disconnected, etc.), he functions as an antihero who (*a*) frustrates the townspeople's and the audience's expectations that his interaction with them will make sense and (*b*) represents a "light," frivolous *homme moyen* of modernity who contrasts with the mayor as a "heavy" representative of Old Russia.

These various meanings of Khlestakov's "real" character and actions have the plot function of "tying together" the play's "collective" representation of a Russian culture that is split between old and new ways. They must be considered in addition to the plot functions lodged in Khlestakov's mistaken identity as the inspector general—the blank screen onto which the townspeople project their understanding of Petersburg. They are the most important components omitted from Mann's interpretation, in which "the situation of the inspector general" is the fundamental, unifying "idea" of the play.

In "Leaving the Theater after the Performance of a New Comedy" Gogol wrote that "it is an idea, a thought that governs a play. Without it, a play has no unity. And anything can tie things together: horror, terrified anticipation, the threat of law looming on the horizon" (V:143/181). The "idea" for a play that Gogol received from Pushkin was the idea of an inspector general as a case of *mistaken identity* in a Russian provincial town. Gogol added to this his conception of the "real" Khlestakov. The resulting "idea" for the comic plot of *The Inspector General* is that a provincial Russian town is visited by the "real" Khlestakov who is mistaken for an inspector general from Petersburg.

The plot engendered by this dramatic relationship is complex because all of Khlestakov's interactions with the town are double, engaging both of his identities. The plot can best be analyzed by beginning at the beginning, where its main strands are introduced separately. Act 1 introduces the mayor and his town; act 2 introduces Osip and Khlestakov and begins to develop the interaction between the mayor on the one hand and the two basic aspects of Khlestakov on the other—the town's version and the audience's version; act 3 deepens this interaction, and so on.

At the beginning of act 1 the mayor narrates his view of his town as he thinks aloud about how it might be reviewed by the inspector general who is on his way from Petersburg. He thinks first of how the town does not comply with standards of orderliness, seemliness, and propriety—standards that he associates with Petersburg bureaucracy but not with his town. He advises each of his fellow bureaucrats "to see to it that everything at your place is *prilichno* [presentable or proper]."[5] At the same time he narrates vividly detailed little scenes of unseemliness and impropriety in each of their domains. He advises Zemlianika that at the hospital "the nightcaps should be clean, and the patients should not look like blacksmiths . . . and that it's not good that the patients smoke such strong tobacco that you sneeze your head off as soon as you walk in the door" (IV:13/56); and he advises the judge, Liapkin-Tiapkin: "In your antechamber where the petitioners present themselves, the guards have been raising geese, and the little goslings are always poking their necks under people's feet. Of course it's laudable for anyone to take up animal husbandry, but why should a guard get into it? It's just that in a place like that, you know, it's *neprilichno* [not proper]" (IV:13/57).

The mayor also describes certain characters at the lower ranks of the town bureaucracy as innately improper or unseemly in their body odor, their facial gestures, or their actions. For example, he warns the judge about his clerk: "No doubt he's a knowledgeable man, but he gives off such a smell that you would think he had just walked out of a distillery. That won't do either. . . . If it's his natural odor as he claims, there are remedies: you can advise him to eat onion, or garlic, or something else" (IV:14/57). The superintendent of schools is warned about the "strange actions" of his schoolteachers:

> I realize they're learned people, educated in various colleges, but they have some very strange ways about them. Naturally, the sort of thing that goes along with the teaching profession. One of them—what's his name?—the one with the fat face—he can't get up in front of a class without grimacing, like this (*the mayor grimaces*). Then he starts smoothing his beard out with his fingers underneath his tie. (IV:15/58)

A similar case is the history teacher, whose "head's crammed with information . . . only he gets so worked up when he's lecturing he forgets himself" (IV:15/59). The mayor describes a lecture by the history teacher on Alexander the Great: "He was all right on the Assyrians and the Babylonians, but as soon as he came to Alexander the Great, I can't tell you what happened to him; I thought the school was on fire. He bolted from his desk, grabbed a chair, and with all his might smashed it against the floor. Of course, Alexander the Great was a hero, but why break chairs?" (IV:15/59).

Although the mayor relates all these instances of uncontrolled and unseemly behavior as defects the town officials should correct in order to gain the approval of the inspector general from Petersburg, he also agrees with his fellow officials that the life of the town is essentially out of their control, moved by an unruly nature or a "God who moves in mysterious ways." When, for example, the superintendent of schools tells the mayor that he has already reprimanded the history teacher but to no avail, the mayor acknowledges that it would be futile to try to control mad behavior such as the fat-faced teacher's grimaces or the history teacher's lectures on Alexander the Great: "It's true, God moves in mysterious ways. An educated man turns out to be a drunk or he makes faces that would scare the saints" (IV:15/59).

Although Zemlianika's and the mayor's resignation to nature are clearly being satirized here as examples of bureaucratic neglect, the play also encourages its audience to take some pleasure in the mayor's vision of the uncontrolled vitality of Russian provincial life (as Gogol's characterization of the untamed "bear" Sobakevich is pleasurable in *Dead Souls*).

At the end of act 1, after the mayor has been led to believe that the inspector general has already arrived in his town in the person of Khlestakov, he stops thinking about how he and his colleagues might be implicated for bureaucratic neglect and begins desperately casting about for ways to cover up his guilt for such clear-cut crimes as extortion and embezzlement. Contemplation of his own guilt always leads him in a circle: thoughts of cover-ups and evasions of punishment are followed by thoughts of further "sins": "Oh, oh, oh, I've sinned, I've sinned a lot (*picks up a hatbox instead of his hat*). Dear God, let me off the hook this time, and I'll light such a candle for You . . . it'll be enormous. I'll make every son-of-a-bitch of a merchant come across with a ton of wax. Oh my God, my God!" (IV:23/66).

As the mayor rushes off to confront Khlestakov at the inn at the end of act 1, he has already revealed himself as a provincial philosopher of sorts, burdened with fear that he will be condemned for the chaotic disorder of the town or that his own sins will be discovered and punished, and yet also arguing persuasively that the town is anarchically resilient to ordering and that he is morally incorrigible. His position is analogous to that of Fedor Karamazov, who at the beginning of *The Brothers Karamazov* rushes off to meet the saintly Father Zossima at the monastery in an attempt to resolve whether there is some higher authority that can judge him guilty for his sins and his unseemliness, or whether the unseemly and evil laws of nature prevail. The mayor hopes to meet an inspector general who will be corrupt like himself and can be bribed into not punishing him. But he is so burdened with philosophical doubt and uncertainty that he might also welcome a clear and absolute judgment of his guilt from a higher authority.

Who then is the Khlestakov character who awaits the mayor at the inn? In his article "On Khlestakov," Iurii Lotman identifies the "real" Khlestakov as the hero of the play and, focusing on his drunken monologue about Petersburg at the beginning of act 3, defines him as a liar. He interprets Khlestakov's lying as a typical form of social behavior within Russia's elite at the beginning of the nineteenth century. Such lying, according to Lotman, reflects the tension between various kinds of "ambition" (to rise in the bureaucracy, to change the world, etc.) and the reality of an "irregular public life" in which some people work ploddingly to advance their careers while others rise effortlessly to high positions through "connections."[6] In his case study of the actual historical figure, Zavalishin, whose public lies about his role in history were as extravagant as Khlestakov's, Lotman attributes Zavalishin's extravagant public lying to a strong, self-loving ego's need to assert its "ambitious dreams" in "imagined deeds." However, according to Lotman, "Khlestakov is another story. The source of his lying is an unremitting contempt for himself. Lying intoxicates Khlestakov because, in his imaginary world, he can *cease to be himself*, escape from himself, become someone else. . . . The split personality which was to become the central focus of Dostoevskii's *Double* . . . was already present in Khlestakov."[7]

Lotman's study is valuable in its analysis of the sociocultural context that produced acute "status anxiety" within elite Russian society at the time Gogol and young Dostoevsky were writing. Its analysis of public lying that has its source in the liar's "unremitting contempt for himself" applies perfectly to the lying, impersonations, and delusions of grandeur that characterize a number of the heroes of Gogol's Petersburg stories, from "The Diary of a Madman" to "The Overcoat," and that can also be found in Dostoevsky's work, beginning with *The Double*. However, it is not true that Khlestakov himself suffers from status anxiety and low self-esteem.

When Khlestakov is introduced along with his serf, Osip, at the beginning of act 2, he is revealed as a person who can pass easily back and forth across the boundary between the provinces and Petersburg without experiencing any anxiety that he would have to change his identity as he makes this transition. Osip's opening monologue in act 2 introduces this notion of a relaxed, pleasurable, anxiety-free transition between the provinces and Petersburg. He compares country life to the life of Petersburg in terms of the different pleasures these places afford him. "Things are easier back in the village," he thinks, "not so much going on, but less to worry about. Find yourself a woman and lie around all day stuffing yourself on home cooking" (IV:26/68). On the other hand, he thinks, "when you come right down to it, there's no place like Peter. If you got the cash, life's nice 'n refined—teeayters, dancing dogs for your pleasure, the works!"

(IV:26/68). Rather than being cowed by a sense of inferiority to the various other classes of people he meets in Petersburg, Osip enjoys the carnivalesque mixing and leveling of different social classes on the city streets, where "the shopkeepers in the market call you 'sir'! On the ferry you get to rub elbows with a government official. Feel like company? Just drop into any store: some soldier'll chew your ear about army life, or tell you what the stars in the sky mean. An officer's lady will come traipsing in, maybe a chambermaid . . . and what a chambermaid! Wow! (*Bursts out laughing, shaking his head*)" (IV:26–27/68–69).

Osip has developed no ambition to be anyone other than a peasant as he mixes with other classes on the Petersburg streets. His amorous thoughts shift easily from the "officer's lady," who would be inaccessible to him by virtue of class differences, to the more accessible chambermaid; his tastes in food remain simple ("God! What I wouldn't give for a bowl of cabbage soup," IV:27/69); and generally, all the pleasures of Petersburg that he catalogs are accessible to him as a peasant.

Khlestakov is similar to Osip in that he too has enjoyed the entertainment that Petersburg society offers anyone "if you got the cash." He has engaged in conspicuous consumption, presenting himself in public as a person with more money and more refined taste than he actually has. Osip mimics his master's pretentious spending habits: "Osip, book me a room, the best they've got, and order a first-rate dinner. I can't stomach bad cooking; I've got to have the best" (IV:26/68). However, it would be incorrect to conclude, following Lotman's analysis, that Khlestakov is attempting to escape from a contemptible, low sense of himself as he squanders his money in Petersburg. Although Khlestakov has not enjoyed working in Petersburg, he has obviously enjoyed spending his money there. Osip reports: "Catch him going to the office! He'll be strutting along the avenoo or out playing cards" (IV:27/69).

Another basic characteristic of Khlestakov's, one that distinguishes him from Osip, is that he does not care how much money he has. He embodies the cyclical set of cultural attitudes that fuels the modern capitalist system: pleasure in the process of spending money; pleasure in the "status symbol" value of what one buys; acceptance of the penury to which one's spending cycle reduces one; and, finally, a gambler's sense of optimism that there will be more money in the future and the spending cycle will start over again. He is like Nozdrev of *Dead Souls* in that he does not seem to mind where he is in this cycle. While suffering hunger pains in his hotel room at the beginning of act 2, he recalls with pleasure the experience of losing all his money to a gambler, he looks forward with pleasure to the opportunity of gambling again, and he expresses his careless, mindless self-satisfaction in his distracted whistling at the end of his speech:

> It's terrible, being so hungry. I thought a walk would make my hunger pass. No, dammit, it won't go away. Now if it wasn't for that fling in Penza I'd have enough money to get home. That infantry officer really put one over on me. Amazing the way the son-of-a-bitch plays cards. He sat in for no more than a quarter of an hour and cleaned me out. Still, I'm dying to have another crack at him. Just haven't had the chance yet. What a grubby town! The grocers won't give anything on credit. How stingy can you get! (*Whistles, first from "Robert le diable," then "Red Sarafan," and finally nothing in particular.*) (IV:29/70)

Khlestakov's carefree lack of concern about where he is and what position he occupies in society can also be attributed to more primary psychological attributes of frivolity, stupidity, and indifference to everything in life except certain routine, mundane pleasures such as eating, cardplaying, and flirting with women. Frivolity is evident in his short attention span (he sometimes forgets what he is saying in mid-sentence, and he courts the women Anna Andreevna and Mar'ia Antonovna indiscriminately). Doltish intelligence is betrayed in his tendency to state the obvious and to make statements that merely record the registering of sensory data (for example, when Liapkin-Tiapkin introduces himself as "Judge of the District Court" and Khlestakov responds "So you're the judge" [IV:59/97], we infer that Khlestakov is not making polite conversation but rather slowly registering his perception that Liapkin-Tiapkin is, in fact, the judge).

Khlestakov's simpleminded focus on pleasurable experience is evident in his repeated statements "I like . . . I love . . . I'm wild about . . . " As he says at the beginning of act 3 after being wined and dined by the director of charities: "I like the way you show the visitors the sights of the city" (IV:45/85); or, as he says when the town officials begin to bribe him in act 4: "I've grown very fond of this little town" (IV:60/98). He expresses nothing but pleasure in most of the lines he delivers to Anna Andreevna and Mar'ia Antonovna:

> KHLESTAKOV, *bowing.* How delighted I am, madam, to have the pleasure of your acquaintance.
>
> ANNA. It's even more of a pleasure for us to meet you.
>
> KHLESTAKOV, *posturing.* Oh no, madam, it's far more pleasant for me.

ANNA. How can you say that, sir! You've only trying to flatter us. Please be seated.

KHLESTAKOV. Standing near you, madam, is joy itself. But if you insist, I'll sit. . . . How delighted I am at last to be sitting beside you. (IV:47/87)

Constantly attuned to the little mundane pleasures of life, Khlestakov is, at the same time, indifferent and dispassionate, whimsically attuned now to this possible source of pleasure, now to that, like a child in a toy store, first courting Mar'ia Antonovna, then courting Anna Andreevna, then proposing to Mar'ia Antonovna, and then whimsically dropping both women and exiting the town. This whimsical, detached orientation toward pleasure is evident in Khlestakov's bribe-taking scenes in act 4. He "*likes*" being given money; it "*is pleasing*" to him to be plied with bribes by all the officials of the town, and then by the merchants too. And yet he is so fundamentally indifferent to this experience that he is barely able to keep up his end of the bribe-taking ritual, and even forgets to ask for the bribe on one occasion.

Did Gogol articulate a social type or prototype in this set of psychological features (frivolity, stupidity, mundane hedonism, indifference) attributed to Khlestakov? Or is Khlestakov's minimal personality more of an antihero-as-literary-device, the equivalent in drama to Ivan Shponka's character in prose? Or finally, does his minimal personality function primarily to frustrate the townspeople's appeal to the inspector general for some sort of absolute revelation of the truth?

There is no doubt that Khlestakov's personality comically frustrates the townspeople's desire that he reveal himself as the powerful and authoritative person they assume the inspector general to be. It is also true that the gaps and absences in his identity challenge the audience's norms for what would constitute a human character. As to whether this minimal personality articulates a social prototype, it seems possible that Gogol did conceive of Khlestakov as a modern everyman, comparable, in certain respects, to Pushkin's creation of his little hero Evgenii in *The Bronze Horseman* a few years earlier, or, a few years later, to Gogol's own creation of Akakii Akakievich in "The Overcoat."

Evgenii, Khlestakov, and Akakii are similar, first of all, in that they are self-satisfied in spite of their minimal personalities (this *samodovol'nost'* [self-satisfaction] is what distinguishes them from Gogol's madman or Dostoevsky's Goliadkin). Second, they are similar in that they make such small demands on life: Evgenii can be satisfied by a secure "little position" in the Petersburg bureaucracy and by a modest, lower-middle-class domestic life in the suburbs with Parasha; Akakii could be satisfied by his copying and then by his overcoat; and Khlestakov, as we have seen, reaps many small pleasures in life and is willing to take the good with the bad (even as he contemplates starvation at the inn, his Petersburg pants give him pleasure: "It'll be rough though, if he won't give me anything to eat. I never dreamed I could feel so hungry. Maybe I can raise some cash on my clothes? Sell my pants? No, I'd rather starve" [IV:30/71]).

Khlestakov is also like the Evgenii-Akakii prototype in that in spite of the small demands that he makes upon life, he ultimately realizes that Petersburg is an insufferable place and rejects it. Evgenii and Akakii reach the tragic understanding that they should not have suffered the insufferable conditions of Peter's city, and they go insane as they rebel against these conditions. Between the lines of Khlestakov's monologue about Petersburg we can read a comic-satiric variant of the Akakii-Evgenii story. Consider, for example, the beginning of the monologue, first as Khlestakov delivers it, and then as it can be reconstructed as his actual experience:

> Of course, there's no comparing [the country] with the capital. Ah, Petersburg! That's the life. You may think all I do is transcribe documents. Not at all. I'm on a friendly footing with my department head. He pats me on the back and says, "Come on over for dinner, my good man." I only drop in at the office for a minute or so, merely to issue instructions—"Do this like this, that like that"—and before you know it, the clerks are scratching away like a pack of rats. "Scr, Scr, Scr." They even wanted to promote me, but I said to myself, "Why?" The doorman runs after me with a brush. "Allow me, sir," he says, "may I polish your shoes?" (IV:48/88)

If one reads through the lines, the same passage reveals the wretchedness of Khlestakov's life in Petersburg:

> Ah, Petersburg! What a wretched life. All I do is transcribe documents. I'm *not* on a friendly footing with my department head. He *does not* pat me on the back and *does not* say "Come on over for dinner, my good man." I go into the office *from early morning until evening* and all I do is *receive* instructions—"Do this like this and that like that"—and before you know it *we* clerks are scratching away like a pack of rats. "Scr, Scr, Scr." They did *not* want to promote me, and I said to myself, "Why?" The doorman runs after *other people (but not me)* with a brush. "Allow me, sir," he says, "may I polish your shoes?"

In the following passage, it is not even necessary to read between the lines to understand Khlestakov's narrative as a straightforward account of public humiliation on the one hand and lack of public recognition on the other; it is only necessary to infer that the words "There goes Khlestakov!" were spoken jeeringly, not with respect:

> I'm not one to stand on ceremony. In fact, I always do my best to slip by unnoticed. But it's impossible to escape attention. simply impossible! The minute I step out the door, people shout, "There goes Khlestakov!" Once I was even taken for the commander-in-chief. The soldiers leaped out of the guardhouse and presented arms. The officer, who's a great friend of mine, said to me later, "You know, old man, we actually took you for the commander-in-chief." (IV:48/88)

Some of Khlestakov's narrative is devoted not to the pain and humiliation of his life in the ministry but to the pleasures of Petersburg's entertainment culture. For example, his description of a high-society party is grounded in the mundane *realia* of experience to which he had access. We can infer that he ate watermelons in Petersburg, but that they did not cost seven hundred rubles. We can infer that he ate soup with French names, but that this soup was not "straight off the boat from Paris." And from Osip we know that he spent much of his time playing cards, but that his friends did not include the foreign minister and the French and German ambassadors.

> Words can't describe parties in the capital. I'll have a watermelon on the table that sells for seven hundred rubles! A tureen of soup straight off the boat from Paris! You lift the lid, and the aroma—ah! There's nothing in the world to compare to it. I'm at a party every day of the week. We have our own card game: the foreign minister, the French ambassador, and the German ambassador—and me. We play till we're exhausted. It's incredible! I'm barely able to drag myself up to my room on the fourth floor and say to the cook, "Hey, Mavrushka, take my coat." What am I blabbering about? I forgot, I live on the first floor. (IV:49/89)

Clearly, Khlestakov is unlike Akakii and Evgenii in that his mundane need for pleasure could be fulfilled by Petersburg's nightlife, and the basic Nozdrev-like resiliency of his character allowed him to escape from his downtrodden state as petty bureaucrat to the pleasurable condition of eating at restaurants, cardplaying, and so on. But the parts of Khlestakov's narrative that focus on his life in the bureaucracy reveal that even the fatuously self-satisfied, resilient, indifferent Khlestakov could not endure his ministry's denial of his minimal demands for a sense of power, dignity, and self-worth. He presents himself as a person who must get back to Petersburg to soak up more of its culture, yet it is significant that he left the city of his own accord before his money ran out (IV:26/68); and it is clear that he intends never to return there to work (IV:35/77).

Khlestakov's monologue in act 3 provides a good example of how interpretations of *The Inspector General* vary according to whether the audience understands the "real" Khlestakov primarily as a blank screen onto which the townspeople project their notions of the power and authority of Petersburg or whether the audience views him as a complex, concrete character bearing with him experience of Petersburg that challenges the townspeople's expectations in a concrete way.

Looking at Khlestakov-the-inspector-general-from-Petersburg narrative from the townspeople's point of view, it is appropriate that the audience should miss the fact that he is telling us a story about intolerable debasement and humiliation at the hands of the Petersburg bureaucracy and of his frivolous pursuit of pleasure in Petersburg's "teeayters" and restaurants. Identifying with the townspeople, we tremble in awe and terror at the degree of power he says he has in Petersburg. Burdened with feelings (expressed by the mayor in act 1) that our own lives are chaotic and anarchic, we want this awesome power to assert its authority over us. We want to subjugate ourselves to it, as we do when we all go to present our bribes to Khlestakov in act 4. For us, this subjugation of ourselves to Khlestakov-the-head-of-the-ministry is a quasi-religious act in which we are empowered and affirmed. Bobchinskii speaks for us all when he says: "I humbly beg you, sir, when you return to the capital, tell all those great gentlemen—the senators and admirals and all the rest—say, 'Your Excellency or Your Highness, in such and such a town there lives a man called Pyotr Ivanovich Bobchinsky.' Be sure to tell them, 'Pyotr Ivanovich Bobchinsky lives there' " (IV:66–67/104).

If, from our detached ironic position in the audience, we view the "real" Khlestakov simply as "not the inspector general," then the townspeople's religious zeal in bowing down to him appears to us as simply a comic-pathetic revelation of provincial Russia's need to subject itself to the all-powerful earthly authority that it thinks might exist in Petersburg. However, if from our ironic, detached position we view the "real" Khlestakov as a person who has lived inside the Petersburg bureaucracy and whose most minimal human needs have been denied there, then the provincials' desire to subject themselves to the political power of Petersburg appears even more concretely pathetic. As an average, everyman representative of the real contemporary Petersburg, the "real" Khlestakov concretely asserts the hollowness of Petersburg's claim to authority in Russian culture.

Interpretations of the ending of *The Inspector General* are influenced by the extent to which Khlestakov is viewed as a representative of the average contemporary reality of Petersburg in the collective plot of the play. At the end, the "real" inspector general's authority is suspect if it is grounded in the reality to which the "real" Khlestakov has introduced us. The interpretation of the ending most consistent with our interpretation of Khlestakov would identify the inspector general who appears at the end not as a real representative of Petersburg's political power but as an ideal deity with power and authority that have not yet been revealed to humanity. By crossing the boundary that separates Petersburg from the provinces, Khlestakov forces a religious, as opposed to a political, resolution to the collective plot of the play.

Robert Louis Jackson

Gogol's "The Portrait": The Simultaneity of Madness, Naturalism, and the Supernatural

IN "LE DANTYU as a Beacon," the artist-typographer Ilia Zdanevich's fifth drama (or *dra*, as he called his productions), published in Paris and dated 1923, two of the main characters are painters. The hero-painter is, in fact, based on a "real" artist by the name of Mikhail Le Dantyu who died in 1917. In the *dra* this real painter is contrasted with a villain-painter who is a "realist."

The villain-artist paints a portrait of a dead woman: it is described as the "living image of her." In contrast, the hero-artist, the "real" Mikhail Le Dantyu, paints an "unlike" portrait of the dead woman.

In the *dra* both portraits come to life. When the unlike portrait touches the dead woman, she comes to life. Then the unlike portrait kills her, setting off a series of murders, which are finally resolved by the resurrection of the forces of life.

We have no difficulty in recognizing in Zdanevich's *dra* a parodic inversion of Gogol's "The Portrait." In that tale, in its second part, a religious painter, desiring to introduce the "Prince of Darkness" into one of his religious epics, strives to paint the portrait of a demonic moneylender, more precisely the Antichrist, with "scrupulous exactitude." He succeeds in creating a living—that is, a dead—image of him. "Temnye glaza . . . starika gliadeli tak zhivo i vmeste mertvenno" ("The dark eyes of the old man looked out in such a lifelike and yet dead way," III:405). The moneylender dies. The character of the painter changes for the worse. He escapes the baneful influence of the portrait, finally, by giving it away, entering a monastery, and consecrating himself to God.

The power of the Antichrist, however, continues to live in the portrait and to bedevil all those who come into contact with it. In the first version of the story the portrait is the harbinger of the Apocalypse. The painter's son—he tells his father's tale in the second part of the story—finds the portrait but fails to destroy it. The portrait disappears again. Evil turns out to be elusive.

In the first version of "The Portrait" Gogol foregrounds the action of the supernatural, while posing the aesthetic theme of the relation of art to reality. In the second version of his tale he foregrounds the aesthetic theme. Here he by no means abandons the supernatural, but, as though following Pushkin's recipe for the fantastic, integrates the supernatural into the aesthetic and psychological drama in such a way as to make it difficult for the reader to know whether it is the power of the supernatural or the failure of the painter's aesthetic that brings about the evil portrait and, with it, the direct entrance of the Antichrist into the world.

Here I should like to focus on the way the categories of the fantastic (or supernatural), the aesthetic, and the psychological interact, indeed, at times seem identical with one another in Gogol's "The Portrait."

The misfortune of the painter of the portrait and of those who look at it may be summed up in Nietzsche's epigram: "And when you gaze long into an abyss, the abyss also gazes back into you" ("Und wenn du lange in einen Abgrund blickst, blickt der Abgrund auch in dich hinein").[1] In Gogol's case the look would have to be understood, on the aesthetic plane, as obsessive concern with imitation of an object, that is, with "naturalism." Gazing into the eyes of the moneylender in an effort to capture every detail, the painter finds these eyes gazing hypnotically back into his own. The result of the painter's effort to capture the living image of the moneylender is that he becomes a prisoner, as it were, of the "evil eye." He experiences in turn a psychological crisis.

On the fantastic plane of the story's action the effort to imitate reality results in the reification of the evil spirit of the moneylender. The devil breaks through the defenses of everyday reality. In purely aesthetic terms the painter's attempt to reproduce reality with absolute exactitude leads to the "super" natural, to a kind of magic realism, to a picture of reality, finally, that not only pushes realism to its limits and beyond but evokes in the viewer a disturbing sense of the uncanny, the unnatural, the grotesque. The viewer, full of apprehension and anxiety, finds himself on the threshold of the supernatural or fantastic. Instead of elevating his spirit, the portrait plunges him into serious distress or depression. He experiences a psychological crisis.

In the first part of the story Chartkov—the painter who discovers the evil portrait in a secondhand shop—experiences this confusion of feelings. Even before he sees the portrait, his eye is drawn to somber paintings with dark green lacquer and yellow frames; one of them is given over, ominously, to the depiction of "sovershenno krasnyi vecher pokhozhii na zarevo pozhara" ("an absolutely red evening, like the glow of a conflagration," III:79).

It is not clear at this moment whether the portrait influences Chartkov's mental state or whether Chartkov's mental state influences his way of looking at the paintings and his surroundings in general. Significantly, as he walks off in the twilight his thoughts take on a "gloomy cast" ("mysli ego . . . omrachilis'," III:83). "The devil take it," he says, "it's a rotten world!" ("Chert poberi! gadko na svete!" III:83). But is it a rotten world, or do things simply appear in a rotten light? Whatever the answer, Chartkov feels "absolutely numb to everything" ("polnyi beschuvstviia ko vsemu," III:83). The devil seems already in him, hardening his heart; a devilish glow and devil's shadows are in the air ("krasnyi svet vechernei zari ostavalsia eshche na polovine neba. . . . Poloprozrachnye legkie *teni khvostami* padali na zemliu" ["the red light of sunset still remained on half the sky. . . . Half-transparent light *shadows* fell *tail-down* on the earth," III:83, emphasis added]). Chartkov speaks of a "strange light" ("somnitel'nyi svet"), but again it is not clear whether it is the "light" ("svet") that is "somnitel'nyi" or whether the world ("svet") itself has been "somnitel'nyi," that is, "strange" or "questionable" in the eyes of the viewer. In this brilliant entrance to his story Gogol no doubt intends to suggest both the impact of the devil on Chartkov and the presence of a demonic vision in him.

In the nocturnal light of the moon, Chartkov again examines the portrait. "Whether because of the light of the moon, carrying with it the delirium of dreams and enfolding everything in other images opposed to positive day, or something else," he becomes frightened. He picks up the portrait and looks with horror at the eyes: "That was no longer a copy from nature, it had the kind of strange vitality that might have illumined the face of a dead man risen from the grave." "This was no longer art; it destroyed the harmony of the portrait itself." Instead of feeling "lofty pleasure" Chartkov is overcome by a "feeling of anguish and pain" ("boleznennoe, tomitel'noe chuvstvo"). Why is it, he wonders, that "a faithful, slavish imitation of nature," the depiction of something "objectively and coolly, without feeling any particular sympathy for it," must necessarily confront the observer "in all its terrible reality." Even lowly nature in a true work of art, he ruminates, "appears in a kind of light." And yet the same work of another artist appears as "low and sordid" "without anything that shed a luster" ("net v nei chego-to ozariaiushchego"). "There is no sun in the sky" ("Net na nebe solntsa," III:87–88).

In Gogol's aesthetic the light of the "moon" and the light of the "sun" have real properties; however, they are also metaphors for artistic light: the lofty light of a noble idea or ideal (the sun) or the "questionable light" ("somnitel'nyi svet") of spiritless vision (the moon). In artistic terms, the light of the sun and the light of the moon disclose different realities in the world and in man. "Lofty cognition," the narrator observes in the first version of "The Portrait," creates "sacred works." Here "great art lifts the cover from heaven and shows man the part of his own inner world which is filled with sounds and sacred mysteries" (III:424). But the same cover that conceals the divine heavens also (as in Tiutchev's "Den' i noch' " ["Day and Night"] conceals the "nameless abyss." In the first version of the story the narrator makes plain that a "line" ("cherta") or "boundary" ("granitsa") separates these two worlds. The artist crosses it at his peril, that is, he crosses over the line (*cherta*) into the realm of the devil (*chert*). Looking at the portrait, Chartkov asks himself:

> What is this? . . . art or some supernatural sorcery which has eluded the laws of nature? What a strange, what an inconceivable task! Or is there for man some boundary to which higher cognition leads and which, once he has crossed it, he is already stealing something uncreatable by the labor of man, tearing something alive out of the life that animates the original? Why is it that this crossing of the boundary set as a limit for the imagination is so horrible? Or is it that beyond imagination, beyond creative inspiration, reality at length follows—that horrible reality into which imagination springs from its axis in consequence of some accidental push, that horrible reality which appears to him who thirsts for it when, desiring to comprehend the beauty of man, he arms himself with an anatomist's scalpel, lays bare the interior and beholds the repulsiveness of man. Inconceivable! Such an astonishing, horrible animation! Or is excessively close imitation of nature just as cloying as a dish that has an excessively sweet taste? (III:406)

In this strange passage we are struck, among other things, by the notion of *imagination sprung from its axis by some accidental push* ("deistvitel'nost', na kotoruiu soskakivaet voobrazhenie s svoei osi kakim-to postoronnim tolchkom"). Here is a phrase that would appear to have both aesthetic and psychological interest. The vision of a "horrible reality," whether as conceived by the painter or as perceived by the viewer of the painting, seems linked with some kind of psychological trauma. The movement of "cognition" beyond a certain boundary is plainly experienced as a psychic jolt or dislocation. In both versions of the story the perception of horrible reality is linked with "a disturbed imagination" ("potrevozhennoe voobrazhenie," III:408). There is a sense of "tearing something alive out of life," "as though the eyes had been cut out of a living man"

(III:87). The "faithful, slavish imitation of nature," Gogol writes in a parallel passage in the second version of the story, is like a "transgression" ("prostupok"); it affects you "like a piercing, discordant scream" (III:88). Instead of experiencing pleasure, Chartkov, looking at the picture, is overcome by "a feeling of anguish and pain" ("boleznennoe, tomitel'noe chuvstvo," III:87). He is convinced, finally, that "his imagination was completely disordered [*rasstroeno*] and was presenting to him in the form of a dream his own agitated thoughts" (III:410). This sense of inner disorder the narrator compares to the "wild feeling" one experiences "at the appearance of oddities [*strannosti*] that represent the disorder of nature, or rather, some kind of madness of nature" (III:405).

In short, the sense of madness in nature and in the portrait is paralleled by a sense of wildness, pain, disorder, and, ultimately, madness in the individual. Chartkov, for example, experiences a severe breakdown. Psychic disorder in him reaches an extreme form: completely disordered visions end up in "fits of rage and madness." Death follows. The painter of the portrait also frequently experiences a "surge" of "despairing, violent thoughts." "This somber state of soul . . . drove him to seek out the black side of man" (III:438).

In both versions of the story the action of the supernatural, a false aesthetic, and greed are advanced as motivations for the artist's sense of psychological disorder, his despair, his moral disintegration. Yet I would suggest that Gogol is also broadly hinting that disturbing aesthetic visions may also be motivated by psychological disorder, some traumatic internal event, some "accidental push" causing "imagination to spring from its axis."

Let us ask another question: What, in moral and aesthetic terms, is this imagination-sprung-from-its-axis? It is imagination devoid of moral or spiritual striving or context; it is what Gogol might have called *secular imagination*, imagination responsive chiefly to a despiritualized and disintegrated material world; it is imagination that discloses a world of terror and madness, a disgusting world, "all that which lies, like a black sediment, in the depths of man, and which is destroyed and banished by education, noble acts and the contemplation of the beautiful" (III:438). Secular imagination perceives a landscape or nature that evokes a "wild feeling" ("dikoe chuvstvo"), that kind of inexplicable sensation we feel at the appearance of oddities representing "the disorder or, rather, some kind of madness of nature" (III:405).

Gogol's implicit distinction between two kinds of "imagination" (or two kinds of "cognition"), a higher and a lower, a lofty and a secular one, later finds embodiment in Dostoevsky's pseudo-grotesque tale "Bobok." The tipsy, half-mad narrator of that work has a vision of a decaying underworld of corpses. This underworld is precisely Gogol's "horrible reality"—a despiritualized realm, the so-called disgusting anatomy of the body, the "black sediment in the depths of man" of which Gogol speaks in his story. Dostoevsky conceives the vision or hallucinations of his narrator not as the result of the supernatural but, on the one hand, as the result of a mental breakdown and, on the other, as the result of a naturalistic aesthetic that is incapable of serving the higher and fruitful realms and purposes of art. Fantasy as Dostoevsky exhibits it in "Bobok" is a parody of higher or idealistic fantasy; the fantasy of a materialist, it gives expression not to a sense of self-renewing boundless reality but to the secular imagination of man before a bounded, self-consuming reality.[2] It is not surprising that Gogol's aesthetic of two kinds of imagination should be echoed in Dostoevsky's most Gogolian work, "Bobok": in this work the problem of naturalistic realism is explored on both the aesthetic and philosophical planes. Not surprising, too, is the fact that the bizarre hero of this work is named Ivan Ivanovich.

The imagination that has sprung from its axis conceives and perceives a distorted, inharmonious, despiritualized world. The crossing of aesthetic limits is also a crossing of moral-spiritual boundaries. In opening the door to the aesthetically "super" natural, one also in Gogol's world opens the door to evil in the form of the occult and supernatural. Here, too, it is noteworthy that Gogol depicts the appearance or occurrence of the supernatural as a form of violence. At the end of his tale, the painter of the portrait (in the first version of the story) explains that the Antichrist has long wanted to "come into the world, but has been unable to because he can come only in a supernatural manner."

> But in our world everything is created in such a way that everything happens in a natural way, and thus [the Antichrist] has no means of breaking into the world [*emu nikakie sily . . . ne pomogut prorvat'sia v mir*]. But our earth is ashes before the creator. By its laws it must be destroyed, and with every day the laws of nature will become weaker and therefore the boundaries holding back the supernatural more accessible. (III:443)

The notion of the Antichrist (or supernatural or demonic or black spirit) "breaking into the world" parallels the trauma of imagination sprung from its axis. The individual experiences this "breaking in" as psychic violence, ultimately as madness. The mind of man is opened up, as it were, to the devil, to the disgusting world of the dead, a world in which imagination expresses itself only in "super" naturalistic ways. The disorder of art, the disorder of nature, and the disorder of society are completed by the disorder of the mind. Only two things can follow: disfiguration (death) or transfiguration (resurrection). Both of these variants are given in "The Portrait": Chartkov perishes in madness; on his deathbed he has hallucinations in which he sees eyes staring at him everywhere. The painter of the portrait, however, overcomes evil and aberration by casting the portrait away and by abandoning the world; he enters a monastery and consecrates his art to God.

To conclude: Gogol in "The Portrait" seems to be reflecting upon his own art, his own strange, disturbed, "super" natural intuitions of reality and upon the state of mind, aesthetic and psychological, that summons up his monsters from the deep. As we have seen, psychic illness in the story is attributed in part to the evil influence of the portrait, that is, to the supernatural; socially, it is attributed to the evil of gold; aesthetically, to a false conception of the relation of art and reality. The door is at least open, I suggest, to a conception of psychic disorder itself as responsible for the vision of evil.

Susanne Fusso

The Landscape of *Arabesques*

IN GOGOL'S 1835 collection *Arabesques*, landscape is destiny. According to Gogol's historical scheme, the character of a people is deeply affected by the geography of its homeland, and even forms of government are dictated by the lay of the land. The preoccupation with landscape in *Arabesques* is more than just a thematic one, however. Like many works of art, *Arabesques* itself contains the clue to how it is written and how it is to be read. It is no coincidence that the right way to read *Arabesques* is most vividly expressed as the right way to view a landscape, for early Romantic English theories of landscape gardening are central not only to *Arabesques* but to *Dead Souls*, the work for which *Arabesques* in many ways serves as both introduction and gloss.

Gogol's letters about *Arabesques* at the time of its publication are characteristically apologetic. To Pogodin he writes, "I am sending you my omnium-gatherum [*vsiakaia vsiachina*]. Smooth it out and pat it down a bit: there is much that is childish in it, and I have tried to throw it out into the world as soon as possible, so as to throw all the old stuff out of my desk at the same time, and to brush myself off and start a new life."[1] The impulse to take Gogol at his word, to regard *Arabesques* as a work whose composition is dictated solely by what manuscripts happened to be lying on his desk one day in 1834, has betrayed itself in the attitudes of critics and editors from the time of the work's publication. Gogol himself, in his 1842 *Collected Works*, set the precedent for the destruction of the integrity of *Arabesques* by separating the fictional pieces from the nonfictional. This separation was also observed in the 14-volume Academy edition, sending Viktor Shklovskii back to the Tikhnonravov edition to recapture the work's original shape.[2] Even the recent Ardis translation of *Arabesques*, billed on its cover as the "first complete English translation," omits the two fictional fragments "Chapter from a Historical Novel" ("Glava iz istoricheskogo romana") and "The Captive"

("Plennik").[3] The omission is a serious one, for along with "A Glance at the Composition of Little Russia," presented as the first chapter of an entire history of the Ukraine, and the internally fragmentary "The Diary of a Madman," published in *Arabesques* as "Scraps from the Diary of a Madman" ("Klochki iz zapisok sumasshedshego"), the historical fragments exemplify the discontinuity and incompletion that are the subject of philosophical and aesthetic inquiry elsewhere in the text.

Critics like Shklovskii and Donald Fanger have resisted the urge to ignore the distinctive unity of *Arabesques*.[4] They may find their warrant not only in the external evidence of Gogol's careful assembly of the work's parts but in the clues to the proper way to read the text that are offered within the work itself. In the essay "On the Middle Ages" Gogol writes:

> People have looked [at the history of the Middle Ages] as at a pile of dissonant, heterogeneous events, as a crowd of fragmented and senseless movements that have no main thread that would combine them into a single whole. In fact its terrible, unusual complexity cannot help but seem chaotic at first, but look more attentively and deeply, and you will find a connection, and a goal, and a direction; however I will not deny that in order to know how to find all this you must be gifted with the kind of sensitivity that few historians possess. (VIII:16)

Throughout *Arabesques*, whether the subject is history, geography, or art, Gogol reiterates the need not only to apprehend multifarious, individual, partial detail but to use one's intellectual powers and artistic sensitivity to assemble the seemingly fragmentary data of experience into a unified whole.[5] The two mental operations are likened at one point to two ways of perceiving a landscape: "You cannot come to know a city completely by walking through all its streets: for this you must go up to an elevated place from which it would be entirely visible, as if on your palm [*kak na ladoni*]" (VIII:30). Neither the intimate, close-up perception of detail (walking through the streets) nor the panoramic overview (standing on a height) is sufficient for a true conception of the whole. For Gogol, detail without overview is embodied in the demonic fragmentation of nineteenth-century life ("vsia drob' prikhotei i naslazhdenii, nad vydumkami kotorykh lomaet golovu nash XIX vek" ["the whole fractionality of whims and enjoyments which our nineteenth century exhausts itself to invent"], VIII:12). But overview without differentiation leads to monotony and excessive abstraction, as in the panoramic paintings that Gogol opposes to those of Briullov: "They are like views from a distance; there is only a general expression in them. We feel only the terrible situation of the whole crowd, but we do not see a person in whose face there would be the whole horror of the destruction he himself has seen" (VIII:110). The all-embracing genius of Briullov has been made possible only by the nineteenth century's obsession with parts, with the perfection of the individual subcategories of the painter's art: "[Briullov] strives to capture nature with a giant's embraces and squeezes it with the passion of a lover. Perhaps he has been greatly helped in this by the fragmented working-out in parts which the nineteenth century prepared for him. Perhaps if he had appeared earlier, Briullov would not have achieved that many-sided and at the same time full and colossal striving" (VIII:113). The only way for Briullov to compose large-scale canvases that have the look of truth is by taking advantage of the nineteenth century's minute observation of nature: "They have noticed such secret phenomena as no one ever suspected before. All that nature that a man often sees, that surrounds him and lives with him, all that visible nature, all those trivialities [*vsia eta meloch'*] that the great artists disdained, have achieved an amazing truth and perfection" (VIII:107). The negative side of this minute observation is that it takes the form of "notes, materials, fresh thoughts" of the kind a traveler enters in his notebook (VIII:107); in Gogol's view, Briullov is destined to make the unified work of art for which the nineteenth century has made the sketches.

The need to shift back and forth between the perception of detail and the perception of the whole accounts for the repeated appearance in *Arabesques* of optical lenses, with their power to diminish and magnify. There is the telescope, through which one must look at a building from a distance in order to make sure that its parts are in the proper proportion (VIII:59). There is the convex lens that reflects an entire landscape in miniature, the image for Pushkin's all-encompassing word: "In him Russian nature, the Russian soul, the Russian language, the Russian character were reflected with the same purity, the same purified beauty, with which a landscape is reflected on the convex surface of an optical lens" (VIII:50). The converse of the operation of the telescope and convex mirror, which present a large whole in a manageably compact and surveyable form, is the operation of the microscope, which enlarges parts to the point where new worlds of detail and ornament, invisible to the naked eye, are revealed. In "The Captive," one of the two fragments from a historical novel that are included in *Arabesques*, the eyes of a prisoner in a dungeon project the wondrous images of microscopically observed reality onto the utter blackness that surrounds him:

> He implanted himself into the darkness with all his senses. And then a completely new, strange world unfolded before him: bright streams started to appear to him in the gloom—the last remembrance of light! These streams took on a multitude of various patterns and colors. . . . These multicolored patterns took on the appearance either of a gaudy shawl, or of undulating marble, or finally that appearance that strikes us with its marvelous unusualness, when we look at a part of the little wing or leg of an insect through a microscope. (III:306)

Gogol ends the *Arabesques* version of this fragment immediately after this passage, and with good reason: the proliferating patterns of ornament produced on the prisoner's retina are not just a superfluous growth on the surface of a historical adventure tale. They provide the fragment with its most important reason for being in *Arabesques*, the very title of which reminds us that the meandering, capricious line of Islamic ornament, which had such a powerful hold on the imagination of German Romanticism, is in some sense central to the plan of Gogol's work. The problem of relating Islamic geometric ornament to certain types of argument and exposition has already been investigated by Howard Stern in his book on Walter Benjamin, and his conclusions are particularly relevant to Gogol's *Arabesques*. Stern begins with an astonishingly Gogolian passage in Benjamin which speaks of the difference between seeing a landscape from a height (in Benjamin's case, an airplane) and coming to know it by walking through it. For Benjamin the two types of knowledge are analogous to reading a text versus copying it. The pedestrian and the copyist construct their panoramic knowledge of the whole through their fragmented encounter with "a strict succession of partial views."[6] The model for Benjamin's road must be, in Stern's words, "a *line* that in some reasonable sense covers an *area;* for if the contrast of pedestrian and aviator is to be meaningful, it must be possible for the pedestrian to acquire knowledge, however fragmented and paradoxical, of the entire terrain" (p. 54). One solution is the Sierpiński line, a figure described by the mathematician Wacław Sierpiński in 1912. The theoretical limit of the recursive procedure that produces the Sierpiński line is a continuous line that completely fills a square (see fig. 1). In crudest terms, it is a line so crooked that, without intersecting itself, it transcends its one-dimensionality and begins to cover an area.

The relevance to the peculiar nature of Gogol's *Arabesques* of the line that mediates between one-dimensionality and two-dimensionality is further illuminated by Benjamin's comparison of Arabian architecture and ornament to a particular form of argument that he labels the tractatus. Like an Arabian building, the tractatus gives no

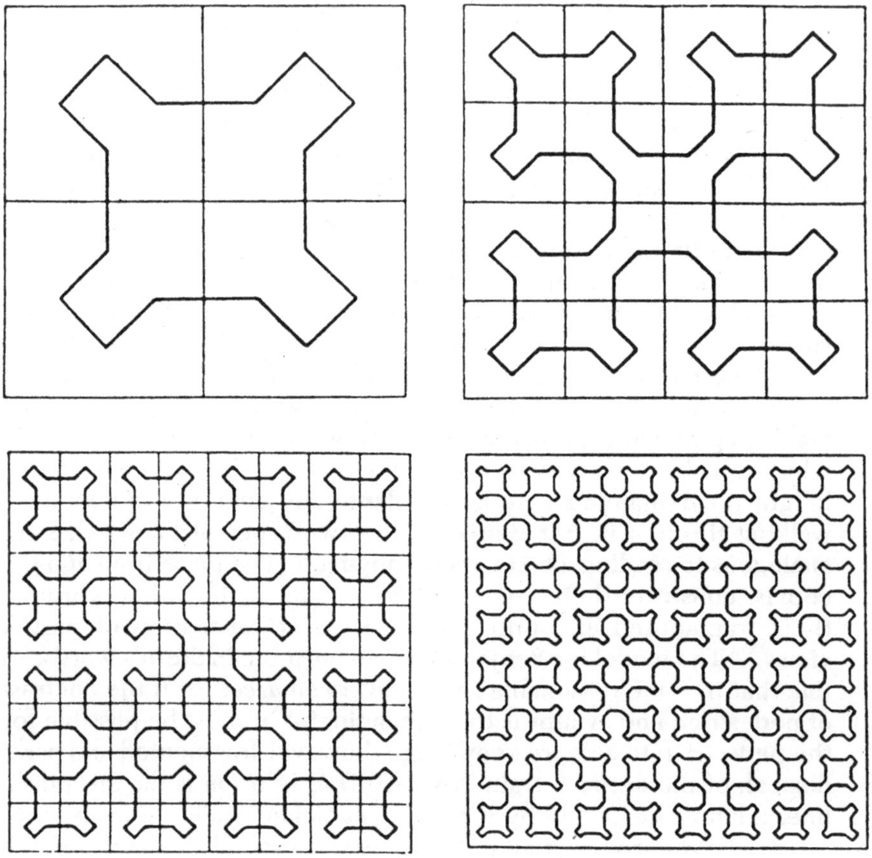

Figure 1. The Sierpiński Line

clue to its structure from without; one must enter the courtyard to see the articulation of the building's parts. As Stern writes, "The tractatus does not immediately reveal its structure or contents; one needs to wander around in it to discover its governing principle" (p. 56). Its facade is covered not with pictorial representations but, in Benjamin's words, "with unbroken, proliferating arabesques. In the ornamental density of this presentation the distinction between thematic and excursive expositions is abolished."[7] If a thematic essay is one that covers a certain conceptual area, and an excursive or digressive essay is one that ignores thematic coherence and follows its own willful, meandering line, then the tractatus, in which the distinction between these two types of exposition is abolished, must resemble Sierpiński's model, which mediates between line and area. In Stern's words, "Related areas will not necessarily be treated together . . . , but eventually the entire surface will be covered by one meandering line of development" (p. 57).

Benjamin's definition of the tractatus can, without too much difficulty, be applied to Gogol's *Arabesques*. As we wander through the landscape of *Arabesques*, we keep encountering the same objects and ideas—Gothic cathedrals, Greek marbles, the beginnings of the modern era, the education of the young—from different viewpoints and in different contexts, both fictional and nonfictional. It would be theoretically possible to compose a thematically coherent essay on, say, the vocation of the artist, by assembling bits from "On the Teaching of World History," "The Portrait," "A Few Words about Pushkin," "On Present-Day Architecture," "Nevsky Prospect," and "The Last Day of Pompeii." When read actively and attentively, the meandering arabesques of Gogol's thought begin to map out areas of thematic coherence.

It is clear by now that there is a congruence between macro- and microlevels of the text of *Arabesques*. A work whose apparent fragmentation and discontinuity mask an inner unity takes as one of its major subjects the need to combine close examination of individual parts with a panoramic survey of the whole. The same congruence holds with reference to the unusually complex, dense, and capriciously meandering line that appears in Islamic ornament. Such a line not only is the structural principle for Gogol's work but becomes the subject of explicit comment within the text. It appears in its most striking form in the essay on architecture. Gogol calls for the expansion of the architect's repertory of shapes to accommodate complex ornaments, based on our new understanding of nature "in all its secret phenomena": "Must everything encountered in nature always be only the column, dome, and arch? How many other forms have we not even touched! How a straight line can break and change direction, how a crooked one can bend, how many new decorations can be introduced, which not one architect has yet entered into his codex!" (VIII:74).

Strangely enough, Gogol's words have recently been echoed by Benoit Mandelbrot, the inventor of a new way of looking at shapes in nature. In his "casebook and manifesto," *The Fractal Geometry of Nature*, Mandelbrot writes, "Clouds are not spheres, mountains are not cones, coastlines are not circles, and bark is not smooth, nor does lightning travel in a straight line. . . . many patterns of Nature are so irregular and fragmented that, compared with [standard geometry] Nature exhibits not simply a higher degree but an altogether different level of complexity."[8] Mandelbrot has found a method of modeling and defining the apparently messy shapes of nature, shapes with fractional dimension: lines so crooked that they exceed one dimension and approach two, surfaces so rough that they exceed two dimensions and approach three. Like the text of *Arabesques*, fractal shapes resemble themselves at all levels of generality and on every scale: whether regarded through a microscope or a telescope, the degree of roughness of these seemingly chaotic outlines and shapes remains constant.

Gogol's taste for the maximally irregular shapes encountered in nature is shared with, and in part derived from, the theorists of the picturesque as it was elaborated in the late eighteenth and early nineteenth centuries in England, particularly in the writings of Sir Uvedale Price. Price was concerned both to define the picturesque in relation to Edmund Burke's categories of the sublime and the beautiful, and to discredit the trend in English gardening exemplified by the work of Lancelot "Capability" Brown. Gogol's works give evidence that he was at least indirectly familiar with the ideas of Burke, Brown, and Price.[9]

In his *Philosophical Inquiry into the Origin of Our Ideas of the Sublime and Beautiful* (1756), Burke defines the sublime as a quality that inspires astonishment and horror. Some of the characteristics required to make a landscape sublime are darkness, vastness, and suggestions of danger. A steep precipice crowned by magnificent oaks, with violent waves crashing on the rocks at its feet, is quintessentially sublime. Beauty, on the other hand, is characterized by delicacy, smoothness, gentle curves, and gradual variation. In Burke's summary:

> On the whole, the qualities of beauty, as they are merely sensible qualities, are the following: First, to be comparatively small. Secondly, to

> be smooth. Thirdly, to have a variety in the direction of the parts; but, fourthly, to have those parts not angular, but melted, as it were, into each other. Fifthly, to be of a delicate frame, without any remarkable appearance of strength. Sixthly, to have its colors clear and bright, but not very strong and glaring.[10]

Gogol's awareness of the category of the sublime is reflected in his association of vastness and extreme height with astonishment: "A building must rise immeasurably, almost above the head of the viewer; he should stand, struck by sudden astonishment, hardly in a condition to encompass its height with his eyes. . . . The word *breadth* must disappear. Here the single legislative word is *height*" (VIII:62, 65). Compare Burke: "Extension is either in length, height, or depth. Of these the length strikes least; a hundred yards of even ground will never work such an effect as a tower a hundred yards high, or a rock or mountain of that altitude" (p. 147). As for the category of the beautiful, we need only read Price's description of a woman in whom Burke's idea of beauty has been taken to its extreme to recognize the egglike smoothness, roundness, and whiteness of the governor's daughter in *Dead Souls*:

> . . . hardly any mark of eyebrow; the hair, from the lightness of its colour, and from the silky softness of its quality, giving scarce any idea of roughness; the complexion of a pure, and almost transparent whiteness, with hardly a tinge of red; the eyes of the mildest blue, and the expression equally mild,—you would then approach very nearly to insipidity, but still without destroying beauty.[11]

The school of landscape gardening exemplified by Capability Brown, realizing the impossibility of creating the sublime by artificial means, concentrated on producing the effect of the beautiful. The straight lines, avenues of trees, and rectangular shapes of the formal garden were replaced by serpentine, gently curving streams and paths winding through immaculately trimmed lawns, with rounded, widely spaced clumps of trees. Brown's gardens were meant to seem more artless and natural than the Renaissance Italian garden or the formal plantings of seventeenth-century France. As Price pointed out, however, a smooth, regular curve is no less unnatural than a straight line and much less imposing (1:231). The monotony of the serpentine curve, the bunchy plantation of "clumps" of trees, and in particular Brown's insistence on leaving the manor house exposed on all sides with nothing but grass surrounding it created an effect of monotony and baldness that was ridiculed by the advocates of the picturesque. In the words of Richard Payne Knight, they "shave the goddess whom they come to dress."[12] In *Dead Souls* it is quite clear that Manilov's English garden has been planted by a follower of Brown:

> The manor house stood exposed all by itself, on an elevation open to all the winds that might take it into their heads to blow; the slope of the hill on which it stood was clothed in clipped turf. On it two or three flowerbeds with lilac and yellow acacia bushes were scattered about in the English fashion; five or six birches in small clumps raised here and there their sparse, small-leaved tops. (VI:22)

Manilov's grounds deviate from Brown's prescriptions only in the gaudy coloring of the summerhouse, which should of course be painted the purest white.

In 1794, partly in response to the "shaven goddesses" that were being perpetrated on the English countryside in the name of Burke's idea of the beautiful, Sir Uvedale Price published his *Essays on the Picturesque as Compared with the Sublime and the Beautiful.* Here he defined the picturesque as a third category distinct from the sublime and the beautiful but at times partaking of both. In his scheme the cardinal qualities of the picturesque are sudden variation, as opposed to the gradual variation characteristic of beauty, and intricacy, a quality of line and shape antithetical to Capability Brown's smooth and regular curves: "Intricacy in landscape might be defined as *that disposition of objects which, by a partial and uncertain concealment, excites and nourishes curiosity*" (1:22). The effect of intricacy is produced by allowing the naturally complicated outlines and shapes of freely growing vegetation to efface the regular outlines created by man. Price's description of a picturesque scene provides a vivid illustration of what sudden variation and intricacy mean in terms of visual effects:

> The ground itself in these lanes, is as much varied in form, tint, and light and shade, as the plants that grow upon it; this, as usual, instead of owing any thing to art, is, on the contrary, occasioned by accident and neglect. . . . [The] hollows are frequently overgrown with wild roses, with honeysuckles, periwincles, and other trailing plants, which with their flowers and pendent branches have quite a different effect when hanging loosely over one of these recesses, opposed to its deep shade, and mixed with the fantastic roots of trees and the varied tints of the soil, from that which they produce when they are trimmed into bushes, or crawl along a shrubbery, where the ground has been worked into one uniform slope. (1:27–28)

According to the memoirs of P. V. Annenkov, Gogol understood the aesthetic value of intricacy in landscape:

> Once he said to me, "If I were a painter, I would choose a special sort of landscape. What trees and landscapes they paint today! Everything is clear and sorted out, the master has read it through and the spectator follows him mechanically [*vsë . . . prochteno masterom, a zritel' po skladam za nim idet*]. I would enchain [*stsepit'*] tree with tree, entangle [*pereputat'*] the branches, let light show through where no one expects it, that is the kind of landscape one should paint!"[13]

The emphasis here on taking the spectator by surprise with unexpected combinations of light and shade is fully consonant with Price's conception of the picturesque.

The word *picturesque*, which came into wide use at the end of the eighteenth century, has of course as one of its connotations the idea of copying pictures. Indeed, the gardening practice of the time was heavily influenced by the landscape paintings of Salvator Rosa, Claude Lorrain, and others. But in giving his definition of the picturesque, Price introduces a refinement designed to guard against restricting the category to purely visual phenomena. For him the picturesque refers to "the turn of mind common to painters" (1:44), the kind of thing painters are struck by and take delight in. Thus the qualities of the picturesque may be encountered by all the senses, not just vision. Without his qualification of the term, Price admits, it would be ludicrous to call a capricious movement by Scarlatti or Haydn "picturesque," yet, in his words, "such a movement, from its sudden, unexpected, and abrupt transitions,—from a certain playful wildness of character and appearance of irregularity, is no less analogous to similar scenery in nature, than the concerto or the chorus, to what is grand or beautiful to the eye" (1:46). Following Price we may seek the picturesque in verbal art as well as in painting and music.

The aesthetic of intricacy and sudden variation is both preached and practiced throughout *Arabesques*. In the essay on architecture, the need for sharp contrast is explicitly linked to the picturesque garden:

> True effect is contained in sharp opposition; beauty is never so bright and evident, as in contrast. . . . The more monuments there are in a city of different types of architecture, the more interesting it is; the more often it forces one to examine it, to stop with pleasure at every step. How would it be if in an English garden instead of continual, unexpected views a stroller would find the very same path or, at least, one so similar in its surroundings to what had been seen before that it seems long familiar? (VIII:64)[14]

The point of *Arabesques*, and of works within *Arabesques* such as "Nevsky Prospect," is to avoid such monotony at all costs. We have already seen how the intricate, more-than-one-dimensional line abolishes the distinction between thematic and digressive exposition in *Arabesques*; sudden variation is just as powerful an organizing principle. "Nevsky Prospect" is about neither the high-Romantic fate of Piskarev nor the low-farcical anecdote of Pirogov but rather the point at which the two meet in jarring, genre-crunching contrast.

Price's emphasis on the curiosity aroused by intricacy and sudden variation, with their "partial and uncertain concealment" and exhilarating confrontations of opposites, finds its counterpart in *Arabesques*. For Gogol, curiosity is the emblem of youth, that "freshness" that causes the narrator of *Dead Souls* to guess the lives of people met on the street. *Arabesques* is a work written by a young man (his preface apologizes in advance for the errors caused by his youthful haste), about youth (both the youth of civilization and the youth of such characters as Chertkov and Piskarev), with a young audience in mind (the schoolboy targets of the lessons on history and geography). In the essay on the Middle Ages Gogol explicitly links sudden variation with the arousal of curiosity, insisting that the merging of the classical and modern worlds, the chaos in which petrified fragments of Roman law mix with the amorphous beginnings of modern European society, is "more interesting for us and arouse[s] our curiosity more than the immobile time of the universal Roman empire" (VIII:15). The partial concealment of intricacy, which obscures smooth and regular outline, is just as important for teaching geography: "Strict analytical systematics cannot be retained in the head of a youth. . . . A child can only retain a system when he doesn't see it with his eyes, when it is artfully hidden from him" (VIII:105).

Elsewhere Gogol seems to realize that the preference for the irregular, for the detour over the straight path, is not restricted to youth. In the middle of the essay on architecture, which ends with its celebration of the infinitely capricious lines found in nature, Gogol chides humanity for its attraction to the crooked road: "Man's mind and taste present a strange phenomenon: before attaining the truth, he will make so many detours, will cause so many incongruities, irregularities, so much that is false, that later he himself will be amazed at his slow-wittedness" (VIII:69). This can only remind us of a famous passage in *Dead Souls* regarding man's preference for obscure concealment over bald, illuminated truth:

> What crooked, overgrown, narrow, impassable roads, leading far astray, has humanity chosen in trying to attain eternal truth, while before him has been open the entire straight path, like a path leading to a magnificent temple intended as a king's mansion! It is wider and

> more splendid than all other paths, it is lit up by the sun and illuminated all night by lamps; but people have streamed past it in deep darkness. And how many times, already guided by significance descended from the heavens, have they all the same managed to recoil and go astray, managed in broad daylight to again end up in the impassable backwoods, have managed to again send a blind fog into each other's eyes. (VI:210–11)

The irony of this passage is that the preference for the crooked, obscure, and intricately winding path over the straight, brightly illuminated, and immediately apprehensible one is not just a moral or cognitive preference but an aesthetic one. Moreover, it is a preference that is both encouraged and satisfied by Gogol in his artistic practice.

We have now arrived at the goal toward which my crooked path has been tending—Pliushkin's garden, the apotheosis of the picturesque and the aesthetic heart of *Dead Souls*. The description of Pliushkin's overgrown garden beautifully captures the effects of varied texture and light and of freely growing, interlacing branches and vines that for Price are the hallmarks of the picturesque. The narrator's conclusion to the scene formulates the source of its power:

> In a word, everything was somehow desolately beautiful [*pustynno-khorosho*], as neither nature nor art could invent, but as happens only when they unite together, when nature passes her final chisel over the often senselessly piled-up work of man, lightens the heavy masses, destroys its crudely perceptible regularity and the beggarly holes through which the uncovered, bare plan peeps through, and gives a marvelous warmth to everything that has been created in the coolness of measured purity and neatness. (VI:113)[15]

This collaboration between man and nature is what Price prescribes as the ideal foundation of picturesque landscape gardening. The gardener should not only study and imitate the effects of accident and neglect but allow room in his scheme for them to play an active role (III:35). Unlike other arts, the art of landscape gardening must reserve a special place for accident, according to Price, because the medium in which it works is living vegetation: "Trees and plants of every kind . . . should have room to spread in various degrees, and in various directions, and then accident will produce unthought-of varieties and beauties, without injuring the general design" (III:36).

It is clear from the description of Pliushkin's garden that when nature is allowed to collaborate with man the result is not just a synchronically static composition of light, color, and shadow but a complex record of diachronic change. The wildly spreading trees and bushes, crumbling summerhouse, and storm-damaged birch tell a story of past growth, decay, and disaster. In effect, the picturesque garden is not just landscape but history. What is more, Pliushkin's garden holds the record not only of this generalized change and accident but of Chichikov's personal fate. Through a subtle system of verbal echoes, Chichikov's fatal encounter with the governor's daughter is encoded into the garden scene. Her Burkean beauty, the smooth white roundness that stands out against the murky ballroom crowd, is present in the damaged birch tree: "Belyi kolossal'nyi stvol berezy . . . podymalsia iz etoi zelenoi gushchi i kruglilsia na vozdukhe, kak pravil'naia mramornaia, sverkaiushchaia kolonna" ("The colossal white trunk of a birch tree . . . rose out of that green thicket and was rounded in the air like a regular marble, gleaming column," VI:112–13). The sun's irradiation of her translucent skin at her first encounter with Chichikov is here repeated on a young maple leaf: "Solntse prevrashchalo ego vdrug v prozrachnyi i ognennyi, chudno siiavshii v etoi gustoi temnote" ("The sun suddenly rendered it transparent and fiery, marvelously shining in that thick darkness," VI:113). Finally and most importantly, the intricate interlacing of the garden's leaves and branches—"pereputavshiesia i skrestivshiesia list'ia i such'ia" ("leaves and twigs that entangled and crisscrossed," VI:113)—reprises the entanglement of Chichikov's fate with that of the governor's daughter, "kogda . . . ikh ekipazhi tak stranno stolknulis', pereputavshis' upriazh'iu" ("when their carriages so strangely collided, entangling the harnesses," VI:166).[16]

To be sure, the type of historiography modeled by the picturesque garden is not a scholarly or a scientific one. Like the "chronicle of the world" (VIII:73) represented by architecture, or the "living chronicle" of Ukrainian folk songs (VIII:91), like *Arabesques* itself, it is a fragmented, partially concealed record that demands a complementary act of imagination on the part of the viewer or reader.

Arabesques is itself a chronicle of Gogol's indecision in the early 1830s over what was to be his proper field of activity, scholarship or art. By the time it was published, Gogol was no longer wavering between history and art: he had embraced art decisively. Significantly, *Arabesques* ends, not with the final sober, scholarly lines of "On the Movements of Peoples at the End of the Fifth Century," but with the fictional ravings of the madman Poprishchin. Viewed in the context of *Arabesques*, Poprishchin is a parody of the serious historian who appears elsewhere in the work. His quest for and examination of reliable documents (in the form of dogs' letters) travesty the historian's activity; at the end of his researches he announces, "Teper' ia vizhu vsë, kak na ladoni" ("Now I see everything as if on the palm of my hand," III:208). As befits a historian gone mad, he ends by writing himself into history as a "great man," the king of Spain. Poprishchin's obsession with "getting the facts" sets him on a road that leads straight to the madhouse. Gogol's journey through the landscape of *Arabesques*, which has as its destination Poprishchin's dream of escape, is a winding, overgrown path out of the ordered regularity of scholarship into the intricacy and sudden variation of his artistic vision.

Mikhail Weiskopf

The Bird Troika and the Chariot of the Soul: Plato and Gogol

THE PROBLEM of Platonism in Gogol's work has long attracted the attention of critics. The first to discuss it were, in the beginning of the century, Innokentii Annenskii and S. K. Shambinago; later V. Zenkovskii related Gogol's artistic types to Platonic ideas, and ten years ago, Jesse Zeldin raised the question of the Platonic nature of Gogolian aesthetics.[1] But what exactly does Platonism mean here? To what degree is Gogol's Platonism a question of his actual familiarity with Plato's texts, and how much of it is due to a passive adaptation of various Neoplatonic ideas of the Romantic period? This problem can only be solved by a literary-historical and textual analysis. As long as the comparison of particular texts is replaced by a tempting but loose and unprovable use of metaphors, we are in danger of losing both the philosophical and literary-critical particulars of the subject completely. That is the case, for example, with the famous image of the cave in the seventh book of the *Republic.* Shambinago calls the world of the heroes of *Marriage* "the cave," and Zeldin uses the word to designate the sad landscape of Mirgorod and the landowners' Russia of *Dead Souls.* And this virtually exhausts the comparative analysis. It is not surprising that the direct proof of Gogol's Platonism is based on his early sketch "Woman," inasmuch as it contains an imagined dialogue between Plato and the youth Telecles. However, Gogol's Plato bears no relationship whatever to the real one, with the exception of vague references to the preexistence of the soul and equally vague hints at Plato's broad homosexual theme. Undoubtedly V. Gippius was closer to the truth when he said that "Woman" "arose out of Platonism as understood by the German philosophers," that is, from modernized Neoplatonism.[2]

But in Russia there was also another many-layered tradition of the reception of Plato, created both by classicism and by Russian

Orthodox theology, itself deeply affected by Neoplatonic tendencies.[3] The impressive result of this dual attention to Plato was an edition of his works undertaken in the 1780s by the priests Ioann Sidorovskii and Matvei Pakhomov. Furthermore, it was precisely the Neoplatonic aspects of Orthodoxy that assisted the rapid assimilation of theosophic doctrines by the Russian Masonic milieu at the end of the eighteenth and in the first quarter of the nineteenth centuries, when Plato, acclaimed by the Masons, blended unhindered into the receptive and kindred surroundings of "hermetic philosophy," which preached the search for hidden wisdom and the merging of the soul with the deity.[4] In this system Plato was grouped with Neo-Gnostic writers like Jakob Boehme and Louis Claude de Saint Martin. As to the reflection of Platonism in Russian literature, in the eighteenth century it was for the most part limited to the social utopian themes of the *Republic,* mixed with the story of Atlantis from the *Timaeus* and *Critias.*[5]

Such was the national substratum of the Russian "Lovers of Wisdom"—an alloy of Eastern theology and European mysticism—that, in its turn, prepared the ground for the assimilation of Schelling's Neoplatonizing philosophy.[6] By the 1820s, according to N.K. Kozmin in his book on Nikolai Nadezhdin, thanks to Romanticism, literary interest in Plato "had entered a new stage of growth; politics were put aside . . . ; the sensual world as the illusory reflection of the immortal world of ideas; poetic creation as an act . . . of inspiration bordering on ecstasy . . . —these are the points that attract the new literary theoreticians to ancient philosophy."[7] In other words, attention was now turned to the *Ion, Phaedrus,* and the image of the cave from the *Republic.*

In the circles of the "Lovers of Wisdom," where the names of "dear Plato and Schelling"[8] were confidently united and Romantic imitations of Platonic dialogues were written (by Venevitinov and others), the thought of a new translation of their favorite Greek philosopher often came up—probably a result of Cousin's infectious example.[9] But it was not they who acquainted a broad readership with this new Plato. In 1826 Nikolai Polevoi published a retelling of Plato's metaphor of the cave under the title "Supreme Bliss" in the *Moscow Telegraph.* But a much more important role was evidently played by Nadezhdin, whose Romantic idealism was mixed with the philosophical and theological teaching he had received at the Moscow Theological Academy.[10] In two extensive articles published in 1830 in the *European Messenger*—"The Ideology of Plato's Teaching" and "Plato's Metaphysics"—he did not limit himself to a new description of the cave but recounted in detail the contents of the *Phaedrus* and *Timaeus*, enriching their interpretation with some characteristic conjectures.

Soon after this, another imitation of the Platonic dialogue appeared in the *Literary Gazette*—Gogol's "Woman," although it was a great deal closer to Nadezhdin than to Plato. It responded to one of the central tenets of Nadezhdin's article "Plato's Metaphysics." The world of phenomena, Nadezhdin declared in connection with the Platonic demiurge in *Timaeus*, is "the imprint of the ideas or the product itself of the Almighty Artist" or Architect—God. It is the vocation of every "true artist" to follow him.[11] The motif of God-the-artist that entered Romanticism under the influence of Saint Martin and Karl von Eckartshausen had a clearly synonymous "Sophiological" semantics, which was of course felt in Nadezhdin's interpretation of the "Divine Mind" as well; compare the biblical image of Wisdom the Artist, or of art as the usual function of Sophia in the patristic literature. In Russia, Saint Martin's understanding of Sophia was superimposed on the Orthodox worship of her, reinforced by the iconography and penetrating into the liturgy.[12]

This "Sophiological" interpretation of Plato was combined by Nadezhdin with Schellingian aesthetics, in which the comprehension of the Platonic idea of the artistic work was taken to mean self-contemplation, the self-revelation of the absolute, the merging of the finite with the infinite, of the subjective with the objective. For Romantic writers, the aesthetic overflowed into an erotic Sophia-based metaphysics, and, consequently, Nadezhdin's interpretation of the *Phaedrus* emphasized that the soul of man, drunk with the contemplation of beauty, rises to a "peak" where to the mind "is revealed a secret realm" of ideas approaching the Godhead, "the source of all beings."[13]

We find a similar picture in Gogol's "Woman," in which the Sophiological image of God-the-artist even seems to bifurcate, becoming the artist himself and his logos ("the language of the gods") or Wisdom—the female "idea," attained by the contemplative visionary. The erotic Sophia of Romanticism ripens in the head, the "brow" of the artist, like her pagan predecessor, Athena, born out of the head of Zeus.

> What is woman? *The language of the Gods!* We marvel . . . *at the brow of a man;* but we do not perceive a replica of the gods in him: *we see woman in him* . . . and only in her do we marvel at the gods. She is poetry! *She is thought,* and we are only her embodiment in reality. While the picture is still in the head of the artist . . . it is a woman; when it passes into materiality and is clothed in palpability—it is a

> man. Why does the artist . . . try to turn his immortal idea into gross substance . . . ? Because he is governed by one lofty feeling—to express the divine in materiality itself, to make accessible to people at least a part of the infinite world of its soul, to embody woman in man. (VIII:145–46)[14]

Hence the task of the contemplator "youth" is to penetrate the "infinite world" in order to merge with the deity.

In any case, in this abstract dialogue there is not the least sign of the intense and active relationship to the past that characterizes Gogol's other works of that time. We recall that "Woman" appeared in the beginning of the 1830s, a decade that reworked anew the mystical themes that had prevailed from the eighteenth to the beginning of the nineteenth centuries, at a period when, at the initiative of the same Nadezhdin, the attraction to "synthetic" culture that embraced the best achievements of the past was already clearly making itself felt.[15] The rise of Slavophilism was preceded in the 1830s by the search for national identity, the markedly irrational—in a Romanticized religious Neoplatonic spirit—"Russian idea" (Andrei Kraevskii, Mikhail Pogodin, Stepan Shevyrev, and others). The question of a national philosophy is raised; G. S. Skovoroda is seen as a "Russian Socrates." True, the Greek Socrates also gets some attention: at the end of the decade, a professor of the Petersburg spiritual academy, A. F. Karpov, began work on a new translation of Plato.[16] Russian origins are sought in Byzantine and, by the same token, in Hellenic sources, and in 1836 Gogol sympathetically quotes the opinion of M. P. Pogodin that "Plato's genius . . . is reborn in John Chrysostom" (VIII:192).

Apparently it was after "Woman" that Gogol became truly interested in those of Plato's texts that were available to him in translation. This involvement was, evidently, part of Gogol's general dualism of the first half of the 1830s. Furthermore, according to an immutable tradition, Plato must have served him not only as a philosophical but as a no less grandiose literary authority, as a writer who had clothed his concepts in vivid, attractive images. Therefore it would be logical to look for echoes of Plato's influence in the living structure of the images of Gogol's works. Gogol's dualistic constructions of that time dictated a highly negative treatment of the naturalistic material that he brought into the literary process. This determined in particular the treatment of the theme of the cave in "The Tale of How Ivan Ivanovich Quarreled with Ivan Nikiforovich." I have in mind the total impression of Ivan Nikiforovich's house and of the hanging out of the clothes—the "puppet theater" for the folk set up by "wandering scoundrels." Incidentally, the word *vertep* (puppet theater) also means "cave"; Plato's eighteenth-century translators used the word in that sense.[17]

> The room into which Ivan Ivanovich stepped was *entirely dark* ["sovershenno temna"], because the shutters were closed *and the ray of sun, passing through a hole made in the shutter* ["i solnechnyi luch, prokhodia v dyru, sdelannuiu v stavne"], acquired a rainbow color and, *striking the opposite wall, drew upon it a multicolored landscape of thatched roofs, trees and the clothing hung out in the yard, only all upside down* ["udariaias' v protivostoiashchuiu stenu, risoval na nei pestryi landshaft iz ocheretianykh krysh, derev i razveshannogo na dvore platia, vse tol'ko v obrashchennom vide"]. Because of this the entire room was suffused with a kind of marvelous half-light. (II:231–32)[18]

Compare Plato in Polevoi's translation from book 7 of the *Republic*:

> Imagine people confined in *an underground gloomy habitation* ["podzemnom mrachnom zhilishche"] into whose depths *the daylight barely penetrates through a long opening* ["edva pronikaet dnevnoi svet posredstvom dlinnogo otverstiia"] in the vaults of the cave. . . . *A bright ray, blazing high and far above them falls behind them* ["Iarkii luch, vysoko i daleko nad nimi pylaiushchii, padaet pozadi ikh"]. The prisoners do not even see its path. *It falls on the wall that rises before them, like an opaque curtain on which strange figures are drawn by a magic lantern for the curious rabble* ["On padaet na stenu, pered nimi vozvyshaiushchuiusia, napodobie nepronitsaemogo zanavesa, na kotorom iz volshebnykh fonarei dlia liubopytnoi cherni risuiutsia strannye figury"]. On this wall flit before them various objects, statues, animals, carved of stone or wood, and works of all sorts. . . . Could these inhabitants of the darkness ever see something other than their own shadow which *is drawn on the opposite wall by the ray's glow*? ["siianiem lucha risuietsia na protivopolozhnoi stene?"] (514a)[19]

"The Tale of the Two Ivans," with its image of the sinful earthly city, also considers the civic theme of the *Republic*, although in Gogol's version it takes on a comically lowered character. In the same seventh book, Socrates, returning to the idea of the selection of a ruler from among the guardians, speaks of the love of science as an essential virtue: "They must, my friend, have a keen aptitude for science and be quick to comprehend. . . . [Philosophy] is not for the low-born to attempt, but for the noble" (535b–c). The ignorant, unscrupulous, and unstudious ruler he compares to a lame man of low (folk) origin:

> We will consider a soul *crippled* . . . if it . . . indulgently allows inadvertent lying *and is not embarrassed when it is shown the ignorance in*

> *which it frivolously smeared itself worse than a pig. . . .* He who is not able to distinguish truth from falsehood, be it a private person or the government, without noticing it will attract for one or another purpose, either as friends or as *governors, people who limp on one leg and are lowly.* (535e–536a)

Commenting on this section, translators of the eighteenth century willingly accentuated its allegorical side: "Plato adds that a man *is lame and unwise* who is incapable of action and speculation. Because of this *he chooses as governors those who . . . are schooled in the sciences.* It must further be noted that he excludes the liar from governing for he is as though *one-armed, insufficient and imperfect.*" Plato calls the ignorant "blind and living in a dream, inasmuch as they take the images of things for the things themselves, and he considers it insanity to *entrust the guardianship of a city to a blind man.*"[20]

Gogol's Mirgorod is governed by a *lame mayor* promoted from the ranks, that is, according to Plato, from the guardians of low origin: "He had been shot in the left leg in the last campaign and therefore he would throw it so far to one side as he limped that he undid almost all the work of the right leg" (II:256). The juridical discussion about the pig that has broken "the order of the ranks" exposes the grotesque stupidity and ignorance of the mayor but this does not embarrass him in the least: "Of course, *I have not studied any of the sciences:* I began studying shorthand in the thirtieth year of my life. . . . But my duty," the mayor continues, "is to obey the demands of the government" (II:259). The last assertion, however, does not in the least prevent him from subsequent laxity in interpreting "the law."

It is worth mentioning the other cripples and blind men in the town: its one-eyed, one-armed guard; the lying "deputy" Anton Prokof'evich, who is lame from a dog bite ("Why should I lie? May my arms and legs drop off . . . !" II:269); and "the squint-eyed Ivan Ivanovich," who, together with the mayor, tries to reconcile the heroes. Extending over all Mirgorod, the symbolism of Plato's cave encompasses the whole earthly world, so that the "half-light" of the camera obscura corresponds in the end of the tale to the sad, opaque sky, making possible a negative punning interpretation of *etot svet* ("this world" or "this light") in the final phrase, "Skuchno na etom svete, gospoda!" ("It's boring in this world/this light, gentlemen!").[21]

This worldview, present in the majority of Gogol's works of the 1830s, which caused Chizhevskii to call him a "cosmic satirist," ultimately refers to the Gnostics. Their grateful respect for Plato is combined with hostile rejection of his cosmogony, which reminds them of the biblical one. It is therefore appropriate that at a certain stage

Gogol too entered into a polemic with Plato. This can be found in "The Diary of a Madman," with its thoroughly Gnostic plot of the awakening of the king's son—in the given instance the "King of Spain"—from earthly insanity and his flight beyond the grave to his heavenly father's house.[22] Gogol could have synthesized this plot from traditional mystical sources (such as the *Confessions* of St. Augustine and similar works) as well as from Masonic theosophy, which had been assimilated so easily by Romanticism. For our purposes, it is more interesting that Poprishchin's ruminations about the "lame cask maker" who makes an inferior moon out of "tarred rope and pieces of sap" (III:212) represent a typical Gnostic (more precisely, Valentinian*) parody of the image of the demiurge, the craftsman of the universe who makes the heavenly bodies in Plato's *Timaeus*.[23] According to the *Timaeus*, the world and man are the product of the paternal forming prototype (*pervo-obraz*) and of matter, called the Godmother or the Nurse. The gods, subordinate to the demiurge—the Gnostics called them "pitiful craftsmen"—when creating man, used an abundance of all sorts of ropes, bubbles, and so on, and the disorder of these directly explains both spiritual and the resulting social crimes; for example, "Sexual intemperance is a disease of the soul due chiefly to the moisture and fluidity which is produced in one of the elements by the loose consistency of the bones" (86d).[24] Compare Poprishchin's diagnosis of the social ills and his attacks on the pair of demonic artisans: "It is all ambition, and ambition because under the tongue there is a little bubble and in it a small worm . . . and all this is made by some *barber*. . . . He, together with some *midwife*, wants to spread Mohammedanism over the whole world" (variant of *Arabesques*, III:568). A whole series of such demonic craftsmen appear in all the other tales of the Petersburg cycle as well.

There is also indirect support for the idea that Gogol parodies the *Timaeus* in "The Diary of a Madman." Gnostic mythology assimilated the Platonic demiurge to the Jewish God that was so abhorrent to gnosticism.[25] One of the most important motivations for this conflation was the fact that both Platonism and Judaism created a temporal system articulated by the movements of the heavenly bodies. For the Gnostics the chronotopic order of the universe is an infinite labyrinth of cosmic prisons governed by the Arkhontics† and their Jewish ruler. In Gogol's tale, Poprishchin's attempt to break free from the fetters of chronology is linked to this point of view.[26] The creator of time is precisely the Jewish God, as indicated by the note for "Marchtober the 86th" that was dropped from the original text, al-

*A Gnostic school.
†A Gnostic sect.

though for different reasons, both by Tsar Nicholas's and by the Soviet censors: "But it is incorrect to count the time in weeks. That was introduced by the Jews, because their rabbis wash at that time" (III:566). It would be hard to hint any more clearly at the God of the book of Genesis creating the world in six days and resting on the Sabbath.

It has frequently been remarked that the phantasmagoric flight of Poprishchin in the troika has a lot in common with the flight of the bird troika in *Dead Souls*. The main difference, however, is that, unlike "The Diary of a Madman," or, let us say, the "Tale of the Two Ivans," the novel is permeated not by Gnostic escapism but rather by its opposite in fact, by Romantic Neoplatonic sentiments. Despite the pervasive negative satiric tendency, we do not find the image of the cave here. One might, however, propose that in *Dead Souls* other analogies to the *Republic* could be found. It seems to me that the plot of Gogol's novel originates—with the perceptible mediation of the picaresque novel—in the Russian didactic, allegorical, usually Masonic tale of the eighteenth century, the story of the spirit's wanderings in search of sacred wisdom, sometimes personified by the female "Sophia" image. This literary production, which freely incorporates philosophical and political elements as already mentioned, is always openly—in the spirit of *Tilemakhida**—oriented toward Plato's utopia. Chichikov's journeys as a whole are based on a pattern that shows the effect on Gogol of the Nezhin lessons of Nikolskii, the fervent classicist.

The traveling heroes of Kheraskov, Dmitriev-Mamonov, P. Lvov and others visited various worlds—planets or separate spatial zones—and met the inhabitants, who frequently took on the form of animals.[27] This transfiguration signified the fall and ruinous incarnation of the soul as it had repeatedly been described by Plato. Such works were filled with allegorical figures of all sorts of virtues and evils. These are the direct literary forerunners of Gogol's landowners, whose psychological types reveal the familiar contours of the old allegories. Having visited a series of corrupt and weak kingdoms, the eighteenth-century hero, gradually cleansing his soul of earthly "passions" and temptations, would finally find sacred wisdom. The political proponent, so to speak, of this wisdom would be a tsar's counselor or the unchanging patriarchal "holy tsar," nobly governing his agrarian kingdom.[28] The idea of the "holy tsar," supported by biblical reminiscences, also goes back to Plato.[29]

**Tilemakhida* is V. K. Trediakovskii's 1766 translation of François Fénelon's *Télémaque* (1699), a didactic romance based on the voyage of Telemachus in Homer's *Odyssey*.

Chichikov involuntarily takes the same purifying path, in turn moving from "Zamanilovka," the swinish Sobakeviches, and other dead souls to the estate of the most wise and tsarlike philosophizer Kostanzhoglo, and then to the pious Murazov. But although the distant ideological source of the second volume is the same Platonic utopia, no actual traces of its influence are visible in the work. The author of *Dead Souls* revamped the old journey novel in the mode of Romantic dynamism, deepening the metaphysical symbolism of the road. Accordingly, the center of gravity moved to the Romantic Plato—in particular, to the *Phaedrus.* The closest impetus here could have been provided by Shevyrev's *Theory of Poetry,* published in 1836, soon after Gogol began working on his novel. Shevyrev linked the erotic pathos of the *Phaedrus* to the Romantic idea of the return of the poet-prophet's winged soul to his heavenly homeland "of true beauty."[30] The erotico-aesthetic theme of Plato in *Dead Souls* unfolds in the same direction. This, of course, does not mean that Gogol did not permit himself the kind of comic play with Platonic motifs that was so much a part of his talent, and that furthermore was in the eighteenth-century tradition of combining respect for classical authorities with an ironic travesty of them.

The semantics of the famous troika have interested many scholars. Andrei Belyi in particular has pointed out the hidden psychological resemblance between the horses harnessed to Chichikov's carriage and their master. Belyi understands the horses as Chichikov's "capabilities." One of them, personified as the "sly horse," is dappled, concentrating in himself the qualities of Chichikov the scoundrel: "He doesn't take you where you need to go, so that the troika goes sideways, causing nonsense."[31] The source of the image appears to be the section of the *Phaedrus,* retold in detail by Nadezhdin, in which, in Nadezhdin's words, the "human makeup" is compared to a "carriage, drawn by the horses; the soul . . . to the coachwoman holding the reins." The Platonic characterization of the horses is very much like Gogol's.[32] The white horse, signifying for Plato the reasonable side of the soul, is "a lover of glory, but with temperance and modesty; one that consorts with genuine renown, and needs no whip, being driven by the word of command alone. The other . . . with . . . black skin . . . consort[s] with wantonness and vainglory; shaggy of ear, deaf, and hard to control with whip and goad" (253d–e, pp. 499–500). Compare this to Gogol:

> This dappled[33] horse was extremely sly and would just pretend to be pulling, while the bay shaft horse and the chestnut trace horse . . .

worked wholeheartedly, so that you could even see in their eyes the pleasure they received from it. "Go on and fool around, I'll outfool you!" Selifan would say, getting up and cracking the whip at the lazy-bones. "You do your duty, you German pantaloon! The bay is a respectable horse, he fulfils his duty . . . and the Chairman is a good horse too . . . Hey! What are ya shaking your ears for? Listen when you're spoken to, you fool!" (VI:40)

In the *Phaedrus* the chariots of the gods rise to the vault of the heavens unhindered, perceiving what is beyond the boundary of the sky, "while the others move with difficulty, because the horse disposed to evil pulls with his whole weight towards the earth and grieves his driver, if the latter is the one who trained him badly" (247b). Compare Selifan's words: "I won't teach you anything bad, you ignorant churl" (VI:40). In order to turn toward heaven, says Socrates, "man's soul that has learned to love wisdom or combined it with being in love with a youth" (249a) must become winged anew. Seized by erotic ecstasy, the soul, at the sight of earthly beauty, recalls the divine prototype of beauty; this gives strength to the nature of the wing.

> Now when the driver beholds the person of the beloved, . . . the obedient steed . . . refrains from leaping upon the beloved. But his fellow, heeding no more the driver's goad or whip . . . , forces them to approach the loved one and remind him of the delights of love's commerce. . . . Now they are quite close and behold the spectacle of the beloved flashing upon them. At that sight the driver's memory goes back to that form of beauty, and he sees her once again enthroned by the side of temperance . . . , then in awe and reverence he falls upon his back, and therewith is compelled to pull the reins so violently that he brings both steeds down on their haunches . . . the good horse in shame and horror drenches the whole soul with sweat, while the other, . . . bursts into angry abuse, . . . struggling and neighing and pulling until he compels them a second time to approach the beloved and renew their offer—and when they have come close, *with head down and tail stretched out he takes the bit between his teeth and shamelessly plunges on.* (254a–d, p. 500; emphasis added)

We recall that after his fateful visit to Nozdrev, Chichikov bumps into the carriage of the governor's daughter:

> Selifan started trying to push the carriage back . . . , but it was impossible, everything got tangled. The dappled horse sniffed his new friends that were on both sides of him with curiosity. Meanwhile the ladies sitting in the carriage gazed at all this with expressions of terror. . . . One was already an old lady, the other was young. . . . Everything . . . in her was so lovely that our hero looked at her . . . and paid no

attention to the confusion going on between the horses and the coachmen. . . . Selifan pulled on the reins . . . the horses stumbled backward a bit and then again got entangled, stepping among the traces. In this circumstance the dappled horse liked his new acquaintances so well that *he had no desire to get out of the shafts . . . and, laying his muzzle on the neck of his new friend, seemed to whisper something right in his ear*, probably some terrible nonsense, because the new arrival kept twitching his ears. (VI:90–91)

The last phrase of the quotation is also closely associated with the section of the *Phaedrus* that tells about a meeting between two horses, one talkative and the other silent. I will again use Sidorovskii and Pakhomov's colorful eighteenth-century translation:

> The lover's audacious horse, appealing to the driver, requests from him a little enjoyment for the great labor he has undertaken; the horse of the beloved *does not know how to utter a single word*, but, expressing . . . puzzlement, apprises the beloved of his good will. . . . But his yoke-fellow and driver object to this, persuaded by shame and reason. (256a)[34]

Gogol furthermore decisively gives material form to those motifs that because of their abstract nature do not acquire a clear hypostasis in Plato. For example, the Platonic combination of beauty and reason is here personified in the paired image of the two women.

The scene of the meeting concludes similarly in both texts. In the *Phaedrus* the first contact is broken: "The driver . . . jerks back the bit in the mouth of the wanton horse with an even stronger pull, bespatters his railing tongue and his jaws with blood, and forcing him down on legs and haunches delivers him over to anguish" (254e, p. 500). In *Dead Souls:* "They untied the harnesses; a few pokes in the muzzle of the dappled horse made him retreat"; the shaft-horse, pushed by Uncle Miniai, "bent down almost to the ground"; "steam rose from the horses" (VI:91–92).

In Gogol's novel it is a question of love as an act of memory. This Platonic motif was also given form by Nadezhdin and Shevyrev in their recountings of the *Phaedrus*. After the meeting with the governor's daughter at the ball, the astonished Chichikov resembles a man who "tries to remember what he has forgotten. . . . It seems as if he has everything he needs, but some unknown spirit seems to whisper in his ear that he has forgotten something" (VI:167).

The discovery of the ability to love in Chichikov makes psychologically possible his troika's subsequent acquisition of wings, but the erotic impulse selects another object—Russia. As in the *Phaedrus*, love in *Dead Souls* is only a means of reaching another, nonsexual goal. For Plato, it is the world of infinite ideas perceived by the gods and by those driving the carriage of the soul: "It is there that true being dwells, *without color or shape,* that cannot be touched; reason alone, the soul's pilot, can behold it" (247c, p. 494; emphasis added).

Gogol transfers the invisibility and unformedness of the immaterial Platonic essence to Russia: "Rus! Rus! I see you, from my wonderful, beautiful distance I see you: poor, abandoned and unwelcoming. . . . Everything in you is *open, empty and flat* [*otkryto-pustynno i rovno*]" (VI:220).

The further pathos of Rus is clearly related not only to the *Phaedrus* but to the declamatory, Romantic "Woman," which contains the elementary sophiological triad: the infinite female "idea" turns into a "painting," which, "clothed in tangibility," turns into a male image. The reverse movement, naturally, is built on ascent, and its ultimate goal is disembodiment.

"And if unintentionally the eyes of a youth who passionately understands art strike it," says Plato in "Woman," "what do they find in the immortal painting of the artist? Do they see the materiality of it? No! It disappears, and before them is revealed the *boundless, infinite, disembodied idea* of the artist" (VIII:146; emphasis added). Then the painting is penetrated by a song expressing the liberation and flight upward of the soul, which enters into the same magical mysterious contact with the soul of the artist that in *Dead Souls* is discovered between the poet and Rus: "With what living *songs* his spiritual strings will speak then! How brightly they will respond in him, as if *to a call of the fatherland,* both rushing away irrevocably and approaching irresistibly! How bodilessly *his soul will embrace the soul of the artist!* How they will merge in an inexpressible *spiritual kiss!*" (VIII:146).

The same reverse sequence is presented in the last chapter of *Dead Souls:* "materiality"—the flat painting (the idea)—the song, and spiritual ecstasy (a sequence in principle corresponding to the Romantic hierarchy of arts in the article "Sculpture, Painting and Music"). Furthermore, in distinction to "Woman," with its sculptural Alcinoë (who nonetheless exists on an equal footing with the ideal world), aestheticized plasticity in the novel is uncompromisingly rejected and is "displaced" by Rus. The essence of the dematerialized idea of country is revealed, not to the gaze of the bustling world seduced by earthly beauties, but to the spiritual gaze. To the pagan sensual-sculptural beauty of the European mountainous landscape, to the Catholic sculpturality of Italy, is juxtaposed "the open, deserted" plain of Russia, which turns it into a spiritualized, flattened picture akin to an icon:[35]

> Like dots, like little marks, your low cities stick up among the valleys unobtrusively. . . . But what incomprehensible, secret strength draws one to you? Why can a . . . *song* be heard? What is there in it, in this song? What *calls* and sobs, and seizes the heart? *What sounds . . . kiss and stream into the soul and twine around my heart?* Rus! . . . what incomprehensible link lies concealed between us? (VI:220–21)

> Oh, my Rus! *May holy God kiss you all over.* (manuscript variant, VI:548)

The remarks about "dots" and "little marks" of cities relate this two-dimensional Rus to a geographical map as well, that is, with the printed idea of space. In addition to Gogol's own passion for geography, this might reflect Nadezhdin's thoughts about the concept of Divine Reason in Plato: "The world of ideas is nothing other than a full, all-encompassing *sketch* of the future arrangement of the world," and Belinskii's metaphor (in "Literary Dreams," 1834): "All the art of the poet should consist in placing the reader at a vantage point from which he could see all nature in abbreviated form, in miniature, like the *whole earth on a map.*"[36] In Gogol, to be sure, it is not a matter of localization but the opposite, of the broadening of space, perceived from a limitless height by the poet-visionary.[37] All the negative definitions of Rus point to the central one—her infinite plains, identified with the "boundless idea" of "Woman": "What does this boundless expanse prophesy? Will it not be here, will it not be in you that *boundless thought* will be born, when you yourself are without end? Is it not here that there should be a hero, where there is space for him to unfold and move around? . . . Ooh! What a sparkling, marvelous, distance *unknown to the earth!* Rus!" (VI:221).

The motif of the "hero" (*bogatyr*) (recalling the "coarse materiality" of the male image in "Woman") certainly contradicts the insistence on disembodiment, for it is linked with the opposite, utopian purpose of *Dead Souls*—to embody the "thought," merging the unearthly distance with the "mighty expanse" of Russia. In addition, as scholars have already shown, the "hero" is clearly associated with the narrator himself; he in turn takes on a sacred, unearthly status. Compare the mystical overtones in the rough drafts of the novel that make clearer the comparison of his image with the gods of the *Phaedrus*: "Is there *anywhere a god* or a man to tell me what I feel gazing at these . . . endless steppes? . . . Ooh! What great thoughts carry me along! [Cf. Plato's "helmsman"-mind.] Holy powers! Into what distance! Into what glittering, marvelous distance, unknown to the earth? What am I? *Am I a man?* Ekh!" (VI:643). Rising up together with Russia into metaphysical spaces,[38] the narrator communes with lofty Wisdom; Rus itself becomes Sophia providing him with prophetic knowledge.[39]

The Gnostic Neoplatonic variations on the erotic theme of the upward flight of the soul, its merging with the infinite, and its affinity with the divine absolute were everywhere present in the patristic writings, in theosophy, and, finally, in Romantic literature—from its "poetic ecstasy" to the love lyric, whose genetic connection to the *Phaedrus* Shevyrev pointed out in 1836.

Love is the "homeland of the soul," Gogol's Plato says. Unconsciously following the ancient tradition adapted by Romanticism, Gogol understands Platonic ideas to mean the engendered logos-thoughts of God, and the rush of suprasensory essences into the world as a nostalgia for the "ethereal bosom." In *Dead Souls* the earthly homeland is identified with the heavenly. This positive nostalgic mystique of Rus is accompanied by the pathos of denial, the rejection by it of the rest of the world. Rus itself becomes a troika, a pure becoming that removes, destroys all earthly boundaries: "And something terrifying is contained in this rapid flashing, in which each disappearing object cannot be discerned." "Rus, whither are you rushing, answer? She doesn't answer" (VI:246–47). Thus Gogol resolves the problem posed by Russian historiosophy of the 1830s and 1840s: the Russian idea is itself infinity, undefinedness, that is, the Romantic idea as such.

Having become the herald of mystical Rus, Gogol also took upon himself the mission of the practical instructor of the real, earthly Russia, a mission familiar to us from the instructional allegorical novels of the eighteenth century. Their theme of acquiring a wise soul-saving word as a reflection of the "inner word" Gogol transformed into a Romantic idea of the poet's calling.

In the same year that the *Theory of Poetry* appeared (1836), Shevyrev also published his *History of Poetry* (the censors passed it on 21 December 1835), which Gogol esteemed highly (see VIII:199). In it Shevyrev wrote:

> I would like to catch in the language of the people the people's secret thought, the center of all their actions; I would like to find in their language that basic sound of the soul that is taken by the people from the depths of the soul and which they sustain in general harmony with

> all mankind. Every true poet, the poet understood by his people, will surely catch that sound and will express that soul in words on behalf of his whole people.[40]

The Romantic voice of the people, while replacing the inner word of the Masonic mystics of the eighteenth century, continued to have a functional attraction. For Gogol, Plato's *Phaedrus* continued to serve as a guide to action in this too, but its theory of eloquence was combined in *Dead Souls* with the Christian Neoplatonic concept of the resurrecting Logos in its Romantic form. Registering the psychic typology of the people in all its content, from the unprintable word heard by the hero on the road to the "infinite song," Gogol wanted to proclaim in reply his own creating and transfiguring word of the Romantic poet when he promised Russia "the stately thunder of other speeches" (VI:135). The right to instruct and to prophesy was dependent on his prior self-analysis, and equally on his knowledge of the souls of his future audience; that is why *Dead Souls* is, on the one hand, the history "of my own soul" and the "spiritual truth" of the author (VIII:292, 294) and, on the other, the result of his observations on the linguistic, psychological, and social condition of Russia. It is not even a book but live speech; Gogol promises that before its future Russian heroes, "all the virtuous people of other tribes will seem as dead as the book seems before the living word!" (VI:223). Gogol's ideal is fruitful dialogue with the readers, who receive the status of critical questioners and interlocutors. The writer must learn from "people occupied with the business of life itself" (VIII:287). The soul of Russia will respond with a word addressed to him, the author of *Dead Souls*. The degree of his disappointment at the publication of the novel is understandable: "If at least one soul had responded! It could have been anyone. And even intelligently! . . . On *Dead Souls* a whole crowd of readers could have written *another book, incomparably more interesting than* Dead Souls, which could have taught not only me but the readers themselves" (VIII:287, emphasis added).

All this is taken from the *Phaedrus*, traditionally considered one of the most important authorities on ancient rhetoric. Deliberating on eloquence, Socrates speaks of the superiority of the living word over the written. A true creation is the sort of discourse "that goes together with knowledge, and is written in the soul of the learner" (276a, p, 521). It is the "living speech, the original of which the written discourse may fairly be called a kind of image" (276a). The lover of wisdom composes his works "with a knowledge of the truth, can defend his statements when challenged, and can demonstrate the inferiority of his writings out of his own mouth" (278c, p. 524). "*The dialectician selects a soul of the right type, and in it he plants and sows his words founded on knowledge, words which can defend both themselves and him who planted them,* words which instead of remaining barren *contain a seed whence new words grow up in new characters, whereby the seed is vouchsafed immortality*" (277a, p. 522; emphasis added). For Gogol the wordlessness of the mass of readers was a terrifying sign of their spiritual deadness. Continuing to complain about the fate of his poem, he exclaims: "If only one soul had spoken out for all to hear! It is exactly as if everything had died, as if Russia really was inhabited not by living but by some kind of dead souls."

The influence of the *Phaedrus* can be found in another place as well. Socrates remarks:

> Since the function of oratory is in fact to influence men's souls, the intending orator must know what types of soul there are. Now these are of a determinate number, and their variety results in a variety of individuals. To the types of soul thus discriminated there corresponds a determinate number of types of discourse. Hence a certain type of hearer will be easy to persuade by a certain type of speech to take such and such action for such and such reason, while another type will be hard to persuade. . . . and when . . . he has . . . grasped the right occasions for speaking and for keeping quiet, and has come to recognize the right and the wrong time for the brachylogy, the pathetic passage, the exacerbation, and all the rest of his accomplishments—then and not till then has he well and truly achieved the art. (271c–272a, p. 517)

Gogol gave Chichikov just such a virtuoso ability to adapt to the soul of one or another listener; furthermore, for Plato's quantity of kinds of soul he sometimes substituted the quantity of souls belonging to Chichikov's interlocutors: "First of all he would find out how many peasant souls each one of them had . . . , and then only would he find out what their name and patronymic was" (VI:16). "In conversations . . . he was able to flatter everyone very artfully" (VI:12). "Whatever the conversation was about, he was always able to keep it up: if the subject was a stud farm, he spoke about stud farms . . . ; if they spoke about virtue, he would discuss virtue very well, even with tears in his eyes" (VI:17). Gogol tried to use his accumulated psychological experience in his letters too, including the ones that were published in *Selected Passages*, that essay of the sacralized teaching of all Russia. Adjusting his teaching to the character of his addressees, he often simply gave them individualized instructions in the style of a kind of positive Chichikovism. In essence, *Dead Souls* itself was designed to serve as a broad mnemonic of the typology of souls.

It is hardly necessary to repeat here that Gogol's novel took on a paradigmatic significance for Russian culture. But if today we continue to speak about the constant Neoplatonic tendencies of Russian philosophy on the one hand, and about its deep dependence on the national literary tradition on the other hand, then, when applied to Gogol, this dependence appears as a dim and indirect return of reflective Russian thought to its deformed original source—Plato.

Translated by Priscilla Meyer

Katherine Lahti

Artificiality and Nature in Gogol's *Dead Souls*

THE COURSE this paper will follow should be clear from its title. It will point out an opposition in the text of Gogol's *Dead Souls,* demonstrate that certain moments in the text are actually elaborations of this opposition, and lastly show how the author ultimately reconciles the two poles. The opposition is one between artificiality and nature, surely an intuitable distinction, yet one the author articulates for the reader at the conclusion of his well-known description of Pliushkin's garden:

> In a word all was beautiful as neither nature nor art can contrive, beautiful as it only is when these two come together, with nature giving the final touch of her chisel to the work of man (that more often than not he has piled up anyhow), alleviating its bulky agglomeration and suppressing both its crudely obvious regularity and the miserable gaps through which its stark background [or *plan*] clearly showed and casting a wonderful warmth over all that had been evolved in the bleakness of measured neatness and propriety. (VI:113)[1]

This explicit rendering of the opposition supplies some attributes of Gogol's conceptions of artificiality (here of *art*) and of nature as exhibited in *Dead Souls:* art is contrived and cold while nature is full of wonder and is warming; art is made and accumulated while nature moves itself.

As places where things are both artificial and natural, gardens are important in *Dead Souls.* In Pliushkin's garden the forces of nature are ascending. The opposite is the case with the first garden Gogol describes. Upon arriving in the town of N., the hero of the novel, Chichikov, cases the town a bit before evening. We read, "He also looked into the town park, which consisted of some spindly trees which had not taken root properly and which were propped up from below by triangular supports very beautifully painted with green oil paint" (VI:11/21). As in this citation, where a few unwell little scraps of nature are overwhelmed by attending artifacts, Gogol consistently depicts artifacts and natural things in discord, and, as in the citation given above, the tension created by the disunity is the source of much of Gogol's humor in *Dead Souls*.

The techniques of opposition are numerous. Artifacts and natural things are physically juxtaposed, as when the road upon which Chichikov's carriage is rolling changes from cobblestone to dirt at the border between town and country.[2] Characters in the work gravitate toward one or the other, as when Korobochka repeatedly asks Chichikov to buy honey and jute instead of his desired goods, and when Chichikov consistently declines to touch Nozdrev's dogs (VI:50–55, 68–78/59–64, 77–87). As will be elaborated below, Gogol contrasts the characters' use of natural and artificial, constructed speech. He uses similes and metaphors that awkwardly portray some natural thing as an artifact or vice versa. Since the publication of Carl Proffer's study on the Gogolian simile, it has become a commonplace of Gogol criticism that the characters in *Dead Souls* are dehumanized as the author compares them with inanimate, or at least nonhuman, entities.[3] Proffer's work is part of a greater tendency in Gogol criticism which uses two categories borrowed from Russian grammar, the categories of animacy and inanimacy, to describe entities in the text and ultimately to interpret its title, *Dead Souls*. Although the opposition between animacy and inanimacy does function in the text (for instance the narrator states explicitly that Sobakevich shows no emotion, as if his soul were beyond the mountains ([VI:101/109–10]), the opposition between nature and artifact, after subsuming under its own categories much material that other critics classify as either animate or inanimate, proceeds to explain more in the text and, I believe, leads to more interesting conclusions.

Even when not presenting them in opposition to natural things, Gogol underscores the artificial quality of artifacts by showing them in the process of being made. Typically, the narrator states what the raw material was, describes the work performed on that raw material, supplies the names of the tools used, and gives the name of the finished product. Very early on in the first chapter Chichikov removes a woolen scarf that the narrator says is rainbow-colored and is of the sort "that wives make for their husbands with their own hands" (VI:9/19). The very quantity of similar accounts of the production of fabric and garments is impressive. The reader finds Chichikov praising the governor's purse embroidery to Manilova, who is herself a great crocheter of purses and other surprises. It can be assumed that neither knows the countess enamored of Nozdrev who embroidered a certain tobacco pouch for him after falling in love with him somewhere on the post road. Korobochka keeps an unpicked housecoat in a drawer and is planning on turning it into a dress in the event that the one she is currently wearing gets scorched during her baking. In a portrait hanging on a wall in Korobochka's house, a man is wearing a uniform with red cuffs of the sort they used to sew on during the reign of Paul I. She bemoans the fact that two girls she sold used to weave napkins for her. The account of the rise and fall of Pliushkin's estate presents, among other manufacturing endeavors, the rise and fall of his fabric mill. Surely the crown of all this sartorial activity appears in the ninth chapter when the lady-who-is-nice-in-every-possible-way and the lady-who-is-just-plain-nice discuss clothing construction in a conversation that continues for two pages (VI: 24–28, 75, 45, 47, 52, 117–19, 180–82/36–38, 84, 54, 56, 61, 126–29, 190–91). Besides impressing the reader with these marked representations of the production of dry goods, which echo Gogol's short story "The Overcoat," *Dead Souls* is conducive to being read as a catalog of any and all kinds of human production, be it the production of buildings, of carriages, of paper documents, or even of a pretty face or a confidence scheme.[4]

Even artifacts that appear in the text as ready-made come equipped with an implicit reference to their production: a past passive participle. In what amounts to yet another representation of clothes, the narrator recounts the entrance of Sobakevich's wife: "Voshla khoziaika, dama ves'ma vysokaia, v cheptse s lentami, perekrashennymi domashneiu kraskoiu" ("The lady of the house entered, a quite tall woman, in a bonnet with ribbons which were redyed with home dye," VI:95).[5] The participle in the phrase "perekrashennymi domashneiu kraskoiu" ("redyed with home dye") indicates, yet does not represent, the process of the cap's production. Through such use of past passive participial phrases, the narrator can communicate to the reader the raw material used to make a given thing, the type of work done to make it, the person who made the thing, and the tools that were used in the process. A great number of nouns in *Dead Souls*—they usually (but not always) represent inanimate things—carry at least one of these indicators of the process that brought them into being. A page of text without at least a few of them is truly an anomaly. Animacy or inanimacy of all things is determined in advance by the grammatical system of the Russian language; Gogol, however, directs us to see entities in the text as being either agents or patients, a status he determines and expresses in a number of ways, including the use of this particular grammatical form.

The world in *Dead Souls* is one filled with things that are specifically the products of human endeavors and is filled with them to the noticeable exclusion of anything natural. Andrei Belyi takes note of this quality when he writes about the overwhelming number of things, the "veshchnost'" ("thingness") and the "nagromozhdenie . . . sushchestvitel'nykh" ("piling up of substantives") in *Dead Souls*.[6] Often literal heaps that appear in the plot of the text as artifacts are described as being piled, stored, and hoarded. Heaps of things appear stylistically in *Dead Souls* when Gogol provides long lists of man-made things, one after the other. He typically takes the reader into the heart of a man-made thing only to show more artifact. This is the case in the famous description of Chichikov's trunk, in which the reader is taken on tour of all its little compartments and shown the objects therein (VI:55–56/65). Gogol's descriptions of characters in the novel follow a similar course. Characters frequently exist only as the artifacts that surround them, for example, the young man we meet in the first scene of the novel: "And moreover, as the carriage drove up to the inn, a young man chanced to pass wearing white twill trousers that were very tight and short and a swallow-tail coat with claims to fashion from under which a shirtfront was visible fastened with a Tula bronze pin in the shape of a pistol"(VI:7).[7] After this description, which gets progressively more detailed but which never leaves the subject of the character's clothes to touch on the person himself, the young man disappears from the text, never to be met again.

Gogol shows artifacts being built in *Dead Souls*, yet he just as often shows them in a state of decline. The famous discussion between the two Russian muzhiks over the durability of a certain wheel begins the parade of man-made things that are wearing out, breaking, decaying, getting dirty, or becoming weathered. In his book about *Dead Souls*, James Woodward refers to this kind of decay as a manifestation of the force of nature.[8] I can agree with him somewhat, for nature is responsible for much of the decline of artifacts in *Dead Souls*. However, I part ways with him when he proceeds to assert that in *Dead Souls* Gogol is decrying nature as the realm where aging, decay, and death are possible. Woodward finds death in natural things by seeing each individual thing in nature in isolation from the living system of which it is a part. This is not an approach encouraged in *Dead Souls*, especially considering the regenerative quality attributed to nature in the Pliushkin garden scene, in which Gogol seems to be embracing the conception of nature shared by many Romantics, a conception that life is common to all things in organic nature precisely because they are in a state of flux.[9]

In contending that in *Dead Souls* Gogol shows he believes that artifacts would last forever were it not for the forces of nature, Woodward also asserts that Gogol thought that the uniquely artificial quality of artifacts is eternal, that is, divine. To do so he posits that Gogol respected a category of "the human," which includes both the divine and the artificial, and Woodward himself conflates the two, for example, when he claims that Gogol ascribes more divinity to buildings that are made out of stone than to those made out of wood because stone is less natural.[10] However, I believe that decay is portrayed in *Dead Souls* as an inherent feature of the artifact, not as a violation by nature. Although the weather and the plant and animal kingdoms are portrayed in an antagonistic relation to man-made things, artifacts decay by other than natural causes in *Dead Souls*. Artifacts get worn out by their intended use: for example, Chichikov's suitcase, the paper money that Chichikov gives Sobakevich, and the various items of clothing that are showing shiny spots (VI:8, 107/18, 116). Artifacts simply accidentally break, which is what happens with the three-legged bed on which Petrushka has to sleep, with the torn net in Manilov's pond, with the dress of Korobochka's that might get burned, and with the broken pocket watch that Pliushkin considers giving to Chichikov as an expression of his gratitude (VI:9, 23, 45, 130/18–19, 33, 54, 139). Woodward contends that, despite the absence of anything that could be identified as a force of nature in these examples, they are cases of the "naturalization" of "the human." He defines the natural as being nothing other than physical reality itself and defines "the human" as being something transcendent of that reality. But Gogol provides the reader with absolutely no indication that he believes that any kind of supreme ideals or aspirations are being violated as he presents artifacts in decay. The idea that the motley decaying artifacts Gogol has chosen (the three-legged bed, the wheezing barrel organ, the torn horse collar) could have been—even in their prime—embodiments of supreme aspirations is indeed peculiar.

The decay of artifacts in *Dead Souls* seems to be an illustration of the following, often cited statement from Hegel's *Science of Logic,* "It is rather the very being of finite things, that they contain the seeds of perishing as their own Being-in-Self, and the hour of their birth is the hour of their death."[11] Gogol works with this theme again in "The Overcoat," in which Akakii Akakievich acquires and loses his beloved overcoat on the very same day, bringing the moment of the coat's birth and death so close together as to make the story almost a parody of Hegel's idea.

There are a number of recurring motifs in *Dead Souls* that work off the opposition of artifact and nature. There is one, however, that is almost archetypal: the opposition between the boot and the mud. The boot is first violated by mud when Chichikov is crossing Nozdrev's field: "Chichikov began to feel tired. In many places their feet squelched in water, so low-lying was the ground. At first they took care and stepped gingerly over the puddles, but afterwards, seeing that it made no difference, they walked straight on without bothering to see whether the ground was muddy or not so muddy" (VI:74/ 83).[12]

The image of mud covering our hero's feet echoes another image that occurs just a few sentences earlier in the text where Chichikov meets one of Nozdrev's dogs. " 'Swear' displayed similar friendship toward Chichikov and, raising himself on his hind legs, licked him with his tongue right on the lips, making Chichikov spit at once" (VI:73).[13] Chichikov and this dog are not of the same type, though they would be if the text worked on the opposition between animate and inanimate. In Russian grammar animals historically formed a third class bridging the animate (human) and inanimate categories. Perhaps taking a cue from this, the tendency has been to read Chichikov and Swear's confrontation as one between animate man and less animate dog,[14] but Gogol has set his observant reader up to read the scene otherwise. By this point in the text, the narrator has twice described Chichikov's overly meticulous toilet, with special attention paid to his face washing. Chichikov's face is another artifact. The grotesque is created by violating the boundaries between dirt and cleanliness, between nature and artifact; the dog licking Chichikov's face parallels Chichikov's boots stepping into mud and has nothing to do with animacy or inanimacy.

Chichikov's great plan to acquire wealth is confounded when Nozdrev appears at the ball and announces that Chichikov has been going around the countryside purchasing the papers for serfs who have died. The narrator describes how Chichikov felt at this moment, using a simile that incorporates the boot and the mud: "He began to feel uncomfortable and ill at ease; exactly as if he had stepped into a filthy, stinking puddle with a beautifully polished boot" (VI:173/ 183). Since Gogol has consistently portrayed Chichikov's scheme using boot imagery, when the reader is presented here with the image of a clean boot stepping into the mud, he or she is predisposed to read the simile not only as an expression of how Chichikov felt but as an indication of the demise of his scheme, the decay of his artifact.

The opposition between the boot and the mud enlightens two other scenes in the text. The first involves Pelageya, the little serf girl who shows Chichikov the way back to the main road: " 'Hey, Pelageya!' said the old lady to a girl of about eleven, standing near the steps in a frock of home-dyed linen, with bare feet so thickly covered with fresh mud that they might have been taken for boots from a distance" (VI:58–59/68). Later she gets this mud on Chichikov's carriage while climbing onto it. The second instance is the famous late-night scene at the end of chapter 7, where the quiet release Chichikov feels upon finally completing the purchase of dead serfs is expressed in the famous description of a lieutenant admiring his boots:

> Soon after this everything quieted down and deep slumber enveloped the hostelry; one light alone remained burning and that was in the small window of a certain lieutenant who had arrived from Ryazan and who was apparently a keen amateur of boots inasmuch as he had already acquired four pairs and was persistently trying on a fifth one. Every now and again he would go up to his bed as though he intended to take them off and lie down; but he simply could not; in truth those boots were well made; and for a long while still he kept on revolving his foot and inspecting the dashing cut of an admirably finished heel. (VI:153)[15]

That the boots are artificial is emphasized by the participles in the descriptions: "well made" (*khorosho sshity*) and "admirably finished" (*na divo stachannyi*). There is of course a heavy air of fetishism in this scene. The word *fetish* comes from the Portuguese *feitiço* (artificial or false), which in turn originates from the word *factus*, which produced the English word *artificial*. In *Dead Souls* Gogol asserts the interdependence of precisely the same ideas without referring to Latin roots; he does so with the motif of the overvaluation of the artifact.

The characters in *Dead Souls* are frequently shown fetishizing artifacts, the things they make. The florid assessment of the pitiful city garden that was published in the newspaper, Chichikov's praise of his own round chin, and the undue care with which Korobochka and Pliushkin protect what they have stored away are some of the more memorable examples. In *Life against Death* Norman O. Brown shows that commodity fetishism is nothing other than the transformation of the worthless into the priceless—a process that occurs easily once unnecessary things are assimilated in one's mind with excrement.[16] It would be possible to make a psychoanalytical study of anality in *Dead Souls* that would endeavor to account for the numerous occasions on which things and people fall into the mud or otherwise become dirty; such a study would likewise look at all the cleaning and repair activity in *Dead Souls*. I suspect that such an approach would be very fruitful, since tricksters in primitive mythology, among whose ranks Chichikov could easily be said to count, are traditionally "surrounded by unsublimated and undisguised anality."[17]

Though the present study could accommodate a bit of such analysis (excrement is, after all, the primary human product), to pursue this line of thought would require a realigning of the categories and would complicate matters greatly. Suffice it to say that it is quite likely that Gogol is saying in *Dead Souls* that artifacts are inherently mud (to use a euphemism of sorts), which would account for their ability in the text to attract dirt so readily and for their tendency to turn into mud, that is, to decay.[18] The boot and the mud of my opposition may not be polar opposites at all; they may in fact be the same thing, a thought that compels us to take another look at the mud-shoed peasant girl in chapter 3 as well as at the well-known scene in the beginning of chapter 7 in which Chichikov—as an expression of his joy at the approaching successful completion of his scheme—gleefully kicks his naked bottom with the heel of his foot, which he has just furnished with a boot made out of morocco leather "with cutouts showing inlays of various colors" (VI:135).

Overvaluation of the worthless is the prime motivator of the plot of *Dead Souls,* which moves along almost entirely because of the discrepancy between the artificial and real values of those dead serfs Chichikov is buying. The story of Chichikov's travels and his pursuit of wealth is often considered to be nothing more than an anecdote during the telling of which Gogol can display his virtuosity with the Russian language and in which he artfully hides his real message. Critics have found various ways to discover Gogol's real message while ignoring the plot of the work. By approaching *Dead Souls* as an explication of the opposition between artifact and nature, one can interpret the plot in even its most crudely restated forms. Each of the scenes in which Chichikov proposes his purchase is an exploration of the process of overvaluation. Gogol abstracts this process from the seeming practical purpose it has in the marketplace by making the goods in question worth absolutely nothing in any real sense. To encourage the landowners to want to sell their dead peasants, Chichikov points out the discrepancy between the real value of the dead serfs and their value as fixed on paper, the latter obliging the landowners to pay out money in the form of taxes for something that is worthless. Chichikov then contradicts his own assessment of the serfs by offering to buy them.

The dialogue that ensues between Chichikov and the landowner is, in each case, a working out of the paradox of overvaluation. Korobochka and Nozdrev try to direct Chichikov's willingness to overvalue back to things that do have some value to start with. With the exception of Manilov, all the landowners try to bring overvaluation back to the marketplace, where it belongs, by making the absurd threat that they want to hold out for a better price. To this Chichikov always responds with a strong appeal to the landowner's sense of real value. To Korobochka he replies: "I should think not! It would be a miracle if you could have sold them to anyone, or do you think that there really is any profit to be made out of them?" (VI:51/61). To Nozdrev, who thinks that there must be some future benefit in all this, he says: "And how could I be scheming? You can't get anything out of a trifle like that."[19] And to Sobakevich he says: "After all the goods are zilch. What on earth are they worth? Who needs them?" "Well, you're buying them. It follows they're needed."[20] Gogol plays a lot with the idea of necessity in these buying scenes, pointing up again and again the absurdity of the valuation of the worthless. He even has Chichikov say to Nozdrev at one point, "And what am I, some kind of fool? you just think: why should I want to possess something that I have absolutely no need for?"[21] which would be a refutation of his whole scheme were it not for the fact that these dead serfs do have value *on paper*—something of which Chichikov is very mindful.

Artifacts made out of paper hold an important place in *Dead Souls.* They constitute the medium by which the hero advances toward his goal. What Chichikov wants are lists of dead serfs for which he will hand over paper money, and in chapter 7 these lists and money are turned into deeds of ownership. The reader would probably not draw any conclusions from this if the narrator did not draw special attention to these paper artifacts. At Korobochka's, Sobakevich's, and Pliushkin's estates we read in great detail about the hero and the landowner fussing over the paper, the ink, and the other accoutrements of writing that are then used to make the documents of purchase. All this adds to Chichikov's resemblance to Mephistopheles, who also acquires written documents that will give him souls.[22] In chapter 7 there is a long narration of how Chichikov rewrites his lists, which is followed by Manilov appearing in the town with a list he rewrote himself, the paper drawn with a border and tied up with a pink ribbon (VI:140/149).

The man-made qualities of money are also underlined. We usually hear what material the money is made out of, and Gogol has Sobakevich complain that the money Chichikov gave him is worn out: that is, money decays. The actual production of paper money is indicated at the town meeting in chapter 10 when one of the gentlemen in attendance advances the possibility that Chichikov is a forger (VII:199/208). Chichikov overvalues all paper artifacts, even those that will not make him a rich man. We learn this from the layout of his box, which, as we read several times in the text, contains a special section for used tickets and other scraps of paper. In the first chapter Chichikov compulsively reads a poster that he has removed from a pole:

> [He] took the playbill out of his pocket, moved it nearer to the lighted candle, and began to read it, screwing up his right eye a little as he did so. There was very little of any interest in the bill, however: it announced the performance of a drama by Herr Kotzebue in which the part of Rolla was to be played by Mr. Poplyovin, and that of Cora by Miss Zyablov, the rest of the cast being even less distinguished; however, he read through all their names, getting even to the prices of the stalls and discovering that the playbill had been printed at the printing works of the provincial administration; he then turned the playbill over to find out if there was anything on the back of it, but finding nothing, rubbed his eyes, folded it neatly, and put it in the mahogany box. (VI:12/22)

The text on paper is truly Chichikov's medium of choice. It is also Gogol's.

The text is full of parallels made between Chichikov's scheme and the text of *Dead Souls.* The goods Chichikov is buying and the title of the *poema* have the same name, and Gogol makes his pun several times in the text, as he does when the townspeople ask themselves what dead souls could be: "Whatever can they be [What kind of parable], really, whatever could these dead souls be? There's no logic at all in dead souls" (VI:189).[23] As a way of devaluing the serfs he wants to buy, Chichikov describes them, or his plan to acquire them, as fiction. To Korobochka: "But dead souls are not something of this world at all" (VI:53/62). To Nozdrev: "Well, it's plain and simple, this fantasy came to me" (VI:78).[24] And to Sobakevich: "Still they exist, whereas the others are just a figment of the imagination" (VI:103/112). The fact of the matter is that Chichikov does end up writing a fiction on paper. "We'll write them down as if they were alive," he always says, "kak by zhivye." But this fiction is a pure lie.

Dead Souls is a parade of liars, a magnification of various kinds of verbal deception. The characters use language mainly as a tool they manipulate to get what they want. Chichikov, for instance, changes the way he speaks to conform to the dialect of each of the landowners with whom he wants to do business. He has been called a polyglot who speaks Russian all the while, which is quite on the mark, I think. It is not simply the case that the reader may or may not notice that Chichikov's language changes; Gogol shows him making it change. In the case of Korobochka we read what Chichikov thinks, "Well, it seems this broad's a real blockhead!" and then we hear him speak much more politely, "Just listen to me, ma'am. And you just think this over real good" (VI:52).[25] Inside Pliushkin's house, Gogol presents Chichikov in the process of producing artificial language:

> For a long time he [Chichikov] could not think of words to explain the reason for his visit. He was about to express himself something in this vein, that having heard of his great virtues and the rare qualities of his heart and mind, he had deemed it his duty to pay his homage personally, but he quickly recollected himself, feeling that that would be going a little too far. Casting another sidelong glance at all the things in the room, he felt that the words "virtues" and "rare qualities of heart and mind" could very well be replaced by the words "economy" and "good order." (VI:120–21/130)

In a similar way Gogol often shows his other characters thinking one thing and saying another, and one must never forget the ladies of the town of N. who have cleaned up their language to such an extent as to throw out, according to the narrator, half the words in the Russian language.

There are some characters in *Dead Souls* who do not speak in a constructed language altered to have some desired effect over the listener, who do not lie. They are peasants, though not all of the peasants. A peasant whom Chichikov meets on the road to Pliushkin's estate calls Pliushkin a bad name in Russian, leading the narrator to his famous digression on the Russian language.

> The Russian common people are very fond of strong expressions! And if they do bestow a nickname on someone, it will stick to him all through his life and will pass on to posterity, he will carry it with him into the service and into retirement and to Petersburg and to the ends of the earth. And however much he may try to ennoble his nickname, even if he may get the writing fraternity for a consideration to trace it back to an ancient, princely house, nothing will be of any use: like the loud cawing of a crow it will raise its own croaking voice and proclaim clearly where the bird has flown from. A neatly uttered word is like a word that has been written down and that, according to the Russian proverb, cannot be cut out with an axe. And how wonderfully apt are the sayings that come out of the depths of Russia where there are neither Germans nor Finns nor any other foreign tribes, but everything is indigenous, living and ready Russian wit, which does not fumble for a word or brood over it like a sitting hen, but comes out with it at once and sticks it on at once to be carried like a passport all one's life, and there is no need to add a description of your nose or your lips—you have been drawn from head to foot in one stroke. (VI:108–9/117–18)

This passage speaks of a word that has power to do more than simply to communicate truth or falsehood or to influence the listener. It is a vision of a kind of language that not only tells the truth but creates it.

That words have extracommunicative power is an assertion that surfaces in numerous contexts in numerous cultures. I have found elucidations of this kind of extracommunicative word that correspond particularly well to what Gogol is asserting in *Dead Souls* in the writings of certain eighteenth-century and early nineteenth-century German thinkers. The writings of Herder, Humboldt, and Schelling are useful, as are those of two writers actually mentioned in the text of *Dead Souls:* Eckartshausen and Schiller. Although Gogol parodies and mocks the works of these thinkers, along with all other German undertakings, he seems to embrace their ideas about language. Although I shall cite specific works of specific authors, my contention is only that the work of these men indicates the general context of ideas in which Gogol was working.

Herder and Eckartshausen write of the language of nature in which things determine their names.[26] In contrast to the conception that the word is a transient and arbitrary sign for its referent, an idea with which Gogol plays in *Dead Souls* as he has various characters pick and choose their words, the natural word and its referent are inseparable. Thus, in the passage cited above, the Russian nickname sticks to a person throughout his or her life, and the Russian word cannot be cut out with an ax. I see this assertion that there is a language that is motivated by the nature of things as a retort to the overvaluation of artifacts that Gogol presents in the rest of the text. I realize that I am equating motivated meaning with motivated value here, but this is what Gogol himself does when, to illustrate how *apt* a Russian nickname is, he writes that its *value* cannot be inflated by paying money for fancy genealogical work. The extracommunicative word is motivated because it is the real essence of the thing it names. In a Russian translation of Eckartshausen's *The Journey of Young Kostis,* we read:

> No chto takoe *imia?* Chto znachit *imenovat',* izrekat' imia?
>
> Svoistva, oznachaiushchie sushchnost' veshchi, vo vsei ee obshirnosti, sostavliaiut imia sushchestva v prirode.
>
> But what is a *name?* What does it mean *to name,* to pronounce a name?
>
> The qualities that signify the essence of a thing in all its magnitude are what make up the name of a being in nature.[27]

In like manner, the Russian nickname in the passage quoted above is said to draw a person from head to foot in one stroke. The extracommunicative word is always depicted as a palpable thing, as with our crow in the passage in question.[28] As an interesting aside, let me point out that human speech is often portrayed as a bird in *Dead Souls;* characters own birds that function as symbols of their particular kind of language. It should be noted, however, that according to Eckartshausen and others, extracommunicative language was supposed to be supernational and composed of mysterious words that are unlike words as we know them. What a turn it is for Gogol to assert that this phenomenon is encapsulated in Russian profanity!

Crows are important figures in *Dead Souls.* As shown above, they are the progeny of the language of nature, and they are associated with nature in the one scene in the text where the good qualities of nature are explicitly pointed out, that is, in the description of Pliushkin's garden, where there are crows' nests in the tops of the trees and the narrator remarks that he sees a shadow that looks like a dark bird. In the lyrical passages, which occur with greater frequency as one approaches the end of the novel, Gogol associates crows with the vast Russian countryside through which Chichikov rides. "A song struck up somewhere far away, the tops of pine trees in the mist, the peal of church bells fading away in the distance, crows as thick as flies, and a horizon without an end . . . Russia! Russia!" (VI:220/231). And in the final, "troika passage": "On each side of you the forest flies past with its dark rows of firs and pines, with the thudding of axes and the cawing of crows" (VI:246/258). In both passages the image of the crow signifies both Russia and the extracommunicative language of nature. This association is joined by two other elements: the song of Russia and the text of *Dead Souls.*

At times during the text, peasants appear singing a song that is always described as without end: "After which Selifan, waving his whip about, struck up not what you might call a song, but something long-drawn-out that seemed to go on forever. Everything went into it: all the encouraging and inciting cries with which horses are regaled from one end of Russia to the other, all sorts of adjectives without discrimination just as they happened to come first to his tongue" (VI:42/51). Selifan's song shares two qualities with the bad name the peasant called Pliushkin. Both are uttered without planning ahead, that is, they are motivated by something other than the speaker's intentions; and both are cases of name giving (name-*calling,* actually). These two qualities together lead me to believe that Selifan's song is another example of language in which the relation between the sign and its referent is motivated, a case of natural language. The narrator mentions the endless song of the peasants a second time at Nozdrev's estate: "Some wooden trestles were placed in the middle of the dining-room and two peasants were standing on them and whitewashing the walls and striking up some endless song" (VI:72/

81). The third time he mentions the song, the narrator states explicitly what has been implicit up to now: the song of the peasants is as endless as Russia is horizonless: "That will be the time for you, Volga boatmen, to work with a will! And you will set to work all together just as before you made merry and ran wild, toiling and sweating, towing the barges to the sound of a song as endless as Russia herself" (VI:139/148). The defining characteristics of the peasants' song are that it is uniquely Russian and that it exists in infinite time and space; in so being, it is like a natural thing.[29] It is not produced and it does not decay.

In *Dead Souls* there is a song that emanates from boundless Russia. It, like the songs of the peasants, is said to be as endless as Russia. The narrator asks Russia:

> But what is the incomprehensible, mysterious force that draws me to you? Why does your mournful song, carried along your whole length and breadth from sea to sea, echo and re-echo incessantly in my ears? What is there in it? What is there in that song? What is it that calls, and sobs, and clutches at my heart? What are those sounds that caress me so poignantly, that go straight to my soul and twine about my heart? (VI:220–21/231–32)

Russia and nature's extracommunicative language were conflated in the image of the crow. Russia and the endless song of the peasant are united in the song that emanates from Russia's depths. This constellation of notions, repeated many times in differing combinations throughout the text, creates an overall impression of the existence of something that is distinctly unartificial (i.e., it is not made, it is not overvalued, and it does not decay) and that is linguistic (thus, the *song* and the *word*).

In *Dead Souls* Gogol proposes that *Dead Souls* itself is the manifestation of that unartificial and linguistic entity. The song that sounds from the depths of Russia asks something of the author. The passage quoted directly above continues:

> Russia! What do you want of me? What is that mysterious, hidden bond between us? Why do you look at me like that? And why does everything in you turn eyes full of expectation on me? . . . And menacingly your mighty expanse enfolds me, reflected with terrifying force in the depths of me; my eyes are lighted up with supernatural power—oh, what a glittering, wondrous infinity of space the world knows nothing of! Russia! (VI:221/232)

Gogol represents himself here as reflecting, in his soul, the infinite expanse of Russia. In German Romantic thought, one often finds assertions that such reflection of nature's infinity in the mind of the artist leads to its reflection in the work of art itself.[30] Gogol asserts that the text that he writes reflects the infinite expanses within him, in Russia, and of the song. The narrator promises: "But the reader will learn about all this gradually and in good time, if only he has the patience to read through this very long story, which will assume greater and much vaster dimensions as it nears its end, which crowns all" (VI:19/29). Gogol writes of the expansive dimensions of this text, likening it to his Russia in very distinct verbal echoes. Claims about the text's actual expansiveness aside, the novel is in fact never ending because it lacks a proper ending. The story of Chichikov finds no resolution. Instead, the text opens out in the final, troika passage, in which all the material referents of the narration disappear and the referent of the text becomes a sublime vision of movement, infinity, and inspiration. Gogol has willed his art to become a part of nature.

Frederick T. Griffiths and Stanley J. Rabinowitz

The Death of Gogolian Polyphony: Selected Comments on *Selected Passages from Correspondence with Friends*

IN 1842 GOGOL'S *Dead Souls* left off with the portentous question, Whither Rus'? After five years of failing to offer a suitably monumental answer, presumably the next two canticles of a Russian *Divine Comedy*, Gogol offered his impatient readership *Selected Passages from Correspondence with Friends*, a preliminary, unfictionalized guide to the national destiny and to its literary corollary, Whither Gogol?[1] Among the beneficiaries of this epistolary advice—landowners, the clergy, wives of provincial governors—stand the Russian authors, Gogol chief among them. Over half the text concerns itself with literature and mounts the argument that Gogol's own failure to continue derives from Russia's failure to realize her own identity and find her own language. Gogol ends, in the chapter "Easter Sunday," awaiting a solution from above.

That solution, argues Mikhail Bakhtin in his essay "Epic and Novel," was something that Gogol had already found and lost, though it was not from above: he got caught between his real "novelistic" gifts—rude, satiric, polyphonic—and a paralyzing aspiration toward the other generative principle of literary creation, the "epic," which entails cultural exclusiveness, authoritarianism, and absolute voice. *Dead Souls* succeeded because Gogol's lively, perverse imagination and sharp ear thwarted the high, dull intentions with which he began the project: "The form of his epic Gogol modeled on the *Divine Comedy*; it was in this form that he imagined the greatness of his work lay. But what in fact emerged was Menippean satire. Once having entered the zone of familiar contact he was unable to leave it, and he was unable to transfer into this sphere distanced and positive images."[2] That is, what had been planned as a deadly cultural monolith, Russia's great book, turned into the earthy, engaging satire that gave the Russian novel a firm and unlikely start. But Gogol's "epic" intentions kept him from being heir to that legacy when he tried to write his sequel: "Gogol could not manage the move from Hell to Purgatory and then to Paradise with the same people and in the same work; no continuous transition was possible." Caught between "epic" flights and the rude, close view of the lowly, Gogol "lost Russia . . . he could not find the proper focus on his binoculars."[3]

Bakhtin's category of the "epic" stands in a troublesome relationship to Homer and his influential followers. As written, Dante's *Commedia* serves better as a triumph of the "novelistic" tendency, for here the central tradition gets both sullied and extended by the interanimation of Latin and the vernaculars, the confrontation of the high style (Virgil and scripture) with native satire, and the multivoiced ventriloquisms of a literary hybrid—almost an oxymoron—autobiographical epic. Yet Bakhtin's "epic," that flat, oppressive thing imposed on schoolchildren—a creation of translation, veneration, and cultural conservatism—is just as clearly an operative category in Gogol's thinking and perhaps the source of all his woe. For *Selected Passages* is itself a meditation on his unreachable Dantesque empyrean. With its Preface, *Selected Passages* has thirty-three parts and begins and ends with the theme of pilgrimage toward which part 2 of *Dead Souls* moves. In his last letter, "Easter Sunday," Gogol unmistakably replicates Dante's own moment of emergence from the inferno. As strongly as in the *Divine Comedy*, national destiny is seen to hinge on individual redemption; conversely, human art may be forgiven its imperfections until the Second Coming perfects the world that it depicts. As in the *Purgatorio* and the uncompleted part 2 of *Dead Souls*, the artist becomes emblematic of the rhythms of salvation. Various artists (the starving engraver of "Testament," the painter Ivanov, Gogol himself, even the blind Homer) must suffer through to their reward. Gogol argues that delay itself can be formative, and we may be reminded of the souls learning patience on the ledges of the Mount Purgatory. Redemption comes from loss:

> The second part of *Dead Souls* was burned because it was necessary. "Lest the seed die, it will not live again," says the Apostle. It is first necessary to die in order to be resurrected. . . . Immediately after the flame had carried away the last pages of my book, its content suddenly was resurrected in a purified and lucid form, like the Phoenix from the pyre, and I suddenly saw in what disorder was what I had considered order and harmonious. (VIII:297–98/108–9)[4]

Though the burning of epics is a classical habit (Virgil, Ovid), the sacrifice, to be echoed as the epigraph to *The Brothers Karamazov*, is here presented entirely in terms of Christian immolation and transfiguration.

As Bakhtin suggests, the sources of the problem are already apparent in the triumph of 1842 and Gogol's obtuseness about what he was doing right. Indeed, it is not just in *Dead Souls* that we find them in that year. Carl Proffer has argued that Gogol simultaneously issued other works—"Leaving the Theater after the Performance of a New Comedy" and the revisions of "The Portrait" and "Taras Bulba"—to protect himself from the doubts about his patriotism and artistic seriousness that he knew *Dead Souls* would inevitably provoke.[5] At the same time, Gogol issued a fragment of a projected novel, *Annunziata* (published as "Rome"), that may be even more a sign of things to come. In its short course "Rome" runs through the whole cycle that Bakhtin charts from *Dead Souls* to *Selected Passages*.

This tale of an Italian nobleman begins as a *Bildungsroman* with a tantalizing study of Italian perspectives on French society as they are expressible in a suitably baroque Russian style.[6] Gogol had since 1836 been living mostly in Rome to get perspective on Russia, and this fragment distills the experience. In the wake of the sixteenth-century prophecy of Moscow as Third Rome, the spiritual heir to Rome and Byzantium, Gogol's choice of retreat says something about the high, "epic" calling he felt. Ever the outsider, he will signify his shift of spiritual orientation in *Selected Passages* by replacing Rome with Jerusalem as that place outside of Russia where one can see Russia whole.

At the start of "Rome," however, the national bard seems for once on holiday and has nothing at all to say about Russia. Indeed, the symbolisms of the dilapidated city and the noisy *popolo romano* initially promise something far lighter and more playful. The contrast between the anarchic vitality of Italy, with its jumble of pagan and Christian inheritances, and the arid, secular materialism of the French runs along the axes that Bakhtin sets up between cultural pluralism and exclusiveness, polyphony and a deadening authoritarianism. The essence of Roman street life is, appropriately, a carnival, and the city wears its extraordinary historical and spiritual legacy lightly. But once Annunziata of Albano courses through the text (on a wagon, like Beatrice in the Procession of the Host in *Purgatorio* 30 and the redemptive Ulinka of *Dead Souls*, part 2), the narrative turns inward to soliloquy, a meditation on the rapture of a hillside prospect of the Eternal City. Here the cacophony of the street gives way to a single voice disappearing into itself, leading to the kind of disembodied tonelessness that characterizes the homiletics of *Selected Passages*. Having made that turn, the fiction could not continue, perhaps anticipating the larger false turns that put the cycle of *Dead Souls* at an end.

As might be expected, Bakhtin's terms prove useful for the reading of *Selected Passages*, and this we shall pursue in what follows. More surprisingly, Gogol himself, in the convoluted self-explanation of this work, proves already to have anticipated and refuted much of Bakhtin's analysis, as we shall argue in concluding.

Gogol subsumes his immediate problem of continuing the story of *Dead Souls* into a larger question, What is Art? The painter Ivanov has (like Gogol, in Rome) been sacrificing his career and his life to complete a masterpiece showing the movement of man to Christ, a canvas he cannot complete until that movement finally happens. Gogol at once draws a parallel to himself: "My works are strangely connected to my soul and to my inner education. For more than six years I could do no work for the world. All my work was done within myself and for myself alone" (VIII:333/152). The great strength of Ivanov's work (which Gogol implies also for himself) lies in its directness as spiritual expression; the question of a fit audience may be postponed. Earlier, in talking about the public criticism of *Dead Souls*, he similarly admits that "my heroes are close to the soul because they come from the soul; all my last works are the story of my own soul" (VIII:292/103). Indeed, the one passage of the novel to which he explicitly refers is that moment of lyrical reflection where Chichikov's consciousness and the narrator's seem to merge. Gogol now sits himself down in Chichikov's carriage: "I have never been able to bear the doleful, lacerating sounds of our songs which rush across all of the boundless Russian space. These sounds eat my heart, and I marvel that everyone is not aware of the same thing" (VIII:288/99). The autobiographical substratum of *Dead Souls* now comes clearly and undeniably to view, confirming James M. Holquist's claim that "the specific quality of Gogol's personal experience . . . which is at the center of his life and work, is a radical ontological rendering of self (*Zerrissenheit*)."[7] As we have seen, he brought "Rome" to a similar, if simpler, conclusion (or impasse). In his *apologia* Gogol seems now to be experiencing in all seriousness the process, parodied at the end of *Dead Souls*, of losing track of the boundary between one's own fictions and the phenomenal world from which they derive. It is no longer literary form but salvation history that imposes limits on the utterance, for the text that can redeem society cannot appear, any more than can Ivanov's canvas, until there is a redeemed society to describe.

These rantings of the spiritual and prophetic Gogol show a writer who has thoroughly painted himself into a corner. Having admitted that he writes only about himself and that he desires only spiritual purity, how is the writer ever to tell an interesting story? Yet he claims that he burned the sequel because it was too panegyrical: "To depict some fine characters who are supposed to demonstrate the nobility of our race would lead to nothing. It would only arouse empty pride and vanity" (VIII:298/109).

Already Augustine's *Confessions* shows how the shifting voices of self-examination can complicate and dialogize the most commonplace narrative inheritances—Dido and Aeneas, the Fall of Man, Gethsemane. *Selected Passages*, however, seals off that inner world of subjectivity and confession by presenting the dull regress of the voice talking about the voice talking about the disembodied voice. Casting himself as a conventional Christian Everyman, Gogol lets no personality at all show through, no vivid scene of conversion, no delicious history of sins, no confession of continuing and individuating mortal weaknesses (apart from writer's block) such as St. Augustine, Dante, and others made compelling. Given the confusions of text and world, the writer who creates the text asserts no more individuality than the Creator, whom he simultaneously expresses and assists. The letters, in fact, sound like nothing so much as the epistles of St. Paul, also from abroad, trying to promote faith and support temporal authority until the Second Coming, which in the closed universe of *Selected Passages* seems to be the advent of the sequel to *Dead Souls*.[8] Just as Gogol had to leave Russia to write about it, he seems to confront the task of self-examination as virtually an exile from the self. Like Narcissus, he has vanished into his own reflection, having finally decided that it may be easier to issue a new Gogol than a new *Dead Souls*.

Gogol has also found a way to keep his captious audience at bay by casting them in a kind of closet drama for which he writes all the lines and which by its closure and absoluteness invites no reply. His fear of the audience had always surpassed that of most writers, often causing him to leave town when a new work appeared. The readers closing in on the narrator at the end of part 1 of *Dead Souls*, even as the townspeople close in on Chichikov, are still a humorous fiction. But the earlier joking justifications of his scurrilous characters are now repeated in dead earnest: "My heroes are not at all villains. . . . But the banality of all of them frightened my readers. . . . The Russian is more frightened of his insignificance than of all his vices and shortcomings. . . . None of my readers knew that while laughing at my heroes he was laughing at me" (VIII:293/103–4). Gogol has reversed the comedic stance—"Don't confuse me with my nasty characters!"—taken at the end of part 1 of *Dead Souls* into a demand that readers make that identification.

While *Dead Souls*, part 1, halts the action only occasionally (though increasingly) to address the audience, *Selected Passages* is entirely an address to the readers—conceived of as individual recipients, or as social categories, or as Russia—to the exclusion of the fiction. The invented reader becomes the work's protagonist, but the invented reader is left no place to stand. Self-criticism itself preempts outsiders' opinions. In taking what were in some cases letters that his perplexed, even angry correspondents had received and presenting these messages as exemplary, working them into a pattern, arraying the now anonymous recipients into his own vision of a redeemed Russia—his own City of God—and comparing, then finally confusing their spiritual destiny with his own progress as a writer, Gogol manages to translate the audience from real to hypothetical.

The epistles of St. Paul, when published, had a comparable effect in helping to translate a scattered collection of communions into an enduring ideal of Christendom. In recasting his troublesome audience into his own version of true (that is, Russian) Christendom, Gogol puts them on their best behavior. A communication from writer to reader so ritualized, so immersed in the matrix of religious language and obligatory charity, renders both parties ideal, innocuous, predictable. So inevitable is the Christian scenario, of course, that Gogol can supply everyone's lines—not only for painters and writers but even for wives of provincial governors. In part 1 of *Dead Souls*, Gogol had unexpectedly trapped the readers and the writer himself among the company of dead souls—a wicked but rather winning joke; *Selected Passages* implicates the reader in resurrection, a strategy equally fraught with contradictions that, however, are not now held in suspension by irony. Gogol once had a fine eye for delusions of grandeur, but now the running joke of Captain Kopeikin's letters to the tsar and of Tentetnikov's grand (and soon abandoned) blueprint for the Russian nation realizes itself in earnest. Gogol, while extolling humility, seems in fact to be replicating the animating act of the primal Ventriloquist who brought His creation to life by projecting His Word into it.

With the translation of self and audience into the controllable realm of the ideal comes the eradication of fiction and the assertion of a kind of absolute, authoritative, and monophonic voice. What Ivanov is painting is directly the Truth, mimetic to such an extent that it cannot be completed until its subject matter (i.e., redeemed humanity) completes itself. Gogol's feelings about his own involvement in letters, in particular in epic, can perhaps be read from "*The Odyssey* in Zhukovskii's Translation." The claims made for Homer's epic here come little short of those for the second coming of *Dead Souls*, and writing to Zhukovskii (14 December 1849), Gogol observed, "At times it seems to me that the second volume of *Dead Souls* could serve for the Russian reader as a kind of step toward reading Homer."[9] Though pagan, the *Odyssey* comes to play a central role in salvation history, having been "Christianized, Gogolized and moralized into a conscious social blueprint," as Donald Fanger observes.[10] The *Iliad*, the model for "Taras Bulba," is now for Gogol just "an episode" (VIII:236/32). The *Odyssey*, by contrast, presents all of life. Like Christian revelation itself, it languished misunderstood in Europe, waiting for Russia to discover its ultimate riches. It is now in Zhukovskii's version not just translated but reborn, reincarnated in "the living word" that even its first author did not hear, so that "all Russia might accept as its own"—"a miracle . . . a re-creation, restoration, a resurrection of Homer" (VIII:237/33).

Homer's purpose was not only to affirm "all the bewitching beauty of poetry" but also "to remind man that there is something better and holier in him." Gogol borrows from Dante and other Christian classicists not a little of the prophetic claims for pagan literature as a parallel to and almost an extension of the Old Testament when he talks of how Homer could write "a living and complete book infused by law at a time when there was still neither law nor founders of order" (VIII:240/36). But in seeing the *Odyssey* as the perfect and instructive model of patriarchal society, Gogol virtually manages to unmake it as a fiction. His own earlier tale of the traveling trickster Chichikov itself descended ultimately from that same *Odyssey*, but Gogol now looks squarely at that epic prototype and manages to unsee the fictive, playful, finally skeptical outlook that the reader finds in Homer's epic as much as in *Dead Souls*, part 1. Homer's lively tale becomes thereby the perfect, dull epitome of what Bakhtin would later label "epic." Gogol's escape here from the dilemmas of his own fiction is to deny that fiction exists or, even back to the time of Homer, has ever existed. There is only scripture. Though celebrating the triumph of the life force, Gogol has in the largely imaginary recipients of these unsent letters found himself yet another set of dead souls.

Dead Souls, part 2, implicitly diagnoses its own paralysis: Tentetnikov waits for another fit preceptor to appear, Chichikov waits for some blueprint for rebuilding his soul, Gogol waits for a plan to complete the immense cathedral of letters for which part 1 can serve as cellar.[11] The solution proposed here is not to find another fit guide—the perfect critic that Pushkin should have lived to become—or even to proceed without a guide, but for Gogol to become the critic himself and perhaps not proceed at all. In the pivotal eighteenth chapter, "Four Letters to Divers Persons apropos *Dead Souls*," more or less at the midpoint of the book, Gogol scrutinizes both part 1 and its critics, indeed even applies the allegories of the text to its misguided reception: "And if but one soul had begun to speak out in public! It was exactly as though everything had died out, as though Russia in fact was inhabited not by living but by *Dead Souls*" (VIII:287/97–98). His critics have taken him too literally, especially the "lyric digressions" of the intruding narrator, and accused him of pride for the expansive assertions made. But he bears the responsibility for having issued an ill-made book prematurely, for relying on ironies that were misconstrued.

> Pushkin plays an innocent role in this misadventure: It is enough for me to tell you that when I began to read the first chapters of *Dead Souls* to Pushkin, in the form in which they formerly were, Pushkin, who always laughed at my readings (he loved laughter), slowly became gloomier and gloomier, and finally he was completely somber. When the reading was finished, he uttered in an anguished voice: "God, how sad is our Russia!" This amazed me. Pushkin, who knew Russia so well, had not noticed that it was all a caricature and my own invention. . . . From this time forward I began to think only of how to mitigate the painful impression which *Dead Souls* had produced. (VIII:294/105)

The surrounding discussion suggests that in heightening the ironies and moving the characters closer to the banal, Gogol threatened to irritate the Russian audience all the worse. Alone among mortals, Pushkin perceived Gogol's "principal essence," rivaled by no other writer: "the gift of presenting the banality of life so clearly, of knowing how to depict the banality of a banal man with such force that all the *petty details* which escape the eyes *gleam large* in the eyes" (VIII:292/103). For all Pushkin's insight, his death kept him from seeing everything: "Only afterward was it [Gogol's gift for the banal] deepened in me by its union with some spiritual circumstance. But I was in no condition to reveal it then, even to Pushkin" (VIII:292/103).[12] Gogol speaks as the perfect critic of his own work, of his critics, even of Pushkin's wondrous critical insight. He has become the guide that Pushkin did not live to be.

Even as his reading of the *Odyssey* implies that fiction does not exist and never has, his retrospective profile of Gogol the fiction writer presents that entity as little more than a result of the audience's and his own confusions. When he thought he was inventing fictions, he was actually stumbling upon the great truth about Russia. It is his clumsiness and his clumsiness alone that has upset people; but the Russian truth writes itself without the imagination as an intermediary. In proof of this thesis and in answer to criticism of the troika scene at the end of part 1, he simply rewrites that vision as fact:

> In Russia, now, it is possible to make oneself a hero at every step. Every rank and place demands heroism. . . . I perceive that great vocation which is not now possible for any other people, which is possible for the Russians alone, because before them alone is there such scope and their soul alone is acquainted with heroism—that is why that exclamation was wrenched out of me, and it was taken for vainglory and presumption. (VIII:291–92/102)

To be sure, there is such a thing as literary craftsmanship, and Gogol has nothing good to say about his own, even though critics overlooked his careless stitching together of materials and indecent rush into print. What they have criticized is beyond criticism, for the Russian destiny announces itself, and his own recognition of it was simply wrenched out of him, "an awkward expression of a real feeling" (VIII:289/99).

Literary criticism has produced few experiences odder than hearing this unsurpassed ironist test and reject his work on the touchstone of sincerity and monolithic truth. "My personal thoughts, simple, unpuzzling thoughts, I did not know how to transmit, and I myself gave grounds for these misinterpretations, and on the harmful rather than the useful side" (VIII:291/101). Part 1 "is still no more than a prematurely born child" (VIII:294/106). Gogol does not see his work as a making, a *poema*, but simply something brought out from within, about which the author can at most decide the moment of delivery. Though any creative mind can feel itself as transparent—as inspired, seized, spoken through—that passivity seems strangest from an ironist whose effects depend on such obvious calculation. Though the intruding narrator and the voices within voices of *Dead Souls*, part 1, raise introspection to the level of comedy, we dare not assume that the eternal jokester who can mime and mock such tones of desperate sincerity as we hear in the "lyrical digressions" is not himself at some level, beneath and beyond the giddy play of his levels and levels of irony, desperately sincere. What is most exhilarating about the authorial self of part 1 as it reverberates contradictory voices around itself—the narrator, Chichikov, Russia, Christendom, all clumsily dialogizing and bruising one another—is the deducible sense that here for once is a mind liberated, as ours cannot be, from the killing literalism of introspection. To be sure, there is always a higher and a lower in this struggle, and authoritarianism competes against fervor, but here is a mind capable of leaping from ledge to ledge of its own abyss and looking back at itself without, like the rest of us, being sentenced always to experience consciousness on one flat, literal plain without perspective and without proportion.

Selected Passages deflates that happy myth. Gogol discusses irony purely as a matter of communication, not introspection—a vehicle for Truth rather than a structure of imagination. His discussions of his relations with Pushkin and the Russian audience center on questions of irony; his observations about himself here, as in his earlier letters and in the half-fictionalization of those letters in "Rome," all proceed in the mode of unrelieved literalism. And indeed the faltering of fiction in *Dead Souls*, part 2, and the virtual exorcism of it in *Selected Passages* bring us back to the collapse of fiction and of voice in "Rome," to Gogol narrating without irony. In its own labored and doctrinal terms, the self-abnegation of *Selected Passages* works toward the rapt passivity, the absorption into a perceived grandeur, of the ending of that fragment, with Jerusalem now replacing the Eternal City. The onerousness of the Russian identity in *Selected Passages* and its wondrous absence in "Rome," which has nothing at all to say about things Russian, commonly leave the artist with little to do with the making of illusion: In the latter case he lacks subjects; in *Selected Passages* a cooperatively manifest destiny has already done his work for him. In neither work is the reader constantly on the defensive, as in *Dead Souls*, lest pious affirmations suddenly be overthrown by abrupt shifts of perspective. The perfect critic who writes the letters is no longer Gogol but the daimon who has watched over his shoulder through misspent decades and now flies free to tell the tale or, as Gogol explains it, the "simple unpuzzling thoughts" that have always lurked under his gifts for irony and illusion, gifts for which he now quite credibly claims to have found a cure.

Bakhtin's category of the "polyphonic" usefully illumines the evolution, or we might say attenuation, of the quality of voice in Gogol's writings in his last decade. The voices that begin *Dead Souls* are legion: earthy, pompous, rude, above all contentious as they torture Russian prose into a particular brilliance. The emergent narrator asserts a more consistent literary discourse, and this discourse prevails, largely to the exclusion of dissonance and variety, in the long descriptive stretches of part 2, fragments without drama because there are not enough voices to play it. *Selected Passages* marks the triumph of the monotone, the rejection of polyphony as of irony and the world.

Yet Gogol seems to have anticipated Bakhtin's analysis (or Bakhtin to have appropriated Gogol's), though in diagnosing the same symptoms, Gogol sees salvation rather than incapacity. He is in *Selected Passages*, like Bakhtin, a theorist trying to explain why *Dead Souls* got stalled in the first installment. Like Bakhtin he works from an analysis of language to a survey of literary history. In the penultimate chapter, "On the Essence of Russian Poetry and on Its Originality," Gogol locates quintessential Russianness in Bakhtin's polyglossia, the power of language as it is only now being discovered by the Russians themselves:

> After all, our extraordinary language is itself a secret. In it are all the tones and all the shades, all the transitional sounds from the solidest to the tenderest and softest; it is unlimited and can, living like life, at each hour be constantly enriched, drawing on the one hand, from the sublime terms of the biblical language of the Church, and, on the other, choosing to select accurate terms from the innumerable dialects scattered through our provinces, thus having the possibility in one and the same speech of ascending to heights inaccessible to any other language and of being lowered to a level of simplicity appreciatively felt by the dullest of men. (VIII:408–9/248)

In surveying the history of poetry from Lomonosov to Pushkin and Zhukovskii, Gogol sees as expressive of the Russian character the predominance of those satiric, personalistic, ironic works that figure centrally in Bakhtin's diagnosis of the "novelistic."

Gogol's history organizes itself around an absence: Russian literature does not have at its center a work to bring the pieces together. "It [poetry] accumulates only innumerable little hints of our diverse qualities; it has brought together in one depository various unconnected sides of our many-sided nature" (VIII:404/243). This chapter is Gogol's literary posing of the question, Whither Rus'? But Gogol reverses Bakhtin's direction almost exactly. The lack of a monumental center is not a liberation, a throwing off of the old shackles of the "epic," but a captivity. Heteroglossia, the interanimation of languages, is not an inspiration but an impediment to creativity. Having given themselves over to French and to European writers, the Russians do not know their own language: it remains hidden, fractured, unresolved:

> Our poets have perceived that the time has not yet come to paint us as a whole and brag about us, that we must still be organized, become ourselves and make ourselves Russians. Our nature is still too soft, still

> too unprepared to take the form fitting to it; we have still not had time to take in the total of that multitude of elements of all kinds and all origins brought into our land from every place, an incoherent concurrence of alien forces within us, an unwise result of a concatenation commanded by God. (VIII:404/243)

The inchoate diffuseness of Russian culture is a form of Babel, and Gogol moves to the final chapter, "Easter Sunday," with a vision of the descent of the Holy Spirit recalling the reversing of Babel at Pentecost:

> This [true Russian] speech will pass into every soul, it will not fall on sterile soil. Our poetry will be imbued with an angelic passion and, having struck every string there is in the Russian, it will move the most hardened soul with a holiness with which no power and no instrument in man can contend: it will evoke our Russia for us—our Russian Russia. (VIII:409/248)

Gogol's vision is radically centripetal. It looks, like Pentecost, to the rescinding of difference, to unification. Here we see clearly the Gogol who had left himself no human language to work with, possessed of a theory whose absolute terms prevented him from speaking at the cultural center, from giving Russia the monument that she wanted, by the assumption that that center was unitary, fixed, not just stable but eternal, not entirely of this earth. His radical insistence on throwing off foreign masters—part of the cultural exclusiveness of Bakhtin's "epic"—leaves him with no access to the international tradition that, in a millennial history of compromise and paradox, established Greek epic at the Virgilian center of Roman letters, pagan Virgil as Dante's guide to the Christian afterlife, and Catholic, Italian Dante himself as guide to Chichikov's pilgrimage through the dead as it gave birth to the Russian novel. Gogol had no more to give Russia because he was trying too hard to be Russian.

This straitening into solemnity and consistency does not, pace Bakhtin, constitute a movement from the "novelistic" to the central epics, at least as they got created. From the *Iliad* to the *Commedia* and beyond, they are pandectic, complexly voiced, and, until they fall into the hands of schoolmasters, unpredictable. But what is involved is Bakhtin's form of the "epic"—the flattened textbook Homer of "Taras Bulba," the static historical rapture that ends "Rome," and the intractable didacticism of *Dead Souls*, part two—a tendency that had lurked in Gogol at least since he departed for Rome in 1836 to write Russia's great book. This "epic" exists only in the sacrifice of epic fiction's range and treachery, its evocation of many struggling voices so that one may impressively prevail. The faceless, official discourse at which Gogol finally aimed might satisfy the theoreticians as epic but in fact mimes the voicelessness of scripture.

In a letter of 29 December 1847 Gogol described to Zhukovskii his literary impasse:

> For a long time I have been occupied by the thought of writing a *great work* in which I would present all that is good and all that is bad in [the] Russian man and thereby uncover before us the most obvious *quality* of our Russian nature. Though I have seen and grasped separately many of [its] parts, the plan of the whole has just not unfolded itself to me or taken shape in the form needed for me to begin writing it. (XIV:35)

In describing these uncooperative ideas and structures, he gives no indication that he is waiting for a story to jell or characters to evolve. We seem to be still among the ethical preachments of *Selected Passages*. "At every turn I have felt that I am lacking much, that I still can't tie and untie events, and that I need to learn the structure of the great masters. I've taken them up, starting with our beloved Homer" (XIV:35). Epic was what he wanted to imitate and be remembered for, but no longer what he wanted to write.

Gogol's final drift to literal-minded prophecy, his renunciation of his narratives for some higher, more purely religious and confessional form of artistic expression, anticipates an apparent syndrome that will recur, if never again so acutely, among masters of Russian monumental literature. Propelled by the momentum of his own large creation, Tolstoy rejected *Anna Karenina* (and no doubt *War and Peace* as well) when he insisted to his friend V. V. Strakhov: "I assure you that this abomination does not exist for me and that I am only vexed that there should be people who have need of it."[13] *What Is Art?*—Tolstoy's iconoclastic repudiation of the goals and methods of modern fiction in the name of a simpler, more edifying, and universally accessible aesthetic—could follow only after a statement such as this, much as *Selected Passages* could issue forth only after Gogol claimed in 1845: "I have no love for what I have written and published up to now, and especially *Dead Souls*."[14] What André Gide observes about Dostoevsky applies to other giants of Russian prose: "The literary creator who seeks himself runs a great risk—the risk of finding himself. From then onwards he writes coldly, deliberately, in keeping with the self that he has found. He imitates himself."[15] Gogol is only the first to find himself in this frozen, infernal rut, yet *Selected Passages* gives us a rare insight into that sort of wrong turn and how it could get perceived at the time as the true and only course for the writer and the nation. Bakhtin's description of Gogol's crisis in terms of a loss of polyphony, of irony flattened into authoritarianism, applies broadly and well, but Gogol himself already offers a similar though reversed analysis from within the experience, a vision of heteroglossia not as inspiration but as distraction and threat; of "novelistic" possibility as spiritual immaturity rather than the finest flowering of the human spirit; of polyphony as a Babel awaiting some pentecostal return to the primordial centeredness that Bakhtin sees as the source of the problem. Ironically, the "epic" that Gogol thought he owed Russia, scripture conducted by other means, kept him from completing the *commedia* that he had brilliantly begun.

Alexander Zholkovsky

Rereading Gogol's Miswritten Book: Notes on *Selected Passages from Correspondence with Friends*

AS MY BLOOMIAN title implies territoriality, it must be acknowledged from the start that a number of maps have been charted for Gogol's "artistic space" in general and for *Selected Passages from Correspondence with Friends* in particular.[1] "Forgotten" as these passages may be, they turn out to be sufficiently crowded for *Doppelgänger* to find themselves elbowing each other in the maze.[2] What makes *Selected Passages* so rereadable now is, I think, the current postmodern climate, fostering the different but cognate critical strategies that focus on antiutopian discourse, writing (*écriture*), polyphony, psychoanalysis, reader response, intertextuality, and literature as institution. Such a perspective encourages projecting *Selected Passages* onto a variety of cultural texts, making it a test case for some major theoretical issues, of which I will begin with *skaz*.

1. SKAZ, GOGOL, AND HIS CHARACTERS

The definition of skaz hinges on the distinction between the intellectually and stylistically unreliable narrator and the implied author, who towers above him simply because we the readers cannot imagine an author so stupid and inept. But what about *Selected Passages*, where just that is known to be the case? And how do we then deny Gogol the benefit of stupidity in his best—skaz—writing, whose striking similarity to *Selected Passages* has been noted by Gogol's contemporaries and later critics.[3]

Some crucial boundaries were blurred already in such texts as "The Overcoat," where the absence of a consistent narrative perspective—rather than an identifiable, if flawed, narrator—foregrounds the act of writing itself.[4] *Selected Passages* constitutes a further confusion of author and character-narrator, and in fact Gogol himself admitted that in writing *Selected Passages* he had behaved like a Khlestakov.[5]

The affinity between Gogol and his characters is well known. Gogol, who was famous for impersonating the comic characters of his texts and improvised scenes, has described his creative process as a satirical exorcism of the worst aspects of himself and specified the corresponding literary technique as "demotion from the rank of general to that of enlisted man."[6] Identifying secretly with his lowly alter egos, Gogol often endowed them with "authorial" status (e.g., Khlestakov, Chichikov, Nozdrev, Poprishchin, Akakii, the Postmaster) and ended up as a literary character himself.[7] This conflation began with anecdotes and continued with biographies—genres that treat the writer as character, in Gogol's case as a comic mask.[8] A high point in fictionalizing Gogol qua Gogolian Character was reached in Bunin's short story "Zhilet Pana Mikhol'skogo" ("Mr. Mikhol'skii's Vest," 1934), which depicts Gogol as envious of the article of clothing belonging to the narrator.[9]

Gogol qua Grotesque Author appeared even earlier—in Dostoevsky's *The Village of Stepanchikovo*.[10] Perhaps there was poetic justice in this. After all, it was Gogol who started the game by placing Khlestakov on a friendly footing with Pushkin. And in demoting the author from his privileged position above the characters (in the Bakhtinian sense), Dostoevsky was only following in Gogol's narrative footsteps. Therefore, who else should inaugurate the carnival of professional and would-be writers in Dostoevsky's novels but Gogol, indeed, the Gogol of *Selected Passages*, in the guise of Foma Opiskin, the self-appointed "writer" of books and of the destinies of his entourage?

Foma's very name is emblematic of the author-character oscillation. Dostoevsky probably had in mind the two great Catholic Thomases (discovered by Gogol in the 1840s, Aquinas and à Kempis, especially the latter, whose *De imitatione Christi* Gogol emulated in *Selected Passages*),[11] as well as Foma Grigor'evich, one of the "authors" of *Evenings on a Farm near Dikanka*. In a Gogolian manner (cf. Akakii Akakievich), Foma became Foma Fomich, with a pejorative-diminutive family name, structurally reminiscent of Bashmachkin. Also semantically, *opiska*, "misspelling," evokes Akakii's profession (and the *oshibka*, "mistake," he almost made in copying when he became excited over his new overcoat) and, more generally, his status as a "mis-person." To complete the picture, among the numerous "poor clerks" in the pre-"Overcoat" literature there was one Foma Fomich Openkin, a creation of Bulgarin,[12] the same Bulgarin who, after the failure of "Hanz Kuechelgarten," obtained for its author the position of collegiate registrar (the title that Gogol, in the spirit of Kovalev in "Nevsky Prospect," would sometimes pass off for that of collegiate assessor).[13]

Thus, Gogol started out both as an exalted, but failed, Romantic poet and a "poor clerk" akin to the precursors of his characters. He successfully promoted himself to the rank of author and in the process ambivalently elevated/degraded himself and his characters to the status of Akakii and Khlestakov. By authoring *Selected Passages* from the position of such a character-writer, he effectively set himself up for the grotesque objectification in *Stepanchikovo.*[14]

2. GOGOL'S IDENTITY, WRITING, AND RECEPTION

The oscillations of Gogol's (self-)image stemmed from his problematic sense of identity and its boundaries (as abundantly shown by Donald Fanger). Gogol himself insisted that he was a riddle. He identified completely with his various roles, could wear several facial expressions in one day (and thus elude painterly portrayal), and could change toward a friend overnight.[15] He was pathologically unsure of his performance (e.g., as a lecturer) and slavishly adapted himself to the tastes of his "superiors" (e.g., Pushkin). He partly invented his name, appropriating the semifictitious Gogol' and dropping Ianovskii,[16] and, when traveling, signed it variously as Gonol', Gogel', and so on.[17]

Psychologically, this has been related to Gogol's identification with his mother, his desire to elude her control, and his repressed homosexuality; some memoirs show him knitting (cf. the embroidering governor in *Dead Souls*) and wearing woman's clothes (cf. Pliushkin).[18] Gogol's fragile identity was most likely at the root of his stylistic contrasts; his doubles, impostors, characters lacking selfhood; and his two master themes: metamorphosis, which determined his evolution, and mistaken identity, which permitted such different readings of his life and works. In particular, Gogol's dual orientation toward the literary aristocrats and the lower-brow public, mostly successful, was always fraught with the potential for rift.[19]

A major tension in Gogol's personality was that between nonentity and grandeur. Megalomaniacal in matters great and small, he prided himself on his cultural mission and his knack for buying cheap. He tyrannized his friends, who were supposed to relieve him from menial trifles and expenses and otherwise "cherish" (*leleiat'*) him,[20] imposed penances, and died asking for a ladder to heaven.

He also claimed for himself all possible roles. One contemporary saw him as a typical Ukrainian, *khokhol*, who wants to be everything—musician, painter, actor;[21] and indeed he tried his hand at every literary genre (poetry, short story, epic novel, drama, criticism, journalism, history, testimonial).[22] He admired Senkovskii for being a one-man journal and lovingly ridiculed such a personality in the image of Khlestakov. Gogol's writing has been described as an "orchestra of voices" and a ventriloquist's act.[23] A curious case of ventriloquism is provided by "Leaving the Theater after the Performance of a New Comedy," in which the fictional author eavesdrops and comments on the opinions of viewers that have, of course, been prompted by the real author, intent on prescribing his interpretation of his own play, *The Inspector General*.

This double authorial overkill is a telling manifestation of yet another facet of Gogol's megalomania: desire for total control. Gogol could ill stand the presence of unfamiliar people, wrote out his lectures (or else feigned sickness), and tried to monitor from Europe all the movements and exchanges of information related to him—for instance, the itineraries of acquaintances who could bring him messages or money[24]—as well as the circulation of his letters and the exchange of opinions about himself, instructing his friends how to refute misrepresentations. He was notoriously secretive, traveling under altered names and avoiding contacts with fellow travelers (he would go to such lengths as feigning sleep or pretending not to recognize them), and (like Petrushka) often slept fully dressed—armed, as it were.[25] In correspondence, he "falsified" his motives and personality.[26] He concealed his addresses and changed printers, misleading his associates (e.g., Shevyrev), and consorted with Belinskii's group clandestinely from the Slavophiles.[27] He also had a penchant for destroying his writings: he burned a juvenile novella, a romantic poem, a historical drama (after it put Zhukovskii to sleep),[28] and, twice, the second part of his "epic." Sure enough, after the failure of *Selected Passages* Gogol regretted not having burned *it*.[29] His annihilatory pyrotechnics can be viewed as a will to monopolize his literary rights, and his near-suicidal death as a desperate gesture of control over his very life.

Indeed, most of Gogol's bids for power were always on the brink of collapsing. They achieved control either by destroying their object or by the less dramatic strategy of withdrawal (evidenced by his celibacy, aloofness from mundane matters, avoidance of contacts, and self-imposed exile). In an ambivalent reversal of his manipulativeness—but not of his blissful unconcern for the boundaries of his self[30]—Gogol deliberately surrendered many functions to others. Thus he instructed his friends to pool their efforts, each in his own way, for his sake, and in particular for taking care of his mother.[31] He delegated to Shevyrev all matters of money management and publication, including even the editing of his faulty style and grammar; to his correspondents, the drafting of his future texts;[32] and to censorship, the enforcement of artistic discipline.[33] Before burning *Dead Souls*, Gogol tried to leave the manuscript with A. P. Tolstoy, and the decision what to do with it to the discretion of Filaret and others.[34]

Delegation of power naturally led to situations where others failed Gogol (as, for instance, when A. P. Tolstoy refused to keep the manuscript, effectively enabling Gogol to burn it, or when Aksakov decided not to pass on to Pogodin Gogol's offensive remarks about him)[35]—and to delegation of guilt. Gogol blamed his friends for the advice to publish *Selected Passages*, Aksakov and Annenkov for the faults of the entire public,[36] and the "evil one" (*lukavyi*) for the burning of *Dead Souls*. Thus, the circumstances of this fatal burning are emblematic of both total control and relinquished responsibility.

The same interplay of grandeur, nonentity, and withdrawal determined Gogol's exclusive concentration on writing. He admitted that he did not know Russia,[37] or, for that matter, the Ukraine,[38] and created out of nothing by sheer linguistic prowess, words (e.g., gleaned from the dictionary) being all he required for his work. Gogol's worldly needs were minimal and his existence purely textual, so that there was nothing he could hide (!) from the public. An apotheosis of this rhetorical magic, *Selected Passages* is "purely literary," defined "by style alone,"[39] in a triumph of poetic control at the price of complete withdrawal from reality.

Failure of control and delegation of authority also marked Gogol's relationship with critics. In addition to reviews, he sought private information about responses to his work, especially negative ones; he at first squirmed and rebutted but then adapted his self-image accordingly, letting his literary identity be redefined for him by others.[40] For instance, in *Selected Passages* he did become an ideologist, as Belinskii wanted him to, but, ironically, one of a persuasion prompted by another camp.[41]

Gogol's contradictory person, style, and reception cast a long historical shadow in the form of successive rereadings. Russian literature has since been busy working out Gogol's prophetic slips, with *Selected Passages* the grossest and the latest to be vindicated. The peripeties of Gogol's "tragedy of misdirection" by the critics and of its posthumous consequences for *Selected Passages* have been traced by Paul Debreczeny in his *Nikolay Gogol and Contemporary Critics.* In particular, Debreczeny notes how "Dostoevsky [first] suffered for Belinsky's opinion on [*Selected Passages*, then] . . . was conditioned by Siberian brain-washing to love what he had hated, and eventually accepted Gogol's ideas, allying himself with Apollon Grigor'ev, the only critic who had wholeheartedly supported Gogol" (p. 60). Yet it was the same Dostoevsky who made double-edged fun of Gogol in *The Village of Stepanchikovo.*

The "rehabilitation" of Gogol's oeuvre has proceeded along two main lines, those of form and content, and *Selected Passages* lies at their intersection.

3. *SELECTED PASSAGES* AND THE IMPORTANCE OF WRITING BADLY

In *Selected Passages* Gogol pushed his grandiloquent sermonizing to an extreme. Branded as reactionary by liberal critics and as downright silly by most everyone, his message did find a supporter (in Grigor'ev) and was later endorsed and developed by Dostoevsky, Tolstoy, Rozanov, and others.[42] Gogol's conversion prefigured those of Dostoevsky and Tolstoy, in an early attempt at legitimizing that very Russian blending of fictional and ideological discourse which informed—deformed, in the views of some—the narrative mode of such texts as, say, *War and Peace*, Rozanov's writings, and *Doctor Zhivago.* The effect was not purely ideological but stylistic as well, liberating the direct, aesthetically imperfect voice of the author.[43] Thus, Gogol's notoriously miswritten book was his final and ironic defeat, but, in a sense, its "bad" writing was the best thing about it.[44]

From the start Gogol produced "bad" texts that he had to renounce and destroy.[45] Even in his best prose, critics were quick to point out provincialisms, examples of dubious taste, and ungrammaticalities. His worst mistakes would be edited out, but most of his "irregular" writing remained intact, to be soon recognized as innovative and eventually canonized, when Gogol was proclaimed a modernist *avant la lettre.* His stylistic "failures" were appropriated by the comprehensive cultural revolution of the past hundred years.

"Miscontrolled" writing signaled the liberation of a previously repressed and disciplined "lower" voice, analogous to such manifestations of literary decontrol as the "works" of Koz'ma Prutkov, Leskov's skaz, Dostoevsky's "hurriedly unpolished" manner, the late Leo Tolstoy's deliberately primitive "truth-searching" discourse,[46] Rozanov's homely homilies, Khlebnikov's quasi-graphomaniac poetics,[47] Zoshchenko's coy primitivism, down to Limonov's stark uncouthness, which prompted a traditionalist contemporary's apt formulation: "personazhi pishut," "(now) the characters are doing the writing."[48] In a broader, philosophical sense, this is akin to such modern cultural phenomena as Nietzschean relativization of values, Freudian triple-voicedness of the psyche, and Dostoevskyan-Bakhtinian dialogism.

Is *Selected Passages* then polyphonic? Certainly not in intent, although Gogol did try to pass off his own (real, edited, and fictional) letters for a "correspondence," that is, an exchange of opinions. To be sure, according to Bakhtin, dialogism does not equal the dramatic (or as the case may be, epistolary) mode: the "other" voice is to be heard even in the discourse of a single speaker. This does happen in *Selected Passages*, but the authorial voice dominates all others. Or does it? Thanks to bombast and inconsistencies, its persuasiveness unravels. The decontrol is, of course, involuntary—Gogol is not a Prutkov, but he comes so close to him that some contemporaries believed *Selected Passages* to be "a deliberate Ukrainian prank by which Gogol intended to attract public attention."[49] In other words, the book is "camp," and guilelessly "pure" camp at that, calling for a "campy," postmodernist rereading.[50]

A further twist to this virtual dialogism is given by the nature of the monologic voice. The authorial stance is Domostroi-like, autocratic, pervasively megalomaniacal. Pretending to the role of Russia's official savior,[51] Gogol also resembles Prutkov in the latter's role of senior official and author of "A Project for Introducing Uniformity of Thought in Russia." The relationship between the Tsar/State and the Poet is a master myth of Russian culture. Gogol's variant of this myth envisions a union instead of rebellious opposition, foreshadowing Khlebnikov's (and other avant-gardists') Poetic World Chairmanship.[52]

Indeed, the oxymoronic combination, in *Selected Passages*, of liberatingly bad writing with grandiose political pretension can be compared to the alliance between the avant-garde and totalitarianism. Lest these dystopian overtones sound hollow, we might recall that, not unlike Stalin, the author of *Selected Passages* insists on knowing every woman's *konek* (hobby), in order to manipulate her better, and the names and patronymics of all the important personages in town, in order to "be their friend . . . , to all, without exception" (VIII:311/125).[53] This prophetic anticipation of Big-Brotherly love for every subject has, in fact, materialized in direct literary lineage: it was on the author of *Selected Passages* that Dostoevsky modeled his Foma Fomich, who in turn was an early version of the Grand Inquisitor, a precursor of dystopian rulers.[54]

Furthermore, since according to a recent view, Stalin and Stalinist culture were a runaway version of the Russian avant-garde,[55] such postmodernist refractions as Sasha Sokolov's *Palisandriia* are only natural.[56] The myth of Palisandr Dal'berg—the great graphomaniac, savior of Russia, Kremlin ruler, and repository of all possible roles and attributes—is all the more relevant to the problem since Palisandr mentions Gogol on several occasions, and his "romantically officialese" writing bears distinct traces of Gogolian influence and overtly plays with specific Gogol intertexts, for example, the dead souls scam.[57] Here, finally, Gogol's "camp" is recycled into its highest possible counterpart. *Palisandriia*, too, is shockingly "reactionary" in its affectionate portrayal of the powers that be (Uncle Joseph, for one), held together by its lofty rhetoric alone, and obsessively metaliterary.[58]

The prominence of metaliterary themes in *Selected Passages* is well known and has been solidly covered by Ruth Sobel in *Gogol's Forgotten Book*. I will concentrate here on Letter 21, "Chto takoe gubernatorsha" ("What the Wife of a Provincial Governor Is," VIII:308–21/122–36), whose preoccupation with writing has escaped critical notice because it ostensibly constitutes advice to the *gubernatorsha* on how to serve the public good. Incidentally, this discrepancy between the writer's intended message and the reader's ability to see through it constitutes yet another situation of decontrol, virtual skaz, and polyphony.

4. GRANDEUR, INFORMATION, AND MEDIA MANIPULATION

Letter 21 is a typical Gogol text. The speaker's persona comes across as both self-aggrandizing and self-deprecating. On the one hand, he boasts of his predictions that have come true, his near omniscience, and his close ties to God; poses as the ultimate arbiter who can put everything in order; and demands unconditional obedience. On the other, he admits that he is completely uninformed about the town and Russia in general; that he is not a "vseznaika," a "know-it-all," but just "a fool" ("glup, reshitel'no glup," VIII:319–20/134).[59]

The theme of grandeur is also projected onto the bureaucratic hierarchy (Gogol mentions the infinite ladder of bribery), reflecting both Gogol's love-hate of rank and the addressee's "number one" position in town. At the top, second only to God, Gogol places himself, an ideal order-enforcing official ("chinovnik," VIII:311/125); then comes the *gubernatorsha* (governor's wife), whose good example will trickle down through the ranks,[60] or else she can threaten the unhelpful priests with the names of the bishop, the "supreme government," and the emperor himself. Even spiritual reeducation is metaphorized as law enforcement: the stupid sheep must be driven with the whip of shame and conscience.

Bureaucratic coercion is combined with the techniques of public relations. Gogol plans the manipulative use of balls, dinner invitations, fashions, legalistic procedures, public ostracism, rumors, sermons, and the influence of society women on their husbands. These strategies are to target all social groups—bureaucracy, gentry, women, clergy, merchants, and lower middle class ("meshchanstvo")—with their respective systems of subordination.

All of this hinges on communication. Like an American campaign manager, Gogol charts the flow of data, analyzes ratings, prepares media events, and relies on image manipulation. In fact, the entire fourteen-page letter deals with nothing other than various forms of information processing.

First, information has to be gathered. Gogol delegates this task to his correspondent, who must personally interview every important official (Gogol has ready a questionnaire of three standard questions), supplementing the dossier with information gathered from others; talk with and learn "through and through" ("naskvoz' ") about "the entire female half of the town" (VIII:312/126); and meet with every priest, polling them (as well as the chief of police, with whom a hearty talk is recommended) about every citizen of the middle and lower middle class (some of whom should be interviewed personally). The search for information ends with the scrutiny of all possible "merzosti," "abominations, disgusting things" (VIII:320–21/135).

Second, information must be carefully filed, and Gogol repeatedly instructs his correspondent on the art of note taking. (All the while, Gogol's own text is so repetitive and chaotic that toward the end he has to admit it, but of course he blames it on the addressee: "Everything in [my letter] is haphazard, not in strict logical order, which, however, is your fault," VIII:321/136). Like a "diligent schoolgirl" (VIII:319/134) and "sensible official" and unlike a "passionately chaotic woman" (VIII:311/125), the *gubernatorsha* must start a special notebook and record in it all conversations as accurately as possible, using the margin or separate pieces of paper for additional notes. This activity must be allotted regular hours, yet somehow every conversation must also be taken down right away ("Having found out, go [*otpravliaites'*] to your room and immediately put it all down on paper for me," VIII:312/125)—one more inconsistency typical of the flawed authorial voice of *Selected Passages*. Of course, once reinterpreted as a stylistic pattern, that voice exhibits a subtle use of skaz for maximum effect: the unreliable speaker gets away with making two opposite points.[61]

To return to information processing, gossip is to be recorded too, either "beskhitrostno," "guilelessly, the way it was," or exactly "the way it was reported to you by trustworthy people" (VIII:313/126). All these data must be shared with other "media" personalities, for example, the bishop, but above all with Gogol, who will help put the chaotic information in good order. (Referring to the correspondent's previous letters, he keeps criticizing her for not supplying enough well-processed information—a familiar gesture of delegated guilt.)

But mere streamlining of the information flow is not all. To influence events, information must be manipulated by a panoply of techniques:

—by raising one's own consciousness ("convince yourself that . . . [all your subjects] are your kinsmen and people close to your heart, and then everything will change before you," VIII:310/123–24);

—by prayers (advised of the problems, Gogol will use his personal access to God, who will enlighten him: "[He] might send to my mind the gift of understanding [*vrazumlenie*], and my mind, made understanding by God, might be able to do something better than a mind which has not been made understanding by Him" [VIII:310/124], that is, than the less creative mind of the correspondent);

—by engineering facts and appearances that will be taken as role models and disseminated by fashion and other "aping" mechanisms, "obez'ianstvo" (VIII:309/123; Gogol suggests wearing the same simple dress to parties, refusing to visit a bad official, publicly praising good behavior, and firing offenders);

—by the interviewing strategies (the very course of the conversation will advise the people of their problems and desirable cures);

—by influencing the perceptions of key communicators (the bishop, the wives) in order to enhance the persuasiveness of their acts (sermons, brainwashing of husbands);

—and, above all, by recourse to Gogol's own creative and prophetic gifts, in particular his ability to divine the future (for him, "it is sufficient to observe the present more attentively, and the future will suddenly appear [*vystupit*] all by itself," VIII:320/134).[62]

5. WRITING ABOUT WRITING

The amount of attention Gogol devotes to writing and creativity and the supreme position he reserves for himself make suspect the declared purpose of this writerly pyramid: the improvement of life in the provincial city.[63] On the one hand, all this manipulation of files and images, which sounds like a cross of Stalin's *ars apparatoria* with Nixon's wiretapping and Reagan's Great Communicatorship, brings out Gogol's *mania grandiosa*, his love of rank and control. But even more forcefully, he emerges as absorbed with *écriture*, his main claim to Romantic grandeur. In a curious replay of the "The Diary of a Madman," the writer of *Selected Passages* pretends to the crown of the Poet/Tsar of the City he has blessed with his attention.

Indeed, all this power play is purely literary and Gogolian. The fixation on the minutiae of text production (orderliness, regular hours, special notebooks and scraps of paper, etc.) is reminiscent of Akakii the writer and Petrushka the reader. The process of writing is likely to evoke strong emotions ("If, in the course of the descriptions you will be making for me . . . , our [i.e., Russian] regrettable aspects should strike you too hard and outrage your heart," VIII:316/130) and in compensation yield a legitimate *plaisir du texte* ("pleasure, repose, spiritual relaxation [*razvlechen'e dukha*]," VIII:318/132). Small wonder, since Gogol expects from his correspondent genuine acts of artistic creation. To impress on Gogol (and the bishop) her situation, she must "sketch everything down to the last vivid detail, making it literally appear before [their] eyes, so that your town, as if alive, would constantly abide in [their] thoughts" (VIII:316/130). Like a literary critic, Gogol insists that the images she creates should be graphic and typical,[64] but he allows also for caricature:

> I must have someone *live* [*zhiv'em*] from among them, so that I may observe him from head to foot in all detail. . . . All this information will serve to paint an *exemplary picture* [*primernyj obraz*] . . . of the middle-class person and merchant as they really should be; in a monster you will recognize the ideal of that which, as a caricature, has become a monster. (VIII:317/131)

The literary talents Gogol expects from his correspondent and other women are quite extraordinary:

> If you only know how to speak to them in the language of their souls, . . . to sketch out for a woman a lofty career that the world expects of her today—her heavenly career to be the source which propels us to everything that is right, noble, and honest, to summon man to noble aspirations—[she] will suddenly blaze up . . . , push her husband to the honest fulfilment of his duty, and, tossing her rags aside, convert everyone to action. (VIII:319/133)

These rhetorical talents are, of course, carbon copies of his own rare gift: "If you give me a full understanding of their character . . . , I will tell you in what way . . . it is possible to instigate them: there are secret strings in the Russian, unknown even to himself, which one needs but pluck for him to throb everywhere" (VIII:318/132–33).

In fact, it is Gogol's own, not the *gubernatorsha*'s, activity that is the ultimate goal of all the information processing, and through a thin disguise we recognize Gogol's notorious pleas for material, indeed for ready-made writer's sketches that would enable him to write about Russia: "For my sake, you must . . . begin an examination of your . . . town . . . . I need this" (VIII:311/125). She herself must refrain from any activity other than communicating with Gogol: "For the time being it is better not to hurry; do nothing, even if it seems to you that you can do something. . . . It is better meanwhile to observe closely . . . [and] transmit . . . to me; . . . without that I do not even understand how it is possible to give counsel" (VIII:312/126). Only after having accumulated complete knowledge will Gogol be able to articulate the magic word: "Then will I be able to tell you certain things, and you will see that much of what seemed impossible is possible. . . . Until that time I will say nothing, because I could make a mistake, and I would not want to do that. I would like to speak such words, as would strike the mark precisely" (VIII:313/127).

To this problem of writing block Gogol—in an obvious echo of his failure to finish *Dead Souls*—returns again and again: "In the first place . . . , but . . . my words may be beside the point, it would be better not to pronounce them at all" (VIII:318/132). "I feel that I am beginning to speak of things which are perhaps not at all fitting to your town, . . . but the fault is yours, for you have not conveyed detailed information on anyone to me" (VIII:319/134). To overcome the block, toward the end of the letter he tries to work himself out of it by invoking his ability to prophesy the future through a scrutiny of the present. Then follows a sweeping dip into all the *merzosti* of the present. Or rather, the direction is both downward and upward, for the passage is a characteristically Gogolian exercise in masochistic yet lofty rhetoric, with the root *merz-* repeated thirteen times, five of them in the recurrent phrase "vsmatrivat'sia pobol'she vo vsiakie merzosti," "to scrutinize as much as possible all kinds of abominations" (VIII:320/134)—an incantatory monotony worthy of Stalin. Cleansed from and by the "disgusting" depths, Gogol rises to spiritual clarity and concludes on a hopeful note.

The ending is emblematic of the whole enterprise of *Selected Passages*. Gogol still refrains from pronouncing the Last Judgment—in the same way as with *Dead Souls*, where he in fact ended up offering instead nothing other than *Selected Passages* as a sort of interim report. Pending his attainment of omniscience and the magic Word, he commands his correspondent to "reread the [present] letter five, six times. . . . The substance of my letter must remain totally within you; let my questions be your questions and my desire your desire, so that each word and letter may haunt you and torment you, so long as you have not fulfilled my petition exactly as I wish" (VIII:321/136). The letter comes to verbalize explicitly its metaverbal, metaliterary theme of writing writ large, foregrounding of *écriture*, set toward expression, message for message's self-referential sake.

• • •

Today much of *Selected Passages*, including Letter 21, reads as hilariously funny. As in most of Gogol's texts, this results from the way the speaking voice subverts itself, allowing the reader to see around the speaker. That in *Selected Passages* the character/narrator who is preoccupied with writing but fails to control it is the author himself does not seem to spoil the reader's fun. To account for this response, only a subtle shift in the critical viewpoint is necessary—the one prompted by the figures of Koz'ma Prutkov and Palisandr Dal'berg. All the miswritten book asks for is to be misread into place, and, I believe, the postmodern sensibility, as well as Gogol's insistent pleas for help from readers, suggest just that. Through the "visible to the world," tearfully programmatic message of *Selected Passages* we will then be able to perceive and appreciate its "invisible laughter."

Cathy Popkin

Distended Discourse: Gogol, Jean Paul, and the Poetics of Elaboration

TO GET TO the point: Gogol loves to elaborate. He seems unwilling to introduce even the most peripheral character without expatiating at length on his trousers, the material from which they were made, where that material was purchased, who is the richest man in that fabric-producing town, what kind of fence this affluent gentleman has built, who paints it, how regularly, whether oil-based paint is used, why or why not, and so on. He regales us with page-long catalogs of carriage types, veritable inventories of food and drink, and extended similes of unsurpassed extravagance.

Whatever the point is, Gogol is not one to get straight to it. His prose is distended with details and digressions that threaten to swamp sense and impede narrative progress. This observation is hardly new—it reflects what we have come to recognize as Gogol's style. And ever since the first reviewers of *Dead Souls* derided Gogol for his compulsive stockpiling of things and his equally pathological deployment of irrelevant detail about them, critics have had to contend with this stylistic peculiarity in one way or another.[1]

The morass of minutiae has been read variously as Gogol's commitment to "naturalistic" representation,[2] as a clever way of including "all of Russia,"[3] as a rich source of humor,[4] as an artifact of an earlier attraction to the fantastic,[5] as a network of symbols pointing to something greater,[6] as a general celebration of "plenitude,"[7] as an exhaustive catalog of human vices,[8] as a ruse to distract the tsarist censors from his searing social commentary,[9] as evidence of a propensity for the carnivalistic,[10] as a reflection of widespread linguistic upheaval,[11] and as plain old stylistic excess.[12] But whatever explanation or complaint it has occasioned, Gogol's gift of gab has rarely gone unnoticed.

Robert Maguire has commented that recent scholarship seems to follow two general critical tendencies to contend with Gogol's characteristic excess.[13] The first, to which Maguire himself subscribes, views each detail as inherently meaningful. Although Gogol's fervor for "data" is seldom regarded any more as an index of his realism,[14] his energetic invocation of things and names for things, according to this first point of view, "establishes [them] as . . . solid and unforgettable presence[s] and conditions us to regard any small detail as potentially important." The now famous detail of the bronze pin from Tula (VI:7), for instance, teaches us "that we must sharpen our eyes lest we miss important clues."[15] Reading Gogol, then, becomes a challenge to interpret these abundant "clues," to ferret out these significations and to discern the order and logic in the apparent untidiness, to urge the text to reveal its "secrets."[16] Hence many of the ingenious sense-making ventures of current Gogol criticism; hence Carl Proffer's contention that the apparently gratuitous detail of Gogol's similes is actually scrupulously selected and exceedingly pertinent; hence James Woodward's insistence on the absolute expressiveness of each and every element and the coherence of the whole; hence, also, while very different in approach, Daniel Rancour-Laferriere's psychoanalytic attributions.[17] For the orthodox Freudian there are no accidents and no superfluous details.[18] As Michel Foucault comments in reference to narrative specificity and another kind of orthodoxy, "for the true believer no detail is unimportant." It must be seen precisely as a testimony of faith when Vsevolod Setchkarev declares, in awestruck wonder, that in Gogol, "every little episode, every descriptive stroke, every ever-so-tiny detail has a critical significance for the work as a whole."[19]

But as Naomi Schorr points out, to read in detail in this way is, "however tacitly, to invest the detail with a truth-bearing function, and yet . . . the truth value of the detail is anything but assured."[20] Or, leaving "truth" aside, we might say that the "significance" or even the "substance" of the details—the *solidity* and *presence* averred by Maguire et al.—is anything but assured. If we persist in "sharpening our eyes" on every Gogolian bronze pin that appears only to disappear, we are likely to go blind. Thus, proponents of the second inclination, who might criticize the first as a kind of "semiotic totalitarianism," hesitate to interpret the verbal clutter, even allowing the details to stand as rampant signifiers whose exuberance is quite independent of their well-bracketed signifieds.[21] Donald Fanger, for instance, has posited a "verbal counterreality" that occasions not exegetical engagement but delight in the performance. For Victor Erlich, "language is the only active protagonist" in the Gogolian oeuvre. Sergei Bocharov, too, has pointed to Gogolian "expression without corresponding content," like those items that appear on Soviet menus but are inevitably unavailable.[22] Most recently, A. P. Chudakov as well insists on the radical unmotivatedness of so much of Gogol's material by pointing to the innumerable things that get crowded into the *fabula* with only the flimsiest connection to the story.[23] But even more extreme, he contends, is the swelling of the discourse, most notably in Gogol's famous extended similes. Chudakov compares the path of Gogol's prose to the trajectory of a multistage rocket ship, hurtling ever farther from the center of gravity, the story getting progressively lighter as it discharges each verbal stage. He cites the fabulous example of Chichikov's approach to the Sobakevich estate, identifying each successive stage of remoteness from the original object that prompted the comparison:

> As he drove up to the front porch he noticed two faces that peeped out of the window at almost the same moment: a female one in a bonnet, long and narrow like a cucumber, and a male one, round and broad like (1) Moldavian pumpkins, (2) known as "flagons," (3) which in Russia are made into balalaikas, (4) two-stringed, light balalaikas, the pride and joy of (5) the quick twenty-year-old lad, (6) a flirt and a dandy, winking and whistling at (8) the white-bosomed and white-throated village (7) maidens who (9) gather around to listen to (10) his soft strumming. (VI:94)

The pumpkins, Chudakov remarks, take on a life of their own and metamorphose into a balalaika, which in turn prompts all sorts of information about its construction and who goes in for such instruments, namely the foppish youth, who then acquires multiple characteristics and eventually even an entourage of admiring young lasses with specifications of their own. Chichikov, like the earth the rocket has left behind, has utterly disappeared from view, and the descriptive detail we have been treated to has arguably nothing to tell us about his activities or even his perceptions.[24] And the face that launched the thousand details (and the rocket) has long since vanished from the window and from our minds. "No sooner had the two faces peeped out than they disappeared," the text itself reports, as if commenting on its own discursive procedure.

A. Potebnia had conjectured that this diversion of our attention from the "main thing" has an important effect, to wit, a *calming* one, since the "main thing" is a fairly harassing story. Andrei Belyi, too, suggested that the digressions provide a welcome "lyrical relief." Chudakov restores some of the tension of the digressive trajectory but suggests that this joy ride on the rocket ship is intensely pleasurable; this aspect of Gogol's narration "excites in the reader an especially burning and irresistible fascination." Fanger, too, regards the flights of verbal prodigality as "occasions of delight," as sorties into pure pleasure.[25]

But is all this enforced detouring really so inherently pleasurable? How diverting is all this diversion? Obviously both the semiotic "totalitarians" and "anarchists" consider it great fun. In fact, in a recent informal survey, Slavists who were asked to complete the sentence: "It is (BLANK) to read Gogol," all, with a single exception, responded that "it is *FUN* to read Gogol." The exception, on the other hand, who requested with some urgency that he/she remain anonymous, responded, "It is [audible sigh] *necessary* to read Gogol." I suspect this is less a matter of liking or not liking Gogol than of learning how to like him. A. Slonimskii's documentation of Gogol's *funniness* notwithstanding, the "fun" answer is so axiomatic and so uniform that it is my suspicion that this is at least in part a learned response.[26]

Originally the consensus was considerably less overwhelming: the extended similes that were praised by Aksakov horrified Senkovskii,[27] and while Belinskii rejoiced in the expansiveness of the procedure, its potential to provide extensive information, Masal'skii found the detail extraneous and irritating. Zhukovskii called the experience of the Gogolian text *both* "zabavno i bol'no" ("fun and painful").[28] Earlier in this century, I. Mandel'shtam, too, complained of the "prolixity, irrelevancy, and distraction" of the ubiquitous and endless similes. And though Proffer found the apparent obscurity of the simile material hilarious, Andrei Belyi maintained that he failed to understand what was so funny. Now, in our apparent unanimity on the joys of reading Gogol, we seem to have become one of Stanley Fish's "interpretive communities" with shared explanations, institutionalized procedures, several "usual and customary" ways of characterizing Gogol's excesses that render them tolerable and even self-evident.[29] Iurii Mann notes with some amusement at the earlier misunderstanding that many of the excesses we now cite as proof of Gogol's genius were originally adduced with a "minus sign."[30] We might profitably take equal note of our own reversal of that valence.

Perhaps we should try to reconstruct the greatest challenge in reading Gogol, whether we choose to decipher him or not—namely, to keep reading. It is frustrating to read Gogol. It is annoying to be perpetually derailed. And if we read the opening of "The Overcoat" with no sense of impatience and only a knowing smile at the characteristically Gogolian digression when we are left in the lurch after "V departamente" ("In a certain department," III:141), if our immense erudition obscures that disorientation, then we have lost something to the distortion of *Nachträglichkeit*;[31] we have impoverished the experience of reading Gogol. I am not suggesting that we read Gogol for the plot but only that we should not lose sight of the sensation of being *unable* to do so, of being thwarted by the digressions, by the endless elaboration, by the exhaustiveness which is, after all, exhausting, by a narrative syntax that exhibits about as much connexity as the items on Ivan Nikiforovich's clothesline or the objects ("whatever comes into anyone's head," II:244) hung out to dry on the incomparable Mirgorod fences. Charles Bernheimer suggests that Gogol's prose celebrates literature's prerogative to be discontinuous, but what about the reader's prerogative to discontinue, to throw the thing over in despair?[32]

Roland Barthes, in discussing the very issue of textual pleasure, posits two kinds of reading, a directed one that goes straight to the point, to the *story*, and another that revels in the *discourse*. The first, hungry for answers, says Barthes (in terms singularly appropriate to Gogol), devours; the second is content to graze.[33] Gogol himself attributes his critics' inability to appreciate *Dead Souls* to their greediness for plot, the rapidity and avidity of their reading—their essentially consumerist mentality.[34] The alternative, nondirected mode of reading is suggested by his portrayals of Chichikov's man, Petrushka, who reads "without troubling too much about content" (VI:20), enjoying the phenomenon of reading itself; of Chichikov, who indulges in a thorough perusal of random notices, the contents of which have nothing to offer (VI:12); of Shponka, whose fortune-telling book does little to elucidate his puzzling dream, but who contemplates it "just as a government clerk will read a directory of addresses with great delight several times a day with no ulterior motive, but enormously entertained by the printed list of names" (I:289).

Surely this grazing, this reading "without ulterior motive," without vested interest in content, is in some measure the only hope of negotiating the Gogolian text. But even Gogol cannot quite recommend it with a straight face, and perhaps the consummate inscription of this Kantian *ästhetische Anschauung* (aesthetic contemplation), this placid contemplation *ohne alles Interesse* (without any pragmatic interest), is the image of the spectator on Ivan Nikiforovich's porch who stands by, tranquilly picking his nose (II:238).

Thus when Ivan Ivanovich exhibits an urgent "inquisitiveness" to match his *ac*quisitiveness ("God forbid you should start to tell him about something and not finish the story!" [" . . . da ne doskazhesh' "] II:227), and when his heart throbs with impatience at the police captain's digressions and slowness to "come to the point" (II:257), we cannot help sympathizing. Because the fact is, while we can tolerate a certain amount of delay and disruption, and while deferred gratification has its own rewards, we do have certain desires—for sense, for plot, for end, for direction. Narratives, Peter Brooks tells us in his provocative *Reading for the Plot*, are doubly inhabited by desire: they both tell of desire—for a new coat or a neighbor's gun, for a lost nose or a list of dead serfs—and they "arouse and make use of desire as a dynamic of signification." They excite what Barthes refers to as a reader's "passion for meaning."[35] Gogol, however, goes to well-documented lengths to frustrate the requiting of our passion for sense, signification, and relevance. Nevertheless, it is not clear that we read Gogol more sensibly by renouncing our desire for what he dangles provocatively beyond our reach. In other words, while I concur with critical tendency number two's refusal to posit a hidden meaning everywhere in Gogol's clutter, I would defend as well the urgency of tendency number one's passion for relevance. Can we really read "without ulterior motive"? Can we really achieve the equanimity of Gogol's idle nose picker?

For while narrative, as Barthes reminds us, is by nature dilatory; and while it contrives to keep the enigma open in spite of the reader's craving for closure;[36] and while it never takes the shortest, most direct route between point A and point B, plot being "a kind of arabesque or squiggle toward the end"; still, that detour is "irritation," or, as Brooks claims, a state of appetite and arousal that is tolerable because it looks forward to its satisfaction. "Desire is the wish for the end, for fulfillment," not for excitement without end.[37] Gogol, instead, engages his reader in a kind of perpetual "foreplay."

Given Brooks's obvious penchant for erotic metaphors, he would probably enjoy Chudakov's image of textual pleasure as a speeding rocket ship, but I suspect he might be troubled, as I am in reading Gogol, by the rocket's suggestion of perpetual tumescence, its trajectory into infinite space with no destination and no prospect of coming to rest, no hope of getting to the point. Gogol himself names the problem: "Doezzhai-ne-doedesh' " ("Drive-and-drive-but-you'll-never-arrive," one of Pliushkin's former serfs who no doubt died of despair at wading through the mountains of material); even the name is difficult to read, crowded as it is onto a sheet of paper "scribbled all over, with names as thick as flies" (VI:125). *Doezzhai-ne-doedesh'. Rasskazyvai, da ne doskazhesh'* (telling and telling, but never getting to the end of the story—Ivan Ivanovich's worst nightmare).

Narrative desire is goal oriented: it strives to progress along a coherent path. But in Gogol, "the roadway everywhere [is] in bad shape" (*Dead Souls*, VI:11), and the problems of "getting there" are legion. In the "bewitched place" ("zakoldovannoe mesto") the longer one walks, the farther one's destination recedes into the distance (I:312–13). This is the nature of the place where *words* double uncontrollably. So while bad roads and impeded progress plagued provincial Russia quite independently of Gogol's poetics, the impassibility they figure in his texts parallels vividly our troubled trajectory on the narrative pathway, where the tenor of a simile is a point of departure from which there seems to be no point of arrival.

Nonarrival is almost paradigmatic in Gogol's oeuvre. *Dead Souls* opens with the conviction that Chichikov's wheel *might* make it to Moscow, but it would never get to Kazan (VI:7). More persistently obstructive to Chichikov's progress toward his destination, though, are the machinations of his helmsman. Typical Russian driver that he is, Selifan always speeds along with his eyes closed; and though he inevitably gets somewhere in the end, it is rarely where Chichikov wished to go (VI:43). Perhaps the association of Chichikov and the amputee Captain Kopeikin is not so farfetched after all: the former is at the mercy of his creative driver, the latter subject to those English artificial legs that (according to the postmaster) carry a person so far off to God knows where that he is never to be found anywhere ever again! (VI:205).

All the apologetic protestations of the narrator to the contrary, Selifan is no secondary character. As he misses turns and gets hopelessly entangled en route he enacts and engenders the meanderings of the discourse.[38] By engineering its detours, he traces a path that derails narrative desire and leaves us as far afield as Chichikov. Selifan is not unlike the police captain of Mirgorod, whose gait parallels his digressive speech patterns (he is constitutionally unable to get to the point). Propelled by a defiant left leg that keeps him from advancing purposefully and in a straight line, each time he tries to move forward he (like the narration) "lurches off a long way in the opposite direction" ("The Tale of How Ivan Ivanovich Quarreled with Ivan Nikiforovich," II:256, 272). And while the police captain's slowness to arrive drives Ivan Ivanovich mad with impatience, he himself regularly takes circuitous routes to the adjacent yard (thereby revealing a greater tolerance for producing digression than consuming it). Eventually both he and Ivan Nikiforovich are shown to make only false starts.

The general predicament seems to embody the old New Hampshire adage that "you can't get there from here." Old Granddad in "The Lost Letter" finds himself, after all his travels, back at the very beginning and can only start out yet again (I:190). The sorcerer of "A Terrible Vengeance" rides and rides straight to Kanev but can't seem to get there. Instead he finds himself in Shumsk. So he turns back to Kiev but arrives at another town instead, even farther removed from his goal (I:277). Chub and friend lose the very road in a snowstorm ("Christmas Eve," I:213); Akakii Akakievich walks away from instead of toward his destination (III:152); and the Person of Consequence, who imagined he was going to Karolina Ivanovna's to satisfy his desires, never gets there either (III:173). The only notable arrival is accomplished by Gogol's madman, who "reaches" Spain in a mere half hour (III:211).

All of these images of what Clarence Brown (taking a cue from Wallace Stevens) has dubbed "the not quite realized transit of Gogol' " inscribe our own sense of impeded progress.[39] Thus, when the narrator of the "Two Ivans" makes his final appearance (and final statement) by "passing through" and making haste to travel on, since a case with no verdict, a story with no end in sight ("da ne doskazhesh' ") is "skuchno" (dull, boring) (II:276), we can understand the impulse. The narrator of *Dead Souls* plays on the reader's *need* to arrive at something comprehensible when he promises early on: "But the reader will learn all about this gradually and in good time, if only he has the patience to read the whole work at hand, which is very long and will expand more broadly to still greater enormity as it nears its end, which crowns all" (VI:19). But this promised "crowning end" is the greatest joyride of them all, the speeding troika that, like Chudakov's rocket, is hurtling only God knows where. *Dead Souls*, part 1, ends on a great "kuda?" (whither? where to?). The Gogolian text suppresses arrival, "coming" to rest. Admittedly, volume 2 was to have consummated the affair. But Gogol doesn't get there.

It is not the endinglessness of Gogol's texts that is so troubling, but the apparent endlessness of the middle, the elaboration, the anxiety that, like *doezzhai-ne-doedesh'* (and thanks to *ne-doskazhesh'*), you might never get there. And even though arrival signifies the death of narration, if Freud is right, then beyond the pleasure principle lies the death instinct; we do have a drive toward quiescence, toward an inorganic state of rest.[40] Often, confronting Gogol's compendia of catalogs or explosions of dependent clauses, one despairs of even coming to the end of the sentence.

It is this dynamic of digression and progression, this tension between *infinite* elaboration and *finite* patience that motivates Jean Paul's presence in this undertaking. In his famous *Vorschule der Ästhetik* (*School for Aesthetics*) (1804), he explores precisely the juxtaposition of *das Endliche* and *das Unendliche*, the finite and the infinite, and derives from this confrontation what he considers the most essential element of Romantic *Poesie* (poetic text), namely humor.[41] "Romantic humor," in his much quoted definition, consists in obliterating (and thus transcending) the finite by contrasting it with "endlessness" (5:124–25.31–32). Admittedly, when he talks about ending and endlessness he has something slightly more metaphysical in mind than Brooks's climax. In fact, his terms refer to the anguish of human limitedness in the face of the "idea," that which is infinite; this recognition gives rise not to paroxysms of laughter, but to "that laughter, which contains both pain and grandeur" (5:129.33), not unlike the familiar notion of laughter through tears.

Thus it is not surprising that Slonimskii reaches straight for Jean Paul to open his own treatment of Gogol's humor, and he explores precisely this philosophical aspect. But even more suggestive for Gogol than Jean Paul's programmatic statements is his fiction, in which limitlessness presents a much more concrete problem.

Jean Paul's novels are what the Germans call *ungeheuer*—monstrous. They are massively digressive and infinitely elaborative. They feature a pleonastic tendency to name and rename things many times over; an exuberant attachment to metaphoricity that results in an extended *stufenweise Lösung* (step-by-step dissolve) away from the object of comparison[42] (not unlike the path of the multistage rocket); a tendency to follow the play of sounds wherever they may lead; a passion for gratuitous documentation, calculated to obscure rather than to clarify; excursuses on every subject imaginable that leave even their own subject in the dust—in short, his novels are a nearly perfect embodiment of what Kenneth Burke calls the "hypertrophy of information" and its concomitant "atrophy of form."[43]

"Always digress," Jean Paul urged, and he religiously heeded his own advice. "An author's 'main topic' should be fundamentally just the vehicle and the platform from which to talk about everything else in the world."[44] The result is an encyclopedic "totality" (5:126.32) reminiscent of someone out to include all of Russia, and a kind of stylistic excess whose affinity with Gogol's prose is unmistakable.

What remains unclear is the extent to which Gogol was personally familiar with Jean Paul's novels, except insofar as he seemed to associate reading them with feeling unwell. In a letter to M. P. Balabina, after complaining at length about his own illness and commiserating with her about hers, he wishes her improved health, hoping to find her soon "reading not Jean Paul Richter, but Shakespeare and Pushkin," both of whom, in contrast to Jean Paul, can be read "in a healthy state."[45] It is interesting that Jean Paul's "joyride" (not dissimilar to Gogol's own circuitous itinerary) seems to produce motion sickness in Gogol when he is in the passenger seat; I regard this as partial validation of my own exasperation at being similarly propelled around by Gogol. As we see from the example of Ivan Ivanovich, whose own capacity for "à propos des bottes" non sequitur is great (II:261) but who cannot tolerate any such straying by others, it is much more fun to give than to receive.

Beyond the obvious stylistic similarities, though, are certain Jean Paulean strategies that can help crystallize some of Gogol's concerns, most notably his provocation of and assault on directed, desirous reading. Like Gogol, Jean Paul thematizes reading with and without ulterior motive and, also like Gogol, fights against goal-oriented reading by problematizing arrival. In the well-known formulation in his novel *Flegeljahre* (Years of Indiscretion)[46] (1804–5), art is declared to be "simultaneously road and goal." One must not read "simply to arrive at another spot" (2:653). More tacitly, the novel inscribes its own pragmatic quagmire by opening the text with the "Eröffnung" (opening) of a testament (2:571). In fact, the novel at first coincides with the text of the will, the reading of which perfectly embodies reading with a vested interest, here modeled in the will's reception by the seven presumptive heirs who stand to gain from it. Naturally they are intensely curious, and since this will, like the novel, is swamped with numerous extra leaves, marginal commentary, and clauses beyond measure, this curiosity soon turns to rather keen impatience to get to the main point, their inheritance.[47]

The novel is full of spectators and readers of various sorts who expectantly await outcomes; and the twin protagonists, Walt and Vult, embody respectively (among other things) an ideal, aesthetic, contemplative approach to life and text and a pragmatic, desirous "consumerism." Walt has a great tolerance for "empty stories that lead nowhere" and leafs through manuscripts "idly," while Vult (whose very name is a Latinate invocation of desire) sits "cursing with impatience" (2:615, 622). While Walt is clearly the fair-haired boy of this novel, Vult's Ivan Ivanovich–like "Gier" (simultaneously inquisitiveness, acquisitiveness, and desire) brings him closer to the actual reader of *Flegeljahre*, which, near the end, finally evinces a certain awareness of its own readers' "longing" to get to the point "after so many printed pages" (2:596).

Flegeljahre inscribes not only its own reception but also its production, and the model is generative (and extremely suggestive for Gogol). Not only are we treated to numerous examples of Walt's genre, "Streckvers" (stretch poetry), in which each verse is "pages and pages long" (2:622), but we begin to see how the Jean Paulean text itself is generated by a kind of doubling. In *Flegeljahre*, every Walt engenders a Vult; each character is multiply named (not only because, according to the terms of the will, the beneficiaries must take on additional names, but because the text insists on invoking their names with endless appositives—professional and descriptive—many times over) (Jean Paul, for that matter, multiplies his own name in his translation of the German Johann Paul to the French Jean Paul). The fictional novel within *Flegeljahre* (largely corresponding to the actual one) produced by twin authorship is called a *Doppelroman* (double novel), with a reiterative title that perpetuates the echo (*Hoppelpoppel*) and an alternative name (*oder das Herz* [or the heart]) just for good measure (2:657); the chapters, too, are multiply entitled (each carries a number, the name of an associated mineral, and an aphoristic description).

This model of text production by verbal overdetermination is easily matched by Gogol. Nabokov was only one of many critics to point to the redundancy of expressions like "russkie muzhiki" ("Russian Russian peasants"),[48] and Maguire comments as well on the convulsive naming and renaming of Chichikov's revered vehicle.[49] Whether this gives the carriage greater materiality (as Maguire claims) or simply foregrounds the linguistic transaction of calling it something, the pleonastic urge inevitably delays the carriage's arrival. Despite Jean Paul's own Adamic penchant for bestowing names, pleonasm is a tendency he snidely ascribes to women, who, he claims, have devils in their mouths.[50] Gogol, too, attributes the uncontrollable proliferation of words to devilry: in Dikanka's paradigmatic "bewitched place" words reduplicate and multiply beyond the speaker's control (I:314), and even the most accomplished storyteller is also fond of "treating the devil to nicknames" (I:185), multiplying the names of the multiplier of words himself.

In the works of both authors, this proliferation proceeds not only from a single thing to its multiple names, from a doubling of words for things, but also from a multiplication of the things that generate words. In the *School for Aesthetics* Jean Paul had pointed to the particular ability of combination and juxtaposition—*Witz*—to produce discourse (5:169–73.42–43) (not unlike the "telling bee," the battle of the two narrators in the Dikanka cycle that serves less to differentiate the stories than to generate them; or even the triple generative project of the present conference volume—Gogol × German Romanticism × contemporary literary criticism—calculated to engender more and better discourse than our author in isolation). In Jean Paul's fiction, the verbal plenitude is stimulated, most notably, by the inscription of hoarding, the obsessive accretion of many things, to motivate the naming of many things. Not only do the chapters have several names, but they owe their own great number to the vast collection of minerals in the testator's "cupboard," each of which literally generates the chapter that carries its name, insofar as it pays the author's wage for producing it (2:584). Similarly, in Jean Paul's novel *Siebenkäs* (1796–97), the source of discourse is inevitably a trunk, case, or cupboard of some sort which has been stuffed full and will now be emptied to produce narrative content—from the trunks "full of things" dragged around by ladies, and their mouths full of gossip which they also hasten to "unpack"; to the household cupboard, the contents of which are sold to finance the hero's writing of ever more chapters (2:35, 181, 162).

Gogol's hoarders, too, are legion, and their presence is verbally productive. Pliushkin's plethora of things produces an array of words equally massive and disorderly. Chichikov's *shkatulka* (box), into which he stuffs anything and everything he picks up, and from which nothing is ever discarded, serves a similar (if less extreme) purpose, and the narrator even foregrounds our impatience at the pointless accumulation of things and their accompanying descriptions by offering to "satisfy" our inquisitiveness by giving us a detailed account of the box's internal arrangement as well (VI:55–56). Ivan Ivanovich's fairly anal compulsion to retain the seeds of all the melons he has devoured has as its corollary his delight at painstakingly recording their historical coordinates (II:224). And when Gogol, like his acquisitive character, "lets his eye go roaming around for some new thing" to incorporate into his domain (II:228), the narrator produces from this optical search mission another whopper of a simile before Ivan Ivanovich lights upon his "indispensable thing" (II:234).[51]

Over and over again, hoarding is associated with verbal prodigality, perhaps nowhere more clearly than in the person of Akakii Akakievich, who fanatically hoards his two-kopeck pieces, and who even collects garbage, thanks to his "special talent for passing under windows at the very moment when various rubbish was being thrown out of them, and therefore was constantly carrying away various melon rinds and similar litter on his hat" (III:145). But what accrues in the greatest quantity on and around the figure of this copy clerk is *words*. He provides a pretext for the production of more words and clauses than any reasonable sentence can accommodate (most notably in the page-long extravaganza beginning, "Even at those hours . . . ," III:146). In this seemingly infinite deferral of the main clause, Gogol's own procedure parallels his hero's fundamentally agoraphobic impulse to fill up empty pages with words.

But perhaps the greatest Gogolian hoarder and producer of discourse is Pulkheriia Ivanovna of "Old-World Landowners"; she (apparently like the narrator of her story) is unable to disregard anything that crosses her path (II:17) and (again, like the narrator), "always liked to prepare a store for the future above and beyond what she figured to be necessary for use" (II:19). This excess is reflected in the exhaustive inventory that faithfully reproduces the bounty of her storeroom, from the innumerable sorts of preserves and delicacies she stockpiles in her larder to the multiple types of vodka that render a man "utterly unable to control his tongue" (II:19).

Like the dishes of Nozdrev's cook, who pitches everything at hand into his soup (and provokes the narrator to do the same to his prose) (VI:75); like Rudyi Panko's advertising copy in the preface to his Dikanka tales (concerning the food so luscious that it will make anyone who tastes it *talk* about it to everyone in the world, Panko himself having already "blabbed out of control" on the subject [I:107]); like the repasts throughout Gogol's prose that prompt the narrator to "expatiate on them" ad nauseam (despite his avowed preference for "eating them" [II:271]), food in Gogol's texts seems to have a remarkable tendency to stimulate the tongue beyond its usual transaction with the taste buds.

Hence, the reception of all this discourse is logically cast as consumption—stories are actually baked into pies, after all (I:283), and are "like dumplings to a hungry man" (I:310). But the dilemma of the Gogolian reader/eater is most vividly depicted in the plight of Afanasii Ivanovich, devoted husband of Pulkheriia Ivanovna and indefatigable consumer (like the reader) of poppy-seed pies, salted mushrooms, vodka, dried fish, porridge, mushroom sauce, watermelon jelly, dumplings (naturally), and a great many other things—all before (and inevitably delaying) the main agenda (dinner!) (II:21–23). This gluttony is reflected in the glut of details in the prose, and when Afanasii Ivanovich develops a stomachache in the wake of his tremendous intake, we can relate to his distress.[52] Predictably, the "cure" for the bellyache is to eat some more (II:23), and the reader is served up ever more as well. We wind up engorged like the banquet goers in "The Coach," with acute indigestion and a fervent need to unbutton our waistcoats (which, however, discretion and training forbid—reading Gogol, after all, is "fun") (III:181). Gogol's own terms of overconsumption suggest some of the problems of narrative hoarding. Dante, incidentally, condemns those who hoard and dispense too freely to perpetually wheeling back and forth—in the best Gogolian tradition, Dantean dead souls are doomed never to arrive either; the Italian, at least, has the good sense to regard this as a torment rather than as "fun."[53]

For Jean Paul, too, textual production is inextricably bound up with the culinary. Writing is "Bücherbräuerei"—book-brewing (2:76)—(and the literary brew is appropriately named after the devil, that other great fermenter of words); reviewers are "tasters" (2:159); writing inevitably occasions a dispensation from fasting and a suspension of all rules of "table economy" (2:81); and the ubiquitous "cupboard" that is emptied to finance the writing is the repository of eating utensils.

But again, the Jean Paulean strategy foregrounds an aspect of all this that can be extremely suggestive for reading Gogol. Jean Paul's portrayal of text production as an economy of hoarding and spending emphasizes the phenomenon of conversion of currencies (and this in several senses). First, whereas greedy readers are gripped by the "impulse to convert all content to form" by assigning significance and relevance,[54] Jean Paul (like Gogol) thematizes the *authorial* compulsion to convert all substance into word, into textual plenitude, the sense of which (like the produce of Dikanka) is impossible to disentangle ("razobrat' nel'zía," I:316). Second, Jean Paul's novel emphasizes the economic aspect of this transaction: the conversion from content to word is remunerative. Siebenkäs writes until he accumulates enough paper to balance the sum raised on a herring dish, a soup tureen, a salad bowl, and some plates (2:181) (in the Dickensian spirit of wages by the word); the writer produces hard currency—like the "Morgenstund'," he has "Gold im Mund";[55] and the hero's book itself is converted into the household "food cupboard" (2:165). If *reading* for profit (Martin Price's conversion of content to sense) is problematic, *writing* with a vested interest (converting content to "cents") appears to be the order of the day. Gogol's "scribblers," too, are fueled by silver rubles (unpacked from the ancestral hoard in, naturally, an old trunk) (II:274); and it is ultimately Chichikov's money-making plot that generates the fictional one.

But where does this transactional model leave the reader? *Siebenkäs*, which is constructed largely on the tension between the incentive to digress and the need to finish (and which includes several "extra leaves" condemning the tendency to say too much, while expanding on it indefinitely [2:184]), posits a kind of complicity between writer and reader: "The reader and I have so far worked toward nothing but the conclusion of the book; and now that we are almost there, it is extremely distasteful to both of us. The least I can do is somehow to conceal its end to the best of my ability . . . , and say a few things which, in any case, will lengthen the work a little" (2:553–54). But this alleged dovetailing of interests is plainly as ironic as can be, for there is no profit sharing here. The reader is shortchanged, if not downright exploited.

Barbara Herrnstein Smith argues that narrative is precisely a kind of "transaction" and, as such, is ultimately "subject to the economics of the marketplace."[56] A reader has desires and demands, which finally must be fulfilled in order for the customer to go away satisfied rather than just go away. While a consumer may be willing to sacrifice some ease of access to the "point" in exchange for "the pleasure of getting there," the degree of pleasure experienced in the face of elaborative excess is determined by the extent to which the parties' *interests* are served.[57]

What readers ultimately desire (passionately, if we are to believe Barthes and Brooks) is *sense* (sense both as "meaning" and as pleasurable "sensation"). Ross Chambers understands narrative transaction as *mutual* desire. His formulation, somewhat reminiscent of a *New York Review of Books* personal ad, proclaims "desire to narrate" seeks "desire for narration."[58] Gogol the narrator needs and desires a desirous reader,[59] but persists in playing hard to get. The pleasure is hogged by the autoerotic text generator, the Akakii Akakievich figure, who obsessively makes more and more copies for *himself*, impressed by addressees but never in contact with them. He perpetually *perepisyvaet* (copies) but never *perepisyvaetsia* (corresponds) (producing, in effect, the original purloined letters). Gogol's protestations, as it were, that "the check is in the mail," that the reader will get his (or hers), are difficult to credit.

And if a book is indeed a "Gallehault," a go-between that stimulates desire for "delight" (sensual in both meanings), as the story of Paolo and Francesca in the Dantean subtext suggests, then the Gogolian text might be viewed as a Gallehault that serves the interest of only one party. As a conduit to the pleasures of textual sense, it is as unreliable a source of transport as its various modes of conveyance are of transportation to an end. By arousing desire it refuses to satisfy, it risks being put aside for delights that are accessible. It risks an end to reading that precedes the end of text. It might very well share the fate of that famous book in canto 5, when Dante's lovers opt for a real consummation of their desires: that day, says Francesca, with a most un-Gogolian reticence, "that day we read no more."[60]

Gary Saul Morson

Gogol's Parables of Explanation: Nonsense and Prosaics

"I understand absolutely nothing," said the nose. "Explain it more satisfactorily."
—"The Nose"

Slowly, as slowly as one can possibly imagine, did he [Selifan] go down the stairs, leaving the imprint of his wet boots on the worn steps, and for a long while did he keep scratching away at the nape of his neck. What did this scratching signify? And what was its general portent? . . . God knows, you can't guess. Many and sundry are the things portended when the Russian people scratch the napes of their necks.
—*Dead Souls*

1. THREE IDEAS

IN HIS classic study *The Russian Idea*, Nicholas Berdiaev wrote: "What will interest me in the following pages is not so much the question: what has Russia been from the empirical point of view, as the question: what was the thought of the Creator about Russia, and my concern will be to arrive at a picture of the Russian people which can be grasped by the mind, to arrive at the 'idea' of it."[1] This idea itself—the idea of the Russian idea—has obsessed Russian intellectuals. Berdiaev's own book stands as one of the great expressions of their mad pursuit of total explanation and their frenetic construction of historicist systems that can be readily "grasped by the mind."

Critics of Russian thought, both Russian and Western, have repeatedly stressed the determination with which Russian intellectuals posed the eternal, "accursed questions" and arrived, time and time again, at "final" answers. Nineteenth-century Russian intellectual history offers an encyclopedia of mutually exclusive keys to history, to human life, to ethics—to everything. Viewed from the perspective of God, the apocalypse, or the Laws of History, what is the significance of our lives and of our activity? The fact that each ultimate answer to this question rapidly turned into a penultimate one, and each penultimate one faded into mere historical curiosity, did not prevent new thinkers from making the same claim of finality. Soviet communism has been taken as the culmination, for better or worse, of the Russian idea.

What these Russian philosophies share is an approach I like to call *semiotic totalitarianism*. They are semiotic because they take everything in existence as a sign of some underlying pattern or meaningful system. That system can in principle account for everything, which is why it is totalitarian. The disorder of life as we experience it is felt to be something unnatural or illusory, something that can be seen through, explained away, or interpreted as a mere instantiation of something else that is hidden. Knowledge of that hidden something, if we only had it, would answer all questions. Like Hermann in "The Queen of Spades," who is literally haunted by a secret that will eliminate chance and serve as the "philosopher's stone," many Russian thinkers and novelistic heroes have sought and claimed to have found a mystical certainty, the "key to the mysteries." Dostoevsky's underground man offers and parodies some of the most striking images of this kind of thinking: "We have only to discover these laws of nature. . . . All human actions will then, of course, be tabulated according to these laws, mathematically, like tables of logarithms to 108,000 and entered in a table; or better still there would be published certain edifying works like the present encyclopedic lexicons, in which everything will be so clearly calculated and designated that there will be no more incidents and adventures in the world." These lines, I think, characterize not only the particular systems mentioned by the underground man but also all forms of Russian semiotic totalitarianism.

For all their diversity, Russian intellectual movements have displayed a remarkable similarity in tone and impulse. What Russian Marxism and its apparent opposite, Russian Formalism, share is the faith that chance, freedom, and real originality are illusions, epiphenomena, and, ultimately, mere products of a system. Taking Formalist premises to an extreme, Osip Brik declared that if Pushkin had not created *Eugene Onegin*, someone else would have. As there is such a thing as vulgar Marxism, there is evidently also vulgar Formalism. But even at its more refined moments Formalism produced the "scientific" theory that all of culture is a "system of systems" and that what appears to be chance from the perspective of any one cultural system is in fact the effect of systematic laws operating in another. It was just this aspect of Formalism that, perhaps more than any other, repelled Mikhail Bakhtin, who insisted that the quest for systems was itself a mistake because it denied human "unfinalizability."

Nevertheless, the diversity of such systems is impressive and testifies to the devotion of Russian intellectuals to semiotic totalizing. Petr Chaadaev's whole argument in his "First Philosophical Letter" depends on the idea that Russia stands outside history as defined by eternal underlying laws; the Slavophiles generated numerous models and -isms to show that Russia was, on the contrary, history's chosen nation; Westernizers joined in the game of historiographical algebra, but of course reached different conclusions.

Russian communism and apocalypticism illustrate two more features of this tendency in Russian thought. First, the explanations offered are also soteriologies, systems of salvation. *Everything* depends on them. To be sure, Tolstoy objected that "if we concede that human life can be governed by reason, the possibility of life is destroyed,"[2] and Dostoevsky raised similar objections to utopianism, but the predominant view remained that utopia was the inevitable consequence of true, which is to say absolute, historical knowledge. Second, thought of this type is characteristically extremist. When a Western system is borrowed in this spirit, it is pushed to the limit, beyond recognition by its Western formulators. As Dostoevsky remarked, a Russian intellectual is someone who can read Darwin and conclude he should become a pickpocket. Or we can think of the splendid line Chekhov gives Semyonov-Pishchik in *The Cherry Orchard*: Nietzsche recommends that we forge banknotes. The devil in *Karamazov* offers the apt reply: "That's all very charming; but if you want to swindle why do you want a moral sanction for doing it? But that's our modern Russian all over."[3]

Let us follow Berdiaev and refer to this style of thought as *the Russian idea*. We may then note that the very extremism of a tradition tends to create opposing traditions that question one or another of its enabling assumptions. I would like, for the moment, to mention two ways in which the Russian idea was subject to skeptical scrutiny. The less productive kind of scrutiny accepted the idea that knowledge, to be meaningful, has to explain everything, but questioned the possibility of such knowledge. The result was various forms of radical skepticism, and, to use Turgenev's terms, a series of Hamlets who reply (uncertainly, of course) to the Don Quixotes. The radical skeptics offered an opposite claim: nothing explains anything and the world is pure nonsense or absurdity. As Kirillov observes in *The Possessed*, Christ himself "lived in a lie and died for a lie" and "all the planet is a lie and rests on a lie and on mockery. So then, the very laws of the planet are a lie and the vaudeville of demons. What is there to live for?"[4] From this line of thought derives the radical existentialism so often discovered in Russian literature: the palpable sense of the void and the endlessly repeated myth of Sisyphus. Everything we say about life, all the meaning we find in it, is mere talk, as the underground man says: "But what is to be done if the direct and sole vocation of every intelligent man is babble, the intentional pouring of water through a sieve?"[5]

Precisely because this trend shares the central assumption of semiotic totalitarianism—that meaning to be real must be certain and all-encompassing—I refer to it as the mere "obverse of the Russian idea." To use Sir Isaiah Berlin's terms, this is still a philosophy for hedgehogs, albeit hedgehogs who have become disillusioned.

But Russian thought also generated a much more productive alternative tradition, with its genuine counteridea. The counteridea of Russian literature is what I call *prosaics*, and it has produced some of the most remarkable works of Russian literature and criticism. Arguably, this countertradition, though a minority voice, may constitute the most durable contribution of Russian thought. I have described prosaics in detail elsewhere, but I will mention here that it received its first explicit formulation in Herzen's essay on Robert Owen and in his *From the Other Shore* and its greatest literary expression in *War and Peace* and *Anna Karenina*. Chekhov developed it with special originality; and in Bakhtin's hands, it became a general theory of language, literature, and ethics. Dostoevsky and Turgenev entertained some of its key insights and represented them with some sympathy, but ultimately rejected them.[6]

Although there are a few moments when Gogol seems to be struggling toward a prosaic viewpoint, he belongs on the whole to the other, less productive alternative to the Russian idea. By "less productive" I am emphatically *not* referring to Gogol's aesthetic achievement, but only to the viability of his philosophical position. From an aesthetic standpoint, Gogol must be regarded as one of the greatest writers of nonsense, if not the greatest, in the history of world literature. And perhaps if he had not explored the obverse of the Russian idea so thoroughly and so brilliantly, the sense that a better alternative was needed would not have been so compelling.

2. THE IDEA OF THEORY

> However, there do occur sundry refinements and variations in methods, especially at the present time. . . . In other boarding schools the major subjects may be given in such order that the pianoforte comes first of all, the French language next, and domestic science only after that. And at times it may even so happen that the first order is domestic science . . . then the French language, and the pianoforte only after that. The methods vary.
>
> —*Dead Souls*

If one reason to study the literature of the past is to gain new perspective on the present, then the debate I have been describing may be of special interest to literary scholars today. For literary theory of the past few decades has recapitulated the hermeneutic argument that obsessed nineteenth-century Russian thinkers and has done so, in part, under Russian influence. Our semiotic totalizers have offered us privileged systems of interpretation of various sorts: structuralist, Freudian, Marxist, and others. We have developed our own versions of the Russian algebra, which we might call the Idea of Theory.

One senses the supreme confidence characteristic of this kind of thought in the current phase of exposing the political and moral failings hidden deep in the classic texts of the past. With a certainty that only a Theory could authorize, critics are now in the habit of showing how any classic text discloses to the well-trained theorist a hidden self-subversion. Unbeknownst to its author, the text reveals its true agenda and, in the process, inadvertently confirms current political prejudices.

But what, apart from a Theory, could lead critics to believe that they are wiser than all the classics and that those classics point inevitably to the theorists' own beliefs? In *War and Peace* Tolstoy remarks that "there is no one in present-day Russian literature, from schoolboy essayist to learned historian, who does not cast his little stone at Alexander for the things he did wrong at this period of his reign," and if we substitute, let us say, Shakespeare for Alexander, we have a fair description of a good deal of current literary theory. But all that such judgments show, Tolstoy replies, is that Alexander (or Shakespeare) "did not have the same conception of the welfare of humanity . . . as a present-day history professor," who will, in turn, find himself declared reactionary by his successors, perhaps with the same confidence.[7]

Tolstoy's point here is that judgments of this sort are essentially *apocalyptic* in nature, for two reasons. First, they presume the sort of knowledge available only at the end of history when future experience could not outdate present judgments. Second, they depend on the sort of certainty of values that only a final Revelation of meaning could warrant. Shakespeare saw as through a glass darkly, but we see as face-to-face.

In America, too, theoretically grounded certainty has generated its obverse, a radical skepticism. Radical skeptics agree that knowledge to be real must be based on absolutely certain foundations but deny that such foundations are possible. Within the debate so framed, the skeptics often have the upper hand, because they can point to unseen weaknesses and unforeseen consequences of the systematizers' formulations. The structuralists saw meaning as the product of oppositions within a system, and their poststructuralist critics spelled out the unsettling implications of culture as a prison house of language. The systematizers often respond not only by calling the skeptics reactionary but also, and more profoundly, by pointing to the ease with which skepticism has itself become a system with its own mechanically repeatable methods. We are all familiar with the sort of poststructuralist reading that finds systematic meaninglessness, "mirrors reflecting mirrors," and indefinite postponement of significance in every text. System returns in inverted form: the return of the obsessed.

A dizzying sequence of neologisms and terminological matrices has been formulated to produce these interpretations. As Gogol would say, "The methods vary."

And in fact the logic of this debate, between idea and its mirror image, is already present in *Dead Souls* and in Gogol's stories. Perhaps one reason the Formalists loved Gogol so much is that, after all, there could be no better illustration than "dead souls" of the idea that meaning or value is not in some mysterious way substantial but is merely the product of a system of differences. Could there be a better illustration than "The Overcoat" that we live in a prison house of language? The Formalists liked to point to the concept of the "zero ending"—an absence that is meaningful only because of a system—as proof that systems do govern. Could anything have exemplified meaningful absences or social "zero endings" more aptly than dead souls? In a weird way, *Dead Souls* is both a structuralist argument and, in its very absurdity, a poststructuralist refutation.

Iurii Tynianov's own story "Lieutenant Kizhe," which is clearly indebted both to Gogol and to Formalist theory, should make the link between the two crystal clear. If you recall, one person who does not exist comes into a brilliant paper existence, while another, who discovers that he is officially dead, accepts this judgment, because it comes from infallible authority. Descartes notwithstanding, he thinks that he is not. What Gogol makes even clearer than Tynianov is the deconstructive turn such reasoning invites, the sense in which it turns all of us into impostors of our own (necessarily counterfeit) selves.

3. THE TRUE HERO OF *DEAD SOULS*

> But man is so fond of systems and abstract deductions that he is ready to distort the truth intentionally, he is ready to deny what he can see and hear just to justify his logic.
> —Dostoevsky, *Notes from Underground*

From the perspective of the Russian debate on explanatory systems, Gogol's most resonant works are "The Nose" and *Dead Souls*. Presenting in especially pure form Gogol's recurrent themes and techniques, they place the greatest emphasis on the nature of meaning and value. *Dead Souls* and "The Nose" are hermeneutic (and axiological) parables.

As a parable, *Dead Souls* belongs not to the tradition of the great nineteenth-century novel but to the much longer tradition of Menippean satire. It resembles the *Satyricon, The Golden Ass*, and the heterogeneous works of Lucian a good deal more closely than it resembles *Père Goriot, Middlemarch*, and *Anna Karenina*. In the modern world, it is closest to Sterne, Diderot, and, especially, Voltaire's parodic philosophical tales. We could look at it this way: "The Nose" is a short philosophical tale, like Voltaire's story of the Good Brahmin and "Micromegas"; *Candide* and *Dead Souls* expand the concerns of these shorter narratives to novel length without becoming psychological or realistic novels. All return to themes and rely on techniques developed in Lucian's "Philosophies for Sale" and his *Dialogues of the Dead*, titles that could be given to Gogol's works as well. If one looks forward, one sees this tradition of parodic philosophical narratives, which first reached significant form in the Menippean satires of antiquity, extending to Mark Twain's *Letters from the Earth*, Stanislaw Lem's *Cyberiad*, and Borges's *Labyrinths*. The realism and psychology of the novel—even the philosophical novel—would not allow for the free play of ideas, the examination of abstract problems, and the parodic treatment of philosophies "for sale" that are the hallmark of the Menippean parable.

The ideas treated in "The Nose" and *Dead Souls* concern the possibility, or rather the impossibility, of explanation. In Gogol's world, an infinite number of explanations, most of which contradict each other, are possible for every phenomenon, and there is no good way to choose among them. Systems grapple with the absurd, and the absurd wins.

In Gogol's narratives we encounter a potentially infinite variety of models that first fail and then collapse into a stifling uniformity. That is one reason Gogol so often uses the rhetorical trope of marveling at differences without a difference (a radish with its head turned upward and a radish with its head turned downward). Tales often begin in a world praised for its diversity but end with the recognition that it's all the same, that "it's boring in this world, gentlemen." In my youth, says the narrator of *Dead Souls*, "everything would bring me to a stop and amaze me" (VI:110/135).[8] But now, he confesses, "I drive up apathetically to every unfamiliar village and look apathetically at its vulgar appearance; to my time-chilled gaze things seem bleak, and I am not amused" (VI:111/137). Passages like these intimate the potential Kafka in Gogol, the element of cosmic despair that is inseparable from his humor. That despair arises in large part from the emptiness of all interpretation and the impossibility of true understanding.

Inadequate interpretive methods multiply like maggots in *Dead Souls*. Scholars have stressed the influence of Sterne's fiction on Gogol, an influence they quite properly detect in his use of sentimental and mock-sentimental rhetoric, his obsession with noses, and his clever improvisations with metaliterary devices. For our present purposes, however, what is most important is Sterne's concern with mad systems that purportedly explain everything and exhibit what might be called "hermeneutic resistance": strategies that prevent counterevidence or self-contradiction from counting. Like so many interpretive schemes of our own times, the ones described in *Tristram Shandy* strive for unfalsifiability, even at the cost of the emptiness necessarily entailed by total closure to evidence. Given the choice between possible refutation and definite tautology, between the risk of testing and a trivial unfalsifiability, Sterne's systematizers opt for the latter while never quite renouncing the claims that only the former could justify. This pattern, of course, is an all-too-familiar one.

Because the claims of totally closed interpretive schemes are empty, their defenders often create an imposing mechanism of description and a complex structure of symmetrical arguments that distract attention from their absent center. Like the world of Gogol itself, they body forth an absence, give apparent form to the void. Their well-developed kinds of hermeneutic resistance keep vision focused on the intricate but ultimately pointless *process* of explanation.

In Sterne, the master of systems is Walter Shandy. Walter's obsessive systematizing is important, Tristram tells us, not for the odd opinions to which it leads but rather

> as a warning to the learned reader against the indiscreet reception of such guests, who, after a free and undisturbed entrance, for some years, into our brains,—at length claim a kind of settlement there,—working sometimes like yeast;—but more generally after the manner of the gentle passions, beginning in jest,—but ending in downright earnest.
>
> Whether this was the case of the singularity of my father's notions,—or that his judgment, at length, became the dupe of his wit;—or how far, in many of his notions, he might, tho' odd, be absolutely right;—the reader, as he comes at them, shall decide. All that I maintain here, is that in this one, of the influence of Christian names, however it gain'd footing, he was serious;—he was all uniformity;—*he was systematical, and, like all systematick reasoners, he would move both heaven and earth, and twist and torture every thing in nature to support his hypothesis*. (Emphasis added)[9]

We might compare this passage to a key digression in *Dead Souls*:

> There is nothing unusual about the fact that both ladies became at last utterly convinced of that which hitherto they had merely assumed and known to be a mere assumption. Our fraternity—we intelligent people, as we style ourselves—acts in almost the same way, and our learned ratiocinations serve as a proof of this. At first the scholar, when it comes to such things, will steal up on them as a most arrant knave, cringing and wheedling: he'll start off timidly, moderately; he'll start off by posing a most modest query: Is this not derived from that? Is it not from this locality that such-and-such a country received its name? Or: Does not this document appertain to another, later period? Or: Do we not have to understand, under the name of this nation, that other nation? Without losing any time, he will cite this ancient writer and that, and no sooner does he perceive some hint or other of what he's after, or simply what seems a hint to him, than he already puts on speed and takes heart, talks with the ancient writers without standing on ceremony, puts questions to them, and even answers for them himself, forgetting altogether that he had started off with a timid assumption. It already seems to him that he perceives the point, that it is clearly evident, and his ratiocination concludes with the words: And it was thus that this event came about! It is such-and-such a nation that

> we must understand under the name of that other! And so it is from this point of view that we must regard the subject. Then he proclaims it for all the world to hear, ex cathedra, and the newly discovered truth is off on its jaunty travels through the world, gathering unto itself followers and devotees. (VI:188/238)

This passage may—and should—cause discomfort to literary critics and theorists. "We intelligent people, as we style ourselves" are, after all, professional explainers, whose wit often gets the better of our judgment. One might say that *Dead Souls* anticipates and "parodies in advance" the subsequent history of its own interpretation. And its real hero, I think, is the "newly discovered Truth," that picaresque rogue who is always with us, whose disguises are endless, and whose jaunty travels take him through all countries and all epochs. Or to be more precise, the hero of *Dead Souls* is the very *process of explanation*, which Gogol here describes at such length: the process that gives birth to such truths and allows them to gather devotees and followers.

That hero is the liveliest character in the book. Part 1 of *Dead Souls* divides neatly in two. The first half, in which Chichikov goes from landowner to landowner with his astonishing proposal to buy nothingness, deals primarily with the nature of value and the process of evaluation. The second half, in which the townspeople try to understand what this story means, what dead souls really are, and who this Chichikov is, centers on meaning and interpretation. Whether the central problem at any given point is value or meaning, what most occupies our attention is the process of explanation itself. The lengthy passage about "the newly discovered truth" occurs in the second half of the book, just as the attempt to understand the riddle of Chichikov and dead souls becomes public and begins to obsess not only individuals but the whole town. It marks the point at which the social dynamics of explanation become a central concern.

The switch of themes from the beginning to the end of the book is really a change of emphasis, inasmuch as problems of meaning do occur in the first half and problems of value arise in the second. Indeed, the ways in which characters try to negotiate the price of nothing in the book's opening chapters reveal the mental habits that combine to produce the pageant of explanations run wild at its close. Gogol begins with relatively simple one-on-one negotiations so that he can develop much more complex patterns later on.

We may regard negotiations over "dead souls" as a kind of thought experiment. They allow us to establish the essential features of value by subtracting everything extraneous, everything specifically pertaining to whatever particular objects might be evaluated.

For there is nothing that pertains to dead souls. If one could establish the right price of dead souls, it is suggested, one would understand value in all its purity. How do the various characters Chichikov encounters react?

Each responds by applying a ready-made system, an *algorithm* of behavior that they use in all circumstances whatsoever and which, after some initial astonishment, they apply to dead souls. Much as Pliushkin's servants must each put on the same pair of boots when they enter his house, so each landowner employs the same method to solve all problems.

Before Chichikov offers to buy a landowner's dead souls, the narrator describes the landowners' habits, obsessions, and algorithms, which are never very complex. Chichikov's job is to learn each person's algorithm, which he does at the beginning of each visit. He must then convince them that this deal is not that different from any other by helping them apply their respective algorithms to this new problem. To the extent that there is a difference, he must show that it works to the seller's advantage. In this way, he can arrive at the lowest possible price. As an expert chameleon, Chichikov is able to adapt to each landowner's way of dealing. He succeeds reasonably well with all except Nozdrev, whose compulsion is the swap and who therefore insists on making the dead souls part of a larger trade, that is, on involving Chichikov in evaluations of something (however fraudulently described) rather than nothing. An exchange of that sort would defeat not only Chichikov's plan but his author's parable of evaluating nothing.

Among those who do eventually sell, Chichikov has the most difficult time with Korobochka. Whereas other landowners recognize the strangeness of the proposed deal, and then can be induced to overcome their suspicion, Korobochka is all suspicion and cannot recognize what is really strange. That is because her way of handling a new situation is to insist that it is *in no way* different in kind from old ones, so why not stick to the old ones, where one at least knows the proper price? She therefore cannot understand the obvious advantages of selling nothing.

Korobochka knows that she has never sold dead souls before, but she cannot recognize that dealing in dead souls is not quite like dealing in hemp. She treats them as a crop like any other except that she does not know their value. That is why she keeps wondering whether she might not be cheated and whether dead souls might not be fetching more than Chichikov is offering. It is also why he only succeeds by at last falling in with her obsession that he (like every visitor) is necessarily a commission merchant and promising to buy her feathers.

Thus, whereas Chichikov must convince Manilov that selling dead souls is really quite similar to selling bast slippers, he must convince Korobochka of the opposite. This time he develops at length the paradox of making nothingness a commodity. Korobochka as always worries that she might "take a loss somehow" (VI:52/61), so he asks her: how can one take a loss on nothing? But she takes all rhetorical questions as serious ones that she cannot answer, just as she classes all goods as agricultural products bought up by commission merchants and all visitors as commission merchants. Nothing can convince her that nothing is nothing. "See here, mother," Chichikov explains anew. "What can they be worth? Look at it this way: why, they're nothing but dust. You take any worthless thing, any least thing at all, now, a common rag, for instance, and even that rag has a value; it will, at the very least, be bought for a paper mill; but this dust, now, is of no use on earth" (VI:52/61).

Chichikov here is actually offering, in abbreviated form, two theories of value that he uses to induce people to sell. One is the substantial theory. Things have value because they are objects with certain properties. They are made of something: "Are your souls made of diamonds, or what?" Chichikov asks Nozdrev (VI:79/97). It follows that something with no substance, "a mere shadow," can have no value; it's mere dust, or less than dust, which at least has some substance. "All that is left of them [the souls] is an insubstantial sound" (VI:102/125); they "have no more substance than a puff of air" (VI:104/127); they are "but a dream" (VI:103/126). Therefore the proper price of dead souls is zero, so anything offered is pure profit for the seller.

Of course, Chichikov himself later implicitly refutes this theory when he ascribes positive qualities to absence. He need not fear a rebellion among his dead souls because they are "extraordinarily docile in character" ("otmenno smirnogo kharaktera," VI:156/195). And Chichikov is right. The absence of certain qualities may itself be a quality, as we know from our own economy, which charges more for decaffeinated than for regular coffee, sells skim milk at a premium, and adds a surcharge for tomatoes without salt. One can sell products not only because of the *in*gredients they contain but also because of the *ex*gredients they "contain." The real logic of "dead souls" is that they are an absence that is indeed a presence.

The other theory alluded to in Chichikov's speech to Korobochka is utilitarian. Things have value because they have use. Since what is useful is presumably properties of the object, the two theories might seem to reduce to one, which is probably why Chichikov can merge them so smoothly. But in fact the theories are quite different because properties are stable but utility varies. Rags would be worth less if there were no paper mills, as oil was worth less before industrialization.

The question Chichikov often asks—what good are they?—is designed to elicit a utilitarian conclusion that dead souls have no use and therefore no value. And if this conclusion is accepted, Chichikov can take the process one step further and point out that dead souls in fact have a *negative* utility inasmuch as taxes must be paid on them; therefore, they have a negative value. Even if dust is useless, possessing it does not make one poorer; but the more dead souls one owns, the less one's property is worth, which is why Pliushkin has a list of his dead souls already made up so he can strike them out at the next census. In some cases, the value of nothing is less than nothing.

This reasoning resurfaces in *Crime and Punishment* when the student whom Raskolnikov overhears applies the utilitarian theory to the life of the old pawnbroker: "Besides, what value has the life of that sickly, stupid, ill-natured old woman in the balance of existence! No more than the life of a louse, of a black beetle, less in fact because the old woman is doing harm." Dostoevsky's genius here was to see that utilitarianism consistently applied not only makes murder permitted but mandates it as virtuous, a point that Ivan Karamazov echoes when he declares that crime is "the inevitable, the most rational, even honorable outcome of his position."[10] This application of utilitarianism to ultimate problems of morality, to people rather than things, is already implicit in Chichikov's haggling over human souls.

The substantial and utilitarian theories of value turn out to be spurious, mere distractions from the central issue, as the shrewdest bargainer, Sobakevich, knows. Sobakevich's algorithm is relentless negativity. In his initial conversation with Manilov, Chichikov illogically praised each of the town's officials as the worthiest of men. When he tries the same technique on Sobakevich, he learns that each, no less illogically, is the least worthy. "I know them all, they're all swindlers, every man jack of them; the whole town is like that, one swindler mounted on a second and using a third one as a whip. Judases, all of them. There is but one—and only one—decent man; that's the Public Prosecutor, and even he, if the truth were to be told, is a swine" (VI:97/119).

What happens in this passage is quite characteristic of each character and each universal interpretive rule. At some point, each rule encounters an apparent exception, and then the speaker must choose between the exception and the method; he always chooses the method, and so there is always but one exception, and that, too, is not an exception. The exact parallel to this passage occurs when Nozdrev, trying to demonstrate how much property he owns, reaches its (evidently exaggerated) boundary and then proclaims that he also owns what is on the other side of the boundary. The claim makes nonsense of the very word boundary—its echo in Russian literature is Dmitrii Karamazov's claim that "all shores meet," which would make them anything but shores—but it preserves the algorithm intact.

For Sobakevich, people simply encumber the earth, which is one reason he can attribute positive qualities only to dead souls, who encumber nothing. In his relentless negativity, Sobakevich even manages to complain about his health because he has never had the slightest illness at all. Trying to get Sobakevich to say *something* positive, Chichikov at last resorts to an assertion that cannot be doubted, that the food at the governor's table—regardless of what it was or how it was prepared—tasted good, at least to Chichikov himself. The implication would seem to be that it makes no sense to doubt assumptions reporting direct sensations—"I feel pain," "it tastes good"—but Sobakevich nevertheless replies, "It just struck you that way" (VI:98/120), thus generating a skepticism beyond that of the most skeptical philosophers. As always in *Dead Souls*, the first rule is to protect the rule. Hermeneutic resistance is absolute.

When one first hears Sobakevich's denunciation of all the officials, one might be inclined to conclude that he is first and foremost a misanthrope, but misanthropy is more a corollary than an axiom of his system. The axiom is closer to negativity per se: name something, and it is objectionable. And even this formulation might be amended when one recalls that Sobakevich does speak well of one thing: his dead souls. In the final analysis, his rule is to treat every situation he encounters as a commercial transaction in which he is haggling over the price. When he has something to sell, he speaks of it positively. Otherwise—his default setting, as we might say today—he reacts like someone asked to buy something. This rule is another reason that Sobakevich is not the least caught off guard by Chichikov's offer and so, in making his astonishing proposal, Chichikov for once loses the considerable advantage of surprise. Not only does Sobakevich get the best price for his absent goods, he even has the presence of mind to take Chichikov's scheme one step further and include a female dead soul on the list by making her name look masculine at first glance. He sells Chichikov a counterfeit dead soul, an absent absence.

Chichikov begins with his usual rhetorical speech about the greatness of Russia, employs his practiced euphemisms, and winds up with his offer to do a favor for his friend by assuming the tax burden. But inasmuch as Sobakevich hears everything as empty rhetoric, as "insubstantial sound" and the semblance of a mirage, he asks, simply, "You need dead souls? . . . They can be found; why not?" (VI:101/124). Chichikov tries his usual theories of value: dead souls have no substance, have no use, except negative use. But Sobakevich, with his methodically negative attitude toward all claimed substantiality or utility, understands value most profoundly and most advantageously:

> "Really, now, what is he up to?" Chichikov thought to himself. "Is he taking me for a fool, or what?" and then added, out loud: "I find it strange, really; it seems as if we were going through some sort of theatrical performance or a comedy; I can't explain it any other way. . . . You are, it seems, a man who is quite intelligent, possessing knowledge and an education. Why, the matter under discussion has no more substance than a puff of air! What can such stuff be worth? Who needs it?"
>
> "There, now, you are buying it, therefore there must be a need for it."
>
> Whereupon Chichikov bit his lip and could not find any answer to make. (VI:103–4/127–28)

Sobakevich seems to understand that use, no less than substance, is irrelevant. *What makes something valuable is that someone desires it.* Why he desires it is irrelevant, at best a way of guessing how something will be evaluated, but not itself a factor constituting its value. Utilitarian theory also makes value vary on the market, but Sobakevich's theory might be called a *pure* market theory.

If value depends purely on desire, what does desire depend on? Why is something regarded as desirable? Here Sobakevich's implicit answer is also quite direct: what makes something desired is its desirability, pure and simple. It is like, let us say, American paper money, which has no gold or silver behind it and does not need to: it is accepted because it is accepted, that is, one accepts it because others accept it, because it is acceptable, and for no other reason. Sobakevich understands that all estimates of value are ultimately of this character.

For those of us who live in a market economy, this theory may not seem quite so disturbing. But one has only to reflect on its extension beyond mere prices to see the horror at which Gogol hints. Here current literary theory offers an illustration in Barbara Herrnstein Smith's market theory of literary value. It is one thing to say that oil or hemp has no intrinsic value, but Shakespeare? Is all we can say about Shakespeare that his plays have value for certain specified purposes for certain people on certain occasions? And what if we were to give the market theory of value a theological turn, as *Dead Souls* constantly invites us to do: what is the pure market value of a human soul? "Really, you hold a human soul at the same value as a boiled turnip!" Sobakevich haggles. "Give me three rubles, at least" (VI:105/129).

Chichikov does at least arrive at a price with Sobakevich, but with Nozdrev he fails utterly. We appreciate one reason why from the very first conversations of Nozdrev with his flaxen fair companion. Nozdrev repeatedly makes an incredible, impossible assertion. His companion doubts it. Nozdrev then offers to place a bet on the truth of his claim. This bet cannot be lost. For how does one verify a factual statement, unless by adducing other facts that cannot be doubted? But Nozdrev is willing to challenge each of these facts with exactly contrary assertions, and when challenged on these, he replies, once again, "Do you want to bet on that?" Verification is threatened by the infinite regress implicit in Nozdrev's algorithm. Honor among thieves may be possible, but agreement with a liar, if he is prepared to lie consistently, is not. Even if an agreement is reached, what is it he will say you agreed to?

To be sure, Nozdrev does not benefit from his method, if by benefit one means become richer. He lies simply in order to lie. His crookedness, remarkably enough, is largely disinterested. Just as Sobakevich is not first and foremost a misanthrope, Nozdrev is not primarily a cheat, and Pliushkin is not primarily a miser. With Pliushkin, perhaps, we can see the pattern most clearly, because he grows continually poorer from his stinginess. That, indeed, is one reason he has so many dead souls and runaways to sell. Here as elsewhere, Gogol's genius lies in taking his point to an extreme. What seems to be a method ruthlessly applied to achieve a goal turns out to be a method ruthlessly applied without a goal: a prison house of method, a structuralist's paradise. For Petrushka, reading is a purely formal exercise that he enjoys without understanding any content at all, and for Pliushkin, stinginess is its own reward. In *Dead Souls*, the algorithm is all.

4. THE EXPLANATORY GAP

> Explaining Metaphysics to the nation—
> I wish he would explain his Explanation.
> —Byron, Dedication to *Don Juan*

When Chichikov's secret becomes known, the townspeople try to explain it. But how is one to explain something that makes no sense? Gogol wants to present the essential workings of the hermeneutic impulse run wild, which is one reason he does not reveal

Chichikov's scheme right away. Most readers today begin the book with this knowledge, but at least insofar as the dead souls are concerned, the initial readers were as much in the dark as the officials of the town. Gogol's point is that one does not have to know the right answer to recognize absurdity in *how* explanations are derived, formulated, and justified.

While Chichikov waits, stationary and ill, at the inn, the book's real hero is active. The town bustles with rumor, conjecture, and reinterpreted interpretations as the Process of Explanation has one more adventure in his jaunty travels around the world.

Once again, the townspeople are offered an anomaly, this time about meaning rather than value. As characters were first invited to evaluate nothing, now they are compelled to interpret it. The two problems are in fact closely related, because to understand the meaning of Chichikov's purchases of nothing, one would have to know why he wants it. And to know that, perhaps it would be helpful to know who Chichikov is. But because Chichikov is a chameleon who reflects the humors of anyone he is with, he, too, is a void to be interpreted. However substantial his person may be, his history, when examined, turns out to be so many vague phrases that leave him unidentified. What is known about him is nothing. The man without qualities and the goods without substance challenge positive description. How does one delineate an absence?

Gogol stresses the problem of explanation—alludes to his true hero—in a number of ways. Before the townspeople realize they have anything to unravel, the author presents Chichikov himself with a few riddles that he would do best to ignore but instead tries to solve. At the beginning of the second half of the book, he receives a poem from an unknown woman who says he should be able to guess her identity when he sees her at the ball. Chichikov tries, but is no more able to establish her identity than the townspeople are later able to determine his.

Chichikov's first real failure in the town is in fact an interpretive one:

> Chichikov became so engrossed in conversations with the ladies, or, to put it better, the ladies engrossed him so and put his head in such a whirl with their conversations, which they peppered with such a lot of the most intricate and refined allegories—all of which had to be resolved, the effort of which caused his forehead to become actually beaded with sweat—that he had forgotten to fulfill an obligation of good manners: that of approaching the hostess first of all. (VI:166/209)

His rudeness precipitates the chain of events that soon drive him from the town. His lapse is not so much his botched attempt to solve the allegories as his indiscreet immersion in the very process of trying. Explanation can be dangerous in itself.

It is also dangerous to the author, we are told. Readers overinterpret or misinterpret everything texts say and so attribute to the poor authors meanings they have not intended. (Here again Gogol speaks with uncanny aptness to current critical practice.) No matter how carefully you try to guard against misreading, Gogol cautions would-be fellow writers, there will always be someone who makes just the mistakes you have tried to preclude plus a few more that have not even occurred to you. For example, whatever fictitious name or imagined qualities an author might give a character—and after all, characters must be described in *some* way or other—some readers will take the character as an allusion to themselves. "It suffices merely to say that there is a stupid man in a certain town, and that is already a personal reflection: a gentleman of respectable appearance will suddenly pounce upon you and set up a shout: 'Why, I, too, am a man, ergo, I, too, am stupid'—in a word, he'll surmise in the wink of an eye just what you're up to" (VI:179/226). Here Gogol puts his arsenal of metaliterary devices at the service of his interpretive parable.

The very presentation of the reader's reaction in the form of an abbreviated syllogism already alludes to the problem of explanation. Of course, the larger irony is that the reader's conclusion here *is* justified precisely *because* it is so illogical: anyone who would reason that badly is indeed stupid. The author's final phrase—"in a word, he'll surmise in the wink of an eye just what you're up to"—completes the self-canceling logic that turns this denial of intent to insult on its head.

To be sure, the simplistic interpretive rule the author describes—take everything as an allusion to oneself—pertains (all readers agree) only to *other*, less enlightened readers. But just as there is, for all our denials, a bit of Chichikov in all of us (VI:245/329), perhaps we, too, are closer to simplistic readers than we care to allow. Is the only difference, perhaps, that our interpretive methods prescribe a few more intermediate steps before their unjustified conclusions?

Most important and most repeatedly, Gogol directs us to his main theme by having the characters constantly allude to the problem of meaning, interpretation, signification. "What in the world could these dead souls signify?" the lady who is agreeable in all respects asks the lady who is simply agreeable, who in turn expresses a desire to discover "that something else hidden here" (VI:184/232, 233). The townspeople strive to account for two "facts"—the real one, concerning the purchase of dead souls, and the phantom one concerning the abduction of the governor's daughter. Itself the product of the interpretive system that purports to explain it, this second "fact" is also a sort of dead soul. And so both types of dead soul "became churned and confounded in their heads in an extraordinarily odd fashion" (VI:189/240) that turns out (the narrator later tells us) to be not so odd at all. "The matter would in no wise explain itself" (VI:189/240):

> There's no logic [*logiki net nikakoi*] to dead souls; how, then, can one buy up dead souls? . . . And what sort of fairy gold [*slepye den'gi*] would he use to buy them with? . . . And how on earth has the Governor's daughter gotten mixed up in this? If he really did want to carry her off, then why did he have to buy up dead souls for that? And if he really wanted to buy up dead souls, then what for would he want to be carrying off the Governor's daughter? Was he after making her a present of these dead souls, or what? And really, when you came down to it, what sort of poppycock [*chto zh za vzdor*] had they spread about the town? . . . And if only there were the least sense to it [*i xot' by kakoi-nibud' smysl byl*]. . . . However, spread it they did, therefore there must be some reason [*kakaia-nibud' prichina*] to it? . . . But what reason [*prichina*] can there be to dead souls? Why there just isn't any [*dazhe i prichiny net*]! (VI:189–90/242)

Reason and logic, sense and nonsense, meaning and the quest for it: these are the themes of *Dead Souls*, the tracks left by the book's true hero. This passage concludes with a list of synonyms for nonsense, that is, for the radically uninterpretable.

Of course, the most ridiculous comment in this passage turns out to be that "there must be some reason" to the rumor or it would not have spread. As Gogol explains, rumors have the most currency, the greatest power to circulate, when there is nothing true about them, when people know there is nothing to them, and when they even conclude each retelling by complaining about the groundless lies people repeat.

The townspeople become hopelessly lost in the labyrinths of the explanatory process. In so doing, they fall into a trap set not by Chichikov, who least of all wants them to try to explain what he is up to, but by the author. Their entrapment results from fear, from resentment over Chichikov's perceived insults, and from the dynamics of spreading rumors; but it results above all from their competition in arriving at the right interpretation. In a duel of explanations, it would appear, the most farfetched have the advantage. Nonsensical arguments are not weeded out, they are, so to speak, weeded *in*.

As scholars form schools, the author tells us, the townspeople form parties, and so they arrive together at nonsense beyond the capacity of any one of them. For them as a group, as for Nozdrev alone, the very process of investigation stimulates the imagination.

The townspeople do just what humanity always does, just what scholars above all do, to solve a problem. They let their interpretive machinery grind away to produce elaborations and refinements, trills and flourishes, or—to use the terms of the two agreeable ladies—scallops and polka dots. Gogol draws the parallel between interpretive and sartorial fashions with disturbing accuracy. But the townspeople only get farther from the truth. The competition of closed systems multiplies their errors.

As we have seen, systems purport to explain facts, but they also create them when needed, which is one reason they can be so hermeneutically resistant. Gogol introduces this theme in the conversation of the agreeable ladies, and, with special brilliance, he does so not when they discuss Chichikov but when they debate the completely extraneous issue of the governor's daughter's complexion. You will recall that one lady insists that the complexion is as white as chalk while the other maintains, with no less conviction, that it is hopelessly rouged. Each cites as evidence how she herself once remarked on the chalkiness or reddening of the girl's face, much as one might defend one's spelling by showing one's own earlier use of the same spelling. The narrator interrupts to insist that such disagreements over basic facts are far from unusual:

> Still, let it not strike the reader as strange that both ladies could not come to an agreement as to what they had seen at almost one and the same time. There really are in this world many things which do have that very peculiarity; if one lady will take a look at them, they turn out to be perfectly white, whereas if another lady takes a look at them they will turn out to be red, red as bilberries. (VI:186/235)

Gogol here raises a question that has since become familiar in the philosophy of science and of history: are there facts independent of perceptual and interpretive frameworks?

The ladies eventually come to an agreement about Chichikov, but not on the basis of any evidence. No, they agree to agree because they need each other's access to current fashions and rumors; because they prefer discomfiting the men to arguing with each other; because they love the shape of their invented narrative; and, above all, because agreement itself gives a story a power it would not otherwise have. Perhaps we have here an allusion to the proof of God's existence by the "universal consent of mankind." Just as money is accepted because it is accepted, and value is produced by the process of evaluation, so conviction is produced by agreement.

Like scholars arguing over a theoretical problem, the town divides into "two diametrically opposed opinions and two diametrically opposed parties were suddenly formed" (VI:191/242). This passage may allude to the debate between the Nosarians and the Antinosarians in *Tristram Shandy*, but it certainly suggests a comparison with the debates of intellectuals. One school—the ladies—clearly and rapidly predominates because their account is more systematic and because they do not allow themselves to doubt. "In this party, it must be remarked to the credit of the ladies, there was incomparably more orderliness and circumspection. . . . In a very short while everything with them took on an animated, definite air, assuming clear and self-evident forms; everything became explained, clarified; in short, the result was a finished little masterpiece in oils" (VI:191/242). Although explanations pertain to content, form is what makes them convincing. In the face of such symmetry, even many of the men defect to the female party. Gogol gives us the dynamics of a theory's triumph or a discipline's founding.

Of course, there are some obvious logical problems with all the explanations that are proposed. To begin with, one might think that an explanation, to qualify as one, would have to be more readily understandable than the thing explained. It should somehow narrow, if not eliminate, the explanatory gap. But the townspeople's theories at best replace one gap with another of equal size. For example, how does the initial hypothesis that Chichikov plans to abduct the governor's daughter clarify his purchase of dead souls, which is the problem that the lady who advances this hypothesis is proposing to solve?

In trying to explain the abduction, the hypothesis that has now become a fact, the men offer still more elaborate theories—about Chichikov's "wife," for instance—that only widen the explanatory gap. Gogol's point is that once one forgets the cardinal principle that explanations must narrow, not widen, the gap in understanding, then the number of possible answers rapidly becomes infinite. Still more unsettling, the effort to choose among any two of them becomes futile or arbitrary. Why could Chichikov not be a counterfeiter, a brigand, Napoleon returned from Elba, the Antichrist, or Captain Kopeikin? Which is more difficult to understand: why Napoleon would sneak into Russia disguised as Chichikov or how Captain Kopeikin could fashion a new arm and leg? Whichever choice one makes, problems can be resolved in an instant: "After all, mechanical ingenuity had reached a very high point of perfection in England, that one could see by the papers where someone had invented wooden legs so ingeniously made that at the mere touch of an imperceptible spring they could carry a man off to God knows what regions, so that thereafter there was no such thing as finding him" (VI:205/274).

These attempts at model building also ignore another cardinal principle of explanation: to account for something in particular, an explanation must be specifically, not universally, applicable. An answer that can be given in advance to all possible questions does not really answer any particular question. To be sure, it is always possible to say of any event that it happened because it was caused, or that it was God's will, or that it is linked with other events of its time, or that it reflects the class struggle, or that it is self-deconstructing. And one may even take the sort of pleasure conferred by supplying one's favorite answer to the unenlightened or sharing it once again with other initiates. But such substitutes for illumination, which are no less common among intellectuals than among anyone else, provide no light at all.

When Gogol describes the townspeople's interest in politics, he mentions the fondness of some for explaining everything as a sign of the Antichrist. No matter what happens, it refers to the apocalypse. The merchants, it appears, were especially obsessed with such explanations "inasmuch as they had utter faith in the prediction of a certain prophet who had been sitting in jail for three years by now. This prophet had come no one knew whence, in bast sandals and an undressed sheepskin that reeked to high heaven of spoilt fish, and had proclaimed that Napoleon was Antichrist and was being kept on a chain of stone behind six walls and beyond seven seas, but that later on he would rend his chain and gain possession of all the world" (VI:206/276). Thus, instead of asking each other, "What price did you get for a measure of oats, father o' mine?" people now ask each other, "Have they let Napoleon slip away from that island again, by any chance?" (VI:206/275). They play with numerology and names in terms of their apocalyptic obsessions. This passage, of course, anticipates Pierre's numerological and apocalyptic enthusiasm in *War and Peace*. In both cases, millenarian sign seeking encapsulates all semiotic totalitarianism and all attempts to find a single meaning for everything.

Still more interesting for Gogol's hermeneutic parable is a different sort of explanatory move. What, we might ask, is the connection of the abduction to the dead souls? To this question, a remarkable answer is readily available: *the connection is that there is no connec-*

tion. The purchase of dead souls is interpreted as a "diversion," a scheme to distract attention, which means its very purpose demands that the two should have no connection with each other. (Of course, the fact that this diversion apparently attracted a lot of needless attention to the supposed abduction does not disturb anyone.) Closely related to this kind of explanation is the model of disguises and aliases: if there is no evidence that Chichikov looks like a romantic hero abducting a young girl, or a brigand, or a counterfeiter, or Napoleon, that only shows he is in disguise. And if there is no evidence that he is in disguise, that only shows how effective the disguise is, thus proving all the more surely that he is in disguise.

This sort of argument works by transforming nonevidence into evidence. The lack of proof becomes the best proof. Or to put the point differently, not only is this argument *about* dead souls, but it also repeats the very logic of "dead souls." In this case, it corresponds perfectly to its topic.

Such reasoning is sometimes referred to as the *argumentum e silentio* (the argument from silence), but I prefer a different term, *argumentum ex animis mortuis*: the argument from dead souls. Gogol is right: it is in fact extremely common in the intellectual, social, and political world. The very fact that there was no evidence for the conspiracy described in *The Protocols of the Elders of Zion* was taken by its circulators as the clearest possible proof that the conspiracy was supremely effective; and when a slander trial in Switzerland ended with the verdict that the *Protocols* were a forgery, its circulators concluded that the verdict demonstrated the universality of the Elders' influence.

Closer to home, Freudians often use the absence of evidence for an intention as proof that the intention is "repressed" and therefore all the more significant. That, indeed, is the beauty of the concept of repression, for either evidence or nonevidence demonstrates it. What we really see here is something that pertains to conspiracy logic per se, which is one reason it also finds a home in Marxist interpretation. When literary theorists produce combinations of Marxist, Freudian, and deconstructive readings, as they now so routinely do, we witness a veritable carnival of dead souls, a vaudeville of absences. The most important thing—critics now routinely argue—is what the poet has *not* said; why has he not posed the question of hegemony? What patriotism is to the scoundrel, the *argumentum ex animis mortuis* is to the scholar.[11]

Given the right interpretive tools, the world is infinitely interpretable. Gogol suggests yet another way in which meanings can multiply as rapidly as rumors, the principle of infinite allegorization.

"The Inspector of the Board of Health suddenly paled, seeing in his imagination God knows what: whether the phrase *dead souls* did not signify those patients who had died in considerable numbers in the infirmaries and similar institutions from an epidemic fever against which no adequate measures had been taken" (VI:193/244). Each of the officials goes through a similar process that involves two easy, if in this case, uncomfortable steps. First, interpret dead souls as an allegory for some *crime of absence*: an act either of significant omission or of commission that results in an absence (a fiction, a counterfeit, fraud, misrepresentation, erasure, or, at the worst, a death, which might itself be covered up with a fiction). Second, apply the allegory to oneself. This second step happens to correspond to what readers habitually do, and so another parallel is implicitly established between the mistakes we laugh at and those we make. The inspector's discovery of this step alters the tenor of the entire interpretive process for all the officials except the postmaster, who, the others explain, had no opportunity for either sins of omission or crimes of absence because his job did not offer sufficient opportunity. In this case, only absence explains the absence of crimes of absence.

Each official applies the inspector's method and each comes to see Chichikov as the undercover agent sent to discover the official's own worst crime. It is never explained *why* an agent would perform allegories of the crimes he investigates. Nevertheless, "all suddenly sought out in themselves such sins as they had not even committed" ("takie grekhi, kakikh dazhe ne bylo," VI:193/245), a line of real genius on Gogol's part. Any good satirist would have been content with people finding allusions to the crimes they had committed, but it takes Gogol to think of allegories of the crimes they had not committed. After all, no matter how many crimes one has committed, there are a much larger number that one has not, which multiplies the possibilities of allegory considerably. And what could be more appropriate than for an undercover agent to allegorize not only crimes of absence but also absent crimes? In the devil chapter of *Karamazov*, Dostoevsky takes this logic one step further when the devil, in suggesting Ivan's guilt for a crime of omission, makes his own nonexistence a living and allegorizable presence, a sort of allegory of the crime and of the very process of assigning an allegorical meaning to it.

By this point, the townspeople have so many algorithms, each capable of generating an infinity of explanations, that any new information about anything can easily be made to pertain to Chichikov. The point is that *nothing is irrelevant, everything is meaningful*: semiotic totalitarianism always makes accident, contingency, and lack of connection merely apparent. They can never be more than a temporary concealment of the "hidden something" underneath. Of course, Chichikov could not be the brigand sought by the governor of a neighboring province, but, on the other hand, has he not said something about having a great number of enemies who had even made attempts on his life? "When they had reasoned all this out and recalled everything, they pondered still more deeply: consequently his life must be in danger; consequently, he was being pursued; consequently, he must have been up to something or other after all. . . . But just who was he in reality?" (VI:195/248). This chain of non sequiturs then accommodates the most disquieting implication, that there might be some connection between the arrival of Chichikov and the appointment of the new governor-general. Once one assumes connection and eliminates "mere coincidence," then one has gone beyond even the need to allegorize; mere simultaneity is enough to establish whatever meaning one wants to find. As Marxists once liked to say, "it is no accident that . . . " Or in the more recent formulation, one can read a given period of a culture's history as one would read a poem.

As Gogol begins this section of *Dead Souls* with his long digression on scholarly interpretation, he closes it with another that suggests we are all guilty of the townspeople's errors (VI:210–11/281–82). It is well known that this sort of metaliterary assault on the reader—"Whom are you laughing at? You're laughing at yourselves"—is not uncommon in Gogol's works. It is perhaps somewhat less familiar that such frame-breaking insults are characteristic of Menippean satire as a genre, with its tendency to assimilate the universe—context, audience, the author himself—into the fictitious world it portrays and mocks.

The narrator of *Dead Souls* allows the reader to object that "all this is absurd! This is utterly preposterous! It's impossible that these officials . . . should go so far astray from the truth, when even the veriest babe can see what the whole business is about!" (VI:210/281). The narrator's answer, for all its characteristically askew syntax and tonality, is uncharacteristically direct and to the point. The chronicle of absurd, blind, and vain explanation readers regard as "impossible" is not only possible but actually quite common; and the readers themselves behave the same way. If they do not see this, it is because they are no less prone than the townspeople to exempt themselves from laughter they direct at others; for "man is openhanded with the word *fool* and is ready to deal it out twenty times a day to his fellow man," who is just like him (VI:210/281). However clever we may be in applying our interpretive systems, we do not step outside them.

As readers, we stand outside the characters' systems and laugh at them, and so we assume that in daily life we behave the same way. The very act of reading provides a false comfort, an unearned exemption from criticism. "It's easy enough for the readers to sit in judgment within their tranquil and lofty retreats, whence they have the whole horizon unobscured before them and can see all that is going on below where a man can see only the object which is near at hand" (VI:210/281), the narrator observes.

This "reader's fallacy," as we might call it, reappears in various forms throughout life. We have numerous ways of adopting a spurious viewpoint that seems to exempt us from criticism applied to others. For example, each generation tends to regard preceding ones with the same sense of superiority that readers assume toward characters. The present, like the frame of reading, allows us to sit in tranquil judgment, but that tranquillity is entirely unearned and unjustified. The present generation—and all generations think of themselves as "present"—surveys the errors and delusions of the past from the calm certainty of values and beliefs that are presumed wiser. (We have once again arrived at current literary theory.)

From the perspective of present wisdom, Gogol observes, one can detect "in the universal chronicle of mankind . . . many unbroken centuries which one would, it seems, like to delete and do away with as unnecessary. Many delusions have overtaken this world, which delusions even a child, apparently, would not be subject to now" (VI:210/281). And how odd this appears, Gogol's narrator continues, because the straight and true path of mankind to "the eternal truth"—to current wisdom, that is—was open for all to see, "lit up by the sun and illumined all night by lights, yet it is past it, in a profound darkness, that men have streamed" (VI:210/282). Like the readers who laugh at the townspeople, the present generation assumes that it

> sees everything clearly now; it wonders at the delusions and laughs at the lack of comprehension of its ancestors, not perceiving that this chronicle is written over with heavenly fire, that every letter therein is calling out to it, that from every direction a piercing forefinger is pointed at it—at it and none other than it, the present generation. But the present generation laughs and, self-reliantly, proudly launches a new succession of delusions, over which its descendants will laugh in their turn, even as the present generation is laughing now. (VI:211/282)

These delusions are, of course, the latest disguises of the real hero of *Dead Souls*.

From the perspective of Gogol's own literary descendants, two important observations may be made concerning this passage. First, the idea that the very position of the reader may be compromising—morally or epistemically—was to have a long and rich career in Russian literature. It led both to the motif of authors renouncing literature (or burning their works, as Gogol did) and to radical experiments designed to overcome or at least make explicit the dangers of "the reader's fallacy." Here Tolstoy above all comes to mind. Bakhtin's theory of polyphony in effect describes a way for both authors and readers to overcome the illegitimate "surplus of knowledge" their position as authors and readers provides. Second, and no less important, the idea that the present always seems to offer an illegitimately privileged perspective was to lead to some of the richest works of Russian historical and antiutopian thought, beginning with Herzen's *From the Other Shore* and extending to Zamyatin's *We*—and beyond. To use Zamyatin's terms, the assumption that the present offers a privileged perspective is equivalent to the belief that a given number is the highest one.

5. PURE ANOMALY AND ABSOLUTE NONSENSE

Dead Souls does eventually offer the correct answer to the townspeople's questions. We learn who Chichikov is and why he wants dead souls. To be sure, this explanation is rather banal and much less interesting than the sprawling mountain of nonsense Gogol piles upon it. As scholars have often noted, Gogol characteristically uses an insipid starting point or trivial anecdote as a pretext. "The Nose," however, omits the pretext and does away with the final explanation. It stands as Gogol's purest, and perhaps most profound, piece of nonsense.

In this respect, "The Nose" goes well beyond "The Diary of a Madman." In the latter, the rich trove of nonsense is, to use the Formalist term, "motivated." For the hero is mad, and his increasingly absurd observations, which soon cease to make sense even in their own nonsensical terms, measure his fall into insanity. If one assumes that dogs can write, then the canine correspondence the hero discovers near the beginning of the story does make a curious sort of sense. But the diary headings at the end of the story—"Martober 86 between day and night" or (still more obviously) "No date. The day had no date"—make no sense in any terms. Increasing insanity therefore becomes a vehicle for exploring more extreme kinds and degrees of nonsense.

But in "The Nose" there is no such vehicle. To be sure, Gogol considered presenting the story as a dream, but he eventually chose—wisely—to offer his nonsense unadorned, unmotivated, and above all unexplained. It stands, arguably, as his richest parable of explanation.

In "The Nose" numerous explanatory systems encounter a series of events that are radically inexplicable. These events simply make no sense whatsoever. Kovalev tries to understand them in order to get his nose back, and critics from Gogol's time to ours have tried to impose an interpretive scheme on the story. Even more than *Dead Souls*, this story parodies in advance the history of its interpretation and transforms its readers into characters in an infinitely extendable frame narrative.

To understand Gogol's main point in "The Nose," it might be helpful to consider a more recent attempt to do something quite similar, Stanislaw Lem's novel-length explanatory parable *The Investigation. The Investigation* is far from Lem's best work, but its very transparency makes it a good glass for viewing Gogol's considerably more complex tale.

The Investigation foregrounds its status as a hermeneutic parable. Its epistemologically minded detectives, who quote philosophy, literature, mathematics, and physics, evidently represent the human effort to explain the world and embody the faith that it is ultimately explicable. They find out otherwise. A bizarre series of events, involving corpses that move—dead souls?—seems to allow for no possible explanation. That much is characteristic of detective stories in general, of course, but in this narrative no hidden causal sequence is uncovered to explain the apparently impossible. On the contrary, what the investigators eventually discover is that the incidents *have no explanation*. They belong to a class of events that are absolutely uncaused. "What if the world isn't scattered around us like a jigsaw puzzle," one detective asks,

> what if it's like a soup with all kinds of things floating around in it, and from time to time some of them get stuck together by chance to make some kind of whole? What if everything that exists is fragmentary, incomplete, aborted, events with ends but no beginnings, events that only have middles, things that have fronts or rears but not both, with us constantly making categories, seeking out, and reconstructing, until we think we can see total love, total betrayal and defeat, although in reality we are all no more than haphazard fractions. . . . On every side of us we see bits of life that are completely beyond our understanding—we label them unusual, but we really don't want to acknowledge them. . . . An infinite number of Things taunt our fondness for Order. Seek, and ye shall find. . . . [12]

Or as another detective remarks, perhaps God exists only from time to time.

The series of events in "The Nose" are even stranger than those in *The Investigation*.[13] Let us dwell for a moment on a few of the questions that a good explanation of this story's plot would have to answer: How does Kovalev lose his nose? If the barber cut it off when he shaved Kovalev on Wednesday, then why, as Kovalev asks, was the nose in its proper place on Thursday? Whether or not the barber cut it off, how did the nose get into the barber's roll? Why is there no scar; why is Kovalev's face "as flat as a pancake"? How does the nose grow to human size, and, still more perplexing, how does it become human? Given that it becomes biologically human, how does it become socially human? How does the nose develop a specific identity and a history—a rank in the service and a set of acquaintances—and what happens to the memory of others to make them think they have known him? Does this perplexing event somehow manage to alter the past? How does the nose become a nose again, and, having done so, how does it resume its proper place on Kovalev's face?

In addition to these problems, there are others of a different kind. "An inexplicable phenomenon takes place" when Kovalev sees the gentleman in uniform get out of his carriage and run up the steps: "What was the horror and at the same time amazement of Kovalev when he recognized that this was his own nose!" (III:54/479).[14] How is this act of *recognition*, which seems to parody recognition scenes throughout the history of literature, accomplished? After all, it is one thing to recognize someone as one's own brother, another to recognize him as one's own nose, however syntactically similar the two constructions might be. For one has seen one's brother before, but one has never seen one's nose as a full-sized person, nor has one heard of such events happening to others. Recognition or learning—and certainly the *shock* of recognition experienced by Kovalev—implies some earlier experience that is similar. What could that experience be? Has Kovalev at one time lost his ear? A special feature of this story is that even to comprehend its incidents in the most literal way is to generate whole other narratives of which there is no explicit mention. Moreover, at least Kovalev knows he has lost a nose when he sees the Nose "disguised" as a government official; but what about the nearsighted policeman (and what has nearsightedness got to do with a problem of recognition of this kind?) who arrests the Nose as it is boarding a stagecoach to Riga?

The narrator uses the phrase "an inexplicable phenomenon" ("iavlenie neiz"iasnimoe") rhetorically as we so often do—to indicate a very *unusual* event. Kovalev, too, sees the event as a sort of freak accident, as a rare piece of bad luck. But that description is itself absurd, because rare events at least have an identifiable, if bizarre, causal chain to explain them. What is absurd about this event is that it is impossible to imagine such a causal chain at all. The event is quite literally, not rhetorically, "inexplicable."

At least Kovalev is amazed, but others do not even see anything strange. When Kovalev first wakes up and asks his servant for water to rub his eyes, the servant does not remark on the change in his face; and the doctor he summons to reattach his nose also reacts as if the problem were commonplace. The narrator, in calling the narrative "improbable," also has in mind something extremely mundane: "How was it that Kovalev did not grasp that he could not advertise about his nose in a newspaper office? I do not mean to say that I should think it is too expensive to advertise . . . but it is improper, awkward, not nice!" (III:75/497).

Thus some see the incidents as ordinary, others as very rare, but only one character, upon hearing of the events, reacts appropriately and can make no sense at all of them: that character is the Nose. " 'I understand absolutely nothing,' said the nose. 'Explain it more satisfactorily' " (III:56/481). When Kovalev tells the Nose that he is only an anatomical feature, the Nose responds as most of us would: he fails to understand, tries to intimidate Kovalev into leaving him alone, and escapes as soon as Kovalev's attention is distracted. In short, the only one who talks sense in "The Nose" is the Nose. The reader's perspective is therefore closest neither to the author's nor to the hero's but to that of the eponymous "phenomenon."

What would it mean to explain this story? Most literally, one might be asking for a causal explanation of the events that would make sense of them. And it should be evident that this is an extremely difficult, if not impossible, thing to do, because very different *sorts* of phenomena have to be accounted for. Whatever caused Kovalev to lose his nose without feeling it and the barber to find it in his breakfast—a lost-and-found plot, however weird—would not, one supposes, go very far toward elucidating how the nose develops a social position. To be sure, one could resort to an all-purpose solution, such as a dream or a demon, but that would be more an abdication than an explanation. For explanations of this sort can account for any sequence of events a priori, that is, one could explain any fantastic narrative as a dream before one knows anything at all about it. For that matter, one could explain realistic stories the same way. Such "solutions" cannot elucidate any particular sequence of events because they elucidate all of them equally well; explaining everything, they explain nothing.

One could ask, moreover, how does one explain the dream? That would be easy if one had a system for doing so—the dream book of some Sigmund Zadeka—but for Gogol a dream is "simply incoherent excerpts, which have no sense, taken from what we have thought and then pasted together to make up a kind of salad."[15] But perhaps the most decisive objection to all-purpose explanations is that they explain the story by taking it away from us, by making it uninteresting; one cannot appreciate the story and think of the answer at the same time. Such a solution would therefore be very different in kind—and completely unsatisfying—from the explanations we are given in *Dead Souls* and *The Inspector General*. In those works, the knowledge of Chichikov's scheme or Khlestakov's identity does not diminish the story, as the "dream" solution impoverishes "The Nose."

Gogol has clearly made every effort to make causal linkage impossible to find. No one, at least, has found it, and we can be readily convinced, I think, that it is not as if Gogol had a causal sequence in mind and has made the story a kind of rebus or riddle. On the contrary, we sense that even if someone should someday find a principle capable of accounting for this weird sequence of events—say, something in theoretical physics as applied to the physiology of growth and consciousness—the explanation would be wrong even if it did fit, perhaps even because it fit. What we have in "The Nose" is a sequence of "inexplicable phenomena" related inexplicably to each other.

In asking for an explanation of the story, one might also have in mind an allegorical interpretation. However they are caused, what do these events mean? Quite different problems afflict the search for this sort of explanation. As causal explanations are impossible to find, allegorical ones are too easy. Multiple, perhaps infinite, interpretations suggest themselves. I think Donald Fanger is correct in his observations about the interpretability of "The Nose":

> Readers in search of profundity have found it there by following their own noses, seeing the story as an indictment of physicality, an orthodox Freudian castration fantasy, a sermon against godlessness, a symbolic comment on the drift away from Orthodox observance, and so on. Most of these interpretations are plausible, and justified to a point, but each is unconvincing because too much of the text escapes it. Gogol has created a puzzle that many keys may fit, but none open. [It is] a trap for the unwary.[16]

These interpretations are unsatisfying if we perform what might be taken as a necessary test for all readings, measuring them against our experience of reading the work itself. Somehow we feel that Gogol could have written a Freudian allegory with a plot similar to that of "The Nose," but that such an interpretation of *this* story is absurd. And we feel in advance that the result would be the same regardless of what hermeneutic algorithm was applied.

The problem is not that the story impedes allegorical interpretation; quite the contrary, the problem is that it offers *no resistance at all* to it. All interpretations are equally possible and so are equally unsatisfying. The fact is that constraints of some sort are necessary for interpretation to proceed productively. To use Wittgenstein's analogy: "We have got on to slippery ice where there is no friction and so in a certain sense the conditions are ideal, but also, just because of that, we are unable to walk. We want to walk: so we need *friction*. Back to the rough ground!"[17]

Gogol gives us the first allegorical interpretation of the story in the story itself. When Kovalev writes to Madame Podtochina to protest what has happened to his nose, she interprets it (understandably enough) not literally but as an allegory of Kovalev's "courtship" of her daughter. "You make some reference to your nose also," she replies. "If you wish me to understand by that that you imagine that I meant to make a long nose at you, that is to give you a formal refusal, I am surprised that you should speak of such a thing" (III:71/493). She does what the townspeople in *Dead Souls* do, what the mayor and officials in *The Inspector General* do, what we all do: she interprets the nonsense in terms of her own obsessions. And what else can she (and we) do? Nevertheless, Kovalev immediately recognizes that her interpretation is incorrect.

Thus causal interpretation is defeated by resistance that seems total and allegorical interpretation by resistance that is absent. Interpretation is possible only in the middle ground, when constraints operate with sufficient power to limit but not completely eliminate alternatives.

Like *Dead Souls*, "The Nose" constantly alludes to the problem of explanation. Kovalev and the narrator frequently refer to events as "inexplicable," much as characters in *Dead Souls* ask, over and over again, what dead souls "signify." The very first thing we learn about Kovalev, before he discovers that his nose is missing, is that he makes a certain sound whenever he wakes up "though he could not himself have explained the reason for his doing so" ("khotia sam ne mog rastolkovat', po kakoi prichine," III:52/477). We learn late in the story that this Plato—Kovalev's first name is Platon—has been sent to the Caucasus several times "to conduct investigations" (III:71/493). The hero of this explanatory parable is a part-time detective, the first important metaphysical detective in Russian literature.

How does an investigator—or anyone—explain an anomaly and take appropriate action with respect to it? The first thing one normally does is to discover what *kind* of an anomaly it is, the system of rules or norms that it violates. Only then can one know what to do. For every system has both a prescribed way to handle violations and a social institution dedicated to that purpose. In short, one *classifies* the anomaly and then *refers* it to the proper professional.

Kovalev tries to do just that, only he cannot figure out what sort of anomaly a nose masquerading as a civil councillor is, and each attempt at classification fails. The better part of the story consists of his attempts to get somebody to accept responsibility for the missing nose, to accept the incidents as a violation of some prescribed jurisdiction, so that action of the appropriate sort can be undertaken. He never succeeds, because this is an anomaly unlike all others. It is a wholly anomalous anomaly, an anomaly to no particular system, a *pure* anomaly.

As an investigator, Kovalev first assumes that the system violated is the law, and so he immediately thinks of the police: "He ordered his clothes to be given to him at once and flew off straight to the police commissioner" (III:53/478). Class the missing nose as a crime—a theft?—and it is clear what to do about it. But on the way to the police, he encounters the nose impersonating a government official. Perhaps what is involved is a violation of bureaucratic procedure, in which case Kovalev should consult the nose's superiors in the service?

Other systems, each with their own predetermined violations, occur to Kovalev. He lost it out of foolishness—"I couldn't have been idiotic enough to lose my nose" (III:54/479)—and so he tries to advertise in the newspaper. There he is told that the problem is medical: "If it is lost, that is a matter for the doctor" (III:61/486). The possibilities multiply: the newspaper man misunderstands and thinks Kovalev is speaking of a runaway serf; Kovalev refers to the event as "some swindle or trickery" (III:60/484); he recalls his rather too close shave at the barber; he wishes that he had only lost the nose in a duel or a battle; and he imagines he might be drunk. The story offers a panoply of systems, anomalies, and corresponding remedies, none of which work. Kovalev at last finds his way to the local police inspector, who reclassifies the problem as a *breach of manners* of which Kovalev himself is guilty: "A respectable person does not have his nose pulled off" (III:63/487).[18]

The narrator continues this classificatory avalanche when he reports on the rumors concerning the nose. People soon began saying that "the nose of a collegiate assessor called Kovalev was walking along Nevsky Prospect at exactly three in the afternoon" (III:71/494), and they flocked to see this "freak of nature" ("igra prirody," III:72/494). There are two problems with this explanation. If "freak of nature" is taken in a narrow sense—as an anomaly to normal natural processes, like the birth of a two-headed calf—then it is hard to see how the social dimensions of the story, such as the nose's position in the service, are clarified. If "freak of nature" is taken (as is more likely) in a broader sense, as a term for all bizarre occurrences, then we have an explanation that does not explain at all. Rather, we have an example of the depressingly familiar practice of renaming something and then assuming one has thereby explained it. Explaining a bizarre event as a freak of nature is like accounting for Einstein's creativity by saying he was a genius or explaining the ways of God by saying they are mysterious. Gogol's point—one commonly made in satires of philosophy from Aristophanes to Molière and Sterne—is that what passes for knowledge is often counterfeit currency taken for true coin, an "insubstantial sound" passed off as substantial, an estate consisting entirely of dead souls.

The adventures of the nose are neither a freak of nature nor a supernatural occurrence nor a delusion: they are not *explicable in any way*. They exceed (but invite) explanation in terms of any system, even an alternative logic. The first sentence of chapter 3 reads: "Absolute nonsense happens in the world" ("Chepukha sovershennaia delaetsia na svete," III:73/495). What we have here is *absolute* nonsense, nonsense that conforms not even to a system of nonsense, as (for instance) the nonsense in Edward Lear or Lewis Carroll does.[19] The world we live in contains such nonsense and is partially shaped by events beyond explanation of any sort. "Despite what anyone may say, such things do happen—not often, but they do happen" (III:75/497).

6. THE ORDINARY

I have stated that Gogol's works belong to the tradition of Menippean satire that extends from Lucian to Lem. But it would be a mistake to overlook a crucial difference between *Dead Souls* and *Dialogues of the Dead*. Gogol's narrative was written during the great age of the psychological and realistic novel, and it insists polemically on the ways it is unlike that genre. Gogol, in short, took advantage of what Bakhtin would call a new "dialogizing background" to give his works a kind of complexity unavailable to his predecessors.

Lack of interiority in characters is a generic desideratum of Menippean satire. Unlike their counterparts in philosophical novels, the heroes of Lucian, Rabelais, and Voltaire embody philosophical positions without any corresponding psychological depth. Menippus in Lucian's dialogues and Candide or Pangloss in *Candide* are wholly two-dimensional, but we do not sense anything missing; we recognize that the authors have purposes different from those of the novel and that they are accomplishing "generic tasks" of a very different kind. In Gogol, however, the lack of interiority is felt precisely as a lack of something that might have been present, that somehow *ought* to be present. We read Gogol *against* the tradition of the novel. And we do so not just because his works happen to have been written in the mid nineteenth century, but because he constantly recalls the novelistic qualities his characters fail to possess. Thus, we sense as typical of *Dead Souls*, but not of *Candide* or *Gulliver's Travels*, descriptions like that of Chichikov's superior in the service: "There was just nothing at all in him, either of wickedness or of goodness, and there was a manifestation of something frightful in this absence of everything" (VI:229/307).

Gogol uses the novel to shape his works negatively. It turns mere absences into palpable voids, which become comic or horrifying because of what, from a novelistic perspective, should be present. Or to put the point differently, Gogol used the new literary milieu in which he wrote to exploit the "generic potential" of Menippean satire in an especially profound way that was largely unavailable to his predecessors.

The effects Gogol derives from this innovation in Menippean satire would seem to be essential to his works' literary power. In these effects we sense what is truly "Gogolian" about Gogol. For example, much of the humor of "The Overcoat" depends on constant reminders of the sort of interior self that Akakii Akakievich *might* have had—the self that Dostoevsky *restores* to Makar Devushkin. The story's plot constantly alludes to romantic stories in which love reveals a person's inner depths, but unlike his counterparts in such stories Akakii has almost as little interiority as his well-lined coat. Just before the coat's "abduction" on his "wedding night," Akakii reveals the first primitive glimmerings of a wandering imagination and an embryonic soul, only to have the narrator call our attention to what has been missing all along: "Why did he smile? Was it because he had come across something quite unfamiliar to him. . . . Though possibly he did not even think that; there is no creeping into a man's soul and finding out what he thinks" (III:159/578). Passages like these, which "bare the device" of *the self that might have been*, recur throughout Gogol's narratives and usually mark a key moment in their complex play of tones.

In *Dead Souls* the absence of an inner self becomes most obviously tangible when the public prosecutor dies. As a corpse, he becomes in reality what he has symbolically been all along, "a body bereft of a soul. Only then did they find out, with regret, that the Public Prosecutor had had a soul, although out of modesty he had never flaunted it" (VI:210/281). Of course, the very title *Dead Souls* constantly reminds readers of what the characters lack and, in the process, takes a sideward glance at all those European novelistic titles naming real people with real depth and specific places that are not like all other places. If Russia had not itself later become the birthplace of the world's greatest psychological novels, if after Gogol there had not appeared Dostoevsky and Tolstoy, we might have come to think of Russian literature as antipsychological fiction "peopled" by "dead souls." Each time the title phrase is used, it suggests an intergeneric dialogue with the European novel, much as its subtitle, *poema*, and numerous poetic passages suggest an intergeneric dialogue with the epic.

Reminders of a lack are so important to Gogol's art that he is able to achieve special power when, contrary to his usual practice, he surprises us, if ever so briefly, with a real living soul. In this way, our laughter at emptiness "reverses direction" and turns into genuine pathos at the end of "The Diary of a Madman." Unexpectedly, we sense that greatest of rarities in Gogol, the real "freak of nature" in his world, a suffering soul. From an artistic standpoint, the effectiveness of this passage derives from a "negation of a negation": we have become used to the absence of a novelistic self, and that absence suddenly disappears.

Since antiquity, generic mixing and "intergeneric dialogues" have been regarded as defining features of Menippean satire. So have paradoxes, particularly those that depend on taking Nothing as a sort of something and absence as a kind of presence. In a sense, then, we might say that Gogol's generic innovation of making the absence of novelness into an essential theme of his works remains deeply and doubly Menippean in spirit. His works are Menippean to their absent core.

Gogol's debt to this ancient genre appears as well in his insistence that *The Inspector General* does have one "honorable, noble character acting over its course. This honorable character is—*laughter*."[20] In *Dead Souls* he also complains that the public "does not recognize that lofty, rapturous laughter is worthy of taking its place side by side with a lofty, lyrical strain" (VI:134/166). Statements of this sort are a trope of Menippean satire, which—unlike other forms of satire—allows for nothing that is exempt from mockery. To those who know Lucian, Gogol's statements might recall numerous passages that make Laughter the only hero. In *Dialogues of the Dead*, for example, Charon and Hermes demand that all souls ferried to Hades must divest themselves of anything that might weigh down the boat. They must strip themselves of everything—not only clothes and ornaments but even the beauty of the body itself; and beyond that, it turns out that even certain apparently intangible qualities or attributes, such as vanity, effeminacy, and fame, add unnecessary ballast and must be cast off. The genre's spokesman, Menippus, laughs at each character forced to give up what he prizes most, and the genre's traditional target, the philosopher, receives a particularly stern order from Hermes:

> You there, off first with your clothes, and then with all this here. Ye gods, what hypocrisy he carries, what ignorance, contentiousness, vanity, unanswerable puzzles, thorny argumentations, and complicated conceptions—yes, and plenty of wasted effort and no little nonsense, and idle talk, and splitting of hairs. . . . Away with your falsehood too, and your pride, and notions of your superiority over the rest of men. If you came on board with all these, not even a battleship would be big enough for you.[21]

In resentment, the philosopher demands that the mocking Menippus also divest himself of his defining qualities—independence, plain speaking, cheerfulness, noble bearing, and above all laughter, which informs them all. But Hermes makes an exception for such qualities alone: "Do nothing of the sort, Menippus; they're light and easy to carry, and useful for the voyage."[22] In choosing as his spokesman the jester Yorick, who above all hates "gravity," Sterne was also situating himself firmly in this tradition. Laughter is the height of human wisdom because it does not weigh things down, because it has almost no gravity.

Menippean satires characteristically mock all philosophies, even those closest to their own ethos, like stoicism. All philosophies are and always will be spurious goods "for sale." In a similar spirit, Gogol mocks not just particular explanatory models but the human capacity for explanation itself. He does not create satires of particular systems in the name of others that might be better, but *Menippean* satires on all human understanding. That is one reason his only positive hero is laughter.

It is for these reasons that I see Gogol as the most profound thinker in the tradition I have called the "obverse of the Russian idea." In this tradition, systems are answered by nonsense, and by nonsense alone. We might put it this way: the generic tradition in which Gogol worked best, the one closest to his own vision and most suitable to his talents, barred him from offering a real alternative to semiotic totalitarianism because real alternatives are not a viable option in Menippean satire. In more recent terms, we could say that Gogol never gets beyond the radically skeptical strain in poststructuralism.

By contrast, the real Russian alternative to semiotic totalitarianism—prosaics—developed a line of thought implicit in the *novel* as a genre.

To see why Gogol was precluded from prosaic insights by his favored genre, it would be helpful to consider the status of the ordinary and the everyday—prosaic life—in his works. The ordinary is central to both Gogol and Tolstoy (or other prosaic thinkers), but its meaning for them could not be more different.

Gogol commented frequently on the importance of describing the trivial, the contemptible, and the low. He praised the sort of artistic vision that could find the extraordinary in the ordinary.[23] In *Dead Souls*, we recall, the narrator defends at length the vocation of the satirist, who, unlike the epic poet, does not conceal "all that fearsome, overwhelming, slimy morass of minutiae [*tina melochei*] that have bogged down our life" (VI:134/166). He laments the vanity of readers who prefer epic portraits of people as heroic to satiric portraits of people as petty. Such readers, we are told, regard the satirist as a slanderer of human nature who is guilty of the shortcomings he attributes to others. They fail to recognize that "equally marvellous are the lenses that are used for contemplating suns and those for revealing to us the motions of insects imperceptible to the naked eye" (VI:134/166). So satirists have defended themselves against criticism, and blamed the shortsightedness of their critics, since antiquity.

In fact, this famous "defense of satire" passage in *Dead Souls* is a web of tropes drawn from the history of satire. Its play of tones is especially complex and its overall import is consequently difficult to fix. On the whole, I am inclined to take it as characteristically Menippean. As we have seen, whereas some satires scourge vices in the name of opposing virtues, Menippean satires tend to exempt nothing from criticism. They leave *no* secure vantage point, and if one is temporarily offered, the reader who seeks to occupy it soon finds that he stands on false ground. The morally and epistemically unsettling quality of this genre derives in large measure from this tendency to leave us no place to stand.

For this reason, Menippean satire typically includes a moment when the satirist turns on the modality of satire itself. The satirist who has been mocking the vanity of others takes pride in his courage or moral purity; he praises himself for his unique immunity to self-deception; he self-righteously denounces others who do not appreciate him. Ambrose Bierce's *Devil's Dictionary* thus defines an egotist as "a person of low taste, more interested in himself than in me."[24] Gulliver's prideful denunciation of the human species, from which he exempts himself, turns on a version of the Menippean paradox: humanity is entirely vicious, and the worst of vices is misanthropy.[25] Or if we were to try to arrive at Gogolian formulations, they might be something like this:

> Sobakevich: There is only one exception to universal vice, and he too is a swine.
> Nozdrev: Believe me, I am telling you as a friend, everyone always lies, myself included.
> Gogol: The universe is a counterfeit of which there is no original.

As an intrinsic part of this Menippean work, the defense of satire passage seems to be infected with tones of self-parody. One may detect them in the passage's overblown rhetoric, which is not much different from Chichikov's: "Fortunate is the wayfarer. . . . Happy is the writer. . . . Not such, however, is the lot, and different is the fate, of the writer who has dared. . . . not his will it be to behold responsive tears and the wholesome rapture of the souls he has stirred" (VI:133–34/164–66). Tonalities of self-pity mark this passage as surely as they do Chichikov's daydreams. We may also recall the obviously parodic use of a narrator's lyricism in "Nevsky Prospect," in the tale of the two Ivans, and in "The Overcoat." Gogol seems to be creating a narrative stance similar to Pushkin's in *Eugene Onegin*. There, too, every voice that the author assumes, every mask he puts on, is subject to subsequent parody, not excluding the voice of the universal parodist who mocks everything.[26]

But however arch this passage may be, and however careful we must be in reading any of Gogol's lyrical digressions, it does seem to present a *vision of the ordinary* that corresponds with Gogol's practice. Though suspicious of its own motives, Menippean satire does tend to focus on "all that fearsome, overwhelming slimy morass of minutiae that have bogged down our life" (VI:134/166). Gogol's greatest works portray the world of *byt* (everyday life) as hopelessly vulgar, nonsensical, and empty. Either the ordinary is beyond meaning entirely or it can be redeemed only by something completely alien to it, a transcendent theological presence. For Gogol, as for all hedgehogs, either meaning is guaranteed or it is a dead soul.

By contrast, prosaics, the Russian counteridea, requires no such guarantees. The world of ordinary life is depicted not as meaningless unless illuminated from beyond but as the only place meaning is to be found, not as requiring redemption but as potentially redeeming. It is as if Tolstoy answered *Dead Souls* by having us contemplate his fully living ones. At the end of *War and Peace*, Pierre at last learns Karatayev's prosaic lesson that meaning is always right before our eyes and so he at last discards the "telescope through which he had till then been gazing over the heads of men, and joyfully surveyed the ever-changing, great, unfathomable, and infinite life around him. And the closer he looked, the happier and more serene he became."[27] When we recall that the narrator of *Dead Souls* can only imagine exchanging a telescope for a microscope, we see the enormous difference between Gogol and Tolstoy, between negation and a real alternative, between the failure of explanation and the vanishing of the question. The difference is partially one of individual vision and experience, and partially the consequence of favored genres. It derives above all from distinct visions of the ordinary.

Notes on the Contributors

Andrei Bitov (Moscow and Leningrad), one of the most important contemporary writers of Russian prose, received the Lenin prize in 1988. His collection of stories *Life in Windy Weather* (ed. Priscilla Meyer) and his novel *Pushkin House* have been published in the United States. *Pushkin House* received the prize for the best foreign novel in France in 1989. The collection *The Teacher of Symmetry* is being translated by Susan Brownsberger, and a book of literary essays, *Life without Us* (trans. Priscilla Meyer), is forthcoming.

Sergei Bocharov (Gorkii Institute of World Literature, Moscow) is a scholar and critic whose interests range from Tolstoy and Dostoevsky to Mikhail Bakhtin. He is now working on an edition of the émigré poet Khodasevich and is assistant editor of the new *Complete Works* of Gogol, now being compiled at the Gorkii Institute. The Gogol conference at Wesleyan was the occasion of Bocharov's first visit to the United States.

Susanne Fusso, Assistant Professor of Russian Language and Literature at Wesleyan University, has a book, *Designing Dead Souls: An Anatomy of Disorder in Gogol*, forthcoming from Stanford University Press. A chapter has appeared in the *Slavic Review* ("*Dead Souls*: Fragment, Parable, Promise"), and a Russian version of her paper in the present volume will appear in the Soviet publication *Gogolevskii sbornik: Materialy i issledovaniia*. She is the co-editor and translator, with Olga Peters Hasty, of *America through Russian Eyes* (Yale University Press, 1988).

Frederick T. Griffiths, Professor of Classics at Amherst College, is the author of *Theocritus at Court* (Leiden: Brill, 1979) and, with Stanley J. Rabinowitz, of *Novel Epics: Gogol, Dostoevsky, and National Narra-*

tive (Northwestern University Press, 1990). He has written on assorted topics in classical and comparative literature.

Robert L. Jackson is Professor of Slavic Languages and Literatures at Yale University. He is a scholar of nineteenth-century Russian literature, especially of Dostoevsky, Turgenev, and Chekhov. His publications include *Dostoevsky's Quest for Form* (Yale University Press, 1965), *The Art of Dostoevsky* (Princeton University Press, 1981), and "Two Views of Gogol' and the Critical Synthesis: Belinskii, Rozanov and Dostoevsky: An Essay in Literary Historical Criticism" (*Russian Literature*, 1984).

John Kopper is Assistant Professor of Russian at Dartmouth College. He is at work on a study of metaphor in Proust, Kafka, Belyi, and Gombrowicz. He has written on Nabokov, Belyi, Aleshkovsky, Pasternak, Kafka, and Shakespeare.

Katherine Lahti is a Ph.D. candidate at Yale University, and Instructor of Russian at Trinity College (Hartford, Connecticut). She is finishing a dissertation on classicism in the works of Vladimir Maiakovskii, and conducting research on theatrical movements of the early twentieth century.

Iurii Mann (Gorkii Institute of World Literature, Moscow) has published extensively on Gogol. His works include "Evoliutsiia gogolevskoi fantastiki" (The evolution of the fantastic in Gogol) (1973), *Poetika Gogolia* (The poetics of Gogol) (Moscow, 1978; 2nd ed. 1988), and *V poiskakh zhivoi dushi: "Mertvye dushi": Pisatel'-Kritika-Chitatel'* (In search of a living soul: *Dead Souls*: writer-critic-reader) (Moscow, 1984). He is chief editor of the new twenty-three-volume *Complete Works* of Gogol, now being compiled at the Gorkii Institute.

Priscilla Meyer is Professor of Russian Language and Literature at Wesleyan University. Her study of Nabokov's *Pale Fire, Find What the Sailor Has Hidden*, was published by Wesleyan University Press in 1988. Her other publications include an edition and translation, with Stephen Rudy, *Dostoevsky and Gogol: Texts and Criticism*; an edition of the stories of Andrei Bitov, *Life in Windy Weather* (Ardis, 1986); and "Dostoevsky, 'Mr. Prokharchin,' and Naturalist Poetics" (*Russian Literature*, 1981). A Russian version of her paper in the present volume will appear in the Soviet publication *Gogolevskii sbornik: Materialy i issledovaniia*.

Gary Saul Morson is Frances Hooper Professor of the Arts and Humanities at Northwestern University. His publications include *The*

Boundaries of Genre: Dostoevsky's "Diary of a Writer" and the Traditions of Literary Utopia (Austin: University of Texas Press, 1981), "The Heresiarch of *Meta*" (on Bakhtin; *PTL*, 1979), *Hidden in Plain View: Narrative and Creative Potentials in "War and Peace"* (Stanford University Press, 1987), and, with Caryl Emerson, *Bakhtin: The Creation of a Prosaics* (Stanford University Press, 1990).

Cathy Popkin is Assistant Professor of Slavic Languages and Literatures at Columbia University. Her book, *The Pragmatics of Insignificance: Chekhov, Zoshchenko, Gogol,* is forthcoming from Stanford University Press.

Stanley J. Rabinowitz, Professor of Russian at Amherst College, has just completed, with Frederick T. Griffiths, a study of the relationship of Gogol's work to the literature of classical antiquity, *Novel Epics: Gogol, Dostoevsky, and National Narrative* (Northwestern University Press, 1990). He is an authority on the work of the symbolist poet and prose writer Fedor Sologub.

Mikhail Weiskopf, Hebrew University (Jerusalem), is working on a study of the semiotic structure of Gogol's plots. He is the author of "Poetika Peterburgskikh povestei Gogolia: Priemy ob"ektivizatsii i gipostazirovaniia" (The poetics of Gogol's Petersburg tales: devices of objectification and hypostatization) (*Slavica Hierosolymitana*, 1978), and "Nos v Kazanskom sobore: O genezise religioznoi temy u Gogolia" (The Nose in the Kazan cathedral: on the genesis of the religious theme in Gogol) (*Wiener slawistischer Almanach*, 1987).

Duffield White, Associate Professor of Russian Language and Literature, Wesleyan University, has published articles on Tolstoy and Alexander Blok and a translation of Boris Eikhenbaum's *Tolstoy in the 1870s* (Ardis, 1982). He is working on a study of the early prose of Tolstoy.

Alexander Zholkovsky, Professor of Slavic Languages and Literatures at the University of Southern California, working in the Soviet tradition of structuralism and semiotics, has applied his analytical model to the work of Pasternak, Pushkin, Okudzhava, Tolstoy, and Zoshchenko, not to mention La Rochefoucauld, Bertrand Russell, and a Soviet cookie wrapper. His most recent works include *Themes and Texts: Toward a Poetics of Expressiveness* (Cornell University Press, 1984) and, with Iu. K. Shcheglov, *Mir avtora i struktura teksta: Stat'i o russkoi literature* (The World of the Author and the Structure of the Text: Essays on Russian Literature) (Tenafly, N.J.: Ermitazh, 1986).

Notes

Introduction

1. Maguire, "Legacy," p. 16. (Full citations to the works cited in this essay are given in the accompanying "Works Cited.")

2. Ibid., p. 37.

3. Some of the major texts of Soviet Gogol scholarship have recently become available even to the non-Russian-speaker; see the selections in George Gibian's edition of *Dead Souls* and in the (less successful) special issue of *Soviet Literature*, as well as the awkward but adequate translation of Anna Yelistratova's comparative study. Maguire has done a great service by translating and editing Gippius's *Gogol*; as William Mills Todd III states, the translation, with its corrected and expanded references, "is generally more useful than the 1924 Russian original" (Todd, p. 256n). (See also Meyer and Rudy, Trahan, and Vinogradov.) The Western scholar has recently been offered an invaluable bibliographical tool, *The Gogol Bulletin* (ed. George Gutsche and Gavriel Shapiro), which from 1985 through 1988 provided a yearly list of publications and dissertations, abstracts of conference papers, and announcements of work in progress on Gogol. (One must hope that it will soon resume publication.) See also the comprehensive bibliography by Philip Frantz.

4. Bibikhin, Gal'tseva, and Rodnianskaia, p. 391. It is now possible for the Soviet reader to obtain firsthand knowledge of Nabokov's anathematized study: a nearly complete translation appeared in *Novyi mir* in 1987. Omitted are Nabokov's examples of mistakes in English translations of Gogol's works, as well as the italicized words in the following sentence: "Ever since Russia began to think, *and up to the time that her mind went blank under the influence of the extraordinary regime she has been enduring for these last twenty-five years*, educated, sensitive and free-minded Russians were acutely aware of

the furtive and clammy touch of poshlust" (Nabokov, *Gogol*, p. 64). An introduction by S. Zalygin first compliments Nabokov on his "aristocratically refined" writing style and then points out that refinement is not a native Russian literary trait: "Here we must remember that the truly great Russian writers—Tolstoy, Dostoevsky, Gogol, and even Chekhov—not only never strove for refinement but even denied the need for it in their work. Chekhov identified refinement with coldness and even considered it a literary defect" (*Novyi mir*, p. 173).

5. Bibikhin et al., p. 394, re Karlinsky, and p. 400, re Fanger.

6. See the *Transactions/Zapiski of the Association of Russian-American Scholars in the USA*, no. 17, devoted to Gogol.

7. Maguire, "Legacy," p. 51. See also his "Gogol's 'Confession.'"

8. See also Bocharov, "O stile Gogolia." A sophisticated linguistic approach to late Gogol is developed in the discourse analysis of Thomas Lahusen.

9. Lotman, "Kopeikin," p. 29.

10. See Mann, *V poiskakh*, pp. 16–17. Perhaps the time has come to find a term (semio-structuralism?) adequate to distinguish the lively and productive school of Soviet (and émigré) structuralism from its moribund Western counterpart, especially since the former is no longer a purely Soviet phenomenon.

11. Fanger, review of Todd's *Fiction and Society*, p. 106.

12. But see Debeaux; Shukman; and the essays by Cathy Popkin and Alexander Zholkovsky in the present volume.

13. Pliashko; Zolotusskii, "'Zapiski sumasshedshego' i 'Severnaia pchela,'" in his *Trepet serdtsa*, pp. 328–44.

Sergei Bocharov, Around "The Nose"

1. S. G. Bocharov, "Zagadka 'Nosa' i taina litsa," in *O khudozhestvennykh mirakh* (Moscow, 1985), pp. 124–60.

2. V. V. Vinogradov, "Naturalisticheskii grotesk: Siuzhet i kompozitsiia povesti Gogolia 'Nos,'" in his *Izbrannye trudy: Poetika russkoi literatury* (Moscow, 1976), pp. 5–44.

3. Innokentii Annenskii, *Kniga otrazhenii* (Moscow, 1979), pp. 19–20.

4. The comparison belongs to G. A. Fedorov and arose during a conversation on the topic of these remarks.

5. Andrei Belyi, *Masterstvo Gogolia* (Moscow and Leningrad, 1934), p. 46.

6. Thomas Mann, "Voyage with Don Quixote" (1934), in his

Essays of Three Decades, trans. H. T. Lowe-Porter (New York: Knopf, 1948), p. 446.

7. Iu. V. Mann, *Poetika Gogolia* (Moscow, 1978), pp. 129, 131.

8. English translations from *The Collected Dialogues of Plato*, ed. Edith Hamilton and Huntington Cairns (Princeton, N.J.: Princeton University Press, 1961), p. 341.

9. See P. A. Florenskii, *Stolp i Utverzhdenie Istiny* (Moscow, 1914), p. 707.

10. V. G. Belinskii, *Sobranie sochinenii*, 8 vols. (Moscow, 1982), 8:283.

11. S. T. Aksakov, *Istoriia moego znakomstva s Gogolem* (Moscow, 1960), p. 171.

12. Ioann Zlatoust (John Chrysostom), *Besedy na Evangelie Matfeia* (Moscow, 1846), p. 371.

13. Mann, *Poetika Gogolia*, p. 160.

14. From Florenskii's cycle of the early 1920s, "U vodorazdelov mysli" ("At the Watersheds of Thought"), as quoted by A. S. Trubachev and N. K. Bonetskaia in their introduction to P. A. Florenskii, "O literature," *Voprosy literatury*, 1988, no. 1:150. In general the analysis of the face as a special reality has attracted the attention of the revival in philosophical anthropology in the twentieth century. Among Russian thinkers see esp. Florenskii; and V. V. Rozanov, *V mire neiasnogo i nereshennogo*, 2nd ed. (St. Petersburg, 1904), pp. 1–2.

15. P. A. Florenskii, "Ikonostas," *Bogoslovskie trudy* 9 (1972):92.

16. Ibid., p. 94.

17. Iu. V. Mann, "Eshche raz o moste Manilova i 'taine litsa,' " in his *Dialektika khudozhestvennogo obraza* (Moscow, 1987), p. 270.

18. "But the nose seemed to be made of wood and fell to the table with such a strange sound, as if it were a cork" (III:68).

19. Annenskii, *Kniga otrazhenii*, pp. 226–27.

20. In a recent study, the German scholar Hildegund Schreier defined this inside out logic of Gogol's comic depictions as his *negative anthropology*. See Schreier, *Gogol's religiöses Weltbild und sein literarisches Werk: Zur Antagonie zwischen Kunst und Tendenz* (Munich: O. Sagner, 1977).

21. A. M. Bukharev, *Tri pis'ma k N. V. Gogoliu, pisannye v 1848 godu* (St. Petersburg, 1861), p. 145.

22. "It is true that he made his appearance as only a weak thinker; however, he was a thinker-artist, with the same questions that he developed as an artist-thinker." Apollon Grigor'ev, *Russkaia estetika i kritika 40-50-kh godov XIX veka* (Moscow, 1982), p. 108.

23. See Bocharov, "Zagadka 'Nosa,' " pp. 134–36.

24. This is yet another variant of the idea of the monument in Russian literature, along with the "monuments" of Derzhavin, Pushkin, Baratynskii, Briusov, Khodasevich, etc.

25. Vladimir Losskii, "Ocherk misticheskogo bogosloviia Vostochnoi Tserkvi," *Bogoslovskie trudy* 8 (1972): 65–66.

26. According to S. S. Averintsev, " 'Analiticheskaia psikhologiia' K.-G. Iunga i zakonomernosti tvorcheskoi fantazii," *Voprosy literatury*, 1970, no. 3:129.

27. Ibid., pp. 130, 137.

28. Mikhail Bakhtin, *Problemy poetiki Dostoevskogo* (Moscow, 1963), p. 79.

29. F. M. Dostoevskii, *Polnoe sobranie sochinenii*, 30 vols. (Leningrad, 1984), 26:139.

30. Ibid., 13:302.

31. See the articles and notes of A. F. Khizhdeu and I. I. Sreznevskii from 1833 to 1835 in *Zaporozhskaia Starina, Utrenniaia Zvezda,* and *Teleskop.* Gogol read *Zaporozhskaia Starina* and commented on it in letters to Sreznevskii (X:298–99, 321, 480). Skovoroda's texts were published from the end of the eighteenth century, and particularly in the 1830s in Moscow.

32. Iurii Loshchits, *Skovoroda* (Moscow, 1972), p. 217. E. A. Smirnova has also remarked on the echoes of Skovoroda in Gogol's aesthetics, in connection with the significance of the culture of the Ukrainian baroque. See her *Poema Gogolia "Mertvye dushi"* (Leningrad, 1987), pp. 62–63.

33. Hryhoryi Skovoroda, *Tvory*, 2 vols. (Kiev, 1961), 1:32. Future citations to this work, all to vol. 1, are in the text.

34. V. F. Ern, *Grigorii Savvich Skovoroda: Zhizn' i uchenie* (Moscow, 1912), p. 336.

35. See Mikhail Bakhtin, "Rable i Gogol'," in his *Voprosy literatury i estetiki: Issledovaniia raznykh let* (Moscow, 1975), p. 489.

36. Ern, *Skovoroda*, p. 338.

37. Viacheslav V. Ivanov, *Borozdy i mezhi* (Moscow, 1916), p. 17.

John Kopper, The "Thing-in-Itself" in Gogol's Aesthetics

I am indebted to the anonymous referee who sagely expressed bewilderment at my using philosophical "interest" as a criterion of aesthetic judgment and have excised places in my argument where I did so. Nancy Millichap Davies of Humanities Computing at Dartmouth College helped greatly with the technical production of this essay.

1. Vladimir Nabokov, *Nikolai Gogol* (London: Poetry London, 1947), pp. 36–37. Note also Nabokov's barb, "At his worst, as in his Ukrainian stuff, [Gogol] is a worthless writer," in *Strong Opinions* (New York: Vintage International, 1990), p. 103.

2. For nuanced discussion and criticism of Kant's "thing-in-itself" see Paul Guyer, *Kant and the Claims of Knowledge* (Cambridge: Cambridge University Press, 1987), pp. 333–44; and J. N. Findlay, *Kant and the Transcendental Object: A Hermeneutic Study* (Oxford: Clarendon, 1981), pp. 1–28, 180–90. Both studies excel in tracing the evolution of Kantian concepts, Guyer relying on early works like the *Nova Delucidatio* (1755) and the *Dissertation of 1770*, Findlay on the *Opus Postumum* (written 1796–1803, pub. 1920). See also Justus Hartnack, *Kant's Theory of Knowledge* (London: Macmillan, 1968), pp. 89–91.

3. Immanuel Kant, *Critique of Pure Reason*, trans. F. Max Müller (Garden City, N.Y.: Anchor Books, 1966), p. 199.

4. Ibid., p. 217.

5. Immanuel Kant, *Prolegomena to Any Future Metaphysics*, trans. Paul Carus and James W. Ellington (Indianapolis: Hackett, 1977), pp. 33–34.

6. A. Robert Caponigri and Ralph McInerny, *A History of Western Philosophy*, 5 vols. (Notre Dame, Ind.: University of Notre Dame Press, 1963), vol. 3, A. Robert Caponigri, *Philosophy from the Renaissance to the Romantic Age*, pp. 478–80, 495–500.

7. Belinskii and Bakunin learned their Hegel in Stankevich's Moscow circle, which oriented its discussions toward Hegel beginning in 1837. Bakunin swiftly lost his Hegelianism when he confronted Marx and the Left Hegelians in the early 1840s. Belinskii's Hegelian period was even briefer: 1837–40. Herzen came under the spell of Hegelianism on his return from internal exile in 1840. Always an eclectic student of Hegel, Herzen finally abjured him following the failure of the revolutions of 1848.

8. John Watson, *Schelling's Transcendental Idealism* (Chicago: S. C. Griggs, 1882), pp. 208–17; and Frederick Copleston, *A History of Philosophy*, 9 vols. (New York: Paulist Press, 1963), vol. 7, *Fichte to Nietzsche*, p. 121.

9. F. W. J. Schelling, *The Philosophy of Art*, trans. Douglas W. Stott (Minneapolis: University of Minnesota Press, 1989), p. 45.

10. Charles Taylor, *Hegel* (Cambridge: Cambridge University Press, 1975), pp. 474–75.

11. Kant, *Critique of Pure Reason*, p. 201.

12. See, e.g., Leonard J. Kent's introduction to his edition of Gogol's stories, *The Collected Tales and Plays of Nikolai Gogol* (New York: Pantheon, 1964), p. xxv; Jesse Zeldin, *Nikolai Gogol's Quest for Beauty: An Exploration into His Works* (Lawrence: Regents Press of Kansas, 1978), p. 6; N. L. Stepanov, "Romanticheskii mir Gogolia," in *K istorii russkogo romantizma*, ed. Iu. V. Mann, I. G. Neupokoeva, and U. R. Fokht (Moscow, 1973), p. 199 (hereafter cited as Mann, *K istorii*); and Dmitrii Merezhkovskii, "Gogol and the Devil," in *Gogol from the Twentieth Century*, ed. and trans. Robert A. Maguire (Princeton, N. J.: Princeton University Press, 1974), pp. 57–58. Andrei Belyi gives a psychobiographical interpretation of Gogol's devils:

> The plot's lack of clarity . . . personified by the necessity of introducing into the story the "devil" (an "impure" power) and illuminated by the traditions of a recently sovereign Romanticism, was manifested as a clarity, however fallacious. The "devil" was necessary to Gogol in order to give an accounting of himself *to* himself [*otchitat'sia pered soboiu samim*]. It is a "deus ex machina."

Belyi, *Masterstvo Gogolia* (Munich: Wilhelm Fink, 1969), p. 190, emphasis added.

13. In the Russian story "Prince Danila Govorila," e.g., the old women who tell the sister to make magic dolls are not witches, nor is the sister who makes them, yet they all inhabit a sphere where magic is possible. Aleksandr Afanas'ev, ed., *Russian Fairy Tales*, trans. Norbert Guterman (New York: Pantheon, 1973), pp. 351–56. In "Maria Morevna" the metamorphoses of birds into knights are unmotivated, and the supernatural intervention of the animals in herding up Baba Yaga's horses has no sorcerer or sorceress behind it. Ibid., pp. 553–62.

14. The furniture of two parallel fictional worlds is commonly kept apart by authors, as Alice's experience in England/Wonderland exemplifies, or Dorothy's in Kansas/the Land of Oz. But occasionally the *realia* of one world can cross into another. Nabokov often uses this device, which he perhaps learned from "A Bewitched Place." In "The Thunderstorm" the hero provides the thundergod's chariot with a rusty wheel from a baby carriage in his courtyard, and in "The Visit to the Museum" the trappings of an émigré world—franc notes and letters from Paris—must be frantically shed by the hero after his magical transmigration to Soviet Leningrad.

15. English translations from Gogol's stories, emended slightly where necessary, are from Kent's *Collected Tales and Plays of Nikolai*

Gogol. References to the English text follow references to the Russian, separated by a slash. Unless indicated to the contrary, all other translations are mine.

16. Cf. Johann Georg Hamann's idea that language represents, in the words of Frederick Copleston, "a communication of God, a divine revelation." See Copleston, *Western Philosophy*, vol. 6, *Wolff to Kant*, p. 136.

17. *Master and Margarita* uses this topos in the aftermath of the Variety magic show, when the ruble notes conjured up by Fagot turn into bottled-water labels and the fashionable clothes he has produced disappear.

18. Exceptions are Mann, in his article "Evoliutsiia gogolevskoi fantastiki," in Mann, *K istorii*, pp. 219–58; and Nabokov, in his lecture on "The Overcoat," in his *Lectures on Russian Literature* (New York: Harcourt, Brace, Jovanovich, 1981), pp. 54–60).

19. Ludwig Tieck's "Eckbert the Fair" (1797) has a similarly abrupt ending, made top-heavy through explanation.

20. For a more generous reading of "A Terrible Vengeance" see Donald Fanger, *The Creation of Nikolai Gogol* (Cambridge, Mass.: Harvard University Press, 1979), pp. 93, 237–38.

21. "Ivan Shponka" is rightly considered the sport among the *Dikanka* stories. See, e.g., ibid., p. 93. Nabokov considers it the redeeming gem in an otherwise dangerously misdirected fictional project. Nabokov, *Nikolai Gogol*, pp. 37–39. It represents a style of humor—the non sequitur elevated to a principle of emplotment—that Gogol mined with stunning virtuosity, especially in *The Inspector General*. But Gogol's impressive mastery of Sterne can overshadow other features of the *Dikanka* collection; in particular, his cultivation of an unreachable noumenon shows Gogol as an innovator.

22. The story suffers from a conflict between its chief mode of representation—allegory—and the idea posed by the allegory, the impossibility of transit between phenomenal and noumenal worlds. While the conclusion of the story establishes the noumenon as real but unknowable, the allegorical vehicle requires faith that a symbolic order *can* function and that one world can be bodied forth through the conventional understanding of another. These aesthetic inconsistencies aside, however, the plot of "Vii" is simple to follow.

23. For another theory of the "gaze" see Fanger, *Creation of Gogol*, pp. 252–56. Note also V. V. Ivanov's anthropological study of the categories of the seen and unseen in "Vii." Ivanov interprets the polarity as a figure for death and documents its widespread use in other cultures. Viacheslav V. Ivanov, "Kategoriia 'vidimogo' i

'nevidimogo' v tekste: Eshche raz o vostochnoslavianskikh fol'klornykh paralleliakh k gogolevskomu 'Viiu,' " in *Structure of Texts and Semiotics of Culture*, ed. Jan van der Eng and Mojmir Grygar (The Hague: Mouton, 1973), pp. 151–76. Jesse Zeldin gives an alternative reading of the Philosopher's end: "Aesthetic refusal (the philosopher looked upon the face of Vii and took him for truth) has reaped its reward in death." Zeldin, *Gogol's Quest for Beauty*, p. 27. This reading seems more appropriate to Nabokov's horror stories—*Invitation to a Beheading* and *Bend Sinister*—where credulity in the face of evil empowers evil.

24. Immanuel Kant, *The Critique of Judgement*, trans. James Creed Meredith (Oxford: Clarendon, 1952), pp. 14, 18, 15, 38. See also Caponigri, *Philosophy from the Renaissance*, pp. 460–61.

25. F. W. J. Schelling, *System of Transcendental Idealism (1800)*, trans. Peter Heath (Charlottesville: University Press of Virginia, 1978), p. 225.

26. "In the midst of the fearful kingdom of forces, and in the midst of the sacred kingdom of laws, the aesthetic impulse to form is at work, unnoticed, on the building of a third joyous kingdom of play and of semblance, in which man is relieved of the shackles of circumstance, and released from all that might be called constraint, alike in the physical and in the moral sphere." Friedrich Schiller, *On the Aesthetic Education of Man*, trans. Elizabeth M. Wilkinson and L. A. Willoughby (Oxford: Clarendon, 1967), p. 215; see also pp. 79–109.

27. Ibid., p. 215.

28. In this light it is easier to see why the Germans were "received" by the Russians in a special order, with Kant reserved for the end of the century. Schelling probably won rapid and enduring popularity because his later work, written after 1800, was explicitly religious. In particular, his doctrine of immanence may have matched the Russian Orthodox fascination with the Transfiguration. But with the growth of the Slavophile and Westernizer movements in the late 1830s and 1840s the first comprehensive and critical reformulation of German thought took place. Hegel's philosophy of state responded to the crisis over the nature of government that erupted under Nicholas I, and it briefly helped catalyze the political debate. Although both Schelling's and Hegel's philosophies were outdated positions by mid century, they presaged the Russian fondness for totalizing systems that would surface again in the radicalism of the 1860s and in Marxism. Insofar as Kant offered chiefly a legacy of epistemological skepticism, he gave little to Russians—or to Europeans as a whole—until a renewed interest in the possibilities of tran-

scendental philosophy brought them to retrace the steps that had led to the Romantic aesthetic of perception.

29. For a discussion of Gogol's exposure to German philosophy see E. N. Kupreianova, "N. V. Gogol'," in *Istoriia russkoi literatury: Ot sentimentalizma k romantizmu i realizmu*, 2 vols. (Leningrad, 1981), 2:535; and Stepanov's remarks in Mann, *K istoriii*, pp. 188–93.

30. Cf. Mann, speaking of changes in the appearance of the nose: "No artist could capture this metaphorphosis since he would be knowingly commissioned [*zavedomo prizvan*] to render visible that which must remain elusive and unexplained." Mann, "Evoliutsiia," p. 234.

31. Ibid.

32. Stepanov, "Mir Gogolia," p. 216.

33. Belyi, *Masterstvo Gogolia*, p. 25.

34. Maguire, *Gogol from the Twentieth Century*, p. 11; Belyi, *Masterstvo Gogolia*, p. 28.

35. I. F. Volkov, "Osnovnye problemy izucheniia romantizma," in Mann, *K istorii*, pp. 24–25.

36. Stepanov, "Mir Gogolia," p. 209.

37. Belyi, *Masterstvo Gogolia*, p. 189; M. B. Khrapchenko, *Nikolai Gogol': Literaturnyi put': Velichie pisatelia* (revision of *Tvorchestvo Gogolia*) (Moscow, 1984), pp. 113–14.

38. Mann, "Evoliutsiia," pp. 243–55.

39. Iu. V. Mann, *Poetika russkogo romantizma* (Moscow, 1976), p. 337.

40. Belyi, *Masterstvo Gogolia*, pp. 10–22, 16.

41. For a history of *typologies* of Romanticism, including those of Belinskii and Gorkii, see Volkov, "Osnovnye problemy," pp. 5–36.

42. Using very similar terms Michel Riffaterre argues that the ambiguity of syllepsis has determinate textual effects. See his *Fictional Truth* (Baltimore, Md.: Johns Hopkins University Press, 1990).

43. Iurii Lotman, *The Structure of the Artistic Text*, trans. G. Lenhoff and R. Vroon (Ann Arbor: Michigan Slavic Contributions, 1977), pp. 32–49.

44. Lotman's description of the two semantic relationships demonstrates the curious alliance between the Romantic movement and rational idealism, the school of Descartes and Leibniz that Kant was concerned to refute. Romanticism endorses the possibility that a world can be "thought," but it promotes nonrational means of thinking.

45. This noumenal world is apparently the property of reader

and narrator but not necessarily of characters, as the very different experiences of Cincinnatus in *Invitation to a Beheading*, Sineusov and Adam Falter in *Solus Rex*, Fedor Godunov-Cherdyntsev in *The Gift*, John Shade in *Pale Fire*, and the titular hero of "Lance" go toward showing. Nabokov's guiding correlative for the noumenal experience is Dantean: the kingdom of death. While Fedor, Sineusov, and John Shade are frustrated in their respective efforts to commune with their dead father, wife, and daughter, and Cincinnatus appears to reach a noumenal realm only by being "executed" in the phenomenal, Lance accomplishes a grueling but successful passage between the two planes, and Adam Falter, in Nabokov's best homage to Gogol, seems to reach the "thing-in-itself," an unnameable something that drives him mad. In *Bend Sinister* Nabokov uses another device for expressing the noumenal. The author lifts his character up out of the plot, something Molly Bloom begs Joyce to do during her night soliloquy: "O Jamesy let me up out of this." (James Joyce, *Ulysses*, ed. Hans Walter Gabler [New York: Random House, 1986], p. 633.) But a noumenon clearly identified with the world of the author is obviously not the "thing-in-itself."

For a contemporary effort to resuscitate the "thing-in-itself" in critical discourse, cf. Kristeva's use of the term *chora*, a prelinguistic ground that supports discourse but is apprehensible only as a logical construct. Julia Kristeva, *Revolution in Poetic Language*, trans. Margaret Waller (New York: Columbia University Press, 1984), pp. 25–28.

46. Kafka, incidentally, regaled his friends by reading his works aloud and was renowned in his lifetime as a master of the oral art. He differs from Gogol in emphasizing the ethical nature of confrontations with the "thing-in-itself." The monster into which Gregor Samsa is metamorphosed is presumably the "thing-in-itself" (Kafka gave one clue when he wrote that the monster could not be drawn, i.e., represented), but the family's failure to deal with it in *any* dimension is certainly a moral failure. In other texts, like "Before the Law," *The Trial*, and *The Castle*, the very ascription of power to an invisible dimension of experience invests that dimension with a power that would otherwise not be present. Thus one's attitude toward noumenal experience of any sort becomes a moral act.

It is a sign perhaps of his belonging to a "post-Kantian world" that the immanentist Michel Foucault—although he retains a philosophical property of the "thing-in-itself" in arguing that power cannot be *traced*—refuses to acknowledge that power emanates from a separate dimension of experience.

47. In closing, I wanted to suggest some points for investigation.

First, I have ignored a major aspect of German aesthetics which is related to the phenomenon/noumenon polarity. This would be teleology. Here are some brief propositions. Gogol's art, unlike the ideal art of all the German philosophers of his day, is obviously *not* teleogically complete. Art for Gogol is a determinate, and purposeful, *dis*integration. The Gogolian fragment is a sign of teleological insufficiency, and the metamorphosis a metaphorical perversion of the formative power of art. Gogol represents Petersburg as a Hegelian system, a teleological machine in Russian history which revolts him. Compare the *Athenaeum Fragments* of the Schlegel brothers, many of whose sallies are launched against the Kantian system.

Second, the best metaphor for Gogol's philosophical position might be "metaphysics of the sublime." In the aesthetic of the sublime—if we pick up only the Kantian and English Romantic end of a centuries-long discourse—the sublime is opposed to the beautiful. The sublime is terrifying, not consoling, a quantitative overpowering, not a qualitative engagement of the senses. It is experienced by man in nature and makes him feel helpless. It is chaotic, not well formed; formless, not formative. As such, the experience of the sublime can be registered within art but is obviously opposed to art itself. But let us suppose that Gogol's art is itself the sublime, designed to terrify, overwhelm, and render helpless, to posit sources of authority that remain shapeless because they may not be known.

Priscilla Meyer, False Pretenders and the Spiritual City

1. Konstantin Mochul'skii, *Dukhovnyi put' Gogolia* (Paris, YMCA Press, 1934). V. D. Nosov, *"Kliuch" k Gogoliu* (London: Overseas Publishing Interchange, 1985) also takes Gogol at his word and treats Gogol's religious views seriously.

2. Sergei Bocharov, "Zagadka 'Nosa' i taina litsa," in *Gogol', istoriia i sovremennost'*, ed. V. V. Kozhinov et al. (Moscow, 1985). See also his article in the present volume.

3. Iurii Vladimirovich Mann, "Evoliutsiia gogolevskoi fantastiki," in *K istorii russkogo romantizma*, ed. Iu. V. Mann, I. G. Neupokoeva, and U. R. Fokht (Moscow, 1973), pp. 219–58; and Mann, *Poetika Gogolia* (Moscow, 1978).

4. Boris A. Uspenskii, "Tsar and Pretender: *Samozvanchestvo* or Royal Imposture in Russia as a Cultural-Historical Phenomenon," in *The Semiotics of Russian Culture*, ed. Ann Shukman (Ann Arbor: Michigan Slavic Contributions, 1984), pp. 259–92.

5. A. N. Afanas'ev, *Drevo zhizni* (Moscow, 1982), p. 438.

6. Iurii M. Lotman, "Problema khudozhestvennogo prostranstva v proze Gogolia," *Trudy po russkoi i slavianskoi filologii*, no. 11 (Tartu, 1968): 5–50, on p. 18.

7. Viacheslav V. Ivanov, "Ob odnoi paralleli k Gogolevskomu Viiu," in *Trudy po znakovym sistemam*, no. 284 (Tartu, 1971), pp. 133–42, 141–42.

8. Afanas'ev, *Drevo*, p. 389.

9. See Mann's enumeration of actions associated with the diabolic in Gogol's work in "Evoliutsiia gogolevskoi fantastiki"; and Lotman's discussion of frenzied motion in "Problema khudozhestvennogo prostranstva."

10. The song contains the image of binding up the "head" with metal staves like a barrel. Ivanov traces this image to an Abkhazian epic. "Ob odnoi paralleli," p. 142.

11. As is suggested in Iurii Mann's study of mute scenes and immobility in Gogol's work in the present volume.

12. Dmitrii Chizhevskii, "About Gogol's *Overcoat*" [1938], in *Dostoevsky and Gogol*, ed. P. Meyer and S. Rudy (Ann Arbor, Mich: Ardis, 1979), pp. 137–60.

13. An analysis of the relationship of "The Nose" to "Vii" reveals the same methods of reversal. See Priscilla Meyer, "Features of the Demonic: 'Vii' and 'The Nose,' " paper delivered at the annual AATSEEL convention, Washington, D.C., December, 1988.

14. In the final draft of "The Overcoat," Gogol made the ghost's identity ambiguous. The ghost is, however, sufficiently identified with Akakii, both by earlier drafts and within the text, to reward discussion based on the assumption that the ghost is his.

15. The same connection of clothing, rank, eros, noses, and masquerade is made in "The Diary of a Madman" when Poprishchin inveighs against his competitor for the hand of the boss's daughter: "After all, just because you're a court chamberlain you don't get a third eye in your forehead. After all, his nose isn't made of gold, but it's just like mine. . . . Maybe I'm some count or general, and only seem to be a titular councillor?" (III: 206).

Iurii Mann, Gogol's Poetics of Petrification

1. See Roman Iakobson [Jakobson], *Raboty po poetike* (Moscow, 1987); Jakobson, *Puškin and His Sculptural Myth*, trans. and ed. John Burbank (The Hague: Mouton, 1975).

2. A Gogolian parallel to this phenomenon is the behavior of the fatal "portrait." But this analogy is not complete: the portrait is not

"dead"; part of the life of the mysterious usurer has been miraculously retained in his image.

3. Alexander Pushkin, *Eugene Onegin*, trans. Charles Johnston (Harmondsworth: Penguin, 1979), p. 176.

4. Iurii Mann, *Poetika Gogolia* (Moscow, 1978), p. 117.

5. It is interesting that the very expression *mute scene* was already used before *The Inspector General*, precisely in connection with Pushkin. A reviewer of *Ruslan and Liudmila* noted with regard to one passage that "with the experience of an old artist the young author made use of Vladimir's position, knew how to make of it a tragic 'mute scene.' " *Syn otechestva*, 1820, no. 64:82.

6. Cited in the introductory article by V. V. Ivanov in Jakobson, *Raboty po poetike*, p. 16.

7. S. P. Shevyrev, in *Moskvitianin*, 1851, no. 1:110.

8. Jakobson, *Raboty po poetike*, pp. 166–67.

9. Andrei Belyi, *Masterstvo Gogolia* (Moscow and Leningrad, 1934), p. 319.

10. Belyi, letter to Meyerhold, in V. E. Meierkhol'd, *Perepiska, 1896–1939* (Moscow, 1976), p. 257.

11. Erast Garin, *S Meierkhol'dom (vospominaniia)* (Moscow, 1974), p. 176.

Duffield White, Khlestakov as Representative of Petersburg

1. Nikolai V. Gogol, "Leaving the Theater after a Performance of a New Comedy," in *The Theater of Nikolai Gogol*, ed. Milton Ehre, trans. Milton Ehre and Fruma Gottschalk (Chicago: University of Chicago Press, 1980), p. 181. This collection includes English translations of Gogol's plays and of critical essays and letters referring to the plays. References to the English text follow references to the Russian text, separated by a slash. "Leaving the Theater" is Gogol's most illuminating critical commentary on *The Inspector General*.

2. V. V. Ivanov, "Gogol's *Inspector General* and the Comedy of Aristophanes," in *Gogol from the Twentieth Century*, ed. Robert Maguire (Princeton, N. J.: Princeton University Press, 1974), p. 201.

3. Iurii V. Mann, *Komediia Gogolia "Revizor"* (Moscow, 1966), p. 11. Future citations to this work are in the text. The translations are mine.

4. V. V. Gippius, "Problematika i kompozitsiia 'Revizora,' " in *N. V. Gogol': Materialy i issledovaniia*, 2 vols. (Moscow and Leningrad, 1936). This quotation is from Robert Maguire's translation, en-

titled "*The Inspector General*: Structure and Problems," in *Gogol from the Twentieth Century*, p. 231.

5. *The Inspector General*, IV:13; p. 56. In instances when my interpretation hinges on words or phrases of the original text that have not been literally translated by Ehre and Gottschalk I have slightly revised their translation in a more literal direction.

6. Iu. M. Lotman, "O Khlestakove," *Trudy po russkoi i slavianskoi filologii*, no. 26 (Tartu, 1975): 19–53. These quotations are from Louisa Vinton's translation; "Concerning Khlestakov," in *The Semiotics of Russian Cultural History*, ed. Alexander D. Nakhimovsky and Alice Stone Nakhimovsky (Ithaca, N. Y., and London: Cornell University Press, 1985), pp. 158–60.

7. Ibid., p. 162.

Robert Louis Jackson, Gogol's "The Portrait"

1. Friedrich Nietzsche, *Jenseits von Gut und Böse*, no. 146, in *Werke*, 2 vols. (Munich: Carl Hanser, 1967), 2:70.

2. For a discussion of this problem see Robert Louis Jackson, "Some Considerations on 'The Dream of a Ridiculous Man' and 'Bobok,' from the Aesthetic Point of View," in his *The Art of Dostoevsky: Deliriums and Nocturnes* (Princeton, N. J.: Princeton University Press, 1981), pp. 288–303.

Susanne Fusso, The Landscape of Arabesques

1. VIII:748. Unless otherwise indicated, all translations are mine.

2. Viktor Shklovskii, *Povesti o proze*, vol. 2, *V kotorom rasskazyvaetsia o russkoi proze* (Moscow, 1966), p. 6.

3. Nikolai V. Gogol, *Arabesques*, trans. Alexander Tulloch (Ann Arbor, Mich: Ardis, 1982).

4. See Donald Fanger, *The Creation of Nikolai Gogol* (Cambridge, Mass.: Harvard University Press, 1979), pp. 58–72.

5. See Iurii V. Mann, *Poetika Gogolia*, 2nd ed. (Moscow, 1988), pp. 267–76.

6. Howard Stern, *Gegenbild, Reihenfolge, Sprung: An Essay on Related Figures of Argument in Walter Benjamin* (Bern: Peter Lang, 1982), p. 52. Further citations to this work are in the text.

7. Walter Benjamin, *Reflections: Essays, Aphorisms, Autobiographical Writings*, trans. Edmund Jephcott (New York: Harcourt Brace Jovanovich, 1978), p. 82.

8. Benoit Mandelbrot, *The Fractal Geometry of Nature* (San Francisco: W. H. Freeman, 1977), p. 1.

9. For an excellent introduction to the picturesque see Christopher Hussey, *The Picturesque: Studies in a Point of View* (London: Frank Cass, 1967). While the present essay was in press, an article appeared in *Slavic Review* dealing with Russian garden theory from a historical and political perspective: Priscilla R. Roosevelt, "Tatiana's Garden: Noble Sensibilities and Estate Park Design in the Romantic Era," *Slavic Review* 49 (1990): 335–49.

10. Edmund Burke, *Works*, vol. 1 (Boston: Little, Brown, 1871), p. 197.

11. Uvedale Price, *Essays on the Picturesque, as Compared with the Sublime and the Beautiful; and on the Use of Studying Pictures for the Purpose of Improving Real Landscape*, 3 vols. (London: J. Mawman, 1810), 1:205–6. Further citations, to volume and page number, are in the text.

12. Richard Payne Knight, *The Landscape: A Didactic Poem* (London: W. Bulmer, 1795), p. 23.

13. P. V. Annenkov, "N. V. Gogol' v Rime letom 1841 goda," in *Gogol' v vospominaniiakh sovremennikov*, ed. N. L. Brodskii, et al. (Moscow, 1952), p. 283. See also Annenkov's account of Gogol's enjoyment of scenery: "At the summerhouse of Princess Z. Volkonskaia, which rested against an old Roman aqueduct that served it as a terrace, he would lie on his back . . . and look at the blue sky, at the dead and magnificent Roman campagna, for hours at a time. It was the same at Tivoli, in the thick vegetation that surrounds its *cascatelli*; he would sit somewhere in a thicket and fix his sharp-sighted, motionless eyes on the dark foliage that falls in clumps down the cliffs, and would remain motionless for whole hours, with inflamed cheeks" (p. 276). Annenkov's memories may of course be influenced in retrospect by the impact of Gogol's fictional vision of Pliushkin's garden.

14. This monotonously recurring landscape has already been described in *Arabesques*, in the "Chapter from a Historical Novel." In an attempt to escape the torments visited upon him by a supernaturally enlivened pine tree, an evil lord packs up his household and moves. No matter how far he goes, however, he keeps ending up in the same place: the same forest, the same buildings, the same retributive pine tree (III:310–21). The notion of the picturesque garden as a place of "continual, unexpected views" is beautifully expressed in V. A. Zhukovskii's "Slavianka (Elegiia)" (1815). Likhachev brilliantly analyzes the Romantic garden as the locus of "a striving toward movement, toward changes in time, in the seasons of the year, in the

hours of the day, toward various kinds of borderline phenomena in nature," but fails to draw a clear distinction between the garden practice of Pope, Walpole, Brown, and Repton on the one hand and the theories of Price and Knight on the other, lumping them all together under the rubric "peizazhnyi" ("landscape") or "romanticheskii sad" ("romantic garden"). D. S. Likhachev, *Poeziia sadov: K semantike sadovo-parkovykh stilei* (Leningrad, 1982), pp. 200–291.

15. P. A. Pletnev was the first to recognize the centrality of this passage to the aesthetic system of *Dead Souls*: "Ego kniga tochno etot sad" ("His book is like this garden"). Pletnev, *Sochineniia i perepiska*, vol. 3, ed. Ia. Grot (St. Petersburg, 1885), p. 493; and see Fanger, *Creation of Gogol*, p. 175. Following Pletnev, Siniavskii, in his chapter entitled "The Geography of Prose," adumbrates the homology between Gogol's landscape descriptions and his prose: "Gogol's style seeks direct comparisons in landscape, in order to attest to itself in a materially perceptible form." Abram Terts [Andrei Siniavskii], *V teni Gogolia* (Paris: Sintaksis, 1981), p. 342. Siniavskii's meditation leads him not to the picturesque but to the Baroque (pp. 347–51).

Gogol's moral to the scene of Pliushkin's garden is textually close to a passage in A. I. Galich's influential *Opyt nauki iziashchnogo* (*Essay on the Science of the Fine Arts*, 1825): "But the idea of beauty . . . is just as little exhausted by works of art as by works of nature. For if in the first case we see only lifeless phantoms, in the second we find neither a free idea nor a fitting form. Which is why the beautiful [*iziashchnoe*] . . . unfolds in full radiance only when nature meets with art and gives its beautiful phantoms a beautiful life and soul." In *Russkie esteticheskie traktaty pervoi treti XIX veka*, ed. Z. A. Kamenskii, 2 vols. (Moscow, 1974), 2:231.

16. The echoes between the scene of Pliushkin's garden and scenes involving the governor's daughter (and other fatal women) can be seen most clearly by presenting the evidence in columns:

Pliushkin's Garden	*Governor's Daughter (and Other Women)*
The colossal white trunk of a birch tree . . . rose out of that green thicket	only she alone showed white, and emerged transparent and bright out of the murky and opaque crowd (VI:169)
on its snowy whiteness	the oval of her face . . . showed white with a sort of transparent whiteness (VI:90)

and was rounded in the air	the pretty oval of her face was rounded (VI:90) with the enchantingly rounded oval of her face (VI:166)
the tenacious (*tsepkie*) little hooks	"[the glitter of women] will hook on (*zatsepit*) to your heart" (VI:164)
a hollow, yawning like a dark maw (*past'*)	abyss (*propast'*), disappeared (*propalo*) (passim, associated with the fatal danger of women)
leaves and twigs that entangled and crisscrossed	their carriages so strangely collided, entangling the harnesses (VI:166)
the young branch of a maple, which stretched out its green leaf-paws, under one of which the sun, having gotten there God knows how, suddenly rendered it transparent and fiery, marvelously shining in that thick darkness (VI:112–13)	The pretty oval of her face was rounded like a nice fresh little egg, and like it, it showed white with a sort of transparent whiteness, when, fresh, . . . it . . . lets the rays of the shining sun pass through it; her nice delicate little ears could also be seen through, glowing with the warm light that penetrated them (VI:90).

The intentionality of these correspondences is suggested by the fact that the words "kruglilsia na vozdukhe" ("was rounded in the air"), "temnaia past' " ("dark maw"), "pereputavshiesia" ("that entangled"), and "molodaia" ("young") belong to late revisions of the garden scene.

Mikhail Weiskopf, Plato and Gogol

I would like to express my appreciation to Victor Erlich, Iurii V. Mann, Priscilla Meyer, Stanley Rabinowitz, and the other participants of the conference who made many valuable comments during the discussion of my paper.

1. See Annenskii's remarks about the Gogolian "world of ideas" or about Platonic Eros in "Old World Landowners," *Khudozhestven-*

nyi idealizm Gogolia (1902), in Innokentii Annenskii, *Kniga otrazhenii* (Moscow, 1979), pp. 217–18, 220; S. K. Shambinago, *Trilogiia romantizma* (Moscow, 1911), p. 76; V. Zen'kovskii, *N. V. Gogol'* (Paris, 1964), p. 80; Jesse Zeldin, *Nikolai Gogol's Quest for Beauty: An Exploration into His Works* (Lawrence: University Press of Kansas, 1978), pp. 3, 37–38.

2. Vasilii Gippius, *Gogol'* (Leningrad, 1924), p. 42.

3. "The whole of Eastern Orthodoxy was nurtured on Plato, struggled with it, was plagued by it." Archimandrite Kipriian, *Antropologiia sviatogo Grigoriia Palamy* (Paris, YMCA Press, 1950), p. 48.

4. See, e.g., the works of I. V. Lopukhin, "Dukhovnyi rytsar' " and "Nekotorye cherty o vnutrennei tserkvi," in *Materialy po istorii russkogo masonstva 18 veka*, no. 1 (Moscow, 1913), pp. 17–29, 49–62.

5. See V. V. Sipovskii, *Ocherki iz istorii russkogo romana*, vol. 1, no. 1 (18th c.) (St. Petersburg, 1909), pp. 124, 560.

6. For a discussion of the epigonic dependence of the Lovers of Wisdom on Martinism and Western theosophy, a dependence that facilitated their assimilation of Schelling's mystic tendencies, see James H. Billington, *The Icon and the Axe: An Interpretive History of Russian Culture* (New York: Knopf, 1966), pp. 309–13. On Russian Orthodoxy in this context see also Sarah Pratt, *Russian Metaphysical Romanticism: The Poetry of Tiutchev and Boratynskii* (Stanford: Stanford University Press, 1984), pp. 21–22.

7. N. K. Kozmin, *N. I. Nadezhdin: Zhizn' i nauchno-literaturnaia deiatel'nost', 1804–1836* (St. Petersburg, 1912), pp. 74–75.

8. A. Koshelev's formulation. See P. N. Sakulin, *Iz istorii russkogo idealizma: Kniaz' Odoevskii, myslitel', pisatel'*, vol. 1 (Moscow, 1913), p. 321. Cf. Gogol in "Hans Kuechelgarten": "Platon i Shiller svoenravyi" ("Plato and wayward Schiller," I:84) (in Russia, Schiller was considered a Romantic).

9. See Sakulin, *Iz istorii*, pp. 103–4. On the cult of Plato among the Lovers of Wisdom see also V. F. Odoevskii, *Russkie nochi* (Leningrad, 1975), pp. 191, 263.

10. "Of all the thinkers of the ancient world, Nadezhdin preferred Plato. It is an understandable fact. On the one hand, there was the influence of his theological education, the effect of the desire to bring the philosophical propositions into accord with the truths of the Holy Writ . . . , on the other, the very name Plato had been surrounded by a halo since the end of the 18th century." Kozmin, *Nadezhdin*, p. 73. In the academy, the study of philosophy was conducted on a rather confused religious and Neoplatonic basis. Here

they simultaneously studied Plotinus, the Neo-Gnostic Baader, and Schelling—not his *Naturphilosophie* but his Neoplatonic tract "Philosophy and Religion." The professor of philosophy Golubinskii liked to emphasize in German idealism "the revelation of ideas long since reigning in Eastern philosophy." Later Nadezhdin, in the spirit of his teachers, "tried to reconcile Christian teaching with the newest findings of German philosophy." Kozmin, *Nadezhdin,* pp. 17, 73, 352; and also Z. A. Kamenskii, *N. I. Nadezhdin* (Moscow, 1984), pp. 7–8.

11. Quoted from Kozmin's detailed account, *Nadezhdin,* p. 79.

12. See, e.g., S. Durylin, *Rikhard Vagner i Rossiia: O Vagnere i budushchikh putiakh iskusstva* (Moscow, 1913), pp. 31–32. It is characteristic that Nadezhdin himself studied the Orthodox symbology of Saint Sophia with the same fervor with which, after the Masons, he translated Orphic hymns, underlining their "kinship with Neoplatonic philosophy." Kozmin, *Nadezhdin,* pp. 18, 57–61.

13. Kozmin, *Nadezhdin,* p. 78.

14. Here and in all further citations in this article, the italics are mine.

15. See I. I. Zamotin, *Romantizm dvadtsatykh godov 19 stoletiia v russkoi literature,* vol. 1 (Moscow, 1911), pp. 304, 363. For more detail about *narodnost'* (national roots) see G. Spet, *Ocherk razvitiia russkoi filosofii* (Petrograd, 1922), vol. 1.

16. For more detail see V. Rozanov, "Zametki o vazhneishikh techeniiakh russkoi filosofskoi mysli v sviazi s nashei perevodnoi literaturoi po filosofii," *Voprosy filosofii i psikhologii* (Moscow, 1890), book 3, pp. 4–8.

17. "Imagine an underground *vertep* . . . in which . . . people abide." "Platonova Grazhdanstva, ili O pravednom, kniga sed'maja," in *Tvorenii velemudrogo Platona,* trans. Ioann Ioannovich Sidorovskii and Matvei Sergeevich Pakhomov, 3 vols. (St. Petersburg, 1780–85), vol. 2 (1783), p. 737.

18. Readers of Garnett's English translation should note that "marvelous" (*chudnyi*) is rendered as "uncanny," and "half-light" (*polusvet*) as "twilight."—TRANS.

19. "The Supreme Blessing [from Plato's works]," *Moscow Telegraph,* published by Nikolai Polevoi, vol. 9 (1826), no. 2, pp. 11–12.

20. Plato, Sidorovskii and Pakhomov trans., *Tvorenii velemudrogo Platona,* p. 735.

21. Another important ideological source for "The Two Ivans," as well as for many of Gogol's other works, was G. S. Skovoroda. For more detail on this topic, as well as on Gogol's gnosticism, see Mikhail Weiskopf, "Gogol' i Skovoroda: Problema 'vneshnego cheloveka' " (in press); and Weiskopf, " 'Nos' v kazanskom sobore: O

genezise religioznoj temy u Gogolja," *Wiener slawistischer Almanach* 19 (1987): 26, 33–36.

22. About this universal Gnostic subject see Hans Jonas, *The Gnostic Religion: The Message of the Alien God and the Beginnings of Christianity* (Boston: Beacon Press, 1958), pp. 49–82.

23. Ibid., p. 191.

24. Plato, *The Collected Dialogues, Including the Letters*, ed. Edith Hamilton and Huntington Cairns (Princeton, N. J.: Princeton University Press, 1961), p. 1206. All subsequent citations to Plato are from this edition unless otherwise indicated.

25. Jonas, pp. 43–44.

26. One might consider this a response to the Slavic book of Enoch, but it must be taken into account that the latter was published after Gogol's death. The Gnostic understanding of time as a prison was, however, revived by Masonic theosophy. Cf.: "Time is the weapon of human sufferings, a powerful barrier preventing us from uniting with the primal Source. Time . . . imprisons our immortal soul as if in a dungeon." G. Eckartshausen, *Kliuch k tainstvam natury*, 4 parts (St. Petersburg, 1804), pt. 2, p. 237. On the cosmic prison (in a negative astrological vein typical of gnosticism) see, e.g., the Russian Mason and mystic Glinka (1830): "Alas! The world draws me! I am oppressed *by the attraction of the stars* and, aware of my *captivity* and bemoaning it, I drag myself around the slippery abyss. Break free, my soul, of these binding relations, And, free as a spirit, as a genius, fly to the suprastellar regions." F. N. Glinka, *Izbrannye proizvedeniia* (Leningrad, 1957), p. 388.

27. Sipovskii, *Ocherki*, pp. 85–92, 121–24, 558.

28. Ibid., pp. 137, 564–66.

29. Plato, Sidorovskii and Pakhomov trans., *Tvorenii velemudrogo Platona*, p. 339.

30. Stepan Shevyrev, *Teoriia poezii v istoricheskom razvitii u drevnikh i novykh narodov*, 2nd ed. (St. Petersburg, 1887), p. 19.

31. Andrei Belyi, *Masterstvo Gogolia* (Moscow, 1934), p. 95.

32. The analogy made here between the troika and the Platonic chariot of the soul represents a somewhat extended version of a fragment from a paper about Gogol's ideological sources that I read at the Australian National University in Canberra (Fall 1986). However, S. G. Bocharov, who participated in the current conference, kindly informed me that the possibility of this analogy had been briefly mentioned in a new book on *Dead Souls* by E. A. Smirnova (*Poema Gogolia "Mertvye dushi,"* ed. S. G. Bocharov [Leningrad, 1987]) that had then just appeared. Hence I will consider the follow-

ing comparison of the bird troika with the chariot from the *Phaedrus* as further demonstration of the thesis proposed by Smirnova.

33. "Dappled"—spotted, of impure color. In the notebooks the horse was called grey; cf. the grey kitten in "Old-World Landowners," which evolves out of the terrible black cat of *Dikanka* and preserves its former demonic symbolism.

34. Plato, Sidorovskii and Pakhomov trans., *Tvorenii velemudrogo Platona*, p. 199.

35. Cf. the icon of country in "Life," which forms the compositional center of *Arabesques*: "But Rome stopped and fixed its eagle eyes on the east. Greece too turned its beautiful eyes, moist with pleasure . . . , to the east. *The soil is rocky; the people humble; a sparsely populated* village has nestled against the *bare* hills, occasionally, irregularly shaded by a *dried out* fig tree. *Behind a low and dilapidated* fence stands a donkey. In a wooden cradle lies the Child; over Him the virgin Mother bends and gazes at Him with eyes filled with tears. . . . Ancient Egypt meditates . . . lowers its pyramids; beautiful Greece looks on uneasily; Rome lowers its eyes . . . Ararat bends down" (VIII:84). Here the same humble landscape as in Gogol's Russia reigns, although infinity is only implied by the sense of the scene. The proud bas-relief of the neighboring pagan countries "bows," bends before Judaea, and these lands look at her with a feeling recalling the gaze with which "other peoples and kingdoms" accompany rushing Rus. The spiritual fatherland of mankind (the Virgin, the archetypical image of the mother) is localized in the country that, by its emphatic humility, anticipates the Slavophile ideal of Russia. Another development of the motif is introduced in the finale of "The Diary of a Madman," where the hero's "mother" is clearly associated with the empress of heaven, and primordial rural Russia with the heavenly homeland, as it is later in *Dead Souls*.

36. Kozmin, *Nadezhdin*, p. 79; V. G. Belinskii, *Estetika i literaturnaia kritika*, vol. 1 (Moscow, 1959), p. 49.

37. Gogol here applied the method of the disembodiment of space characteristic of Romantic artists like Caspar David Friedrich. The point of view in their landscapes is moved upward, above the object depicted, into the same "distance" as Gogol's description of Rus, and the landscape of the plains disappears into infinity. See Charles Rosen and Henri Zerner, *Romanticism and Realism: The Mythology of Nineteenth Century Art* (London and New York: W. W. Norton, 1985), p. 34.

38. Zeldin has perceptively noted here the motif of "Mount Tabor light" (*favorskogo sveta*), pointing out as well the mystical nature

of the troika's motion (although he refrained from a more detailed study of the question). See Zeldin, *Gogol's Quest*, pp. 190–91.

39. Precisely this "Sophiological" semantics is contained in the seemingly strange image directly preceding the tirade about the boundless idea: "And I still stand there immobile, full of wonder, but already *a menacing cloud full of impending rains shades my head*" (VI:221). I find in this a curious resonance with one of the standard motifs of Masonic Neoplatonism. Cf.: "For *Wisdom is the steam* of the glory of the power of God, the pure *effusion* of the glory of God the Almighty." Eckartshausen, *Kliuch*, pt. 1, p. 206.

40. Stepan Shevyrev, *Istoriia poezii* (Moscow, 1835), vol. 1, p. 44.

Katherine Lahti, Artificiality and Nature in *Dead Souls*

The ideas for this essay were first elaborated in my honors thesis at Wesleyan University, "Artifact and Nature in Gogol's *Dead Souls*," written in 1981 under the direction of Priscilla Meyer.

1. Vladimir Nabokov, *Nikolai Gogol* (Norfolk, Conn.: New Directions, 1944), pp. 88–89. Here and elsewhere I shall make use of Nabokov's excellent translations of passages from Gogol's works that appear in this biography. For the sake of accessibility, other translations will be from the Penguin edition: Nikolai Gogol, *Dead Souls*, trans. David Magarshack (New York: Penguin Books, 1961). The passage quoted here appears on p. 122 in the Magarshack translation. References to Magarshack will follow references to the Russian text, separated by a slash. When not otherwise indicated, translations are my own.

2. "It was not without relief that the black-and-white striped toll-gate barrier was seen looming in the distance, for it was a sign that, like any other instrument of torture, the cobbled roadway was coming to an end; and after striking his head rather violently several times against the box of the carriage, Chichikov at last was rolling along on soft ground" (VI:21/31).

3. Carl R. Proffer, *The Simile and Gogol's "Dead Souls"* (The Hague: Mouton, 1967).

4. Clothes and buildings make up the bulk of artifacts in *Dead Souls*. To round off the food-clothing-shelter trinity, it is tempting to look at food production in *Dead Souls* as the production of an artifact. Food does in fact bear many similarities to other artifacts in *Dead Souls*. We see people in the process of preparing it; it is described

with past passive participles; and it is hoarded, and it decays (at Pliushkin's estate). Sobakevich and Korobochka, the two landowners who are most involved in the production of artifacts, are also the two who pay the most attention to their cooking. However, people's relation to food is basically different from their relation to other artifacts. Food is the one unquestionably necessary artifact. To talk about food in light of artifact versus nature would therefore involve making judgments about more or less natural (i.e., *necessary*) types of foods. The role of food as an artifact in *Dead Souls* will not be dealt with here.

5. Magarshack's version is on p. 104.

6. Andrei Belyi, *Masterstvo Gogolia* (Moscow, 1934), pp. 152–55.

7. Nabokov, *Nikolai Gogol*, p. 75. Magarshack's version is on pp. 17–18.

8. James B. Woodward, *Gogol's "Dead Souls"* (Princeton, N. J.: Princeton University Press, 1978), pp. 110–27.

9. This is the vision of nature that Schelling ends up embracing in the following passage, which is otherwise about the emergence of the self-conscious ego:

> Hence the intelligence will be able to intuit itself only in an object that has an internal principle of motion within itself. But an object such as this is said to be alive. Hence the intelligence must intuit itself, not merely *qua* organization as such, but as a living organization. But now it appears from this very deduction of life, that the latter must be common to all organic nature, and hence that there can be no distinction between living and nonliving organizations in nature itself. Since the intelligence is to intuit itself as active in the successions throughout the whole of organic nature, every organization must also possess life in the wider sense of the word, that is, must have an inner principle of motion within itself.

F. W. J. von Schelling, *System of Transcendental Idealism*, trans. Peter Heath (Charlottesville: University Press of Virginia, 1978), pp. 124–25.

10. Woodward, *Gogol's "Dead Souls,"* p. 118.

11. G. W. F. Hegel, *Science of Logic*, trans. W. H. Johnson and L. G. Struthers (London: George Allen & Unwin, 1929), 1:142.

12. In an earlier variant of *Dead Souls*, the narrator says that it was only Chichikov who initially took care while walking over the field and that the reason for this was that he wanted to keep his boots clean: "Chichikov, kotoryi stupal snachala ostorozhno, chtoby ne zagriaznit' svoikh sapogov, nakonets uvidel, chto eto ni k chemu ne sluzhit, i brel priamo" ("Chichikov, who at first stepped carefully so

as not to get his boots muddy, finally saw that it was no use, and just slogged ahead," VI:378–79).

13. Magarshack's version is on p. 82.

14. For a very good version of this argument see Iurii Mann, *Poetika Gogolia*, 2nd ed. (Moscow, 1988), pp. 295–97.

15. Nabokov, *Nikolai Gogol*, pp. 82–83. Magarshack's version is on p. 163.

16. Norman O. Brown, *Life against Death*, 2nd ed. (Middletown, Conn.: Wesleyan University Press, 1985), pp. 258–59, 292–93.

17. Ibid., p. 301; Susanne Fusso, "Chichikov on Gogol: The Structure of Oppositions in *Dead Souls*" (Ph.D. diss., Yale University, 1984), pp. 232–42.

18. The best example of artifacts decaying full circle into mud is to be found in the description of the interior of Pliushkin's house. "On the floor in a corner of the room lay a heap of coarser articles unworthy to be placed on a table. It was difficult to make out exactly what was in the heap, for it was so thickly covered with dust that the hands of anyone who touched it began to look like gloves" (VI:115/124). This description of dust-gloves echoes Pelageya's mud-boots.

19. "Da chto zh zateial? iz etakogo pustiaka i zateiat' nichego nel'zia" (VI:78). Magarshack's version is on p. 87.

20. "Ved' predmet prosto: fu-fu. Chto zh on stoit? komu nuzhen?" "Da vot vy pokupaete, stalo byt', nuzhen" (VI:104). Magarshack's version is on p. 112.

21. "Da chto zhe ia, durak, chto li? Ty posudi sam: zachem zhe mne priobretat' veshch', reshitel'no dlia menia nenuzhnuiu?" (VI:81). Magarshack's version is on p. 90.

22. See, e.g., the following speech of Faust in which he bemoans the written contract, mentioning many accoutrements of writing:

Faust. Poor pedant! Must it be in writing too?
Is a man's plighted word a thing unknown to you?
My spoken word must rule my life's whole course
For ever: is this not enough? . . . .
But parchments signed and sealed
Are ghosts that haunt and daunt us; the word dies
Upon the very pen we wield,
And wax and leather tyrannize
Our lives. Well, devil, which is it to be:
Bronze, marble, parchment, paper? Answer me:
What pen, what tool, what chisel shall I use?
The medium is yours to choose!

Johann Wolfgang von Goethe, *Faust*, trans. David Luke (Oxford: Oxford University Press, 1987), I: lines 1716–1719, 1726–1733.

23. Magarshack's version is on p. 199.

24. Magarshack's version is on p. 87.

25. Magarshack's version is on p. 61.

26. Karl von Eckartshausen, *Ausschlüsse zur Magie*, 4 vols. (Munich: Joseph Lentner, 1788–92), 1:28–29.

27. Karl von Eckartshausen, *Puteshestvie mladogo Kostisa ot vostoka k poludniu* [*Kostis Reise von Morgen gegen Mittag*], trans. A. F. Labzin (St. Petersburg, 1801), p. 53.

28. Antoine Faivre, *Eckartshausen et la théosophie chrétienne* (Paris: Librairie C. Klincksieck, 1969), pp. 251–52.

29. See Fusso, "Chichikov on Gogol," pp. 57–70.

30. In Schiller's "Über das Erhabene," we read, "The mimetic creative impulse, which can experience no *impression* without at once striving for a living *expression*, and which sees in every beautiful or vast form of nature a challenge to contend with it, possesses the great advantage over nature of being able to treat as a major purpose and a totality in itself what nature—if she does not heedlessly reject it—in passing sweeps along with her in pursuit of some more immediate purpose of her own." Friedrich von Schiller, *"Naive & Sentimental Poetry" and "On the Sublime,"* trans. Julius A. Elias (New York: Frederick Ungar, 1966), p. 211. For another view on art, nature, and infinity in both see Schelling, *System of Transcendental Idealism*, pp. 229–33.

Frederick T. Griffiths and Stanley J. Rabinowitz, The Death of Gogolian Polyphony

1. Jesse Zeldin argues that *Selected Passages* outlines the ideas of the second part of this trilogy, if not the third as well, and that it "points the way to a regeneration of the 'dead souls' whom he finds in Part One, in much the way that Dante's *Purgatorio* shows the way of salvation for sinners—not a contradiction of *Inferno*, but a part of the same structure in which *Inferno*, *Purgatorio*, and *Paradiso* all have a definite place." Introduction to his translation of *Selected Passages from Correspondence with Friends* (Nashville, Tenn.: Vanderbilt University Press, 1969), p. xv. Andrei Siniavskii (Abram Terts) makes some excellent comments on this topic in his book *V teni Gogolia* (London: Collins, 1975), esp. on pp. 204–7.

2. Mikhail Bakhtin, "Epic and Novel," trans. Caryl Emerson and Michael Holquist, in Bakhtin, *The Dialogic Imagination*, ed. Michael Holquist (Austin: University of Texas Press, 1981), p. 28.

3. Ibid.

4. Translations are by Zeldin, *Selected Passages.* When necessary, we have altered Zeldin's translation to provide more accuracy. References to the English text follow references to the Russian, separated by a slash.

5. Carl Proffer, *The Simile and Gogol's "Dead Souls"* (The Hague: Mouton, 1977), pp. 183–200.

6. So argues Daria Borghese, *Gogol a Roma* (Florence: Sansoni, n.d.), p. 57.

7. James M. Holquist, "The Burden of Prophecy: Gogol's Conception of Russia," *Review of National Literatures* 3, no. 1 (Spring 1972): 41.

8. Holquist (ibid., p. 51) extends the list of possible messianic or prophetic models recalled in Gogol's letters to include John the Baptist and, perhaps, Christ himself.

9. Quoted by Terts, *V teni Gogolia*, p. 295.

10. Donald Fanger, *The Creation of Nikolai Gogol* (Cambridge, Mass.: Harvard University Press, 1979), p. 214.

11. "After having read the whole book [part 1], it seems exactly as though he [the reader] were emerging from some stifling cellar into God's light" (*Selected Passages*, VIII:293/104).

12. One wonders, of course, how Pushkin would have reacted to his newly evangelical friend. Gogol has dealt with this problem retroactively in chapter 10, "On the Theater," by refuting imputations of deism to Pushkin and by rehabilitating him as a Christian. Even Pushkin's 1830 "When out of sport or idle boredom" ("V chasy zabav il' prazdnoi skuki") becomes Christian through the omission of its first stanza (VIII:276/83). One is reminded of the posthumous conversation that Dante would wish for Virgil and fabricates for Statius.

13. Tolstoy to V. V. Strakhov, 1 May 1881, quoted in N. N. Gusev, *Letopis' zhizni i tvorchestva L'va Nikolaevicha Tolstogo* (Moscow, 1958), p. 535.

14. Gogol to A. O. Smirnova, 13 July 1845 (XII:504).

15. André Gide, *Dostoevsky* (New York: New Directions, 1961), p. 50.

Alexander Zholkovsky, Rereading Gogol's Miswritten Book

1. On artistic space see Iu. M. Lotman's article, "Problema khudozhestvennogo prostranstva v proze Gogolia," *Trudy po russkoi i slavianskoi filiologii*, no. 11 (Tartu, 1968): 4–50. Promising avenues of approach to *Selected Passages* have been explored by Paul

Debreczeny, *Nikolay Gogol and His Contemporary Critics, Transactions of the American Philosophical Society*, n. s., vol. 56, pt. 3 (Philadelphia: American Philosophical Society, 1966), pp. 5–68; Abram Terts [Andrei Siniavskii], *V teni Gogolia* (London: Collins, 1975); Donald Fanger, "Gogol and his Reader," in *Literature and Society in Imperial Russia, 1800–1914*, ed. William Mills Todd III (Stanford, Calif.: Stanford University Press, 1978), pp. 61–95; and Fanger, *The Creation of Nikolai Gogol* (Cambridge, Mass.: Harvard University Press, 1979).

2. Cf. Ruth Sobel's title, *Gogol's Forgotten Book: "Selected Passages" and Its Contemporary Readers* (Washington, D.C.: University Press of America, 1981), and the paper by Stanley Rabinowitz and Frederick Griffiths in the present volume.

3. Notably by V. V. Gippius, *Gogol* (Providence, R. I.: Brown University Press, 1963); and Iu. N. Tynianov, "Dostoevskii i Gogol' (k teorii parodii)," in his *Poetika: Istoriia literatury: Kino* (Moscow, 1921; 1977), pp. 198–226.

4. In Fanger's apt formulation, the narration in "The Overcoat" comes from all four directions at once—like the Petersburg wind. *Creation of Gogol*, p. 154.

5. Terts sees the author of *Selected Passages* also as similar to Akakii, Chichikov, and other Gogolian "objects of slaps and mockery." *V teni Gogolia* pp. 12, 61.

6. See *Selected Passages*, Letter 28 (3), VIII:294–95/104–5. All references to *Selected Passages* list the page numbers of the Russian text and, after the slash, the page numbers of the English edition: *Selected Passages from Correspondence with Friends*, trans. Jesse Zeldin (Nashville, Tenn.: Vanderbilt University Press, 1969). Where necessary, the translation has been emended.

The principle of "demotion" is noted by Fanger, *Creation of Gogol*, p. 236. See also Terts on Gogol as a caricature of the figure of Writer. *V teni Gogolia*, pp. 277, 281.

7. See Iu. M. Lotman, "O Khlestakove," *Trudy po russkoi i slavianskoi filologii*, no. 26 (Tartu, 1975): 19–53, 19; Terts, *V teni Gogolia*, pp. 131, 137, 464 (and also pp. 372–74, on the affinity between Gogol's stylistic propensity for accumulation of detail and the greediness of his characters); Fanger, *Creation of Gogol*, pp. 250–51.

8. Among such genres are also literary epigrams (sometimes collected into texts of epic proportions, like A. F. Voeikov's "The Madhouse"), literary epitaphs, and Lermontov's "Death of a Poet" and its progeny.

9. Even discounting its skazlike ambiguity, the story is suggestive of the comic figure Gogol cuts in Russian literary mythology. Cf.

L. I. Arnol'di's memoirs comparing Gogol with his stock of unworn boots to the anonymous episodic character in the last paragraph of chap. 7 of *Dead Souls*, who enjoyed trying on boots in the solitude of his room. See *Gogol' v vospominaniiakh sovremennikov*, ed. S. Mashinskii (Moscow, 1952) (hereafter abbreviated as *GVS*), p. 482; cf. also Gogol's thrifty ways of boot repair (see his letter to S. T. Aksakov, 7 July 1840, *GVS*, pp. 126–27) with those of the Bashmachkins.

10. As shown in Tynianov's now classic article "Dostoevskii i Gogol'."

11. Simon Karlinsky, *The Sexual Labyrinth of Nikolai Gogol* (Cambridge, Mass.: Harvard University Press, 1976), p. 243; Marianna Bogoiavlensky, On the Development of Gogol's Religious Thought (in Russian) (Ann Arbor and London: University Microfilms International, 1981), pp. 51 ff.

12. Gippius, *Gogol*, p. 129.

13. This colorful detail from P. V. Annenkov's memoirs (*GVS*, p. 263) does not seem, however, to be borne out by the records of travelers published in the *Moskovskie vedomosti*. See Iu. V. Mann's commentaries in his edition of P. V. Annenkov, *Literaturnye vospominaniia* (Moscow, 1983), p. 560.

14. For an analysis of an intermediate stage in this process of the characters' emancipation from Gogol's grip and their arrogation of equal authorial rights (making possible his eventual objectification in *Stepanchikovo*), see S. G. Bocharov, "Perekhod ot Gogolia k Dostoevskomu," in his *O khudozhestvennykh mirakh* (Moscow, 1985), pp. 161–209, who focuses on Makar Devushkin's settling scores with the author of Akakii Akakievich.

15. T. G. Pashchenko's memoirs in *GVS*, p. 45; and P. V. Annenkov reporting the words of the painter F. A. Moller and of Gogol, *GVS*, p. 290.

16. See Victor Erlich, *Gogol* (New Haven, Conn., and London: Yale University Press, 1969), p. 8, with a reference to Leon Stillman's "Nikolai Gogol and Ostap Hohol," *Orbis Scriptus: Dmitrii Tschizhewskii zum 70 Geburtstag* (Munich: Wilhelm Fink, 1966), pp. 811–25.

17. Reported by S. T. Aksakov, *GVS*, pp. 137–38, 152. Thus, the Russian joke about distinguishing between Gogol', Gegel' (Hegel), Bebel', Babel', *kabel'* (cable), *kobel'* (male dog), and *suchka* (female dog, bitch) is not devoid of pertinence.

18. Gogol to S. T. Aksakov, 18 Mar. 1843, *GVS*, p. 186; and S. T. Aksakov and D. M. Pogodin, *GVS*, pp. 112, 407.

19. These points have been argued by Gippius; Fanger; Andrei

Belyi, *Masterstvo Gogolia: Issledovanie* (Moscow, 1934); and Paul Debreczeny, "Pushkin and Gogol: A Reassessment," paper presented at the 1985 Pushkin Symposium at New York University, to appear in a volume edited by A. Kodjak, forthcoming from Slavica.

20. He reprimanded them, demanded gratitude for living among them, and expected them to reread, copy, and circulate his letters.

21. Reported by Aksakov, *GVS*, p. 106.

22. Fanger, *Creation of Gogol*, p. 48. Terts compares him to Nozdrev, who claimed as his, *moe*, even what lay beyond his boundaries. *V teni Gogolia*, p. 238.

23. See, respectively, V. V. Vinogradov, *Poetika russkoi literatury: Izbrannye trudy* (Moscow, 1976), p. 191; and Fanger, "Gogol and his Reader," p. 77.

24. Gogol to S. T. Aksakov, May 1843, *GVS*, pp. 202–3.

25. Another shrewd observation by Annenkov, *GVS*, p. 260. Annenkov also discerned his "secretiveness and inclination to rule [*upravliat'*] people." *GVS*, p. 247.

26. V. V. Veresaev's formulation in *Gogol' v zhizni* (Moscow and Petrograd, 1933), p. 5, quoted by Fanger, *Creation of Gogol*, p. 268.

27. See Aksakov and Annenkov in *GVS*, pp. 139, 302, respectively.

28. See F. V. Chizhov and P. V. Annenkov, *GVS*, pp. 229, 282.

29. He said so in a conversation with I. S. Turgenev and M. S. Shchepkin, as reported by the latter's grandson, M. A. Shchepkin, *GVS*, p. 530.

30. Cf. above, n. 22, on the transcendence of boundaries by Nozdrev.

31. Gogol to Aksakov, 18 Mar. 1843, *GVS*, p. 188. This strategy is somewhat reminiscent of Agaf'ia Tikhonovna's wishful combining of her suitors' various features in *Marriage*.

32. See section 5 below. As Terts puts it, "Actually, he is asking the readers to replace him in his authorial role, by sending him in an envelope the missing *Dead Souls*." *V teni Gogolia*, p. 288. On Gogol's idea of writer-reader "coauthorship," see also Iu. V. Mann, *V poiskakh zhivoi dushi* (Moscow, 1984), pp. 240–52.

33. Fanger, "Gogol and His Reader," pp. 71–75; cf. Lev Loseff's provocative theory of censorship, *On the Beneficence of Censorship* (Munich: Otto Sagner, 1984).

34. Testimony of G. P. Danilevskii, N. V. Berg, and A. T. Tarasenkov, *GVS*, pp. 449, 509, 516, respectively.

35. Mashinskii's commentary on Aksakov's memoirs, *GVS*, p. 620.

36. Aksakov's and Annenkov's respective comments in *GVS*, pp. 173, 333.

37. Fanger, *Creation of Gogol*, p. 23; cf. S. T. Aksakov's letter to Gogol, 3 July 1842, in which he reports a contemporary's opinion that the composition of the provincial society in *Dead Souls* is not accurate (*GVS*, p. 158), and Gogol's statement to the same effect in Letter 21 of *Selected Passages* (VIII:311/124).

38. Debreczeny, *Gogol and Contemporary Critics*, p. 6.

39. Gippius, *Gogol*, p. 170; Vsevolod Setchkarev, *Gogol: His Life and Works* (New York: New York University Press, 1965), p. 243.

40. See Annenkov's always perceptive analysis, *GVS*, p. 293.

41. Terts, *V teni Gogolia*, p. 540.

42. This positive view of *Selected Passages* has been canonized in the part of Gogol scholarship that was influenced by the spiritual revival of the Silver Age and exemplified by the scholarship of K. Mochul'skii, *Dukhovnyi put' Gogolia* (1934; Paris: YMCA Press, 1976); and Setchkarev, *Gogol*; see Sobel, *Gogol's Forgotten Book*, pp. 6–8.

43. In this sense, even Chernyshevskii exhibits an unexpected affinity with Gogol. *What Is to Be Done*? is a classic case of bad but culturally influential writing, although the two utopias (on the utopianism of *Selected Passages* see Gippius, *Gogol*, p. 183 ff.; Mochul'skii, *Dukhovnyi put' Gogolia*, p. 99) are very different both in content and in style: whereas the ideologist Chernyshevskii is consistently, if naively, ironic; Gogol, the past master of skaz, is dead serious. Cf. also Terts on Gogol's, Tolstoy's, and Chernyshevskii's rationalism in their religious and utopian thinking. *V teni Gogolia*, pp. 213 ff.

44. Final defeat, because, as Bulgarin's *Northern Bee* correctly predicted, "after this volume nothing further could be expected of Gogol" (quoted in Debreczeny, *Gogol and Contemporary Critics*, p. 53); ironic, because exclusive concentration on writing would be supposed to guarantee a perfect text.

45. Terts sees the origins of Gogol's "bad" prose in his bad poetry, *V teni Gogolia*, pp. 321 ff. "A genius . . . is the one who dares write badly." Ibid., p. 340.

46. Sometimes Tolstoy's style turns quite Akakii-like; see Alexander Zholkovsky, "Lev Tolstoi i Mikhail Zoshchenko kak zerkalo i zazerkal'e russkoi revoliutsii," *Sintaksis* (1986) 16:103–28, p. 116.

47. See Alexander Zholkovsky, "Grafomanstvo kak priem: Lebiadkin, Khlebnikov, Limonov i drugie," in *Velimir Chlebnikov (1885–1922): Myth and Reality*, ed. W. Weststeijn (Amsterdam: Rodopi, 1986), pp. 573–93.

48. Naum Korzhavin in a personal communication. Cf. Fanger's statement that "giving up the freedom of a creator, Gogol took on that of a fictitious character" (*Creation of Gogol*, p. 212), and Terts's

observations on the "deliberate unprepossessiveness and foolishness ["durakovatost' "] of *Selected Passages* (*V teni Gogolia*, p. 84), and on the way *Dead Souls* had already reduced the author to the role of a "belated second-rate character" (ibid., p. 200; see also p. 286).

49. Quoted in Debreczeny, *Gogol and Contemporary Critics*, p. 53.

50. On "camp" see Susan Sontag, "Notes on 'Camp,'" in her *Against Interpretation and Other Essays* (New York: Farrar, Straus & Giroux, 1961), pp. 275–92. Although she draws her examples of camp mostly from fin-de-siècle kitsch, which is very unlike *Selected Passages*, many of her formulations do apply to Gogol's book:

> Camp . . . emphasizes . . . style at the expense of content. . . . Camp which knows itself to be Camp . . . is . . . less satisfying. . . . Camp . . . reeks of self-love . . . , seriousness that fails. . . . The hallmark of Camp is . . . the proper mixture of the exaggerated, the fantastic, the passionate, the naive, . . . the outlandish . . . , the spirit of extravagance . . . , something *démesuré* in the quality of the ambition . . . on the part of one man to do what it takes a generation, a whole culture to accomplish. . . . Camp . . . cannot be taken . . . seriously because it is "too much." . . . A work can be close to Camp, but not make it, because it succeeds. . . . We are better able to enjoy a fantasy . . . when it is not our own. . . . Time liberates the work of art from moral relevance, delivering it over to Camp sensibility. . . . Camp is the glorification of "character" . . . , the unity, the force of the person. . . . The peculiar relation between Camp and homosexuality has to be explained. . . . The discovery of the good taste of bad taste can be liberating. . . . The ultimate Camp statement: it's good because it's awful.

51. Gogol suggested "that the censor Nikitenko, if he approved the book, should be richly rewarded by the government." Debreczeny, *Gogol and Contemporary Critics*, p. 59.

52. In discussing *Selected Passages* Terts draws parallels with Poprishchin's claims to the Spanish throne and with the spirit of the Petrine epoch. *V teni Gogolia*, pp. 65 ff, 646.

53. The obverse of this motif is Bobchinskii's desire in *The Inspector General* that his name be known to the emperor.

54. On Gogol as the Grand Inquisitor see Terts, *V teni Gogolia*, pp. 69–70; cf. Gary Saul Morson, *The Boundaries of Genre: Dostoevsky's "Diary of a Writer" and the Traditions of Literary Utopia* (Austin: University of Texas Press, 1981), pp. 115–41; and Alexander Zholkovsky, "Dreaming Right and Reading Right: Five Keys to One of Ilf and Petrov's Ridiculous Men," *Slavic Review* 48, no. 1 (1989): 36–53.

55. Boris Groys, "Stalinizm kak esteticheskii fenomen," *Sintaksis*

(1987) 17:98–110; Groys, *Gesamtkunstwerk Stalin: Die gespaltene Kultur in der Sowjetunion* (Munich: Carl Hanser, 1988).

56. Sasha Sokolov, *Palisandriia* (Ann Arbor, Mich.: Ardis, 1985); Olga Matich, "Sasha Sokolov's *Palisandriia*: History and Myth," *Russian Review* 45, no. 3 (1986): 415–26; and Alexander Zholkovsky, "The Stylistic Roots of *Palisandriia*," *Canadian-American Slavic Studies* 21, nos. 3–4 (special Sokolov issue, guest edited by D. Barton Johnson) (1987): 369–400.

57. In a variation on both Gogol and Fedorov, Palisandr buys the graves of eminent émigrés to transport back to Russia its glory. Matich, "Sokolov's *Palisandriia*."

58. On the classicist nature of socialist realism see Terts's historic essay "On Socialist Realism," in his *The Trial Begins and On Socialist Realism* (1959; Berkeley and Los Angeles: University of California Press, 1982), pp. 127–219; cf. the painters Komar and Melamid's mock neoclassicist *sots-art* (e.g., *Comrade Stalin and the Muses*). See also Terts on Gogol's links to the eighteenth century and on *Selected Passages* as a sort of *Taras Bulba*. *V teni Gogolia*, pp. 244 ff., 93–94.

59. If his opinion is, after all, unique ("and if there is in me whatever small drop of reason, not possessed by all," a sentence omitted from Zeldin's version), it is, in a characteristic high/low mediation, thanks to his familiarity with "merzosti," "abominations, disgusting things" (VIII:321/135).

60. Cf. the much-quoted principle in *Selected Passages* that love should be transmitted "up through the ranks" ("po nachal'stvu," Letter 28, VIII:366/194).

61. Cf. Goethe's famous observation that Lady Macbeth mentions her children in one scene and childlessness in another.

62. Cf. Chernyshevskii's Vera Pavlovna on carrying things over from the future into the present.

63. The symbolic meaning of this city becomes clear in light of Gogol's retrospective comments, in his "Denouement of *The Inspector General*," on the city portrayed in that play as the Inner City of the Soul. Cf. St. Augustine's City of God, the Utopian City, the "soulful" double entendre in the title of *Dead Souls*, and also the references to the *gubernatorsha*'s soul in the letter under analysis: "You yourself say that I have helped you in the affairs of your soul [*v vashem dushevnom dele*]" (VIII:310/124). "It will be impossible not to love you if your soul is known" (VIII:319/133).

64. Typicality, that crucial concept of the criticism of the time, is also invoked regarding the choice of representative events and rumors to be recorded by the *gubernatorsha*.

Cathy Popkin, Distended Discourse

1. See, e.g., the reviews of *Dead Souls* by K. P. Masal'skii (*Syn otechestva*, 1842, no. 6) and N. A. Polevoi (*Russkii vestnik*, 1842, nos. 5–6). The earlier Dikanka and Mirgorod stories and other works had prompted similar observations from Polevoi and his contemporaries (see Polevoi's review of *Evenings on a Farm near Dikanka* in *Moskovskii telegraf*, 1831, no. 17: 91–95). Some of these objected less to the profusion than to the "dirtiness" of the details: P. M-skii [Iurkevich], review of *Migorod, Severnaia pchela*, 1835, no. 73; and G. Grech, review in *Severnaia pchela*, 1842, no. 137. Others more graciously forgave the accumulation of unnecessary detail as a manifestation of Gogol's "lavish Russian generosity," a laudable propensity to give and give beyond what is called for. S. P. Shevyrev, review of *Dead Souls*, in *Moskvitianin*, 1842, no. 7:207–28.

2. See V. Belinskii, "O russkoi povesti i povestiakh g. Gogolia," *Teleskop*, 1835, no. 26, rpt. in his *Polnoe sobranie sochinenii*, 13 vols. (Moscow, 1953–59), 1:259–307, and "Otvet Moskvitianinu," *Polnoe sobranie*, 10:221–70; and P. A. Pletnev, review of "Rim," *Sovremennik*, 1842, no. 26. Both critics applauded the verisimilitude and perfect representation of life enabled by the inordinate amount of detail.

3. Gogol himself makes this now famous boast of all-inclusiveness, first in his letter to A. S. Pushkin, 7 Oct. 1835 (X:375), and again, later, to V. A. Zhukovskii, 12 Nov. 1836 (XI:74). Iurii Mann makes much of Gogol's intention to grasp the "tseloe" ("entirety"). Mann, *V poiskakh zhivoi dushi: "Mertvye dushi": Pisatel'-kritika-chitatel'* (Moscow, 1984), p. 8. And A. P. Chudakov locates the "intrigue" of Gogol's text in its ingenious "vseokhvatnost' " ("all-inclusiveness") and the "absolute vision" it provides. Chudakov, "Veshch' v mire Gogolia," in *Gogol': Istoriia i sovremennost' (k 175-letiiu so dnia rozhdeniia)*, ed. V. V. Kozhinov et al. (Moscow, 1985), pp. 78–79. Carl Proffer, in turn, treats the distended similes as precisely a means to achieving this ambitious project of all-inclusiveness, motivating the accretion by giving it a point of departure. Proffer, *The Simile and Gogol's "Dead Souls"* (The Hague: Mouton, 1967), p. 81.

4. A. Slonimskii, *Tekhnika komicheskogo u Gogolia* (Petrograd, 1923).

5. In his treatment of Gogol's later work as a kind of attenuated fantastic in the world of *byt* (everyday life), Iurii Mann implies that the radical unmotivatedness of so much of the material, the alogism, and the arbitrary outbursts of characters and narrators alike are ves-

tiges of the more explicit strangeness of the earlier works. The lack of discursive control mirrors the loss of control at the hands of supernatural powers, the more corporeal demons who "scramble everything up." Mann, *Poetika Gogolia*, 2nd ed. (Moscow, 1988), pp. 79, 81, 106, 110–26.

6. Andrei Belyi, *Masterstvo Gogolia* (Moscow and Leningrad, 1934), pp. 94–104.

7. K. S. Aksakov, "Neskol'ko slov o poeme Gogolia 'Pokhozhdeniia Chichikova ili mertvye dushi,'" *Moskva*, 16 June 1842.

8. D. S. Merezhkovskii, *Polnoe sobranie sochinenii*, 24 vols. (St. Petersburg, 1911–14), 10:66. Merezhkovskii saw Gogol's technique of overspecification as a feat of fine moral differentiation.

9. V. Ermilov, *N. V. Gogol'*, 2nd ed. (Moscow, 1953), pp. 186, 212, 213.

10. M. M. Bakhtin, "Rable i Gogol'," in his *Voprosy literatury i estetiki: Issledovaniia raznykh let* (Moscow, 1975), pp. 484–95.

11. Vinogradov points to linguistic development in the thirties and forties and locates Gogol's abuses of verbal decorum in terms of the intermingling of levels of diction. V. V. Vinogradov, "Iazyk Gogolia," in *N. V. Gogol': Materialy i issledovaniia*, ed. V. V. Gippius, 2 vols. (Moscow and Leningrad, 1936; Slavica-Reprint no. 49, Düsseldorf: Brücken-Verlag, 1970), 2:286–88.

12. For an excellent survey of the history of Gogol's reception see Robert A. Maguire's introduction to his *Gogol from the Twentieth Century: Eleven Essays* (Princeton, N. J.: Princeton University Press, 1974), pp. 3–54.

13. Personal communication.

14. A major exception to this has been the Soviet literary establishment, for which social relevance (and, hence, realism) is the primary source of literary value. Soviet critics have traditionally projected a Gogolian oeuvre that exposes the injustices of serfdom, bureaucracy, poverty (and other associated evils of the tsarist regime) and the stultifying *poshlost'* (vulgarity) of contemporary life through a realistic portrayal of these social problems. Today, however, in some of the most imaginative criticism on Gogol, Soviet scholars are presenting his work as anything but straightforward realism; most Western critics as well have dismissed the portrait of Gogol as a realist or naturalist writer. Still, it was in these terms that his contemporaries first discussed (and praised) his work. See Maguire, intro. to *Gogol from the Twentieth Century*, pp. 6, 16–17.

15. Maguire, "Reading *Dead Souls*," *Teaching Language through*

Literature 26 (April 1987): 21, 23. This pin makes its inexplicable appearance on the first page of *Dead Souls*.

16. See Frank Kermode, "Secrets and Narrative Sequence," in *On Narrative*, ed. W. J. T. Mitchell (Chicago: University of Chicago Press, 1981), pp. 91–97.

17. Proffer, *Simile and "Dead Souls,"* pp. 83–86; James Woodward, *Gogol's "Dead Souls"* (Princeton, N. J.: Princeton University Press, 1978); Daniel Rancour-Laferriere, *Out from under Gogol's "Overcoat": A Psychoanalytic Study* (Ann Arbor, Mich.: Ardis, 1982).

18. I. D. Ermakov had, in fact, commented that the proliferation of apparently "irrevelant" detail in Gogol's works provides exactly the same kind of material for interpretation as an analysand's "random" chatter gives the psychoanalyst, namely, the key to underlying meaning. Each and every word of Gogol's, he claimed, is a sign, an indicator of profound significance. Ermakov, *Ocherki po analizu tvorchestva N. V. Gogolia: Organichnost' proizvedenii Gogolia* (Moscow, 1923), pp. 11–12.

19. Michel Foucault, *Discipline and Punish: The Birth of the Prison*, trans. Alan Sheridan (New York: Vintage Books, 1977), pp. 139–40; Vsevolod Setchkarev, *Gogol: His Life and Works*, trans. Robert Kramer (New York: New York University Press, 1965), p. 11.

20. Naomi Schorr, *Reading in Detail: Aesthetics and the Feminine* (New York: Methuen, 1987), p. 7.

21. This tendency traces its most illustrious roots to Eikhenbaum's view of Gogol's plots as an excellent excuse for the deployment of verbal device. See B. Eikhenbaum, "Kak sdelana 'Shinel'' Gogolia," *Skvoz' literaturu* (Leningrad, 1924; rpt. The Hague: Mouton, 1962). Trans. as "How Gogol's 'Overcoat' Is Made," in Maguire, *Gogol from the Twentieth Century*, pp. 269–91.

The phrase *semiotic totalitarianism* is Gary Saul Morson's and refers to the tendency to assign meaning to everything, to see every detail as the sign of an underlying order or system. I refer not only to Morson's *Hidden in Plain View: Narrative and Creative Potentials in "War and Peace"* (Stanford, Calif.: Stanford University Press, 1987), which thematizes the issue of reading for significance, but also to his more recent "Prosaics and Anna Karenina," *Tolstoy Studies Journal* 1 (1988): 1–12, in which he expresses a general suspicion of any perceptual stance that fails to admit the random or accidental. See also his essay in the present volume.

22. Donald Fanger, *The Creation of Nikolai Gogol* (Cambridge, Mass.: Harvard University Press, 1979), p. 235; Victor Erlich, *Gogol* (New Haven, Conn.: Yale University Press, 1969), p. 221; S. G.

Bocharov, "O stile Gogolia," *Teoriia literaturnykh stilei: Tipologiia stilevogo razvitiia novogo vremeni (klassicheskii stil': sootnoshenie garmonii i disgarmonii v stile)*, ed. N. K. Gei et al. (Moscow, 1976), p. 441. Bocharov's formulation comes from Iurii Lotman's characterization of Gogolian space that, in the Petersburg stories, has only "bureaucratic" and no "topographical" reality, reflecting empty administrative assignations rather than concrete, physical space. It is Lotman who cites in this connection Tvardovskii's couplet "Oboznacheno v meniu, / A v nature netu" ("listed on the menu / but nonexistent in reality"). Lotman, "Problema khudozhestvennogo prostranstva v proze Gogolia," *Trudy po russkoi i slavianskoi filologii*, no. 11 (Tartu, 1968):39.

23. Chudakov, "Veshch'," pp. 271–73.

24. Ibid., pp. 273–76.

25. A. A. Potebnia, *Iz zapisok po teorii slovesnosti* (Kharkov, 1905), p. 294; Belyi, *Masterstvo Gogolia*, p. 277; Chudakov, "Veshch'," p. 277; Fanger, *Creation of Gogol*, p. 261.

26. In the words of that inveterate purveyor of axioms, Prince Mirsky, "fun" is what has attracted readers to Gogol "above all," fun that is "simple and unadulterated." D. S. Mirsky, *A History of Russian Literature from Its Beginnings to 1900*, ed. Francis J. Whitfield (New York: Vintage Books, 1958), p. 157.

27. O. I. Senkovskii, "Pokhozhdeniia Chichikova ili Mertvye dushi," *Biblioteka dlia chteniia*, 1842, no. 53:29.

28. V. A. Zhukovskii, diary entry of 6 Jan. 1839, quoted in Mann, *V poiskakh*, p. 42. Zhukovskii's reference to pain is no doubt an expression of anguish and compassion in recognition of some of the more lamentable aspects of Russian life, but I find it captures something of the reading process as well, more effectively than the rhetoric of "unadulterated" fun or unremitting hilarity.

29. I. Mandel'shtam, *O Kharaktere gogolevskogo stilia* (Helsinki, 1902), pp. 75–76; Proffer, *Simile and "Dead Souls,"* p. 78; Belyi, *Masterstvo Gogolia*, p. 70; Stanley Fish, "Introduction, or How I Stopped Worrying and Learned to Love Interpretation," in his *Is There is a Text in This Class*? (Cambridge, Mass.: Harvard University Press, 1980), p. 14.

30. Mann, *Poetika Gogolia*, p. 401. Mann's agenda is clearly to rid the world of the very idea of Gogolian "error."

31. The term *Nachträglichkeit* is Freud's and refers to the retrospective conferral of meaning.

32. Charles C. Bernheimer, "Cloaking the Self: The Literary Space of Gogol's 'Overcoat,'" *PMLA* 90 (1975): 55.

33. Ronald LeBlanc makes effective use of similar terms, positing

a Gogolian distinction between the "gourmand" and the "gourmet," between "manger" and "goûter." LeBlanc, "Dinner with Chichikov: The Fictional Meal as Narrative Device in Gogol's *Dead Souls*," *Modern Language Studies* 18 (1988): 68–80. See also his "Satisfying Khlestakov's Appetite: The Semiotics of Eating in *The Inspector General*," *Slavic Review* 47 (Fall 1988): 483–98. For the *manger/goûter* opposition, LeBlanc credits Ronald Tobin, "Les mets et les mots: Gastronomie et sémiotique dans *L'école des femmes*," *Semiotica* 51 (1984): 135. LeBlanc applies the distinction to feasting characters rather than to reading strategies, but the contrast between gobbling and savoring is suggestive at both levels.

34. Gogol to S. T. Aksakov, 18 Aug. 1842 (XII:91).

35. Peter Brooks, *Reading for the Plot: Design and Intention in Narrative* (New York: Vintage Books, 1984), p. 37; Roland Barthes, "Introduction à l'analyse structurale des récits," *Communications* 8 (1966): 27.

36. Barthes, *S/Z*, trans. Richard Miller (New York: Hill & Wang, 1975), pp. 75–76.

37. Brooks, *Reading for Plot*, pp. 104, 111.

38. Belyi, too, noted that the development of the action owes much to these "bokovye khody," these side trips that lead "away" from the desired destination. *Masterstvo Gogolia*, p. 95.

39. Clarence Brown, "The Not Quite Realized Transit of Gogol'," in *Mnemozina: Studia Literaria Russica in Honorem Vsevolod Setchkarev*, ed. Joachim T. Baer and Norman W. Ingham (Munich: Fink, 1974), pp. 41–45. Judith Deutsch reads these instances of impeded motion rather as windows of opportunity, as moments "to pause on the threshold and glimpse the world beyond." She sees stopping as liberating rather than frustrating. Deutsch, "Perspective from the Threshold: The Troika of *Dead Souls*," *Ulbandus Review* 5 (Fall 1987):14.

40. Brooks, *Reading for Plot*, pp. 51–52.

41. Jean Paul extends Schlegel's famous contention that all poetry is by definition *Romantic* poetry. For Jean Paul, all Romantic poetry is by definition humorous: "Alles muss romantisch, d.h. humoristisch werden." Jean Paul [Johann Paul Friedrich Richter], *Werke*, 6 vols. (Munich: Carl Hanser, 1959–63), 5:127.32. Further citations to this work are in the text, to volume, page number, and, if applicable, section number. The English translations are mine.

42. Bernhard Baumgärtner, "Sprachstruktur in Jean Pauls Roman 'Flegeljahre' " (Ph.D. diss., Friedrich-Alexander-Universität zu Erlangen, 1958), p. 86.

43. Kenneth Burke, *Counter-Statement* (New York: Harcourt, Brace & Co., 1931), p. 183.

44. Jean Paul to Christian Otto, 26 Mar. 1793, in his *Sämtliche Werke*, ed. Eduard Berend, 33 vols. (Weimar: H. Bohlaus Nachfolger, 1927–64), 3(1):375.

45. Gogol to M. P. Balabina, 17 Feb. 1842 (XII:37). G. I. Chudakov does not include Jean Paul in the list of foreign authors known to have been read by Gogol (in translation or in the original). Eight works of Jean Paul's did, however, appear in translation in the 1820s and 1830s in journals Gogol read regularly. Chudakov, *Otnoshenie tvorchestva Gogolia k zapadnoevropeiskim literaturam* (Kiev, 1908), pp. 125–30, 23.

46. There is no apparent canonical translation of this title. The novel has been translated under various titles, including *Walt and Vult; or, The Twins.*

47. Gogol, too, harnesses the palpable logorrhea of legal documents in the interpolated texts in "The Two Ivans"—the various petitions, which constitute a virtuoso performance of aggravated legalese guaranteed to make "any reader cough and sneeze" (II:261). In his earlier novel, *Siebenkäs,* Jean Paul had equated the opening of a testament with the opening of a bottle of champagne, suggesting both the expansiveness of the product and the anticipation of the beneficiary. *Werke* 2:46.

48. Vladimir Nabokov, *Nikolai Gogol* (Norfolk, Conn.: New Directions, 1944), p. 76. Much earlier was S. A. Vengerov, *Sobranie sochinenii,* vol. 2 (St. Petersburg, 1913), p. 139; Belyi makes a point of this as well, in *Masterstvo Gogolia,* p. 82.

49. Maguire, "Reading *Dead Souls,*" p. 21.

50. Jean Paul, *Siebenkäs, Werke* 2:183. The full title of this novel—*Blumen-, Frucht- und Dornenstücke, oder Ehestand, Tod und Hochzeit des Armenadvokaten F. St. Siebenkäs* (Flower, Fruit and Thorn Pieces, or the Married Life, Death, and Wedding of the Advocate of the Poor, F. St. Siebenkäs)—is ample testimony to Jean Paul's penchant for reduplicative naming and infinite elaboration.

51. "All of this, all mixed together, created a very entertaining spectacle for Ivan Ivanovich, while the sunbeams, catching here a blue or a green sleeve, there a red cuff or a piece of gold brocade, or playing on the tip of the sword, turned it into something extraordinary, like the puppet show put on in villages by wandering vagrants, especially when a densely packed crowd looks at King Herod in his golden crown or at Anton leading the goat; behind the scenes the fiddle squeals; a gypsy claps his hands on his lips as on a drum, while the sun is going down and the fresh coolness of the southern

night imperceptively presses itself more insistently against the fresh shoulders and bosoms of the plump village women" (II:229).

52. Simon Karlinsky has aptly described Gogol as a "word glutton." "Portrait of Gogol as a Word Glutton, with Rabelais, Sterne, and Gertrude Stein as Background Figures," *California Slavic Studies* 5 (1970): 169–86).

53. Dante Alighieri, *The Divine Comedy: Inferno*, trans. Allen Mandelbaum (New York: Bantam Books, 1982), canto 7.

54. Martin Price, "The Fictional Contract," in *Literary Theory and Structure (Essays in Honor of William K. Wimsatt)*, ed. Frank Brady, John Palmer, and Martin Price (New Haven, Conn.: Yale University Press, 1973), p. 155.

55. "The morning hour has a mouth full of gold," a proverb in approximately the same spirit as "the early bird gets the worm," only the German one is slightly more explicit about the *monetary* advantage of getting an early start. Jean Paul, *Werke*, 2:159.

56. Barbara Herrnstein Smith, *On the Margins of Discourse: The Relation of Literature to Language* (Chicago: University of Chicago Press, 1978), p. 108.

57. Ibid., pp. 196–97; Barbara Herrnstein Smith, "Narrative Versions, Narrative Theories," in *On Narrative*, ed. Mitchell, p. 230.

58. Ross Chambers, *Story and Situation: Narrative Seduction and the Power of Fiction*, Theory of History and Literature, vol. 12 (Minneapolis: University of Minnesota Press, 1984), p. 11.

59. See Donald Fanger, "Gogol and His Reader," in *Literature and Society in Imperial Russia, 1800–1914*, ed. William Mills Todd III (Stanford, Calif.: Stanford University Press, 1978), pp. 61–95.

60. Dante, *Inferno*, canto 5, line 138.

Gary Saul Morson, Gogol's Parables of Explanation

1. Nicolas Berdyaev [Berdiaev], *The Russian Idea*, trans. R. M. French (Boston: Beacon, 1962), p. 1.

2. Leo Tolstoy, *War and Peace*, trans. Ann Dunnigan (New York: Signet, 1968), p. 1354.

3. Fyodor Dostoevsky, *The Brothers Karamazov*, trans. Constance Garnett (New York: Modern Library, 1950), p. 789.

4. Fyodor Dostoevsky, *The Possessed*, trans. Constance Garnett (New York: Modern Library, 1963), p. 629.

5. Fyodor Dostoevsky, *Notes from Underground*, in *"Notes from Underground" and "The Grand Inquisitor,"* the Garnett translation revised by Ralph E. Matlaw (New York: Dutton, 1960), p. 17.

6. I have discussed the concept of "prosaics" in a number of

articles, including: "Prosaics: An Approach to the Humanities," *American Scholar*, Autumn 1988, pp. 515–28; "Prosaics and *Anna Karenina*," *Tolstoy Studies Journal* 1 (1988): 1–12; "Prosaics, Criticism, and Ethics," *Formations* 5, no. 2 (Summer–Fall 1989): 77–95; and "The Potentials and Hazards of Prosaics," *Tolstoy Studies Journal* 2 (1989): 15–40. The concept is also mentioned in my *Hidden in Plain View: Narrative and Creative Potentials in "War and Peace"* (Stanford, Calif.: Stanford University Press, 1987). It is central to the argument of the book I coauthored with Caryl Emerson, *Mikhail Bakhtin: Creation of a Prosaics* (Stanford, Calif.: Stanford University Press, 1990).

7. Tolstoy, *War and Peace*, pp. 1352, 1353.

8. English translations are from Nikolai V. Gogol, *Dead Souls*, trans. Bernard Guilbert Guerney (New York: Modern Library, 1965). I have occasionally modified the translations for accuracy. References to the English text follow references to the Russian original, separated by a slash.

9. Laurence Sterne, *The Life and Opinions of Tristram Shandy, Gentleman*, ed. James Aiken Work (New York: Odyssey, 1940), p. 53.

10. Fyodor Dostoevsky, *Crime and Punishment*, trans. Constance Garnett (New York: Modern Library, 1950), p. 67; Dostoevsky, *Brothers Karamazov*, p. 79.

11. The argument from significant absence is not always fallacious, of course. If my father has telephoned me every Sunday at 8 P.M. for twenty years and one Sunday I do not receive a call, I would probably be justified in worrying. Nevertheless, this argument becomes fallacious under certain (very common) circumstances and a special suspicion is in order when it is encountered.

Is the absence seen as significant only because it does not mention the investigator's pet theme, and could anyone else use the same reasoning to "detect" a quite different absence? After all, no matter how long a text is, there are an infinite number of things it does not say. Or is the absence one that could be recognized as such by people with different interests at different times? One might reasonably ask someone who claims an absence is significant to provide *some* sort of positive evidence: can he show that a clear pattern of presence is being violated in this particular case? Has an expectation been set up that an omission frustrates? Do we have some equivalent of a sonnet with only thirteen lines, or a rhyme scheme that after many stanzas does not repeat? We would also be justified in rejecting an argument from significant absence when it would be equally possible to make the same claim in the case of presence. It is easiest to detect the abuse of this argument when both evidence and nonevidence can be (or are) used equally well.

12. Stanislaw Lem, *The Investigation*, trans. Adele Milch (New York: Avon, 1974), pp. 179–80.

13. They are also stranger than in Kafka's *Metamorphosis*, which proceeds logically from its initial fantastic premise.

14. English translations are from Nikolai V. Gogol, "The Nose," in *The Collected Tales and Plays of Nicolai Gogol*, The Garnett translation revised by Leonard J. Kent (New York: Modern Library, 1969). All references to Gogol's short stories are to this translation, which has occasionally been modified for accuracy. References to the English text follow references to the Russian original, separated by a slash.

15. Gogol, X:376–77, as cited in Donald Fanger, *The Creation of Nikolai Gogol* (Cambridge, Mass.: Harvard University Press, 1979), p. 119.

16. Fanger, *Creation of Gogol*, p. 120. See also Ann Shukman, "Gogol's *The Nose* or the Devil in the Works," *Nikolay Gogol: Text and Context*, ed. Jane Grayson and Faith Wigzell (New York: St. Martin's, 1989), pp. 64–82.

17. Ludwig Wittgenstein, *Philosophical Investigations*, 3rd ed., trans. G. E. M. Anscombe (New York: Macmillan, 1968), #107, p. 46e.

18. Even more possibilities are of course suggested by the constant punning on idioms involving the word *nose* or other parts of the face. In this story and elsewhere, explanatory nonsense is also generated by Gogol's characteristic use of language—what I like to call "Glagogolitic"—for example, when the syntax runs counter to the logic.

19. For an approach to nonsense as systematic see Michael Holquist, "What Is a Boojum? Nonsense and Modernism," in the Norton Critical Edition of Lewis Carroll, *Alice in Wonderland* (New York: Norton, 1971), pp. 402–18.

20. Milton Ehre, ed., *The Theater of Nikolai Gogol: Plays and Selected Writings* (Chicago: University of Chicago Press, 1980), p. 184.

21. Lucian, *Dialogues of the Dead*, in v. 7 of the 8-vol. Lucian in the Loeb Classical Library, trans. M. D. Macleod (Cambridge, Mass.: Harvard University Press, 1961), p. 111.

22. Ibid., pp. 113–15.

23. For citations from Gogol on the ordinary see Fanger, *Creation of Gogol*, pp. 69–71, 81, 109, 149.

24. Ambrose Bierce, *The Devil's Dictionary* (New York: Doubleday, n.d.), p. 52.

25. Gulliver's prideful denunciation of the human species after his fourth voyage has been central to the debate over whether *Gulliver's Travels* is a work of misanthropy or a satire on misanthropy. As the formulation I have supplied indicates, I think it is both.

26. Most obviously, this happens in canto 1, stanza 46, of Pushkin's *Eugene Onegin*.

27. Tolstoy, *War and Peace*, p. 1320.

Index